Andrea Baricordi
Massimiliano De Giovanni
Andrea Pietroni
Barbara Rossi
Sabrina Tunesi

ANIME

A Guide to Japanese Animation
(1958-1988)

Translated by Adeline D'Opera

Edited & Presented by Claude J. Pelletier
— *Protoculture Addicts* —

PROTOCULTURE

PUBLISHED IN ENGLISH BY

Protoculture Enr., P.O. Box 1433, Station B, Montreal, Quebec, Canada H3B 3L2

Fax: (514) 527-0347 • editor@protoculture.qc.ca • www.protoculture.qc.ca

The original Italian edition was first published in September 1991 (reprinted in January 1994) by Granata Press, Bologna.

Legal Deposit: December 2000
National Library of Quebec
National Library of Canada
ISBN 2-9805759-0-9

Printed in Canada

Canadian Cataloguing in Publication Data

Main entry under title:

Anime: a guide to Japanese animation, 1958-1988

Translated from Italian.
Includes bibliographical references and index.

ISBN 2-9805759-0-9

1. Animated films – Japan – Catalogs. 2. Motion pictures – Japan - Catalogs. 3. Animation (Cinematography) – Japan. 4. Animators – Japan. I. Baricordi, Andrea. II. Pelletier, Claude J., 1962-   . III. Protoculture (Firm).

NC1766.J3A5413 2000   791.43'3   C00-942038-X

CONTENTS

Foreword to Original Edition

You have in your hands the result of an immense amount of work, done across a many-year span by a group of five super-fans (otakus) of Japanese animation. While it sounds like fun, it was really a difficult task, consisting of viewing movies, recollecting old viewings, researching production houses' catalogues, consulting specific books and so forth. This work was made even more difficult, considering the fact that until now no book similar nor as voluminous as this one existed in the world.

Nevertheless this is book is not — as we, editors and authors, are aware — a perfect work, complete in every aspect: Research has been very difficult, often because some production house did not archive their own work, or even due to the fact that these productions (especially older television series) are irreconcilable in terms of versions and release dates.

We eventually achieved what we had promised ourselves — a book, not complete, but as close as objective limits would permit. We have presented the information under an index system which encompasses as much information as possible on anime's production from the very beginning through 1988.

You have in front of you a massive quantity of information, synopses, author's names, titles, series and characters. And you have here, above all, a work intended to be constantly consulted, built to surprise you and expend your knowledge, whether you read it straight through or look up that one elusive fact.

Cover of the Original Edition

Anime, we repeat, is a work of divulgation and consultation. That is why we had to make some decisions concerning transliterating from Japanese, something that might cause some to grimace . We did not, for example, preserve the Japanese tradition of writing a person's last name before their first name. We have, instead, chosen to write name in the occidental style, with the family name last.

In both cases, we have decided to refer to the common use, instead of the actual codification to avoid confusion and consulting difficulty. No Japanese, for instance, will ever say "Rumiko Takahashi", "Lupin" or "Devilman" instead saying "Takahashi Rumiko", "Rupan" and "Debiruman". But what would have been the reaction of uninformed readers if the book had adopted such codification? It would probably require hours and days to become familiar with the mechanics, and this becomes a disadvantage, preventing enjoyment of this book.

Enough digression: before you lie nearly three-hundred pages of entries, images, and plots, an authentic "mare magnum" (vast sea) of fabulous characters and phantasmagoric stories, an enormous fantasy kingdom that awaits discovery and return.

We remind you, however, to dive into this mass of information with restraint — if you take too much, too fast, you could get an indigestion! Please savour.

How to read the entries

Each entry appear in this order:
1) Original Title
2) Literal translation of the original title
3) Production house
4) Category (adventure, comedy, sci-fi, etc.)
5) Number of episodes (for television series only)
6) Release-date (for movies and OAV), or airing-date (for series and television specials)
7) Distribution house (for movie or OAV)
8) English title (if translated and available in North America) [or French title for Québec and France]

Each entry, furthermore, is preceded by a unique number which facilitates searches through the indexes. Besides the number we have also listed the type of production (Series, Special, Movie, or OAV).

A few remarks on Japanese pronunciation

The phonetic transcription of a foreign language is not always easy to understand or to do. Even more in the case of a culture as far as the Japanese culture. To facilitate the reading of the names and words contained in this guide, we chose a transliteration system that is simplified but often used in the West; it omits the reduplication of long vowels (instead of marking them with a macron). Words like "Shoonen" or names like "Ootomo" are transcribed "Shonen" and "Otomo" (the alternative would have been "Shônen" or "Ôtomo"). Here is a guide for the right pronunciation of the few Japanese phonetic groups:

Vowels

a is pronounced like in f*a*ther

e like in g*e*t or p*e*t

i like in macaron*i* (but sometimes not fully sounded)

o like in s*o*lo

u like in bl*u*e or z*u*l*u* (but sometimes not fully sounded)

Semi-Vowels

y is pronounced like **i**, but when put between a consonant and a vowel it stands as a syllable, like **kya** pronounced as in c*a*t

w is pronounced like a quick, consonantized **u**, like in w*o*n

Consonants

Most Japanese consonants have pronunciation relatively close to their English counterparts. The exceptions are:

g is always pronounced hard as in g*e*t

h is always aspirated as in *h*en

n is pronounced in full lenght when alone, and is often pronounced like **m** when followed by a **p**, **b** or **m**

r is pronounced in-between **r** and **l**, sometimes close to **d**

ch is pronounced is in *ch*in

Double consonants are pronounced with a pause (i.e. ki*tt*e pronounced as ki*t t*e).

Presentation (from original edition's inside covers' flaps)

When, in the mid '70s, *UFO Robot Grendizer* appeared for the first time on Italian TV screens, Japanese animation had already been shown before, but the adventures of the mega-robot Goldorak marked the real beginning of a massive invasion that will include, in the following years, cult series like *Candy Candy*, *Lupin III*, *Gundam* and *Lum*. Those beginnings gave rise to controversy not only from the anxious parents and teachers, who saw in the battles of those half-gods dressed in techno-armor a threat for the mind of the young viewers, but also from the numerous detractors, passionate fans of American animation, who found repetitive and badly animated the pitiful adventures of this heroine with the eyes always full of tears. However, the invasion never gave any signs of slowing down, on the contrary, it was attracting more and more the young generation of avid viewers.

Now that Japanese animation is a well established phenomenon and that the fans interest has expended to manga, this work come into being, fruit of a patient and how laborious research on original material not always easy to decipher but, above all, hard to find. It is a guide as complete and exhaustive as possible, including over 1,200 titles and covering thirty years of Japanese animation. It is a filmography that attempts for the first time to put some order, in a systematic but accessible manner, into a production that is massive, varied and in constant evolution. But, in the first place, it is a tribute to all those who, like the young authors of this book, have been moved at least once by the misfortune of *Lady Oscar* or have been fascinated by the victories of *Fist Of The North Star*'s Kenshiro.

Backcover Presentation (from the original edition)

"*Anime*" is the expression used by the Japanese to designate animated features, an art which has, in less than a century, attained an unimaginable popularity in Occident: dozens of specialized publications with millions of copies being printed; a listing of hundreds of titles; television and video productions which reach millions of viewers; a network of theatrical and video releasers rivaling those of major corporations, such as Disney and Warner. This is the reality of Japan, a country capable of creating animated features allying commercial success with technical mastery (Katsuhiro Otomo's now legendary *Akira*, to mention only one). However, *anime* owes its success not only to its massive introduction into foreign markets, but also to its ability to propose, thanks to authors like Osamu Tezuka, Go Nagai, Leiji Matsumoto and Hayao Miyazaki, a high level of technical and stylistic innovations which have gained the favor of the new generations of Occidental viewers. Characters, such as *Goldorak*, *Mazinger*, *Gundam*, *Lady Oscar*, *Lamu* and dozens of others, well known in Occident, have introduced a new narrative dimension, have resurrected, by revitalizing them, genres such as science-fiction, horror and soaps. The consequence of this is that we must, from now on, take into account the importance of *anime* in the animated features' international panorama.

This book was created as a "first contact" with the subject of *anime*, a contribution which, with its chronological and historiographic files, can provide a basic instrument of consultation and investigation to all those impassioned with the extraordinary universe of Japanese animation.

Foreword to English Edition

Since the day I first learned about the existence of this Italian book — *Anime, Guida Al Cinema D'Animazione Giapponese* — I always wanted to translate and publish it in English. However, I had no idea then that it would take me six years, and lots of work, to realize this project.

As a fan of Japanese animation and as someone who professionally writes about anime (I am publishing *Protoculture Addicts*, a magazine dedicated to Japanese animation and comics, since Fall 1987), I have always felt that there was a lack of good references about the subject. Japanese comics, or manga, have been much more studied than anime. The first book that comes to mind when you talk about manga is *Manga! Manga! The World Of Japanese Comics* by Frederik L. Schodt. Since 1983, this book has been the most serious reference about manga, covering its history, authors and thematics. I was hoping that *Anime, A Guide To Japanese Animation* (or *Anime Guide* in short) could be a similar reference for anime.

It was only when I finally got a copy of the Italian book, through one of my contacts in France, that I got confirmation that it was up to my expectation. It was a filmography of the first thirty years (1958-1988) of Japanese animation, listing chronologically over 1,200 titles (movies, TV series and Original Animation Videos) — from *Astroboy* to *Akira*! Each year was introduced with comments on the themes and titles that dominated that particular year. The amount of information offered was mind boggling and the enormity of the work done by the authors was amazing. It really was the most essential anime reference. I was astonished that no one had tried to make this work available in English before.

If the task of translating this book in English was nothing in comparison with the initial gathering of data, it was nevertheless quite an adventure. The first step was to contact the publisher. Through my contact in the publishing industry, I found the address of Granata Press and sent them letters and faxes without getting any answers. Fortunately, a friend attending the book fair of Bologna was able to contact them on my behalf and a publishing agreement was reached not long after. Translating the Italian text into English was more arduous: we had to change translators several times, the work took over two years and ended up being relatively expensive and not totally satisfactory. By the time the rough translation was done, I discovered that the original publisher, Granata, had gone out of business. I tried without success to contact the authors, so the project was shelved. Another two years passed. The authors, now working with Kappa Edizioni, heard that we were interested in publishing the book and contacted us. With a new publishing agreement, I hired a proof-reader to polish our rough translation and started working on the layout. Strangely, this final stage was our thoughest challenge and took much longer than expected.

Designing the layout of the book was relatively easy. I wanted a look that was echoing both the original edition and the presentation of our magazine, *Protoculture Addicts*. I also decided to keep the original cover because I thought it perfectly symbolized the fact that Osamu Tezuka, creator of *Astroboy*, had a leading role for a long time in the early years of the anime industry. He was not only the "God Of Manga," but also had a strong influence on the development of anime. A large part of the layout work was to find pictures to illustrate as many titles as possi-

Intro

1962
1963
1964
1965
1966
1967
1968
1969
1970
1971
1972
1973
1974
1975
1976
1977
1978
1979
1980
1981
1982
1983
1984
1985
1986
1987
1988

Index

ble. Since we didn't had the rights to use the illustrations of the original edition and some Japanese production companies notified us that they didn't want us to use any pictures of their properties, I decided to illustrate the book mostly with the cover art of the North American video releases. We had to research and scan those illustrations. It was not possible to illustrate every title, but the book still has over 400 illustrations.

This stage took us another two years. The proof-reading and the layout were part of a slow process, but most of the delays came from the fact that we had to go forward on the project and manage to produce the magazine at the same time — which, considering our small staff, was very difficult. The vicissitudes of life also conspired to hinder our work with various health and computer problems (data loss, fonts that don't print, etc.). Stress and overwork took a serious toll on our health, but we finally succeeded and you are now holding the result of all this work in your hands.

By publishing this book, our purpose is to make available to all people, fans and scholars alike, the enormous amount of information it contains. It is to make people really understand the anime phenomenon and to place it in its original context. You don't know anime unless you understand how big the industry is in Japan, how it started, and that it is not an homogeneous product, but covers a great variety of subjects and genres. What we have seen here in North America is only a very small fraction of the anime production and, since the anime releasers select the titles they import, it is not representative of what anime really is. This book, without too much analysis, offers you the data that you need to see anime in its global context. All you have to do is dive into this sea of information… However, this book, if essential, is by no means an end, but the beginning, we hope, of more researches and publications on this fascinating subject.

Before going further, we must warn you that, despite the fact it is the most essential anime reference, this book is far form being perfect or exhaustive. First, it was written in the beginning of the '90s and mainly targeted at an Italian readership. We dedicated ourselves to translate the precious information offered by the book and chose not to update it. Also, with the use of illustrations and specific indexes, we tried to put a little more focus on the North American scene, but the comments still relate to the Italian anime market and their perception of anime. Finally, despite all the proof-reading we could do, I am sure there are still plenty of translation mistakes, typos, errors, etc. We did our best and we hope that you will enjoy your reading.

We invite you to send us your comments on the book (you can e-mail to: editor@protoculture.qc.ca with "Anime Guide" as subject). All comments, as well as eventual updates and erratum, will be posted on our web page (www.protoculture.qc.ca) or published in the pages of our magazine *Protoculture Addicts*.

Claude J. Pelletier
Protoculture

FIRST PART:

The Origins and the Sixties

CHAPTER ONE: FROM THE ORIGINS TO 1962

While the actual industry of Japanese animation began in 1958, with Toei Doga's rendition of the ancient Chinese *White Serpent* legend, we must take into consideration the origins of this style of artwork.

Hakujaden (The Legend Of The White Serpent)
© Toei Doga

The history of Japanese animation has its roots in the 18th century, when the theatre of shadows *(utsushie* — cast images) appeared in Japan, and at the beginning of the 19th century, when the process of representing images in movement gained the interest of painters. Among them was Katsushiha Hokusai, who distinguished himself with certain paintings representing the different movements of oriental dance. The first Japanese artists to venture in the world of animation, impressed by the many Western movies shown in their country, were the painter Junichi Kouchi, the caricaturist Oten Shimokawa and Seitaro Kitayama, in charge of the art magazine *Gendai no Yoka*. These three, starting in 1914, worked individually on feature films, based on traditional subjects, that were later produced by Nikkatsu. The level of craftmanship, however, did not allow them to reach notoriety. In 1917, Kitayama produced *Saru Kani Kassen* (*The Crab Takes Revenge on the Monkey*), *The Cat and the Mice* and *The Mischievous Letterbox,* but his first major success came the following year with *Momotaro*, which was the first Japanese cartoons to be shown in the Western world — it played in movie theatres in France. Also in 1917, *Hanahekonai's New Sword* and *The Lazy Sword* were produced, the first cartoons of Junichi Kouchi, who, in the 1920s, simultaneously with Kiichiro Kanai and Sanae Yamamoto, created a great innovation in Japanese animation technique: the use of grey shades. Oten Shimokawa, instead, started out with *Imohawa Mukuzo Genkanban no Maki* (*Mukuzo Imohawa, the Doorman*) and produced in the following years certain feature films about the famous characters of his comic strips, successfully published in major local newspapers. Shimokawa's career was abruptly interrupted because of an eye illness which forced him into an early retirement.

1925 brought the turn of the already mentioned Sanae Yamamoto, who directed *Obasuteyama* (*The Mountain Where the Old Are Abandoned*) and *Ushiwakamuru*, a story about a little samurai. In 1928, the author undertook a profitable collaboration with Kichiro Kanai, with whom he directed *Shitakiri Susume* (*The Sparrows With the Cut Tongues*) and *Issunboshi Chibi Monogatari* (*The Story of the Dwarf Chisibuke*).

Another famous animator who deserves credit for addressing his stories to adults, producing dramas often permeated with erotic elements, was Noburo Ofuji, creator of the feature film *Kujira* (*The Whale*). He made this film by cutting shapes from a special semi-transparent paper (chiyogami) which were layered on various panels of glass to form the illustrations of the characters and the backgrounds, and then photographed frame by frame. The remarkable fluidity of the animation, in relation to the other productions of the time, was enriched by the fascinating effect of the transparency and shadows obtained with this new technique. The movie was soon purchased by a French production firm to be distributed in 1929 in some parts of Europe. Galvanized by this success, Ofuji directed other cartoons, among which came *Sekisho* (*The Control Station*), in 1930, which saw the dawning of sound in his productions and *Katsurahime* (*Princess Katsura*), in 1937, in which he used color for the first time. The arrival of a new technique, imported from America, brought major changes in animation, among which was the introduction of total animation. Yasuji Murata, who made his debut in 1927, is a worthy representative of this technique and owes his success to the movie *Tako no hone* (*The Octopus' Bone*), characterized by a specific style and by the the use of animal-like characters.

The first Japanese talking animation was *Chikara to onna no yononaka* (*The World of Power and of Women*) in 1932, directed by Kenzo Masaoka (known for 1930's *Sarugashima* (*The Island of the Monkeys*)), but it couldn't compete with Walt Disney's films and the notable fluidity of American animation. The humorous story showed the love of a man, married to an oppressive and fat woman, for a delightful typist. The only artist to achieve any success was Yoshitsugu Tanaka. He directed *Entotsuya Pero* (*Pero the Chimney Sweep*), produced by Doeisha, to promote the views of the workers, whose miserable and inhuman conditions became an excellent starting element for a firm social statement. While the involvement of young Japanese cartoonists was strong, no one neglected the pedagogical importance of this new means, and during the Second World War the artists of the Rising Sun created their own animations aimed at war propaganda. The most prolific, surely, was Mitsuyo Seo who directed *The Assault Troops of Sankichi the Monkey*, a feature film on the Japanese-Chinese war, in which the powerful Japanese army attacked an enemy fortress defended without much result by a platoon of Chinese pandas. Afterward, he won his fame thanks to *Momotaro no Umiwashi* (*The Dauntless Sea of Momotaro*) in 1943 and *Momotaro Umi no Shinpei* (*Momotaro: the Gods of the Sea*), in which he presented the Japanese sailors as anthropomorphic animals, training, constructing a landing strip and undertaking the siege of an enemy base in New Guinea. Kenzo Masaoka came to animated film-making in 1939 with *Benkei tai Urashima* (*Benkei Against Urashima*), the story of a priest and a little samurai. In 1943, Michiko Yokoyama proved his great sense of the poetic with *Kumo to Tulip* (*The Spider and the Tulip*), a musical film based on a fairy tale. The star of the film is a delightful ladybug that finds refuge in a tulip to escape from the trap of of a spider in love with her. A raging storm sparked by the divinity of Thunder comes to the aid of our protagonist: only the tulip is saved from the rain and the ladybug, now out of danger, comes out of hiding singing. In 1949 he found new success with *Sakura haru no genso* (*The Cherry Flowers: the Beginning of Spring*), in which some girls wearing kimonos play with puppies and butterflies under blossoming cherry trees, accompanied by German musician Weber's "Invitation to waltz."

After the short feature film *Ko Neko no Rakugaki* (*The Drawings of the Kitten*), Taiji Yabushita, a great animator who now teaches at the Gakuin drawing school in Tokyo, directed for Toei Doga (his own production firm) *Hakujaden*, the first color feature film in the history of Japanese animation. Co-founded with Sanae Yamamoto, another great name in the Japanese panorama since the 20s, the prolific firm produced *Shonen Sarutobi Sasuke*, a movie centered on the traditions of ancient Japan, which showcase the appearance of a courageous *sarutobi* (a ninja at the service of, or in conflict with, the local lords). The little

Shonen Sarutobi Sasuke © Toei Doga

Sasuke, which definitely looked better in the following series produced in 1968 (#0080), appears clumsy and the animation almost never kept up with the rhythm and the rapidity commanded by the plot. In 1960, Osamu Tezuka brought his skills to Toei Doga for the first and only time, for a film called *Saiyuki*, inspired by the stories of the mythical stone monkey, Sun Wukong.

The new decade saw the dawning of an innovative shift in technique as well as in content, which brought Japanese productions up to the level of the schools of other Western countries, like those of Jiri Trnka from Tchecoslovakia, Dusan Vukotic from Yugoslavia, or Jan Lenica and Walerian Borowczyk from Poland. In fact, Yoji Kuri, along with the two illustrators Ryohei Yanagihara and Hiroshi Makabe, formed the group "Sannin no Kai" (The group of the three) that developed new techniques and styles useful to future animators.

The expansion of commercial cinema happened in 1962 and was due to the above-mentioned Osamu Tezuka and his production firm, Mushi. For his first works, the author was forced to work within a very short time frame, producing about one half hour animation per week, at very low cost, which forced him to use certain backgrounds more than once. Despite the success of his first series, *Tetsuwan Atom*, and of the movie *Aru Machikado no Monogatari*, Tezuka, who was experiencing financial problems, had to declare bankrupcy in 1973. It is from then that syndication took control of Mushi. But Tezuka didn't get discouraged and he founded Tezuka Production in 1975, with which he produced works such as *Jumping* (1984), that won first prize at the festival of animated cinema of Zagabria, *Onboro Film* (1985), that won first prize at the Animation Festival of Hiroshima, and *Mori no Densetsu* (1988). These three, however, were experimental films presented in specialized exhibitions and came out on video only in 1991.

Mori No Densetsu ©1987 Tezuka Pro. Packaging & design ©1994 The Right Stuf International, Inc. (Cat.# RS9003).

0001 FILM

HAKUJADEN (*The Legend of the White Serpent*), Toei Doga, fantasy, 78 min., 10/22/1958.

This feature film directed by Taiji Yabushita was taken from an ancient Chinese legend, and won the Special Diploma at the Festival of Cinema for Children in Venice in 1959. The original concept, which shows the tormented love of the main character for a young girl who was previously reincarnated into a white snake, was created by Shin Uchara and the music was composed by Masayoshi Ikeda.

0002 FILM

HYOTANSUZUME (*The Sparrow and the Empty Pumpkin*), Otogi, humour, 65 min., 2/10/1959.

0003 FILM

SHONEN SARUTOBI SASUKE (*Sasuke, the Young Sarutobi*), Toei Doga, adventure/samurai, 83 min., 12/25/1959.

The young Sasuke, son of a skilled ninja who rebelled against the rigid laws of the warrior sect, learns expert fighting techniques from his wise father, and frees the people who are enslaved by the lord of the fief. The film is set in medieval times.

0004 FILM

SAIYUKI (*Voyage Towards the West*), Toei Doga, fantasy, 88 min., 8/14/1960. *Alakazam The Great!*

Shonen Sarutobi Sasuke © Toei Doga

Saiyuki ©1961 Toei Doga.
Alakazam The Great! ©1995 Orion Home Video. All Right Reserved. (Cat.# 50030).

Arabian Night Sinbad No Boken © Toei Doga.

Aru Machikado No Monogatari © Tezuka Production.

Saiyuki was Osamu Tezuka's first feature animation and was inspired by the famous Chinese story of Hiuan Tsane, Sun Wukong. The main character of the story is a little monkey that embarks on a long and tiresome voyage along with bizarre characters, to recover the Sutra, famous scrolls containing sacred scripture. The movie showed in Italy with the American version of the screenplay.

0005 FILM

ANJUTO TO ZUSHIOMARU (*Anju and Zushiomaru*), Toei Doga, historical, 83 min., 7/19/1961.

In medieval Japan, Anju and Zushiomaru, two brothers, sons of a governor fallen from grace, are separated. After numerous adventures, they meet again as adults and are reunited with their mother, whom they thought was dead.

0006 FILM

ARABIAN NIGHT SINDBAD NO BOKEN (*Arabian Nights: the Adventures of Sinbad*), Toei Doga, adventure, 81 min., 7/21/1962.

This is an animated version of the story of Sinbad, the courageous sailor of the South Seas. The original story is taken from the *Thousand and One Nights*, a collection of famous Arab short stories, which have inspired many Japanese productions.

0007 FILM

OTOGI NO SEKAI RYOKO (*Voyage around the Otogi World*), Otogi, documentary, 76 min., 8/25/1962.

Ryuichi Yokoyama, who had founded Otogi in 1955, produced a particularly well-crafted film. It is an anthological film featuring several creations by Otogi's animation staff.

0008 FILM

ARU MACHIKADO NO MONOGATARI (*Stories From a Street Corner*), Mushi, sociological, 38 min., 9/20/1962.

With this simply plotted animated feature film, in which he illustrates certain daily living situations in a Japan at the height of the industrial revolution, Osamu Tezuka inaugurates Mushi, his own production firm. The film has the distinction of having no characters or dialogue, instead using narration based on visual abstractions.

0009 SERIES

MANGA CALENDAR (*The Calendar of Animated Cartoons*), Otogi, documentary, 54 episodes, 25/6/1962 – 4/7/1964.

Contrary to what was reported in articles or by critics of Japanese animation, the credit for having created the first series production does not belong to Mushi with its *Tetsuwan Atom*, but to Otogi who began producing *Manga Calendar* in June 1962.

CHAPTER TWO: 1963

Science-fiction and technology have always been greatly present in Japan, and their presence, even today, determines the success of many animated productions. Certainly, the presence of robots and cyborgs is the element that both enriches and adds a specific uniqueness to the Japanese panorama. Even though we had to wait for the 70s to have a real "robot invasion," it is in 1963 that the foundations were laid.

The year 1963 opened up with the first series made by Mushi, *Tetsuwan Atom*. Born in 1951 as *Atom Taishi* (*Atom the Ambassador*), the character was published without interruption until 1968 in *Shonen Magazine*. In 1959, his adventures had already been adapted in a series of made for television live-action movies starring young actors. The animated cartoon was done in black and white with limited technical expertise and with little professional experience, but it had a powerful emotional range. The main character, one of the most famous of the prolific author, met with great success with the public as well as the critics, so much so that today it still is remembered with nostalgia.

Atom was the first little robot of Japanese animation and, thus, he became a reference for many young authors who in the following years drew from Tezuka's Disney-inspired style and classic plotlines. The character was revived in 1980, thanks to a movie for the big screen. The following year, a color remake of the series was produced.

If *Tetsuwan Atom* represents an important series in the innovative sense, *Tetsujin 28 Go* occupies an important position in animation history for being the first "giant robot" prototype. Created by Mitsuteru Yokoyama, the series, born as a radio serial novel and later adapted in a mini-series of 12 episodes for television, presents all the elements that make up the foundation of this new type of production, named "Robot Animation." In 1963, TCJ produced a first animation series, also in black and white, that was aired until 1967. No particular care was given to the artwork. The look of the robot itself, with its stocky body, small head and disproportionate limbs, as well as the excessive simplicity of the subject — the little Shotaru runs the powerful robot with a ridiculous remote control, almost as if it was an enormous toy — certainly contributed to its limited success. The fact that it introduced such a popular premise, however, makes it worthy of mention, and many now-famous animators no doubt owe their success to Yokoyama and his series. We only have to think of Go Nagai who, starting in the 70s, developed one of the most popular robotic sagas.

In 1980, TMS produced, as Mushi had done with *Tetsuan Atom*, a new color series of *Tetsujin 28 Go*, enriched with a softer design and better animation.

Seeing the increasing success of animated cartoon series, Toei Doga, who had achieved a notable level of quality in some previous feature films, also presented its first series: *Okami Shonen Ken*. Their success built slowly, but their solid foundations bore their fruits a few years later, mainly in the robotic genre, so strongly, that many established authors would still associate their names with Toei Doga.

Another series worthy of mention, *Eight Man*, was taken from a cartoon bearing the same name and saw the light of day with the collaboration of Kuzumasa Irai for the texts

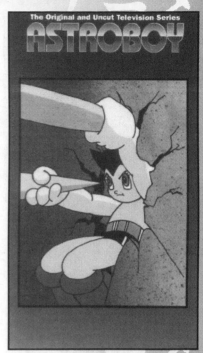

Astroboy ©1964 Suzuki International. English version ©1989 The Right Stuf, Inc.

Astro Boy ©1963 NBC Films, renewed 1991 Suzuki Associates International. Packaging ©1993 The Right Stuf International, Inc.

Gigantor ©1964 Delphi Associates. Packaging © Scott Wheeler Productions

and Jiro Kuwata for the artwork. The main character is, once again, a cyborg (created, like Atom, following the death of the character from which it was modeled) gifted with certain powers, including an ability to effect multiple shape change. This new ability, never seen before in Japan, was rendered in a spectacular way in the animated sequences, which showed a specific change in the character's somatic and physical traits. It became very popular in 1974 with the dawning of one of the best liked superheroes, *Hurricane Polymer*.

0010 FILM
WANPAKU OJI NO OROCHI TAIJI (*The Wicked Prince's Hunt of the Big Snake*), Toei Doga, historical, 85 min., 3/24.

Following the death of his mother Yazanami, Susano the intrepid mercenary embarks on a long and dangerous trip to serve in the army of the emperor Yomi. The movie is the work of Yugo Serikawa, an important artist of the 60s and 70s.

0011 FILM
WAN WAN CHUSHINGURA (*The Faithful Servant Dogs*), Toei Doga, animals/adventure, 81 min., 12/21.

This feature film bears the signature of Hayao Miyazaki, one of the most famous of all Japanese animators. He took on the job of in-betweener (creating the intermediary frames inbetween each key position, which give the fluidity to the characters' movement). This allowed the young Miyazaki to refine his techniques, learning to clean and streamline the animation, as well as reducing the jerkiness of the action.

0012 SERIES
TETSUWAN ATOM (*Iron-Arm Atom*), Mushi, science-fiction, 193 episodes, 1/1/1963 – 12/31/1966. *Astro Boy*.

Tenma, director of the Ministry of Science, builds a robot that looks like his son who died in a car accident. Atom, the result of the perfect marriage between technology and humanity, becomes the defender of planet Earth, fighting against numerous enemies.

0013 SERIES
GINGA SHONENTAI (*The Team of the Children of the Galaxy*), Mushi, science-fiction, 92 episodes, 4/7/1963 – 4/1/1965.

0014 SERIES
SENNIN BURAKU (The Village of the Hermit), TCJ, satire, 9/4/1963 – 2/23/1964.

Taken from Ko Kojimai's original comic strip, the 1963 series presents a unique style. Thanks to the skillful use of satire, *Sennin Buraku* reveals all the vices, weaknesses and corruption of humankind.

0015 SERIES
TETSUJIN 28 GO (*Man of Steel 28*), TCJ, robot, 96 episodes, 10/20/1963 – 5/27/1965. *Gigantor*.

Two scientists, Dr. Shikishima and Dr. Kaneda, arrange for the Institute of Japanese Secret Weapons, to build a robot with peaceful intentions. After 27 attempts, they make a powerful prototype: Tetsujin 28, an enormous humanlike robot, remote controlled by Shotaro, a young boy in possession of the computerized briefcase containing the remote control. The enemies, contrary to future robot series, are not aliens, but groups of gangsters or simply evil individuals. The series is based on the manga by Mitsuteru Yokoyama.

0016 SERIES

EIGHT MAN (id.), TCJ, police/science-fiction, 56 episodes, 11/7/1963 – 12/31/1964. *8ᵗʰ Man*.

Professor Tani transfers the memory of detective Hachiro Azuma into an android with extraordinary abilities. The android can change his facial features due to the elasticity of his skin, and use superpowers to fight against crime. The series is taken from Kazumasa Hirai and Jiro Kwata's comic strip.

0017 SERIES

OKAMI SHONEN KEN (*Ken, The Wolf Child*), Toei Doga, adventure, 86 episodes, 11/25/1963 – 8/16/1965.

The young Ken is raised by a pack of wolves who feed him and take care of him as if he were one of their own. Once grown, he helps his companions maintain peace and serenity in the woods where they live. The series is directed by Sadao Tsukioka.

VIDEO RARITIES PRESENTS

THE GREATEST ADVENTURES OF

8TH MAN

VOL. 1

2 HOURS OF ANIMATED ACTION IN ENGLISH

8ᵗʰ Man ©1990 Video Rarities.

CHAPTER THREE: 1964

There were only three animated series that began in 1964: *Shonen Ninja Kaze No Fujimaru*, *Big X* and *Zero Sen Hayato*. Besides that, only one feature film was produced: *Tetsuwan Atom Uchu No Yusha*, which featured the now famous robot created by Osamu Tezuka.

Shonen Ninja Kaze No Fujimaru was the first animated series to be based on a manga by famous artist Sanpei Shirato. His career began in 1957, and in a very short period of time he became one of the best Japanese screenplay writers and illustrators. Shirato, connoisseur of Japanese history, found his niche in stories focusing on ninjas (like in *Ninpu Kamui Gaiden* (#0097) and *Sasuke* (#0080)), famous hired killers bound to their trainers since childhood. He shows exceptional skill, portraying with extreme realism both the complex world of the ninja, and the battles that they fight because they realize that they are slowly losing their will to become cruel murderers in the hands of local big shots who use them so they won't tarnish their own code of honor. In many cases, Sanpei Shirato compares the past with the present, condemning the problems and contradictions of today's society. The style of drawing is very particular in this series: the artist succeeds in giving expression and dynamic speed to the rapid and precise lines which impart on his works a pictorial quality.

Another series to be taken into consideration is *Big X*, animated version of a famous manga by Osamu Tezuka, who became an appreciated and a solidly recognized author. After *Tetsuwan Atom* and *Ginga Shonintai*, both from 1963, this is the third character from the father of Japanese comic strips to have his own television series. With *Big X*, Tezuka confronts themes linked to studies in genetic engineering. The main character, a gigantic soldier, has been himself created with the help of this discipline with the ultimate goal of confronting the Nazi League. The criticism against the Nazis is clear, as they committed numerous crimes during the last World War in the name of genetic research.

Intro
-1962
1963
1964
1965
1966
1967
1968
1969
1970
1971
1972
1973
1974
1975
1976
1977
1978
1979
1980
1981
1982
1983
1984
1985
1986
1987
1988
Index

The third and final series of this year is *Zero Sen Hayato*, which focusses on a theme seldom used in Japanese animation, the Second World War. Through the action of Zero fighter pilots, Naoki Tsuji brings back the memories of the terrible conflict in order to exalt the patriotic spirit of the Japanese people, who tend to forget those war events because of the dramatic reversal created by the explosion of the atomic bomb, which is much more present in the Japanese imaginary.

Tetsuwan Atom Uchu No Yusha © Tezuka Production.

0018 FILM

TETSUWAN ATOM UCHU NO YUSHA (*Iron-Arm Atom: The Courageous One From Space*), Mushi, science-fiction, 87 min., 7/26.

The film presents the animated movie debut of the famous television series, and confirms the little robot, with his particular charisma, as one of the most popular characters of the 60s.

0019 SERIES

ZERO SEN HAYATO (*Hayato, Zero Fighter Pilot*), P. Prod , war, 41episodes, 1/21 – 10/27/1964.

The actions of the Zero fighter pilots, protagonists of the Second World War, offered Naoki Tsuji a good starting point for the realization of a comic strip marked with patriotic spirit. The animated series is based on this same premise.

Shonen Ninja Kaze No Fujimaru © Toei Doga.

0020 SERIES

SHONEN NINJA KAZE NO FUJIMARU (*Fujimaru, The Young Ninja Of The Wind*), Toei Doga, adventure, 65 episodes, 6/7/1964 – 8/31/1965.

This serial was the first animated productions taken from Sanpei Shirato's manga. Using secret combat techniques and tricks bordering on magic, Fujimaru fights with samurais and evil landlords in an era torn by inner conflicts.

0021 SERIES

BIG X (*id.*), Tokyo Movie, science-fiction, 59 episodes, 8/3/1964 – 9/27/1965.

Based on Osamu Tezuka's original manga, *Big X* is a story about applied genetic engeneering. Professor Asagumo, involved in the study of Big X, a wonderful drug that enlarges the cells of living beings, succeeds in creating a gigantic soldier able to confront the perfidious Nazi League.

Big X © Tezuka Production / TMS.

CHAPTER FOUR: 1965

1965 was an important year for Japanese animation. The productions were mostly geared to a very young public, who eagerly awaited the transposition of their favorite characters from manga to television sets. It was a golden time for Osamu Tezuka, who returned to the small screen with *Shin Takarajima*, already a print best seller, with over six hundred thousand copies sold within the first few days of release. His success was instantaneous and his personal style succeeded in creating original and well-characterized protagonists. Tezuka was the first mangaka to find inspiration in the cartoons of the Fleischer brothers, and the first to impose his strong personal style of graphics and narration which, in the years to come, other manga illustrators will attempted to copy. Tezuka's innovative style was reflected in the animation, contributing to give it the characteristics that many foreign animation companies will later try to imitate with poor results. It is for this reason, above all , that Tezuka is considered, and rightly so, the father of Japanese manga or, as they say in Japan, the "god of manga". He specialized in treating humanitarian, anti-military and environmental themes. In 1951, a work considered fundamental in Tezuka's production started to be published in the pages of *Shonen Magazine*: *Jungle Taitei*. After the enormous success obtained with this manga, a first transposition to animation was done in 1965, which was of great importance: it was one of the first color television series. The animation doesn't fail to live up to expectations. As proof of the success of the series, a sequel to the adventures of the friendly white lion, now an adult, began in 1966. The same year, a feature animated film was made, based on the same characters. Because of the immense popularity of this character, a remake of the first serial was done by Tezuka's staff in 1989 — in February of that year, Tezuka Productions lost its great master.

Gulliver No Uchu Ryoko is the only feature film from this year. It is important to note that Hayao Miyazaki, a young author, destined to occupy a place of great importance in Japanese animation, is part of the crew. His animation is polished, fluid and spectacular. It is not by accident that he is the author of many international hits. Another important debut of this year is due to the prolific Moto Abiko and Hiroshi Fujimoto, better known as Fujiko Fujio, who, with *Obake No Qtaro*, inaugurate a great animation production. Specialized in children's comedy, the authors also deal with the themes related to childhood. Except for very few notable episode, this production centers around stories of science-fiction. It explores the world of superheroes "the American way," in which youngsters, gifted with extraordinary powers and wearing clinging body suits, infest outer space. *Uchu Shonen Soran* inaugurates one of the recurring themes in Japanese animation: orphaned main character searches for their mother, father or brother, confronting never-ending adventures. For Japanese people, these stories have a hidden moral: the demonstration that, counting on one's strength, one can reach any goal. It shouldn't be forgotten that the Japanese people were masters in putting this teaching into practice, a mentality which brought them to rebuild an economic empire on top of the ruins of a devastating war.

The animation industry was still young in this period, but it already understood where to look: the themes became more and more complex, to adapt to a public that was not only composed of children but more mature people with interests specific to their age and tastes.

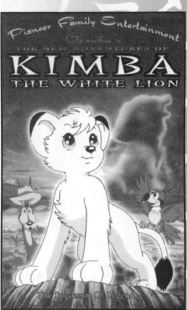

Kimba The White Lion ©1989, 1998 Gakken • Nihon Keizaisha • Tezuka Productions • TV Tokyo. This 1989 remake of *Jungle Taitei* was released in North America in 1998 by Pioneer Entertainment (USA) L.P. (Cat.# PIKB-0001D).

0022 FILM
GULIVER NO UCHU RYOKO (*Gulliver's Space Travels*), Toei Doga, adventure, 80 min., 3/20.

Jonathan Swift has already told us about the adventures of Lemuel Gulliver in the country of the small people of Lilliput, the giants of Brobdingnag, the intelligent horses of Houyhnhnm and on the flying island of Laputa. Here, Toei Doga completes the story sending the famous young traveler in an incredible adventure to the ends of the universe.

0023 SERIES
SUPER JETTER MIRAI KARA KITA SHONEN (*Super Jetter, the Boy Who Came From the Future*), TCJ, science-fiction, 52 episodes, 1/7/1965 – 1/20/1966.

0024 SERIES

UCHU PATROL HOPPER — UCHUKKO JUN (*Hopper Space Patrol: Jun The Little Space-man*), Toei Doga, science-fiction, 44 episodes, 2/1 – 11/29/1965.

0025 SERIES

DOLPHIN OJI (*The Dolphin Prince*), TV Doga, adventure, 13 episodes, 4/4 – 4/18/1965.

First color anime. Toei Doga, already involved in the making of *Kaito Plaid*, was forced to hire new personnel for this production.

0026 SERIES

UCHUJIN PIPI (*Pipi The Spaceman*), TV Doga for the NHK, science-fiction, 52 episodes, 4/8/1965 – 3/3/1966.

0027 SERIES

UCHU SHONEN SORAN (*Soran, The Space Kid*), TCJ, science-fiction, 96 episodes, 5/4/1965 – 2/28/1967.

A child, sole survivor of the destruction of a spaceship that killed his parents, leaves his adoptive planet (on which he learned all the secrets of science) to come back to planet Earth. With a friendly space squirrel as his travelling companion, Soran starts looking for his sister, using the powers acquired in space to do good on Earth.

Uchu Ace © Tatsunoko Pro.

0028 SERIES

UCHU ACE (*The Space Ace*), Tatsunoko, science-fiction, 52 episodes, 5/8/1965 – 4/28/1966.

The survivors of an alien race go looking for a virgin planet on which they will rebuild their civilization. During the trip, a spaceship flown by a young extraterrestrial, abandoning the course, comes to Earth. Gifted with extraordinary powers, the character, created by illustrator Tatsuo Yoshida, presents himself as a champion of justice to help his adoptive planet.

0029 SERIES

KAITO PLAID (*Plaid, The Mysterious Thief*), TV Doga, adventure, 105 episodes, 5/31 – 11/4/1965.

Doctor Plaid is a burglary genius who plans his thefts with extreme precision and fantasy. The many attempts, from the best police agents, fail to stop the mysterious thief.

Yusei Shonen Papi © Eiken.

0030 SERIES

YUSEI SHONEN PAPI (*Papi, the Interplanetary Kid*), TCJ, science-fiction, 52 episodes, 6/3/1965 – 5/27/1966. *Prince Planet.*

The young Papi arrives in our solar system from the far planet Clifton, ready to fight against the Metallizers, evil space pirates.

0031 SERIES

WONDER THREE (*id.*), Mushi, sociological, 52 episodes, 6/6/1965 – 6/27/1966.

With *Wonder Three*, Osamu Tezuka outlines the contradictions of the human race, seen through the eyes of three extraterrestrials disguised as a horse, a duck and a rabbit.

Wonder Three © Tezuka Production.

0032 SERIES

OBAKE NO QTARO (*Qtaro, The Ghost*), Tokyo Movie, humour, 89 episodes, 8/29/1965 – 3/26/1967.

To have a ghost as a friend can really be useful. That's what young Tadashi thinks, when he is chosen by Qtaro to be his discreet tutor. Created by the duo Fujiko Fujio, *Qtaro* introduces the theme of childhood insecurity in a very simple cartoon.

0033 SERIES

JUNGLE TAITEI (*Jungle Emperor*), Mushi, animal/adventure, 52 episodes, 10/6/1965 – 9/28/1966. *Kimba The White Lion.*

Created simultaneously with *Atom*, *Jungle Taitei* was released in both a second television series and a movie in 1966. The series narrates the adventures of Leo, an albino lion cub, forced to become king of the jungle prematurely upon the death of his father, Panja.

0034 SERIES

HUSTLE PUNCH (*id.*), Toei Doga, animal, 26 episodes, 11/1/1965 – 4/25/1966.

Punch, the courageous bear and his animal friends, are forced to fight the brutal incursions of Garigari, the ferocious wolf.

0035 SERIES

TATAKAE! OSPER (*Fight Osper!*), Nihon Oso Eigasha, adventure, 99 episodes, 12/14/1965 – 10/31/1967.

The warlike people of Dorome declare war on Earth. The inhabitants of the sunken continent Mu set against the enemy offensive a terrible warrior: Osper.

0036 SPECIAL

SHIN TAKARAJIMA (*The New Treasure Island*), Mushi, adventure, 52 min., 1/1.

The story is taken from Osamu Tezuka's manga. The main characters are a group of friends involved in the search for a treasure on a mysterious island.

CHAPTER FIVE: 1966

With *Mahotsukai Sally*, Toei Doga unknowingly inaugurated one of the narrative traditions of Japanese animation, which earned even more success later on. The small witches grew rapidly in number, becoming cult series in the 80s with *Maho No Tenshi Creamy Mami* and *Maho No Star Magical Emi.*

The basic concept of the main characters in these series is that they are amateur witches who are sent to our world for a period of apprenticeship, or in other cases, lucky girls who are gifted by Elves or Fairies with magic wands, bracelets or mirrors with which they can transform themselves into whoever or whatever they want.

The most interesting fact is that, over time, the fans of this sort of animation have varied greatly. The little witches, created initially for young girls under the age of ten, have found approval amongst teenagers, probably because of the fascination that these little characters exert, with their power to grow and become fascinating stars while keeping a sense of childhood innocence.

Kimba The White Lion ©1966/2000 Tezuka Production. Packaging ©2000 The Right Stuf International, Inc. All rights reserved (RS7001/08).

Shin Takarajima © Tezuka Production.

Mahotsukai Sally © Hikari Production / Toei Doga.

With Osamu Tezuka's *Tetsuwan Atom*, the public had already shown interest in "mechanical heroes." *Cyborg 009* came out in 1966, confident to obtain a similar success. This movie was inspired by one of Shotaro Ishimori's most famous manga. The superstitious author (he later changed his name to Ishonomori because of the number of signs needed to write the name) narrated the private war of nine people transformed into cyborgs by a mysterious organisation against which they then rebel. The fantastic powers of the nine grabbed audiences: a boy with enhanced speed, a telepathic baby, a big-nosed flying man, a big and strong Indian, a young girl with ultra vision, a human arsenal, a fat flame thrower, a colored man capable of breathing under water and a bald man able to change his appearance formed one of the most innovative teams in the field of Japanese animated science-fiction. They remained in the memory of fans for a long time.

Tezuka's Mushi was particularly busy in 1966, proposing the film and the new series of *Jungle Taitei*, which told the adventures of Leo, the new king of the jungle, caring for the rights and the duties of the animals. The plot details their search for a mysterious tree which bears fruit that tastes like meat.

From the artistic point of view, *Tenrankai No E*, also by Tezuka, is more interesting. The author undertakes the task of making a musical animated film in the Disney style, like *Fantasia*, where classical music and animation are united.

Being effectively a transition year, 1966 brought few innovations in Japanese animation, downright scraping the bottom of the barrel with series like *Tobidase! Bacchiri*, of which the technique, the storyline and the content are quickly forgotten.

0037 FILM
CYBORG 009 (*id.*), Toei Doga, science-fiction, 64 min., 7/21.

Nine people discover, on different occasions, that they are cyborgs gifted with strange powers. Learning that they were built for evil purposes, they unite in a common fight against their creator. Taken from Shotaro Ishimori's manga, the movie narrates the origins of the nine cyborgs.

0038 FILM
JUNGLE TAITEI (*Jungle Emperor*), Mushi, animals, 65 min., 7/31.

The feature film is based on the animated serial. The kindness of the main character and the in-depth screenplay in which the situations switch between humour, introspection and drama brought Tezuka's film recognition at the 19th Children's Film Festival in Venice with the Lion of St. Marc award.

0039 FILM
TENRANKAI NO E (*Paintings In An Exposition*), Mushi, musical, 34 min., 11/11.

The film, which bears Osamu Tezuka's signature, is an animated collage set to the music of *Paintings in an Exposition*, Musorgsky's famous opera. The running theme of the ten satirical episodes, which highlight man's madness, follows the narrative outline of the Zagabrian school.

Jungle Taitei © Tezuka Production.

Tenrankai No E © Tezuka Production.

0040 SERIES

OSOMATSUKUN (*The Little Sosomatsu*), Studio Zero Children Corner, children/humour, 60 episodes, 2/5/1966 – 3/25/1967.

Osomatsu is the main character of Studio Zero's first production. The strength of this series lies in its mix of irony and insanity.

0041 SERIES

RAINBOW SENTAI ROBIN (*Robin The Rainbow Warrior*), Toei Doga, science-fiction, 48 episodes, 4/23/1966 – 3/24/1967.

The courageous Robin and his six friends try to obstruct, with every possible means, the ferocious attacks by the people of the star Palta, who want to conquer the Earth.

0042 SERIES

KAIZOKU OJI (*The Privateer Prince*), Toei Doga, adventure, 31 episodes, 5/2 – 11/28/1966.

0043 SERIES

HARIS NO KAZE (*Haris' Cyclone*), P. Prod., children, 70 episodes, 5/5/ 1966 – 8/31/1967.

Kunimatsu Ishida is a mischevious, troublesome child who attends Haris school. Because of his rebellous character, which shows no sign of calming down, the boy is constantly punished and is considered a scandal by the strict institution.

0044 SERIES

YUSEI KAMEN (*Planetary Mask*), TCJ, science-fiction, 39 episodes, 6/3/1966 – 2/21/1967.

A disastrous galactic war is fought between the army of the Earth and the alien soldiers from the planet Pineron.

0045 SERIES

ROBOTAN (*id.*), Daiko, humour, 103 episodes, 10/1/1966 – 9/27/1968.

The household adventures of the domestic robot Robotan are based on Ken Morita's manga. Morita is a comedy author who doesn't hesitate to give an ironic look at the typical Japanese family, in which a robot happens to be a guest.

0046 SERIES

JUNGLE TAITEI SUSUME! LEO (*Go Leo! Emperor of the Jungle*), Mushi, adventure/animal, 26 episodes, 10/5/1966 – 3/29/1967. *Leo The Lion* [*Le Roi Léo*].

Three months after the feature film, the numerous fans of the white lion could see new adventures of the king of the forest, busy ensuring that all the animals respect his laws.

0047 SERIES

GANBARE! MARINE KID (*Come On! Marine Kid*), TV Doga, adventure, 13 episodes, 10/6 – 12/29/1966. *Marine Boy*.

Produced for Fuji TV for the American market, re-using the characters and the subject of *Dolphin Oji* (#0025), the series was refused by the Japanese broadcasting stations and went to the MTS. Only 13 of the 78 episodes produced were ever shown. In 1967, the first thirteen episodes were proposed again with the new title *Kaitei Shonen Marine* (*Seabottom Marine Boy*).

Jungle Taitei. Susume Leo! © Tezuka Production.

Ganbare! Marine Kid © Fuji TV.

Mahotsukai Sally © Hikari Production / Toei Doga.

0048 SERIES

TOBIDASE! BACCHIRI (*Jump, Bacchiri!*), Nihon Hoso Eigasha, police story, 134 episodes, 11/14/1966 – 4/17/1967.

Bacchiri, a young detective, is a genius who solves cases that even the police can't unravel. The drawings and the animation of the series (10 minutes per episode), are so bad that they make it one of the worst series of the year in spite of its long programming.

0049 SERIES

MAHOTSUKAI SALLY (*Sally The Witch*), Toei Doga, Magic, 92 episodes, 12/5/1966 – 12/30/1968. *Sally The Witch* [*Mini-Fée*].

Inspired by Mitsuteru Yokoyama's manga, *Mahotsukai Sally* is the series that inaugurates the string of "little witches", destined to be hugely successful in the years to come. In this series, a young witch named Sally comes to Earth to study the behavior of human beings. The character design was done by Yoshiyuki Hane.

0050 SPECIAL

SEKAI NO OJA 'KING KONG TAIKAI' (*The King of the World: An Encounter With King Kong*), Toei Doga and Videocraft, adventure, 25 min., 12/31.

The television special is a remake of the famous series of television movies.

CHAPTER SIX: 1967

Once again, Osamu Tezuka reached new hights of popularity thanks to the enormous potential of his mangas that, transposed into animation, become even more captivating. *Goky No Daiboken* and *Ribbon No Kishi* were released in 1967 and both confirm the author's success.

Six years after his first feature film, *Saiyuki*, Tezuka returned with the same theme, this time with a humorous angle. Emphasizing the renewal of a classical subject (later used by many other famous illustrators), he proved his great screenwritting ability with an involving story, characterized by a strong rhythm, and enriched with entertaining and humorous subjects.

Ribbon No Kishi © Tezuka Production.

Always ready to introduce new elements to his numerous fans, the courageous Japanese author also produced *Ribbon No Kishi*, the story of a princess, skilled in the use of the sword, who pretends to be a man in order to ascend to the throne. Saphire, the main character, thus joins the growing ranks of female heroes, demonstrating how little gender matters and how women can do the same things as men even in an extremely male dominated society.

Ogon Bat, a minor series as quality is concerned, also comes out this year. Despite its low production standards, it is nevertheless important, because it features the the first "masked avenger". Created by Takeo Nagamatsu, the series was done in the style of *kamishibai*, a popular show similar in tone to the narration of a story-teller, in which love stories rich with references to both horror and tradition are carefully presented. The main character, a gruesome superhero, combats evil drawing on the strength of his own courage and the samurai code.

The Japanese people's appreciation for horror originated in the Middle Ages when the military class, under the influence of Zen, formed its own culture, which peaked during the Muromachi era (14th to 16th century). Zen buddism differs from other buddist sects in the emphasis it places on personal discipline. Thus it is natural to find both a heroic and tragic tone in the stories linked to civil wars. The accounts of courage and anguish, centered mostly on the lives of warriors, were absorbed the Japanese spirit, indelibly marking the mind of future generations.

The "sports" genre, which became very popular in later years, is introduced for the first time in Japanese animation with a serial about the world of race cars: *Mach Go Go Go*. Although the Japanese national sport is baseball, because of the human fascination with the speed demonstrated by powerful race cars, many other series followed this new lead. The screenplays focused not only on the moment of the race, but also included the private lives of the characters, each of whom had an indispensable place in the story.

0051 FILM

SHONEN JACK TO MAHOTSUKAI (*The Young Jack and the Wizard*), Toei Doga, fairy-tale, 100 min., 3/19.

During a walk in the woods, the young Jack bumps into Kiki, a mysterious girl who flies some sort of helicopter. Through deception, Jack is brought to the devil's castle where he discovers the devil-making machine, which transforms children into little devils. Jack tries to escape, but his little mouse Chuko becomes a victim of the infernal machine.

0052 FILM

CYBORG 009 KAIJU SENSO (*Cyborg 009: The Battle Of The Dinosaurs*), Toei Doga, science-fiction, 60 min., 3/19.

Because of a technical mix-up many prehistoric monsters come back to life, spreading death and destruction. A team of cybernetic fighters, using their powerful abilities, come to the defence of our planet.

0053 FILM

HYOKKORI HYOTANJIMA (*The Friends On Hyotan Island*), Toei Doga, adventure/animals, 61 min., 7/21.

This film presents the adventures of a pack of dogs, including one specimen from each species, sole inhabitants of a fascinating tropical island.

0054 FILM

KYUBI NO KITSUNE TO TOBIMARU (*Tobimaru And The Fox With Nine Tails*), Nihon Doga, 81 min., 10/19.

0055 SERIES

GOKU NO DAIBOKEN (*Goku's Great Adventure*), Mushi, classical/adventure, 39 episodes, 1/7 − 9/30/1967.

Sayiku, the legend of the stone monkey, is redone in an absolutely insane fashion by Osamu Tezuka, in a series directed by Gisaburo Sugii. The jokes are non-stop and the situations paradoxical. The fact that it didn't have much success in Italy is due mainly to

Goku No Daiboken © Tezuka Production.

the public's lack of knowledge of the original legend and thus a misunderstanding of the parody. The character designs are by Shigeru Yamamoto.

0056 SERIES

OGON BAT (*id.*), Daichi Doga, science-fiction, 52 episodes, 4/1/1967 – 3/23/1968.

Young Mary, decoding an ancient inscription, discovers that Ogon Bat (a prince of Atlantide who wear a mask representing a skull) can be awakened from his century-old sleep if someone puts a few drops of water on his chest. Ogon Bat awakens from his sleep and saves human beings from the attacks of the evil doctor Zero. The series was directed by Noboru Ishiguro, with the participation of Nobuhide Morikawa as character designer.

0057 SERIES

KAMINARI BOY A PIKKALIBI (*Pikkalibi, The Thunder Boy*), Mainichi Hoso, humour, 54 episodes, 4/1/1967 – 3/20/1968.

A space incident makes little Pikkalibi, elf of the thunder, fall from heaven. On Earth, the little elf with somewhat bizarre powers is forced to adapt to the different customs of the planet.

0058 SERIES

PAMAN (*id.*), Studio Zero and Tokyo Movie, superheroe/humour, 55 episodes, 4/2/1967 – 4/14/1968.

A group of children and a monkey are chosen by a mysterious masked man to be protectors of their city. Thanks to the elements that give them their super strength and the power of flight, the four children confront both the big and small problems of daily life. The animation is inspired by Fujiko Fujio's manga.

0059 SERIES

MACH GO GO GO (*id.*), Tatsunoko, sport, 52 episodes, 4/2/1967 – 3/31/1968. *Speed Racer*.

The series created by Tatuo Yoshida is the first to feature the sport of car racing as a sport. Go, the main character, drives the super-equipped Mach V car to win races at the limits of reality and to defeat criminal groups. The screenplay, to which Junzo Toriumi, amongst others, contributed, is unfortunately not complemented by Masahiko Suda's poor drawings and Hiroshi Segawa's rushed direction.

Speed Racer ©1966 Trans-Lux Television Corp & K. Fujita Associates, Inc. Package Design ©1990 VidAmerica Group, Inc. All Rights Reserved.

0060 SERIES

RIBBON NO KISHI (*Knight Of Ribbon*), Mushi, adventure, 52 episodes, 4/2/1967 – 4/7/1968. *Prince Saphire*.

The main character, Saphire, mistakingly receives at birth two hearts — one of each gender. Having to hide her femininity under man's clothing in order to ascend to the throne, she is forced to manoeuvre through duels and court intrigues. The series earned enormous success thanks to Osamu Tezuka who ensured its tight direction and who wrote the screenplay with Sadao Miyamoto copying the graphic style of the original manga almost exactly.

Ribbon No Kishi © Tezuka Production.

0061 SERIES

BOKEN GABOTENJIMA (*The Adventures Of Gaboten Island*), TCJ, adventure, 39 episodes, 4/4 – 12/26/1967.

Because of a terrible shipwreck, the young Ryuta lands, with five companions, on the mysterious island of Gaboten. The series follows the themes of Robinson Crusoe, a world-wide classic of literature. It was inspired by the myth that man can survive in a hostile and wild land, inhabited by unpredictable and hidden dangers.

0062 SERIES

KING KONG (*id.*), Toei and Videocraft, adventure, 52 episodes, 4/5 – 10/4/1967. *King Kong*.

The first series made in co-production with the Rankin Bass American production company for the ABC. The designs are by Jack Davis, and the story centers on the adventures of a young boy and his famous gorilla friend.

0063 SERIES

001/7 OYAYUBI TOM (*001/7 Thumb Tom*), Toei and Videocraft, adventure, 26 episodes.

Co-produced, like *King Kong*, with Videocraft, it was broadcast after the first 26 episodes of *King Kong* in the same time slot. It tells the story of a detective and his assistant, accidentaly struck by a shrinking beam. 001/7 (one seventh of a thumb) is a takeoff on the more famous 007. At the end of the series, the final 26 episodes of *King Kong* were broadcast.

0064 SERIES

HANA NO PYUNPYUNMARU (*id.*), Toei Doga, 26 episodes, 7/3 – 9/18/1967.

The adventures of samurais are often shown in Japanese productions, but never before with a humorous angle. For a better example, we will have to wait for the creation of *Ninja Hattorikun*, from the duo Fujiko Fujio. The series about Pyunpyunmaru is nonetheless pleasant.

0065 SERIES

BOKEN SHONEN SHADAR (*The Adventures Of Young Shadar*), Nippon Hoso Eigasha, adventure, 156 episodes, 9/18/1967 – 3/30/1968.

Shadar combats horrendous ghosts and terrifying demons using the power of the light sword, the only weapon capable of defeating them.

0066 SERIES

CHIBIKKO KAIJU YADAMON (*Yadamon, The Little Monster*), P. Prod., humour, 26 episodes, 10/2/1967 – 3/25/1968.

067 SERIES

SKYERS 5 (*id.*), TCJ, science-fiction, 12 episodes, 10/4 – 12/27/1967.

The main characters of this series form a team dedicated to world peace and justice, fighting the menace of the evil Galactic Ghosts.

0068 SERIES

DON KIKKO (*id.*), P. Prod., humour, 21 episodes, 9/7/1967 – 1/25/1968.

0069 SERIES

ORA GUZURA DADO (*Eh, I Am Guzura!*), Tatsunoko, humour, 52 episodes, 10/7/1967 – 9/25/1968. [*Gozura*].

Guzura, a little dragon who came out of an egg, becomes the playmate of a Japanese kid. The main character's name parodise the most famous Japanese monster, Gojira (Godzilla).

Ora Guzura Dado © Tatsunoko Pro.

Gegege No Kitaro © Toei Doga / Fuji TV.

CHAPTER SEVEN: 1968

This seems to be the year of horror. After the repetitive use of American-style science-fiction, four series dedicated to monsters and grim stories are brought to life: *Gegege No Kitaro*, *Kaibutsukun*, *Yokai Ningen Bem* and *Vampire*. The latter was made by the multitalented Osamu Tezuka.

Years before the advent of animated horror (if we exclude Disney's *Skeleton Dance*, which was more humorous than scary, and the occasional use of horror to brighten stories), Japan wins the prize for having dedicated much more efforts to this style, and for having explored its various forms. Inspired by *Kaidan Eiga*, the typical ghost stories of ancient Japan, the authors established the models on which animation bases itself afterward. It is important to note how the designs of the animation inspired by Shigeru Mizuki's manga nevertheless turn out innovative, even if the author's particular traits are cleaned up. Taking cue more from the above mentionned *kamishibai* and the post-war humoristic comic strip of Fleischer and Disney, Mizuki produced *Gegege No Kitaro*, a ludicrous but unique ghost story, by taking the characters and situations of the traditional legends, and re-shapping them in order to make them scary even to the eyes of the new generations.

Straightforward horror can be more easily found in *Yokai Ningen Bem*, the first real example of a Japanese "splatter" cartoon. The colorful adventures of three peculiar protagonists, who were plaguing the television screens of the calm Japanese appartments with poured blood and cut off heads, were a major concern for parents and pedagogues. Bero, Bem and Bera, the main characters of the series, were not good looking at all, but nevertheless exerted a particular fascination on the audiences, who, despite the unquestionably mediocre technique, were glued to their television screen by the story.

Unveiling a radical change of direction, the duo Fujiko Fujio came out with the parody *Kaibutsukun*, centered on the life of a hot-tempered prince of the monsters, gifted with the power of elasticity. In brief episodes of about ten minutes each, presented in groups of two or three at the time (a typical characteristic of Fujiko Fujio's animations), alternately presented classic monsters of every nationality, who, with their own needs, their own obsessions and their own anguish, provided infinite hooks for humorous and ridiculous stories.

Even Osamu Tezuka dove in, attempting an experiment with a mixed technique, based on the simultaneous use of real and animated characters. The brief series that resulted from this is interesting, but not strong enough to gather sufficient ratings for producers and distributors. *Vampire* thus vanished, signalling the first failure of Tezuka. His roundish characters with an innocent look did not fit in horror stories, so drastically that Tezuka very seldomly introduced horrific situations or characters after that, unless treating them with a light and humorous touch, as in *Dracula*.

In the following years, horror was put into perspective and, with Go Nagai, joined to science-fiction, offering bloody battles between giant robots and monstruous alien creatures.

Worthy of mention, even if it is not part of the horror trend, is the interesting detective story from the inexhaustible Shotaro Ishimori, *Sabu To Ichi Torimonohikae*. The main characters are two Sherlock Holmes with almond shaped eyes, operating in Medieval

Japan, often clashing with people holding popular beliefs, old-fashoned opinions and hindering factors such as vendetta and honor, dealing with a kind of unwritten laws, which must be respected nevertheless. Ishimori conceived some brilliant intrigues for his characters, so brilliant that it discouraged other authors to undertake such an enterprise. Suffice it to say that outside Japan very few authors have written historical mystery stories, knowing very well that they would have to combine a rigorously researched setting with credible investigators.

While everyone was trying to surpass one another by creating new types of animation, a more visible Hayao Miyazaki was to be noticed for his collaboration to most of the movies done by Toei Doga. His professional style began to be noticed by many, and when the action sequences of *Taiyo No Oji Hois No Daiboken* ran on the big screens, the audiences were undeniably surprised by the flowing movements of the characters.

This year can thus be considered a year of growth, even if not all the suggestions made have caught on with young authors, who were forced, partly because of the producers, to makes series just for the takings.

0070 FILM

ANDERSEN MONOGATARI MATCH URI NO SHOJO (*Andersen's Stories: The Little Girl With The Matches*), Toei, fairy-tale, 80 min., 3/19.

The young Hans Christian Andersen is a little boy gifted with a lot of imagination. One night, the Lord of Dreams visits him, as a funny little man with an odd-looking hat who takes him on a long trip through the dream world of childhood. Once Andersen comes back to reality, he becomes the friend of a poor little girl who sells matches on a street corner. This last encounter will inspire him as an adult to write one of the most touching fairy-tales ever.

0071 FILM

TAIYO NO OJI HOLS NO DAIBOKEN (*The Great Adventures Of Hols, Prince Of The Sun*), Toei Doga, adventure, 62 min., 7/21.

A nordic village is the victim of the immense power of the evil Gundar, King of the Ice, who wants to subdue the inhabitants of the Arctic land. When the young Hols successfully come back from the kingdom of Death, he discovers the power that light has on the kingdom of Ice, and he engages in a furious battle against it. In Italy, the title of the movie directed by Isao Takahata was changed to *The Great Adventures Of The Little Prince Valient*, to attract the fans of the comic strip *Prince Valiant*, who then found themselves watching a totally different story.

Yaiyo No Oji Hols No Daiboken © Toei Doga.

0072 SERIES

GEGEGE NO KITARO (*Kitaro Gegege*), Toei Doga, grotesque, 65 episodes, 1/3/1968 – 3/30/1969.

Born from the hand of Shigeru Mizuki, Kitaro is a strange boy who lives in a strange world. Constantly in contact with family ghosts, witches, elves and old tomb robbers, Kitaro carries in his empty eye socket the spirit of his father, with whom he tries to find a remedy to the evils done by bizarre ghosts and monsters.

Gegege No Kitaro © Toei Doga / Fuji TV.

Kyoshin No Hoshi © Kajiwara Ikki • Kawasaki Noboru / TMS.

Animal 1 © Kawasaki Noboru / Mushi Production.

0073 SERIES

WANPAKU TANTEIDAN (*The Group Of Clever Detectives*), Mushi, police story, 35 episodes, 2/1 – 9/26/1968.

0074 SERIES

KYOJIN NO HOSHI (*The Star Of The Kyojin*), Tokyo Movie, sport, 182 episodes, 3/30/1968 – 9/18/1971.

Young Hyuma Hoshi is a promising baseball player who wants to become a champion, following his father, Ittetsu. Thanks to intensive training, and the help of his father and coach, Hyuma's dream comes true and he soon becomes the star of the Kyojin team. The series is inspired by Ikki Kajiwara and Noboru Kawasaki's manga, whose style was followed closely by the television version.

0075 SERIES

ANIMAL 1 (*id.*), Mushi, sport/biography, 27 episodes, 4/1 – 9/30/1968.

The sport series presents the story of Azuma Ichiro, a Japanese wrestling olympic champion in the 60s, who became popular worldwide. His life and his many victories constitute the main plot of the anime.

0076 SERIES

CYBORG 009 (*id.*), Toei Doga, science-fiction, 26 episodes, 4/5 – 9/27/1968.

Nine children of various age are kidnapped and transformed into cyborgs by the Lord of the Merchants of Death, to fight in his army. Having escaped from tyranny, the characters, under the guidance of Joe Shimamura 009, rebel against the enemy, overcoming the forces of evil. The story and the characters were created by the author of the original manga, Shotaro Ishimori.

0077 SERIES

AKANECHAN (*Little Akane*), Toei Doga, humour, 26 episodes, 4/6 – 9/29/1968.

Akane is a lively little girl, always ready to get into trouble. The story begins when the main character moves to Tokyo with her family, leaving behind her little country village.

0078 SERIES

FIGHT DA!! PYUTA (*Fight Pyuta!*), Hoso Doga Seisaku, adventure, 26 episodes, 4/6 – 9/28/1968.

Young Pyuta is forced by circumstance to combat the evil people of Ulser, who want to rule the human race.

0079 SERIES

KAIBUTSUKUN (*Little Kaibutsu*), Studio Zero and Tokyo Movie, humour/monsters, 50 episodes, 4/21/1968 – 3/23/1969.

The humorous serial by Moto Abito and Hiroshi Fujimoto, better known as Fujiko Fujio, presents the adventures of Kaibutsu, young prince of the land of monsters, and his friends Franken, Drakula and Warewolf. Having moved to Japan, they meet Hiroshi, a child who soon becomes their friend. A little play on words: Kaibutsu, as well as being the name of the main character, also means "little monster", a suitable name for the prince of the land of monsters.

0080 SERIES

SASUKE (*id.*), adventure/samurai, 29 episodes, 9/3/1968 – 3/25/1969.

Sasuke, with the help of his father, learns ninja techniques in order to defend the oppressed in feudal Japan from the ruling lords. The child is thus forced to combat against very strong warriors who are incredibly skilled in the use of the Katana, shuriken, nunchaku and other powerful weapons. The series is inspired by Sanpei Shirato's manga itself based on the novel by Kazuo Den. The screenplay is by Junzo Tashiro.

0081 SERIES

YUYAKE BANCHO (*The Leader Of The Sunset*), Tokyo TV Doga, adventure, 105 episodes, 10/1/1968 – 3/29/1969.

0082 SERIES

DOKACHIN (*id.*), Tatsunoko, humour, 27 episodes, 10/2/1968 – 3/26/1969.

Asleep for a century, Dokachin wakes up in an ultra-modern Japan. Having lived in the feudal years, the main character finds himself totally unprepared for the frantic way of life of the current Japanese society.

0083 SERIES

SABU TO ICHI TORIMONOHIKAE (*Sabu And Ichi's Investigation*), Mushi, Studio Zero and Toei Doga, detective/historical, 52 episodes, 10/3/1968 – 9/24/1969.

Sabu, a young man looking for adventure, arrives at Edo (Tokyo today) and there meets Saheiji, head of the local police in the district of Ryusenji. Becoming Saheiji's helper, now bedridden because of rheumatism, he meets Ichi, a wise, blind masseuse who help him in the investigations. This kind of Japanese Nero Wolf was created by the always more prolific Shotaro Ishimori.

0084 SERIES

VAMPIRE (*id.*), Mushi, horror, 26 episodes, 10/3/1968 – 3/29/1969.

Vampire is an horror story by Tezuka, inspired by the Western "fantastic" mythology and represents one of the first experiments with the technique mixing animated designs and live-action.

0085 SERIES

YOKAI NINGEN BEM (*Bem, the Human Ghost*), Daichi Doga, horror, 26 episodes, 10/7/1968 – 3/31/1969.

Bem, a vaguely lovecraftian horror serial, is the first cartoon of its type. Amidst ghosts of people who died because of violence and revenge, and demons who thirst for human souls, three beings looking for peace find daily adventures. Although the series is named after Bem, a mysterious man without pupils who possesses the capacity to transform himself into a bestial creature, the real main character is the young Bero, who constantly gets into trouble, which he gets out of only with the help of his older friend and the intervention of the witch Bera. Nuboyoshi Morikawa is part of the executive team for the character design.

Sasuke © Akame Production / Eiken

Dokachin © Tatsunoko Pro.

Vampire © Tezuka Production.

CHAPTER EIGHT: 1969

In March of this year, the feature *Nagagutsu O Haita Neko* was released. The main character of the movie was destined to become the symbol of the Toei Doga: the muzzle of the friendly cat with the boots soon distinguished all the products of the famous production firm.

Animation movies for the big screen are always of major importance and earn the approval of the audiences who fill up the theatres with every new release.

Many characters of television series win the right to appear in the cinema because of their success. An obvious example is *Kyojin No Hoshi,* which has three animated series to its credit (1968, 1977 and 1977), and five feature films distributed within thirteen years (two in 1969, two in 1970 and one in 1982). *The Star Of The Kyojin* plays a fundamental role in the field of animation, and is, in fact, the first animated series in which the main theme was baseball. Japanese people love sports, in any form, and it is not by accident that sports teams are present in every school (with organized fan clubs to support them), and all children must choose which club they wants to join when they register in a school. All the students have the obligation to train every afternoon in the many fields made available by the school. Thus, the whole day is spent in the school that prepares them both physically and psychologically, to face the world. Baseball is the most loved sport, with its millions of fans, which explains the success of *Kyojin No Hoshi*. It mixed spectacular animation with a story not solely about competition, but also one of human emotion.

It is not rare to find sport associated with other types of animation, even the robots. In *UFO Senshi Diapolon*, for example, the members of an American football team each fly an aircraft (a metaphor for team work); in *Daiky Maryu Gaiking* (1976), the pilot of the robot is a baseball player with a deadly throw; in *Magne Robo Ga-kin* (1976), the pilot is a karate expert, and the list goes on and on. The common trait is that the physical perfection obtained through sports is the basis for being a well-balanced individual.

Another animated series taking place in the world of sports is *Tiger Mask*, the story of a wrestler who hides his true identity behind a tiger mask. Not unusualy, real wrestlers appeared as guest stars, like Antonio Inoki, Abdullah the Butcher or Andre the Giant. A sequel to the first *Tiger Mask* series came out in 1981 with a new tiger-man and a new costume. Inspired by the animated series, a young wrestler adopted the same costume for his own fights. An opponent soon imitated him, using the "black" version of the costume.

Kurenai Sanshiro is a clear example of sport glorification combined with a story tinted with drama. Sanshiro is the son of a famous Judo expert who was killed by a rival. The main character looks for the killer to avenge his father, and on the way, encounters enemies and adventures over which he triumphs only after a great deal of combat.

Amongst the sports shown in Japanese animation, there are some reserved only for women, including tennis, gymnastics and volley-ball. It is the latter that begins this trend with *Attack Number 1,* presenting the lives, the loves and the adventures of a women's volley-ball team which aspires to participate in the Olympics. The same themes were re-used in a second series of *Attack Number 1*, produced in 1977, and redone in the more recent *Attacker You!* in 1985.

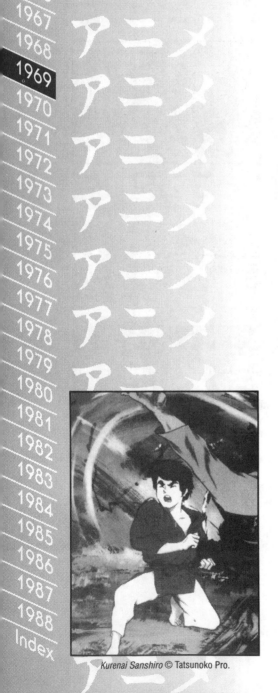

Kurenai Sanshiro © Tatsunoko Pro.

Finally, a fundamental trend, inaugurated by *Mahotsukai Sally* in 1966, finds confirmation in *Himitsu No Akkochan*, another story that has a little girl with magical powers as its main character. Following the success attained by these two heroines, a host of little magicians invaded Japanese television.

0086 FILM

NAGAGUTSU O HAITA NEKO (*The Cat With the Boots*), Toei Doga, fairy-tale, 80 min., 3/18.

Freely adapted from Perrault's fairy-tale, this is certainly the most enjoyable version ever made. Humour is predominant in this feature film due mostly to the characterization of the stupid ogre, who changes character when he changes clothes. The author also borrowed ideas from *Swan Lake* and *Beauty and the Beast*.

0087 FILM

SEN'YA ICHIYA MONOGATARI (*The Thousand And One Nights*), Mushi, fairy-tale, 130 min., 6/14.

The umpteenth remake of a famous story taken from *The Thousand And One Nights* set in the mythical Bagdad, in which Aladdin, the main character, appears more energetic than usual. The feature film was made by Eichi Yamamoto for Mushi, and was distributed by Nihon Herald Eiga, who, after becoming Nihon Herald, produced some animated films of Gisaburo Sugii, among which, we find the memorable *Genji Monogatari* in 1987.

0088 FILM

SORA TOBU YUREISEN (*The Mysterious Flying Saucer*), Toei Doga, adventure, 60 min., 7/20.

Born from the imagination of Shotaro Ishimori, the feature film presents the adventures of a mysterious ghost ship and the main characters, two children and Golem the robot. The movie dwells on a sense of mystery and the action increases as we get closer to the end, where, for the combat scene with the robot, Hayao Miyazaki was given carte-blanche by the author, making it one of the best animated sequences in Japanese cinematography.

0089 FILM

KYOJIN NO HOSHI (*The Star Of The Kyojin*), Tokyo Movie, sport, 88 min., 7/26.

The famous baseball series, celebrating Japan's national sport, was made into this first movie, presenting the adventures of the main character Hyuma Hoshi.

0090 FILM

HIGEKIGA — UKIYOE SEN'ICHIYA (*The Prohibited Picture Novel: The Thousand And One Nights Of An Ukiyo-E*), Leo Productions, erotic, 70 min., 10/29.

A parody of the year's major film success, *Sen'ya Ichiya Monogatari,* from Mushi, tells the story of the ukiyo-e painter Shunsai who, one night, while peeping at a married couple, is inspired to paint an ukiyo-e. The painted characters emerge from the painting at night to commit a murder.

0091 FILM

KYOJIN NO HOSHI YUKE YUKE HYUMA (*The Star Of The Kyojin: Go Go Hyuma*), Tokyo Movie, sport, 70 min., 12/20.

Nagagutsu O Haita Neko © Toei Doga.

Sen'ya Ichiya Monogatari © Tezuka Production.

Sora Tobu Yureisen © Toei Doga.

Intro
-1962
1963
1964
1965
1966
1967
1968
1969
1970
1971
1972
1973
1974
1975
1976
1977
1978
1979
1980
1981
1982
1983
1984
1985
1986
1987
1988
Index

The second chapter of the *Kyojin* sport saga sees the ascension of the young Hyuma to the position of the best player in the team.

Himitsu No Akkochan © Fujio Production / Toei Doga.

0092 SERIES

HIMITSU NO AKKOCHAN (*Little Akko's Secret*), Toei, magic, 94 episodes, 1/6/1969 – 10/26/1970.

During a summer night, a spirit gives Akko a wonderful magic mirror that has the power to transform whoever possesses it into any person or animal. Young Akko uses the mirror to resolve her friends' daily problems in a quiet area of Tokyo.

0093 SERIES

SOBAKASU BUTCH (*The Freckled Butch*), Fuji TV Enterprise, humour, 162 episodes of 5 minutes each, 3/31 – 9/27/1969.

0094 SERIES

UMEBOSHI DENKA (*Denka From The Star Ume*), Studio Zero and Tokyo Movie, science-fiction, 27 episodes, 4/1 – 9/23/1969.

The friendly emperor Denka arrives on Earth from the very distant star Ume. The young Taro welcomes him and shares his house with the odd extra-terrestrial.

0095 SERIES

KURENAI SANSHIRO (*id.*), Tatsunoko, martial arts, 26 episodes, 4/2 – 9/24/1969. [*Judo Boy*].

Young Sanshiro's father is killed by a mysterious man with only one eye during a martial arts competition in the city's harbour. The boy leaves on an exhausting manhunt with only one clue at his disposition — the glass eye lost by the murderer at the scene of the crime. He has to confront many one-eyed people, but only finds the true killer at the very end of the series.

Kurenai Sanshiro © Tatsunoko Pro.

0096 SERIES

MORETSU ATARO (*The Excessive Ataro*), Toei, humour, 13 episodes, 4/4/1969 – 12/25/1970.

0097 SERIES

NINPU KAMUI GAIDEN (*Kamui The Ninja: Stories Other Than The Legend*), TCJ, martial arts/historical, 26 episodes, 4/6 – 9/28/1969.

Kamui is a ninja deserter, a warrior who abandoned the criminal life of a Japanese medieval sect of killers. But his family cannot forgive him and seeks his death, the punishment given to all traitors. But Kamui is one of the best of the ninjas. Uniting his ability with his absolute faith in freedom, the youngster survives the never-ending attacks from the hired killers who persue him. The series was developed from the manga of Sanpei Shirato, a famous author of ninja and samurai stories. Here he described a part of the life of Kamui, absent from his first work, *Kamuiden*.

0098 SERIES

DORORO (*id.*), Mushi, grottesque/historical, 26 episodes, 4/6 – 9/28/1969.

To become king, a samurai makes a pact with the devil. In exchange for the devil's help, he offers his own son's life, a boy then born with the features of a worm. The child get

Dororo © Tezuka Production.

adopted by a craftsman who reconstructed his eyes and other missing body parts in wood. Dororo becomes a skillful fighter and in the course of his adventures, is forced to confront a long series of enemies to recover pieces of his own body. It is taken from Osamu Tezuka's manga.

0099 SERIES
ROPPO YABUREKUN (*id.*), Tokyo Movie, adventure, 130 min., 4/28/1969 – 3/28/1970.

0100 SERIES
OTOKO EPPIKI GAKIDAISHO (*That Bastard Leader Of The Gang Of Children*), Tokyo TV Doga, adventure, 174 episodes of 10 minutes each, 9/29/1969 – 3/28/1970.

0101 SERIES
PINCH TO PUNCH (*Pinch And Punch*), Fuji TV Enterprise, humour, 162 episodes of 5 minutes each, 9/29/1969 – 3/28/1970.

The little Pinch and Punch are two terrible children who orchestrate great practical jokes and put their victims into embarrassing situations.

0102 SERIES
TIGER MASK (*id.*), Toei Doga, sport, 105 episodes, 10/2/1969 – 9/30/1971. [*Le Tigre Masqué*].

Created by Ikki Kajiwara and Naoki Tsuji, *Tiger Mask* is the story of a masked wrestler trained at the "Tiger's Den," a cruel wrestling school that teaches the use of foul play and violence as winning tools. Naoto Date, the wrestler's true identity, does not allow himself, however, to use tricks during his fights, thus becoming the target of the killer wrestlers of the school. Between encounters, Naoto dedicates himself to the children of the orphanage that welcomed him when he was a baby, and to which he gives the major part of the money he gets from winning the various wrestling matches.

Tiger Mask © Toei Doga.

0103 SERIES
SAZAESAN (*id.*), humour, 10/5/1969 – to this day (1590 episodes by the beginning of October 2000).

Created by Machiko Hasegawa, *Sazaesan* first saw the light as a comic strip in a small local newspaper in Fukuoka, but it was soon published in *Asahi Shinbun*, one of the major Japanese dailies. The story centers on the members of a typical Japanese family, made up of Mrs. Sazae, her husband Matsuo Fuguta, her brother Katsuo, her sister Wakame, her son Tara, her mother-in-law Fune and her father-in-law Namihei. The author offers the public a humorous vision of their daily life and brings to life, in a Japanese setting, a series of other characters with particular and distinct personalities, developing their relationships with friends, with strangers and with society itself.

0104 SERIES
HAKUSHON DAIMAHO (*Hakushon, The Great Magician*), Tatsunoko, humour/magic. 52 episodes, 10/5/1969 – 9/27/1970. [*Atchoum! Le Génie / Robert Dans La Bouteille*].

In this parody of the genie in the lamp, adapted to modern times, the fat arabic genie, can be called out of his bottle with a sneeze. His wife and daughter also appear, respectively with a yawn and a hiccup.

Hakushon Daimaho © Tatsunoko Pro.

Attack Number 1 © Chikako Urano / TMS.

Wonder Kun No Hatsuyumeuchu Ryoko
© Tezuka Production.

0105 SERIES

MOOMIN (*id.*), Mushi and Tokyo Movie up to the 26th episode, Tokyo Movie Shinsa from the 27th episode, humour, 65 episodes, 10/5/1969 – 12/27/1970. [*Les Moomins*].

Animated version of the famous hippopotamus from Tove and Lars Jansson's comic strip.

0106 SERIES

ATTACK NUMBER 1 (*id.*), Tokyo Movie, sport, 104 episodes, 12/7/1969 – 11/28/1971. [*Les Attaquantes*].

The first series dedicated to women's sport in Japan is taken from Chikako Urano's manga. Certain students have formed a volley-ball team and count on their captain to lead them as they face the teams in the students' tournament.

0107 SPECIAL

WONDER KUN NO HATSUYUMEUCHU RYOKO (*The First Marvelous Dream In Wonder's Space Trip*), Mushi, adventure, 20 min., 1/2.

SECOND PART
THE SEVENTIES

CHAPTER NINE: 1970

Strongly dominated by series and films inspired by sports, 1970 was one of the years that witnessed the dawning of a radical change of direction in plotline. Together with the heroes we watch the birth of antiheroes, who traveled the calm world of animation with their dark behavior and insanity. It was the time for *Ashita no Joe*, a cult series that achieved an unprecedented success for a sport series in this period, if we exclude *Kyojin no hoshi*, which made history without reaching comparable levels of popularity.

Joe is portrayed as the typical suburban hooligan, totally disinterested in school, devoting his life to brawls and wandering after the deaths of both parents. Joe is "discovered" to be a talented boxer by an old, drunk ex-trainer. Rebelling against all of the advice given by the old man, Joe gets into trouble and ends up in jail. There he learns the basics of boxing by following, after an initial period of disinterest, the lessons sent to him by his faithful trainer. Adversity follows the young man after his exit from jail, culminating with his encounter with his feared rival. This story is interesting in its use of the characters and settings to reflect upon the social misery of the 60s. The graphics are influenced by manga, with the outline of the characters made as though the shading had been drawn with a piece of coal or with a thick marker, not with a paint brush. The animation is simple, quick and balanced and it reaches an excellent level of quality for a series of the 70s, prominent even for today's viewer.

Ashita No Joe © Chiba T. / Takamori A. / Mushi Production.

While movies have been made of *Attack Number 1*, the very famous *Kyojin no hoshi* and *Tiger Mask* with its angular features and dry animation, the sport series *Akakichi no eleven* is the first time we see soccer appear on television. Although it is not of exceptional quality, this cartoon establishes the basic conventions for the portrayal of soccer in Japanese animation, conventions later used by all creators of soccer cartoons. Although the story is based on serious premises, after the first stages of the game, the problems became more and more evident. At this point there are two solutions, either shut off the television set and forget *Akakichi no eleven* forever, or look at it from a new perspective and consider that, if the authors had been more moderate, the animation would have been no different than a real soccer game and there would have been no real point. That is why everything was so highly exaggerated, why a race across the field took at least 15 minutes, training involved kicking rocks and a shot in the goal could sweep away the goal keeper, break through the net and possibly even the wall of the stadium. The excitement of variety was created in a particular way by the presence of "special shots" — already tried with some success in *Attack Number 1* — which strain at the limits of credibility, creating whirlwinds or optical effects that make it impossible to block the ball unless the goal-keeper has the gift of teleporting.

The Tatsunoko seized the opportunity and produced a comedic series that uses judo as a premise even though competition did not feature in the show itself. It is very curious that

this production firm realized the brief success obtained by the duo Fujiko Fujio and attempted to take possession of such outlines to make *Inakappe taisho* and *Tentomushi no uta*. It is even more curious that Tatsunoko's program, this contradictory animation studio, counts amongst its anime almost exclusively crazy humor series or ultra-depressing dramatic stories.

In 1970, *Konchu monogatari minashigo Hutch* was released on the Japanese screens. It is an incredible experiment telling the adventures of a poor, unfortunate little bee (that in the Italian version was passed off as a female) in search of its mother, queen of the villages of insects whose organization was inspired by the customs of medieval Japan, infested with monstrous lizards and spiders that more resembled ancient demons than creatures of this world. The main character gets involved in heartbreaking adventures of survival, blood and death, so much so that it leaves the spectator disconcerted and asking himself if it is worth it to watch a series that expects him to be touched by the death of an ant. Notwithstanding all this, the entomological soap opera was a success and the Tatsunoko gained a point in its favor.

The Toei Doga on the other hand, did not detach itself too much from its original schedule. It continued to propose remakes of literary works and fairy tales. 1970 saw the turn of *Chibikko Remi to meiken Capi*, freely adapted from Hector Malot's *Without Family* (so freely adapted, in fact, that the ending is transformed into an action story) and *Kaitei Sanman Miles*. Even though the latter's title became *Twenty Thousand Leagues Under the Sea* in Italy, Captain Nemo and his Nautilus are nowhere in sight. This movie narrates the story of an invasion by people living underwater. Once again we have to note the unreal practices of certain Italian distributors who, for profit, forged ambiguous titles like *Daimos*, *Son of Goldrake* or *Heidi Becomes a Princess*, completely disorienting those who wanted to see one product and found themselves in front of something totally different.

More interested in the Japanese historical anime, the TCJ proposed the animated series *Norakuro* again, taken from an old manga by Suiko Tagawa that tells the story of a strange war between militarized animals.

Norakuro the dog has been proposed again recently, adapted for a younger public, as a comedy series starring a talking black puppy, companion to a group of young children.

0108 FILM

CHIBIKKO REMI TO MEIKEN CAPI (*Little Remi and the Faithful Dog Capi*), Toei, classic, 81 min., 3/17. [*Rémi – Sans Famille*].

The film, directed by Yugo Serikawa, presents the first animated adaptation of Hector Malot's famous novel, set at the beginning of the century, in which a foundling from France is searching for his parents. Actually sold by his stepfather, he was forced to join a group of traveling musicians and acrobats. After many adventures with them, he finds his mother, who thought he was dead.

0109 FILM

TIGER MASK (*id.*), Toei, sport, 47 min., 3/17. [*Le Tigre Masqué*].

A feature film made following the success obtained by the television series, retelling the most significant episodes.

0110 FILM

YASASHI LION (*The Kind Lion*), Mushi, animal, 26 min., 3/21.

0111 FILM

ATTACK NUMBER 1 (*id.*), Tokyo Movie, sport, 63 min., 3/21.

Made with scenes taken from the first television series devoted to female volleyball.

0112 FILM

KYOJIN NO HOSHI DAI LEAGUE BALL (*The Star of the Kyojin, the Great Sports League*), Tokyo Movie, sport, 100 min., 3/21.

The umpteenth movie devoted to the Kyojin, now a famous baseball team.

0113 FILM

KAITEI SANMAN MILES (*Three Thousand Miles Under the Sea*), Toei Doga, adventure, 60 min., 7/19.

Young Isamu and his loyal cheetah embark in the submarine constructed by Isamu's father to explore the bottom of the sea. Having met the lovely princess Angela, heiress to the throne of the underwater kingdom, the main character helps her get rid of the perfidious Magma 7, exiled by the king because of his crimes. The story is by Shotaro Ishimori.

0114 FILM

TIGER MASK FUKU MEN LEAGUE SEN (*Tiger Mask: War to the League of Masked Wrestlers*), Toei, sport, 53 min., 7/19.

The very strong tiger man is involved in a strenuous fight, combating attacks by the evil wrestlers of the league, but as always, he comes out of it a winner.

0115 FILM

ATTACK NUMBER 1 NAMIDA NO KAITEN RECEIVE (*Attack Number 1: Tearful "Kaiten Receive"*), Tokyo Movie, sport, 59 min., 8/1.

The adventures of the young players and the talented Captain Ayuhara continue, with always more tiring encounters stretching the limits of credibility. To enhance the team, the coach teaches the girls a particular receiving technique, the "kaiten receive."

0116 FILM

KYOJIN NO HOSHI SHUKUMEI NO TAIKETSU (*The Star of the Kyojin: Confrontation Wanted by Destiny*), Tokyo Movie, sport, 61 min., 8/1.

Yet another game from the team of giants. Once again, the young main character brings his team to victory.

0117 FILM

CLEOPATRA (*id.*), Mushi, historical, 22 min., 9/15.

The life of Cleopatra has inspired many literary works around the world and the Japanese people have not been able to resist the pull of the famous Egyptian queen. Daughter of Ptolome XII, she became the protégé of the Roman emperor Julius Caesar to whom she gave a son, Cesarion. She then fell in love with Anthony, with whom she conspired to

Yasashi Lion © Tezuka Production.

Cleopatra © Tezuka Production.

create a new Oriental monarchy to oppose Rome. In the year 31, after Octavian's victory in Azio, Cleopatra committed suicide. Yugo Serikawa's animated feature film presents the most important events of Cleopatra's life in a romantic light.

0118 FILM
ATTACK NUMBER 1 NAMIDA NO SEKAI SHENSHUKEN (*Attack Number 1: World Championship Tears*), Tokyo Movie, sport, 51 min., 12/19.

The volleyball team doesn't give up, and after numerous games, it wins the world championship, spurring great emotion on the part of Japanese athletes.

0119 SERIES
ITAZURA TENSHI CHIPPER (*Chipper the Mischevous Angel*), Fuji TV Enterprise, humor, 240 episodes, 3/30 — 7/21/1970.

0120 SERIES
DOBUTSUMURA MONOGATARI (*The Story of the Animal's Village*), Eiken, animal, 16 episodes, 3/30 — 7/21/1970.

0121 SERIES
ASHITA NO JOE (*Joe, Boxer of Tomorrow*), Mushi, sport, 79 episodes, 4/1 — 9/29/1970.

Ashita No Joe © Chiba T. / Takamori A. / Mushi Production.

Joe is a youngster from the seediest part of Tokyo, an orphan who lives by his wits. One day a drunk bumps into him and, annoyed, Joe punches him away with a strong right hook. The reaction of the old man is totally unexpected, as he is in fact Danbei Tangi, a great boxing coach who retired after a great number of defeats and turned to the bottle. The two realize that they can use each other, Joe interested in scrounging free room and board from the old man, Danbei convinced that he can make of Joe the boxer of tomorrow. The main character pretends to train but in reality, he spends his time doing small burglaries in the suburbs. He is arrested for one of these burglaries. Spending a year in jail, Joe finally understands the importance of friendship and renews his involvement with Danbei, who continues to send him boxing lessons, even in prison. Finally free, the success of the young man is immediate. He soon encounters Ishi Riki, a youngster he first met in jail and who, in the years to come, will become his greatest enemy in the ring. The story is directed by Asao Takamori and Tetsua Chiba amongst others, and the screenplay is by Osamu Dezaki.

0122 SERIES
BAKUHATSU GORO (*Goro the Terrible*), TCJ, humor, 26 episodes, 4/3 — 9/25/1970.

0123 SERIES
KONCHU MONOGATARI MINASHIGO HUTCH (*Insect Story: Hutch, the Orphan*), Tatsunoko, animal, 91 episodes, 4/7/1970 — 12/28/1971. [*Hutchi*].

A majestic beehive dominates a forest, and the worker bees spend every day trying to improve it. Unexpectedly, an attack from the evil wasps forces the little insects to leave their home. In all the confusion, little Hutch is lost and left behind by his companions. Thus begin his adventures in search of his mother, the queen bee. This search brings him, along with the audience, to discover the wonderful world of insects. After numerous travels, little Hutch finds his mother and a new home. The story and the screenplay are from Junzo Toriumi. It was created by Tatsuo Yoshida and directed, amongst others, by Ippei Kuri.

Konchu Monogatari Minashigo Hutch © Tatsunoko Pro.

0124 SERIES

AKAKICHI NO ELEVEN (*The Dark Red Eleven*), Tokyo TV Doga, sport, 52 episodes, 4/13/1970 — 4/5/1971.

The series created by Ikki Kajiwara presents the adventures of Shingo Tamai and ten other children who form a soccer team with him. Their dream, of course, is to win the World Cup. After much training and because of their willpower, the Japanese players finally succeed in making the finals where they meet the Brasilian team.

0125 SERIES

NIHON TANJO (*The Birth of Japan*), Mushi, historical, 5 episodes, 6/10 — 10/24/1970.

In a fantastic voyage through time, a cat and a rat illustrate the evolution of Japan.

0126 SERIES

MANGA JINBUTSUSHI (*Illustrated Stories of Great Individuals*), Office New, Documentary, 365 episodes, 8/1/1970 — 9/30/1971.

0127 SERIES

OTOKO DOAHO! KOSHIEN (*Koshien! Born Male for No Reason*), Tokyo TV Doga, sport, 156 episodes, 9/28/1970 — 3/27/1971.

Koshien was given the name that means 'baseball field' from his grandfather who hoped to make him a champion, but Koshien shows himself to be totally incompetent. . . at least at the beginning.

0128 SERIES

KICK NO ONI (*The Demon of Kick Boxing*), Toei Doga, sport, biography, 26 episodes, 10/2/1970 — 3/26/1971.

Sawamura Tadashi was a great champion of kick boxing and his moves are still remembered today by the Japanese. The Toei Doga thus decided to devote a series to the famous boxer, based entirely on his life.

0129 SERIES

IJIWARU BASAN (*The Spiritual Grandmother*), Knack, humor, 40 episodes, 10/3/1970 — 10/25/1971.

Given the great success of *Sazaesan*, his previous work that is still popular in Japan today, Machiko Hasegawa turns to artistic direction in this new series, where she is still attentive to the vices and virtues of the Japanese people.

0130 SERIES

INAKAPPE TAISHO (*The Young Countryman Leader*), Tatsunoko, humor/sport, 103 episodes, 10/4/1970 — 9/24/1971.

The humorous adventures in this series created by Tatsuo Yoshida are inspired by the life of a famous Japanese judo champion, even if in this show he is transformed into a child and renamed Taisho. The main character is trained by an enterprising cat, Nyanko.

Kick No Oni © Nakashiro K. / Noguchi Production / Kajiwara Production.

Inakappe Taisho © Tatsunoko Pro.

Maho No Makochan © TV Asahi / Toei Doga.

Fushigina Melmo © Tezuka Production.

0131 SERIES

NORAKURO (*id.*), TCJ, humor, 28 episodes, 10/5/1970 — 3/29/1971.

Based on Suiho Tagawa's original manga, the TCJ decided to adapt to animation the war between an army of dogs — in which the courageous Norakuro fights — and a menacing group of monkeys.

0132 SERIES

WARERA SALARY MAN (*We Are Employees*), P. Prod., comedy, 10/7/1970 — 3/31/1971.

0133 SERIES

MAHO NO MAKOCHAN (*Little Magic Mako*), Toei Doga, magic, 48 episodes, 11/2/1970 — 9/27/1971.

Mako the mermaid wants to live as a human to find a young sailor that she saved from drowning. She is then transformed into a young girl and sent to the surface world. Gifted with magic powers that she uses to help people in trouble, Mako adapts rapidly to her new life thanks to the many friends she meets on the dry land. This modern version of The Little Mermaid written by Masahi Tseiji (under the pen name of Urakawa Shinobu) is directed by Yago Serikawa.

CHAPTER TEN: 1971

The fairy-tales present in every culture differ in setting, plot and cultural baggage, but they share fundamentally common themes and values.

The Japanese people, more than any other, find the roots of their own culture in their fairy-tales and popular legends. For centuries, the stories were transmitted from generation to generation through books and oral tradition. Today, in the electronic age, it is easy to see them broadcast on television, and the animated productions of 1971 are a clear example of this.

Ali Baba to yonjuppiki no tozoku is a feature film from the Toei Doga, which presents the lives of the descendants of the characters from the famous *Thousand and One Nights*. The second example is given by *Andersen monogatari*, a 52-episode animated series, in which the numerous characters of the prolific Dane writer run from episode to episode.

The year 1971 marks the debut of another important production by Osamu Tezuka, *Fushigina Melmo*. The father of the Japanese manga is a subtle writer, and he carefully places within his subtext subjects such as, for example, sex and genetics. The series actually narrates the adventures of a young girl who has received a vase full of sugar coated almonds as a gift from her mother. Their strange chemical composition can make her younger or older, according to the color of the candy eaten. Her body grows, but her mental age is always the same. The spectator, together with the main character, learns about the human body and the laws that regulate it. The panorama widens when the young girl discovers that she can transform into any animal desired, eventually going back to the fetal state.

The fundamental animation series made in 1971 is *Lupin Sensei*, which mirrors the success of Monkey Punch's (Kazuhiko Katoh) manga published in 1967. Rapidly becoming a trendsetter, *Lupin sensei* influenced, in both Japan and abroad, more than a generation of fans and features the most famous anti-hero of Japanese animation. He is a burglar, a lady's man and a liar, but above all, he is a genius. It is thus easy to develop a passion for his adventures that never fall into the trap of useless repetition. While this series' success was poor at the beginning, it later became recognized as a classic and movies as well as series succeeded one another without pause up to the present day. A second series about the friendly scoundrel appeared across Japan in 1977 and a third in 1984. Their success was supported by a large number of feature movies. In 1978, *Lupin Sensei Mamoo no Ichihen* debuted, produced by TMS; in 1979, *Lupin Sensei Cagliostro no Shiro*, also produced by TMS; in 1985 *Lupin Sensei Babilon no Ogon Densetsu* was released, and two years later, *Lupin Sensei Fuma Ichizoku no Inbo*. Finally, we have to recall two television specials, *Good-Bye Liberty* made in 1980 and *Hemingway Paper no Nazo* (*The Mystery of Hemingway's Papers*), made in 1990, in which the unpredictable protagonists are involved in the search for a mysterious treasure described in the yellowing pages of an old book by the famous American writer. The image of the anti-hero is also present in other productions, but it never reached the success obtained by *Lupin III*.

Lupin Sansei © Monkey Punch / TMS.

Those who know and follow the productions of the Land of the Rising Sun know that few themes have been neglected in the plots of the countless anime, thus we can't be surprised when we find ourselves in front of *Genshi Shonen Ryu*. The events are set in the prehistoric era, but the themes are more current than ever. Ryu is marginalized because of the color of his skin, a paradoxical situation as the character is white, living in a world of people with dark colored skin. The theme of the quest, one dear to the Japanese people, is used. Ryu is in search of his mother who, instead of killing him at birth, as was the custom for every child born with white skin, had abandoned him hoping he would find a better future.

To conclude, *Sasurai no Taiyo* is worthy of mention because of the debut of one of the greats in animation, Yoshikazu Yasahiko, who soon specialized in character design, contributing to the realization of some of the most important works in Japanese animation.

0134 FILM

ATTACK NUMBER 1 NAMIDA NO PHOENIX (*Attack Number 1: The Tearful Phoenix*), Tokyo Movie, sport, 54 min., 3/17.

The film about the team's rise to the World Championship title sees the Japanese team involved in harsh training under the guidance of Hongo, the unyielding trainer who invariably remains insensitive to the feelings and the needs of the young volleyball players.

0135 FILM

DOBUTSU TAKARAJIMA (*Treasure Island, Animal Version*), Toei Doga, animal, 78 min., 3/20.

This is an odd rendition of Stevenson's story that inserts animals amongst the human characters, mostly among the crew of the pirate ship. The plot involves an emotional and entertaining treasure hunt in the natural settings of the mysterious island. The movie, directed by Hiroshi Ikeda, features Naozumi Yamamoto's soundtrack. Amongst the illustrators, there is also Hayao Miyazaki, whose signature is a guaranteed success.

0136 FILM

NINPU KAMUI GAIDEN (*Ninja Kamui, Stories Other than the Legend*), Eiken, adventure, 88 min., 3/20.

Kamui is a young ninja who joined the Iga war sect in the hope of bettering his social standing. An expert in his field, he quits when he realizes that his work is only that of a hired killer, but the sect is unforgiving and tries to kill him. Kamui is forced to run away and hide, without ever being able to attach himself to a place or to a woman, always pursued by ruthless killers. Kamui's voyage is destined to never end, in a continuous fight to survive. The movie is inspired by Sanpei Shirato's manga.

0137 FILM

ALI BABA TO YONJUPPIKI NO TOZOKU (*Ali Baba and the Forty Thieves*), Toei Doga, fairy-tale, 55 min., 7/18. [*Ali Baba Et Les 40 Voleurs*].

Ali Baba To Yonjuppiki No Tozoku © Toei Doga.

A descendant of Ali Baba has become a despotic tyrant, thanks to the riches stolen from the forty thieves by his ancestor. Having the genie of Aladdin's lamp in his possession, he wants to clean the city of a band of 38 cats, one rat and a young boy, descendant of the chief of the band of forty thieves. The latter will do anything and everything to give the treasures extorted through heavy taxation back to the people. Hayao Miyazaki who collaborated on the drawings, left the Toei Doga after this movie. It is produced by Hiroshi Okawa with the help of Mokihisa Yamamoto for the screenplay, Saburo Yokoi for the set design and Seichiro Uno for the soundtrack. The movie is directed by Hiroshi Shidara.

0138 FILM

MANGA EIGA TANJO NIHON MANGA EIGA HATTATSUSHI (*The Story and Development of Japanese Animated Cartoons*), Nihon Doga, documentary, 29 min., 9/11.

0139 FILM

TIGER MASK KUROI MAJIN (*Tiger Mask, the Black Demon*), Toei, sport, 25 min.

Another brief animated film featuring the most significant moments of the television series devoted to the masked wrestler. A new story was created by the same staff in 1981.

0140 SERIES

KABATOTTO (*id.*), Tatsunoko, animal, 558 episodes, 1/1/1971 —9/30/1972.

Kabatotto © Tatsunoko Pro.

A humorous series for children made up of brief episodes, it features the more or less peaceful adventures of a hippopotamus with an idiotic expression and of his little bird friend, the permanent tenant and cleaner of the pachyderm. The series' characters don't talk, the events instead detailed by an attentive narrator.

0141 SERIES

ANDERSEN MONOGATARI (*Andersen's Stories*), Mushi, fairy-tale, 52 episodes, 2/15 — 12/26/1971.

The series features a trip through the famous fairy-tales of the prolific Danish author, who seems to have found a host of admirators even in the land of the Rising Sun.

0142 SERIES

CHINGO MUCHA BE (*The Extravagant Mucha Be*), Tokyo Movie, humor, 46 episodes, 2/15 — 3/22/1971.

Mucha, the main character of the series, follows the patterns of the classic super hero with the double identity. By day he is a mild mannered person who lives in a welcoming house, while by night, he becomes the defender of good, at the service of justice.

0143 SERIES

ANIMENTARY — KETSUDAN (*The Decision — Animation Plus Documentary*), Tatsunoko, drama, 25 episodes, 4/3 — 9/25/1971.

This is the diary of the events that brought Japan to enter the Second World War, a dramatic series which combines deep tones and moments of reflection.

Animentary: Ketsudan © Tatsunoko Pro.

0144 SERIES

SASUKAI NO TAIYO (*The Vagabond Sun*), Mushi, soap-opera, 26 episodes, 4/8 — 9/30/1971.

Mikki and Jane are two aspiring singers. The former obtains success thanks to gifts from her rich parents, who give in to all of their daughter's whims. The latter instead becomes famous after many sacrifices and because of her inborn talent. The twist in this series directed by Kaisuke Fujikawa, which marks the debut of Yasuhiko Yoshigawa as assistant illustrator, resides in the fact that the two main characters, unbeknownst to all, were switched at birth.

0145 SERIES

SHIN OBAKE NO QTARO (*Qtaro the Ghost, New Series*), Tokyo Movie, humor, 70 episodes, 9/1/1971 — 12/27/1972.

The friendly adventures of Qtaro the ghost continue. The duo Fujiko Fujio doesn't lack in imagination and originality in making new adventures studded with jokes and stunts for the young Tadashi and his otherworldly companion.

0146 SERIES

TENSAI BAKABON (*The Idiot Genius*), Tokyo Movie, 40 episodes, humor, 9/25/1971 — 6/24/1972.

Fujio Akatsuka, one of the most popular authors of the humorous manga, publishes the adventures of his lucky character in many of the major Japanese newspapers. Even today, *Tensai bakabon* continues to be known and loved by different generations. The main character is the head of a typical family, like many others that characterize this genre.

0147 SERIES

SEKAI MONOSHIRI RYOKO (*The Instructive Trip Around the World*), Office Uni, documentary, 1006 episodes, 10/1/1971 — 12/31/1974.

0148 SERIES

FUSHIGINA MELMO (*The Marvelous Melmo*), Tezuka, magic, 26 episodes, 10/3/1971 — 3/26/1972.

Fushigina Melmo © Tezuka Production.

A young mother dies, leaving her own two children alone in the world. In paradise, she obtains — as a gift from God — a vase containing sugar-coated almonds that will help her daughter in her daily life. The red candies take ten years off of the age of those who eat them, the blue ones add ten years. Thus the little Melmo can look after her little brother as an adult, constantly getting into trouble because her mind and emotions remain those of a child. Moreover, when she combines the candies, she regresses back to a fetal state and is given the chance to be reborn into any desired animal species. The series is inspired by Osamu Tezuka's manga.

0149 SERIES

SARUTOBI ECCHAN (*The Sarutobi Ecchan*), Toei Doga, humor, 26 episodes, 10/4/1971 — 3/27/1972.

Ecchan is a little girl with a sharp tongue and quick wit. Gifted with incredible powers, she jumps and runs like a real ninja. Her adventures happen in the Japan of today. The series features the debut of Shotaro Ishimori as creator and screenplay writer. Yugo Serikawa is amongst the directors and the soundtrack is by Seichiro Uno.

0150 SERIES

APACHE YAKYUGUN (*Apache's Baseball Team*), Toei Doga, sport, 26 episodes, 10/6/1971 — 3/29/1972.

0151 SERIES

KUNIMATSUSAMA NO OTORIDAI (*Mr. Kunimatsu Passes*), Mushi, humor, 46 episodes, 10/6/1971 — 9/25/1972.

Kunimatsu Ishida, the rebellious student of *Haris no Kaze* (made in 1966), continues to rage on the Japanese screens in this new animated production, which features a good quantity of humorous elements in contrast to the preceding one.

0152 SERIES

SHIN GEGEGE NO KITARO (*Kitaro Gegege — New Series*), Toei Doga, grotesque, 45 episodes, 10/7/1971 — 9/28/1972.

After the well-received series from 1968, the gruesome adventures of Kitaro and his horrifying companions, as created by Shigeru Mizuki, continue.

0153 SERIES

SHIN SKYERS 5 (*Skyers 5 — New Series*), TCJ, science-fiction, 26 episodes, 10/7/1971 — 3/30/1972.

Four years after the initial series, TCJ presents the second chapter of the adventures of the Skyers 5 team, continuing to oppose evil and halt alien attacks.

0154 SERIES

LUPIN SENSEI (*Lupin III*), Tokyo Movie, adventure, 23 episodes, 10/24/1971 — 3/26/1972.

One of the most fun and longest running characters in Japanese animation is without doubt Lupin III, nephew of Arsene Lupin, the famous gentleman burglar created by French writter Maurice Leblanc. Lupin III works with the infallible gunman Daisuke Jigen and sword expert Goemon Ishikawa. Fujiko Mine, the beautiful but unreliable young woman and the inspector Zenigata, fierce enemy of the main character, are also part of the group of extraordinary characters created by Monkey Punch (the pen name of Kazuhiko Kato) and drawn by Yasuo Otsuka.

Lupin Sansei © Monkey Punch / TMS.

0155 SERIES

GENSHI SHONEN RYU (*Ryu, the Primitive Young Man*), Toei Doga, adventure, 22 episodes, 10/30/1971 — 3/25/1972.

Ryu is a young man from the prehistoric era born with white skin in a country where everyone is dark-skinned. As the years go by, during the search for his mother, Ryu faces the difficulties of life in a hostile environment, often dealing with racism and ravenous dinosaurs, including the gigantic tyrannosaur. Shotaro Ishimori's latest subject offers more proof of his inborn capacity to present different styles with ease. The series is inspired by the manga *Ryu no michi* by Ishimori Shotaro, although all the science-fiction elements were taken out.

CHAPTER ELEVEN: 1972

Japanese animation owes part of its worldwide success to illustrator Go Nagai who often shocked the Japanese public, proposing themes linked to sex and violence, many of which proved too innovative for the traditionalistic culture of Japan.

In 1972 two of the most important series of his vast production empire were launched: *Devilman* and *Mazinger Z*. The two characters revolutionized the approach to Japanese cartoons, not so much for the originality of the subjects (which more often than not appeared common and similar), but for the author's particular brand of "bad taste." Even if the shows were presented in very different ways, they both proposed violence as the only means to fight evil, and both are made with an unrefined, rather careless art style, albeit very strong characterizations of the individual characters.

Thanks to the support of the famous production firm Toei Doga, Nagai transposed the setting and the characters of *Devilman* into an animated series aimed at the general public, produced almost simultaneously with the manga (the first television episode appeared just one month after the fortunate publishing of the manga), the story is not only presented in an extremely softened fashion, but it distorts and changes the entire screenplay, betraying the strong revolutionary spirit of the film for a feeling of vague impatience. *Devilman* nonetheless signaled the beginning of a new trend that presented horror themes and gloomy settings, painted in dark and melancholic tones, satisfying the public's taste for black humor and the grotesque.

Nagai's stories are based on a perverse combination of sadism and horrifying violence that often diverges from the subject to flow into a pure exercise of disgust. For this reason, in Japan as well as in the rest of the world, countless numbers of moralistic and conformist associations have tried, without success, to obstruct the evolution of the Nagai phenomenon.

Astroganger © Knack.

Gatchaman ©1994 Tatsunoko Production Co., Ltd. Package Design ©1997 Urban Vision Entertainment. This 1994 OAV revamped *Gatchaman* for the nineties without compromising the design of the original series. (Cat.# UV1003)

Almost simultaneously, *Mazinger Z* was presented on the Japanese television networks. It is a story marked, in the very basics, by a spirit of war, but is also rich in new assumptions. After traveling with the little androids possessing their own conscience and consciousness and the giant remote controlled robots, we bear witness, in this series, to the union of the human and the technological. The robot is flown by a young boy who, aboard a flying device, the pilder, inserts himself in Mazinger's head, personally participating in the battles. One of the fundamental concepts that shines through in Nagai's lexicon is the importance of teamwork. Koji Kabuto fights alongside two minor robots, Boss Borot and Aphrodite A, who more often than not prove to be useless against the enemy attacks, but who nonetheless remain important to the context of the episode. As well as being the first robot of female appearance, Aphrodite is piloted by a young girl who takes part without fear in the battles. Japanese animation is no longer a hegemony of courageous samurais in uniform, but also includes heroines with strong personalities who, as equals to men, have rights and duties in the defense of Planet Earth.

This anime, which appeared in Italy in January 1980, after the success of certain other Japanese series, is the first chapter of a famous saga involving Nagai's favorite robots: Great Mazinger, Grendizer and Getter Robot, although the latter is involved in a less explicit manner. In Italy, the series were presented in a different chronological order, with the added aggravation of modified character names, making the story even more difficult to follow.

Astroganger turned out somewhat differently, with an anachronistic style when compared to the above-mentioned robots. The main character, an automaton with an all too simple design, destroys his enemies using punches and kicks, common methods that don't make the most of the potential of a genre in constant evolution that drew public interest only with difficulty. In a series with poor themes and stories, the variation in the concept of the little main character who is absorbed into the body of the robot is certainly not sufficient to make the work stand out.

Finally, two words on *Kagaku ninjatai Gatchaman*, produced by Tatsunoko on subjects by Tatsuo Yoshida. The history of this series underlines the incredible strictness and rigidity of American censorship commissions, especially compared to those in Italy. After it passed through the very strict procedures to gather the necessary American approval, the story was filtered and changed to be utterly boring, with modifications that didn't only change the dialogue and eliminate the violence, but which altered the entire sense of the work. Almost one third of the footage was redone and edited in with some original sequences, following a new screenplay written by Jameson Brewer. The new series, which presented the American national spirit in its frustrating entirety, as well as featuring new characters with horribly pessimistic attitudes — especially the little robot 7 Zark 7 — offers a horrendous matching of two completely different styles, notwithstanding the fact that the American producers attempted to imitate the Japanese style of animation. The battle scenes not suitable for an American public were set on other planets or totally eliminated. Moreover, the theme of death was never dealt with, for fear of creating panic amongst the American audiences. Italy was fortunate enough to see both the original and modified series, enabling them to objectively judge the validity of the changes made in the original version.

0156 FILM
NAGAGUTSU SANJUSHI (*The Three Booted Musketeers*), Toei Doga, adventure, 53 min., 3/18.

One more installment in the fantastic adventure of Perrault the Cat, constantly pursued by a hired killer sent by the big cat, who wants to kill him to avenge past insults. This time, the endless escape brings our protagonist to the Wild West where he befriends the young sheriff Jim, who is secretly trying to oppose the plans of a local lord, whose intentions are to control the entire city.

0157 FILM
MAKEN LINER 0011 HENSHIN SEYO (*Magic Dog Liner 0011, Transform!*), Toei Doga, science fiction, 53 min., 7/16.

Created by genius Hiroshi Sasagawa who gave us the famous *Shinzo ningen Cashern* in 1973, the film presents the adventures of an extraordinary cyborg dog at the service of good.

0158 FILM
PANDA KOPANDA (*Panda, Little Panda*), Tokyo Movie, animal, 33 min., 12/17.

Hayao Miyazaki's first original creation features the daily adventures of two friendly asian bears, father and son. In this brief anime, a funny looking little girl with two red braids is used as a supporting character. Her character design was taken from the "setei" (preparatory sketches) of *Nagutsushita no Pippi* (*Pippi Longstockings*), which was never produced.

Panda Kopanda © TMS.

0159 SERIES
KASHI NO KI MOKKU (*Kokku made of Oak*), Tatsunoko, classic, 52 episodes, 1/4 – 12/26/1972. [*Pinocchio*].

This Japanese animated version of the story of Pinocchio does not, for the most part, stick to the novel written by Collodi. The main character's name is changed to Mokku, and the stories, created by Tatsuo Yoshida and written by Junzo Toriumi and Akiyoshi Sakai, were more often than not invented ex novo. The drawings are by Sadao Miyamoto, Masayuki Hayashi and Kazuhiko Udagawa, under the artistic direction of Ippei Kuri.

0160 SERIES
SHIN MOOMIN (*Moomin — New Series*), Mushi, humor, 1/9 — 12/31/1972.

Kashi No Ki Mokku © Tatsunoko Pro.

0161 SERIES
SEIGI O AISURU MONO GEKKO KAMEN (*Gekko Kamen, the Man Who Loves Justice*), Knack, science fiction, 39 episodes, 1/10 — 10/2/1972. Moon Mask Rider.

Riding in on his powerful motorcycle, a young detective transforms into Gekko Kamen, the masked super hero, to oppose and defeat the criminal organizations. The animated series, inspired by Yasunoni Kawauchi's original cartoon, was joined by Nobuhiro Osaseko as director and character designer.

0162 SERIES
UMI NO TRITON (*Triton from the Sea*), Animation Staff Room, adventure, 27 episodes, 4/1 — 9/30/1972.

Little Toriton's parents die while attempting to rebel against the cruel Poseidon, king of the sea, who imposes his will on the inhabitants of the sea. Helped by Lakar, a female dolphin

Umi No Triton © Westcape Corporation.

with great abilities and by Pipi, a young siren, the young protagonist takes on the difficult inheritance of his parents. The story is by Osamu Tezuka and was produced by Yoshinobu Nishizaki.

0163 SERIES
MAHOTSUKAI CHAPPY (*Chappy the Magician*), Toei Doga, magic, 39 episodes, 4/3 — 12/25/1972.

Coming from the world of magic, the little Chappy moves to Earth with her family and begins to live as a human being. Magic, an ability common on her world, remains in her power and often, in the most difficult situations, she makes good use of it. The series doesn't present particularly well done animation, nor a brilliant story, even though director Yugo Serikawa and character designer Nobuya Takahashi take part in the project.

0164 SERIES
AKADO SUZUNOSUKE (*id.*), Tokyo Movie, adventure, 52 episodes, 4/5/1972 — 3/28/1973.

The series is the animated transposition of a famous radio drama of the 50s, originally written by Tsunayoshi Takeuchi. It presents the adventures of a young samurai, Suzunosuke, who fights against invaders to protect his country. The designs and the storyboard are from Hayao Miyazaki and Osamu Dezaki.

0165 SERIES
MUNCHEN E NO MICHI (*The Road to Monaco*), Nihon TV Doga, documentary, 16 episodes, 4/23 — 8/20/1972.

0166 SERIES
DEVILMAN (*id.*), Toei Doga, horror, 39 episodes, 7/8/1972 — 4/7/1973. *Devilman*.

After his death, Akira is possessed by a being sent from the Tribe of the Demons to spread death and terror in the world. But his love for Mikki, a young woman, leads Devilman to betray his people. Because of his rebellion, Devilman becomes the target of those who once were his allies. The show was released almost simultaneously with the manga, but Devilman only vaguely respects the original idea, resulting in a faded version. The list of screenplay writers includes Masaki Tsuji. It is directed by Tomaharu Katsumata and Akehi Masayuki.

0167 SERIES
MON CHERICO COCO (*id.*), Nihon TV Doga, humor, 14 episodes, 8/27 — 11/26/1972.

0168 SERIES
KAGAKU NINJATAI GATCHAMAN (*Science Ninja Team Gatchaman*), Tatsunoko, science fiction, 105 episodes, 10/1/1972 — 9/29/1974. *Battle of the Planets / G-Force*.

Ken the eagle, Joe the condor, Jun the swan, Jinpei the swallow and Ryo the owl form the space patrol Gatchaman, and aboard the spaceship God Phoenix, they combat the invading Galactors. Their adventures created by Tatsuo Yoshida had two sequels in 1978 and in 1979. The drawings are by Ippei Kuri and it is directed by Hiroshi Sasagawa.

0169 SERIES
ASTROGANGER (*id.*), Knack, robot, 26 episodes, 10/4/1972 — 3/28/1973.

Kagaku Ninjatai Gatchaman © Tatsunoko Pro.

An extraterrestrial who escaped the destruction of her planet is thrown down on Earth and is rescued by a scientist. They soon fall in love, marry and together have a baby named Kantaro. After a few years, Earth is threatened by the same beings who had destroyed the woman's planet. The couple creates a gigantic robot that watches over the population of the planet. Thanks to a special metal bar brought back by the woman in her space travels, Astroganger, an immense robot, gifted with intelligence, comes to life. The Earth suffers the first attack and Kantaro's parents die, leaving their son at the controls of the powerful robot. The fated end of the war changes, thanks to the mechanical hero who sacrifices himself for the good of humanity. Before he is destroyed, however, Astroganger arranges things so that his little friend goes back to Earth with a space disk. Eiji Tanaka is the character designer, the project was led by Seiichi Nishimo. The direction is entrusted to Masashi Nitta, with a screenplay by Tetsuhisa Tsusukawa.

Astroganger © Knack.

0170 SERIES

KAIKETSU TAMAGON (*Tamagon Resolves Everything*), Tatsunoko, humor, 195 episodes, 10/5/1972 — 9/28/1973.

A little dragon named Tamagon helps people in difficulty with his eccentric eggs, from which are born monsters capable of performing many services — such as washing clothes — for the always busy Japanese homemakers. The episodes directed by Hiroshi Sasagawa last only five minutes, which explains the great number of episodes produced. Yuji Nunokawa heads the staff of animators.

Kaiketsu Tamagon © Tatsunoko Pro.

0171 SERIES

HAZEDON (*id.*), Soeisha, adventure, 26 episodes, 10/5/1972 —3/29/1973.

After the death of his father, Haze, the young Hazedon decides to leave on a long trip in the South Seas, in search of adventures and new dreams.

0172 SERIES

ONBU OBAKE (*The Ghost That Likes to Be Carried On One's Shoulder*), Eiken, mythological, 52 episodes, 10/7/1972 —9/29/1973.

Onbu is a little green eyed spirit who likes to do the back stroke in the sky. One day, he is picked up by an old woman and starts his life amongst the humans. This series recalls the style of Fujiko Fujio.

0173 SERIES

DOKONJOGAERU (*The Persistent Frog*), Tokyo Movie, humor, 103 episodes, 10/7/1972 — 9/29/1974.

Hiroshi is a turbulent young high school boy. When not causing his own trouble, he is involved in the most unthinkable situations by his friend, a friendly wide-eyed frog that is accidentally 'stamped' on his sweater.

0174 SERIES

MAZINGER Z (*id.*), Toei Doga, robot, 92 episodes, 12/3/1972 — 9/1/1974. *Tranzor Z.*

Mazinger Z is a giant robot that old Dr. Kabuto has secretly built to stop the evil Dr. Hell, once his colleague, from conquering the Earth. Dr. Hell has the power to do it, thanks to

Intro
-1962
1963
1964
1965
1966
1967
1968
1969
1970
1971
1972
1973
1974
1975
1976
1977
1978
1979
1980
1981
1982
1983
1984
1985
1986
1987
1988
Index

monstrous devices created by the Cretan civilization and found by the two scientists during an archeological expedition. Dr. Kabuto is a victim of the first attack by his ex- colleague, and leaves the Mazinger Z as an inheritance to his grandson Koji, without having a chance to give the boy any instructions. The death of his grandfather makes the young man want to seek revenge. After many failed attempts, Koji succeeds in entering the robot's head with the Pilder, a little flying device that gives him access to the robot's functions. Aphrodite A, a female robot with feminine features piloted by Sayaka Yumi and Boss Borot, a clumsy toylike robot driven by a fat suburban hooligan, also appear in the series as helpers to Mazinger. The screenplay for Go Nagai's series is by Susumu Takahisa and Keisuke Fujikawa and it is skillfully directed by Yugo Serikawa, Tomoharu Katsumata, Nobuo Onuki and Bonjin Nagaki. The character design is by Yoshiyuki Hane, while the soundtrack is composed by Shunsuke Kibuchi.

CHAPTER TWELVE: 1973

After having created so many humorous characters for children, the duo Fujiko Fujio finally began work on animating *Doraemon*, the robot cat with incredible abilities. 1973 saw the explosion of this character's popularity, audiences warming to the cat who becomes the best friend of all Japanese children. The producers were easily persuaded to sell the rights to the picture, making the most of one of the most extensive merchandising setups ever made, only comparable to the recent case of *Dr. Slump's* Arale Chan.

The appeal of the blue talking cat finds its basis in his friendliness towards and protection of his little human friend Nobita, with whom the young television viewers unconsciously identify. At this point it is necessary to remind ourselves that the sale of stuffed, life-size plush Doraemon surpassed that of any other product inspired by the animation.

This does not take away from the fact that, commercial discourse aside, while *Doraemon* is one of the true money makers of Japanese cartoons, it also brought a feeling of light and hope into the angst-filled 70s. A particular train bears its logo, set up to be both an exhibition devoted to the show and a wheeled playground for young children..

Having become by now a fixed trend, female sport discovers in this period one of its most successful expressions, *Ace o nerae!* A melodramatic soap opera, this animation presents the world of sports and particularly of tennis, as a type of golden jail in which happiness and success can only be reached at the cost of physical and personal sufferings.

A series of OAVs were produced at the end of the 80s, which remade *Ace o nerae!* as a science-fiction program, in which training robots were used instead of tennis rackets. The title, clearly a parody, was *Top o nerae!*

Suffering as an art form was featured in the interesting *Koya no shonen Isamu*, an American-style western with the Japanese tormented son in search of his parents. A sense of reflection was added to the beautiful scenery remenicient of the old classics. Issues were treated in a straightforward manner and without a great deal of angst, such as the racism that the main character faced as the son of Indian and Japanese parents. But young Isamu does not joke, and his ability with a gun soon surfaces when it is time to settle the dangerous situations that were commonplace in the old West.

Ace O Nerae! © S. Yamamoto / TMS.

Along the same lines of discussion of subtle racism, *Shingo ningen Cashern* features the anguished life of a youngster forced to transform into an indestructible cyborg to save the world from the invasion of an army of robots. Cashern's sadness is endemic for a number of reasons. First of all, the robots were created by his father, who was later enslaved by them, then his mother is locked in a mechanical swan and transformed into a robot. Finally, although he is fighting the evil androids, Cashern has to stay away from the human beings that he is protecting, because of the fear that the citizens hold for any type of robot. Even *Microid S* features cyborg children or, more accurately, insect children who put their unfortunate condition at the service of humanity. The story's basics recall Shotaro Ishimori's *cyborg 009*, even if, from the second episode on, it takes on its own characteristics. It almost seems that a subtle hint of ancient wisdom is carefully concealed in these types of stories, a warning not to grieve if life is sometimes cruel, because everyone was created for a reason and is therefore useful to the community.

The cyborgs are treated in a more lighthearted way in *Miracle shojo Limit Chan*, closer in style to the 'little witches' genre than to science fiction, as the resources of the main character are only used to give special powers to a young girl substituting, for once, technology for magic. So, Limit spends most of her time resolving local problems and seldom runs into excessively mean criminals.

Such is not the case with the provocative *Cutie Honey* created by animation's bad boy, Go Nagai. Always caught up in breathtaking fights and involuntary — or not — stripteases (which tended to increase viewer numbers immensely), the android Hewine is one of the first attempts to bring eroticism in animation, even if in small doses. This tame erotica gave way to the advent of Cream Lemon, an adult anime, in the middle of the 80s.

Nagai then collaborated with Toei Doga to produce a film called *Mazinger Z tai Devilman*, a favorite with fans of the 'giant robot' genre, in which the author's two most famous characters meet, offering proof of their existence in a common universe.

Going from Nagai's demons to science fiction archeology, the Toei Doga churned out *Babil nisei*, an interesting tale that features a simple high school student who discovers that he is one of the fundamental pillars of an ancient dynasty, which has now disappeared. As such, he must fight an endless war, along with certain eccentric adventure companions, including an aquatic robot, a pterodactyl and a panther girl.

And so, while the major parts of production firms dedicated themselves to action films and series, the Tatsunoko — now adding their entry with *Shinzo ningen Cashern* — came up with *Kerokko Demetan*, an animal soap opera which tried to emulate the success of *Konchu monogatari minashigo Hutch*. The main character, a small frog of humble origins, manages, in every episode, to get himself in trouble to save his friends. While not as dramatic as the previous bee story, *Kerokko Demetan* nonetheless tried to extract some tears from the television viewers who, having already been suckered in to feeling for the deaths of ants and grasshoppers in 1970, feel even more embarrassed about caring for a green frog afflicted with love torments.

Casshan Robot Hunter ©1994 Harmony Gold U.S.A. / Tatsunoko Production Co. Ltd. Package Design ©1995 Streamline Enterprises, Inc & Orion Home Video. All Rights Reserved. This 1994 OAV updates the original series. (Cat.# 91383)

Babel II ©1994 Mitsuteru Yokoyama / Hikara Production / Sohbi Planning / TEEUP. Package Design ©1995 Streamline Enterprises, Inc & Orion Home Video. This 1994 OAV updates the original series. (Cat.# 91003)

Kerokko Demetan © Tatsunoko Pro. English version ©1989 Harmony Gold U.S.A, Inc / Tatsunoko Prod. Co., Ltd. All Rights Reserved. Atwork ©1999 Plaza Entert., Inc. Package ©MCMXCIX Image Entertainment, Inc.

0175 FILM

PANDA NO DAIBOKEN (*The Great Adventures of Panda*), Teoi Doga, animal, 50 min., 3/17.

Yugo Serikawa's new feature film is aimed at a public essentially composed of teenagers and features the story of a gracious and sweet panda and his animal friends. The author was trying to wrest the title of Japanese feature film master from Taiji Yabushita, famous amongst other things, for the film *Hakujaden* in 1958.

0176 FILM

PANDA KOPANDA AMEFURI SAKUSU NO MAKI (*Panda, Little Panda, the Chapter of the Rained-on Circus*), Tokyo Movie, animal, 38 min., 3/17.

Hayao Miyazaki releases the new adventures of the little panda who was adopted by young Mimiko, nicknamed Mimi by her friends. The two inseparable characters face the joys and sorrows of life together.

0177 FILM

NIHON MANGA EIGA HATTATSUSHI — ANIME SHINGASHO (*The New Illustrated Agenda of Animated Cartoons — History of the Development of Japanese Animation Cinema*), Nihon Doga, documentary, 40 min., 3/31.

0178 FILM

KANASHIMI NO BELADONNA (*The Tragedy of Belladonna*), Mushi, adventure, 98 min., 6/30.

Taken from a novel by Jules Michelet, the animated film features the adventures of a young woman, Jeanne, in Medieval France, at the time of the witch hunts. The feature film, the last one made by Tezuka with Mushi, aimed at an adult public, was produced by the new president of Mushi, Eichi Kawabata and directed by Eichi Yamamoto.

0179 FILM

MAZINGER Z TAI DEVILMAN (*Mazinger Against Devilman*), Toei Doga, robot, 43 min., 7/18. [*Devilman Contre Mazinger Z*].

Special episode that links two of Go Nagai's most dated series, in which Doctor Hell forces the tribe of Demons to join in his fight against Mazinger Z. Devilman's answer is to form an alliance with the pilot of the robot to save the Earth. Special episodes like this one were produced for the occasion of the "Manga matsuri" Animation Festival.

0180 SERIES

BABIL NISEI (*Babil the Second*), Toei Doga, science fiction, 39 episodes, 1/1 — 9/24/1973.

Babil Nisei © Hikari Production / TV Asahi / Toei Doga.

An extraterrestrial comes to our planet at the time of the Babylonians and builds a base under the surface of the Earth to prevent an attack from the evil Yomi. Years pass and Koichi, the character descended from the alien, unaware of his heritage, is brought inside the hidden base by Roden, a mysterious young girl. With the help of Ropuros, a powerful pterodactyl, Poseidon, a gigantic robot that lives at the bottom of the sea and Roden, capable of transforming into a panther, the young Koichi defeats his eternal enemy Yomi, using his own ESP powers. The animated series taken from Mitsuteru Yokoyama's manga had the skillful Shingo Araki as character designer, enriching the artistic value of the production with his great vision and talent. Takeshi Tamiya directed the series.

0181 SERIES

KEROKKO DEMETAN (*Demetan the Frog*), Tatsunoko, animal, 38 episodes, 1/2 — 9/25/1973. *The Brave Frog.*

Demetan is a young frog who falls in love with Ranatan, the daughter of the king of the pond. This causes him a number of problems, as he is the son of a poor craftsman. Demetan's decisive role in freeing the pond from a gigantic and tyrannical cat fish resolved the crisis, breaking the social barriers to the joy of everyone in the pond. The series was supervised in collaboration with Masayoki Hayashi and Hiroshi Kawabata, while the direction was entrusted to Hiroshi Sasagawa, with the story by Junzo Toriumi and screenplay by Akiyoshi Sakai.

0182 SERIES

YAMANEZUMI ROCKY CHICK (*Rocky Chuck, the Mountain Rat*), Zuiyo, animal, 52 episodes, 1/7 — 12/30/1973.

Zawazawa, a village situated in the mountains, is populated by many animals. Their adventures constitute the basis for this new series by Zuiyo Production.

0183 SERIES

JUNGLE KUROBE (*Kurobe From the Jungle*), Tokyo Movie, animal, 31 episodes, 3/2 — 9/28/1973.

0184 SERIES

DORAEMON (*id.*), Nihon TV Doga, humor, 27 episodes, 4/1 — 9/30/1973.

Nobita is a lazy and careless young boy who has no interests other than playing and sleeping. One day Doraemon the robot cat from the future appears on his desk with his time-travelling machine, and Nobita's life radically changes. Using a different gadget from the cat's bottomless pocket every day, Nobita learns that it is more convenient to count on one's own strengths than to wait for help from anyone else. Created by Fujiko Fujio, Doraemon is one of Japan's most popular and most liked children's characters.

0185 SERIES

WANSAKUN (*The Little Wansa*), Mushi, animal/humor, 26 episodes, 4/2 — 9/24/1973.

Mushi's last production from the original story by Osamu Tezuka, before the latter's abandonment of the product and the company's reorganization. The humor is enriched by an excellent soundtrack.

0186 SERIES

KOYA NO SHONEN ISAMU (*Isamu, the Boy From the Wild Prairie*), Tokyo Movie, western/adventure, 52 episodes, 4/4/1973 — 3/27/1974. [*Willie Boy*].

Son of Japanese and Indian parents, Isamu Wataru becomes a skilled sharpshooter to confront the dangers of the Wild West. During his desperate search for his father, the youngster must face one of the worst plagues of all times, racism. The original story is by Noboru Kawasaki and Koji Yamakawa. The design supervision of the series is by Shigenori Yoshida while the animation is by Hayao Miyazaki.

Kerokko Demetan © Tatsunoko Pro.

Wansakun © Tezuka Production.

Koya No Shonen Isamu © TMS.

Microid S © Tezuka Production / TV Asahi / Toei Doga.

Zero Tester © J.D. / Tohoku Shinsha.

Shinzo Ningen Cashern © Tatsunoko Pro.

0187 SERIES

MICROID S (*id.*), Toei Doga, science fiction, 25 episodes, 4/7 — 10/6/1973.

Three youngsters, Yanna, Akeba and Mamgo, are submitted to an experiment by the Gidoron, a race of deadly insects, that will shrink the children considerably. After rebelling, using their new super powers, they combat the creatures to save the human race. The series is inspired by Osamu Tezuka's Microid Z manga. It was transformed into Microid S by request of Seiko, a sponsor. It was directed by Masayuki Akehi and the characters designed by Hiroshi Wagatsuma.

0188 SERIES

CHARGE MAN KEN (*id.*), Knack, science fiction, 130 episodes, 7/1/1973 — 12/30/1974.

The series set in the 21st century features a group of soldiers captained by the courageous and powerful Ken who fights for the freedom of human race.

0189 SERIES

ZERO TESTER (*id.*), Tohoku Shinsha, science fiction, 60 episodes, 10/1/1973 — 12/30/1974.

Fuyuki, Go, Lisa and Captain Tetsuji are a fighting group formed to defend planet Earth.

0190 SERIES

MIRACLE SHOJO LIMIT CHAN (*Limit, the Miraculous Little Girl*), Toei Doga, science fiction, 25 episodes, 10/1/1973 — 3/25/1974.

After the premature death of his daughter, a scientist decides to build a perfectly identical copy of her, including her mind, in his laboratory. Thus Limit is born, a beautiful robot girl forced to hide her mechanical condition even to her closest friends, whom she often helps with her special powers. Shinji Nagashima, author of the manga, worked on both the subject and the screenplay, Kazuo Komatsubara realized the character design while Shunsuke Kikuchi and Tokiko Iwatani composed the soundtrack.

0191 SERIES

SHINZO NINGEN CASHERN (*Cashern, the Man With the New Body*), Tatsunoko, science fiction, 35 episodes, 10/2/1973 — 6/25/1974.

The famous series is directed by Hiroshi Sasagawa. To be able to destroy the evil robots that have taken command of the Earth, the scientist that had invented them transforms his son, Cashern, into a powerful android warrior. Both Luna, the daughter of a renowned professor and the boy's love interest, and Flanders, faithful robot dog capable of transforming himself into powerful space ships, fight at Cashern's side. Tasuo Yoshida and Yoshitaka Amano realized the character design.

0192 SERIES

KARATE RAKA ICHIDAI (*The Karate Clown*), Tokyo Movie, sport, 47 episodes, 10/3/1973 — 9/25/1974.

Taken from a manga by Tsunoda Jiro and Ikki Kajiwara, the series presents the entertaining adventures of a karate expert who, between laughs, aspires to the world championship title. Ironically, the story is inspired by the life of Oyama, a real-life great champion.

0193 SERIES

DOROMON ENMAKUN (*Dororon, Little Judge From Hell*), Toei Doga, magic/horror, 25 episodes, 10/4/1973 — 3/28/1974.

0194 SERIES

ACE O NERAE! (*Point to the Ace!*), Tokyo Movie, sport, 26 episodes, 10/5/1973 — 3/29/1974. [*Jeu, Set Et Match*].

Hiromi Oka, a high school student, practices diligently to be able to participate in the most prestigious tournaments, following the example set by her idol, the champion Reika. Driven by her coach to give up her social life in exchange for achievements in sports, the young woman neglects her love for Todo, also a good tennis player. The original manga that inspired the television series directed by Osamu Dezaki was designed by the capable Sumika Yamamoto.

0195 SERIES

BOKEN KOROBOKKURU (*The Adventures of Korobokkuru*), Eiken, fairy tale, 26 episodes, 10/6/1973 — 3/30/1974

The Korobokkuru are very little gnomes who live in the Japanese mountains. Only a few centimeters high, the human world looks immense and mysterious to them. Therefore, the three little main characters decide to explore it. Fortunately, they soon befriend a child who protects them from the dangers of a life not made for them. The series, aimed at a younger public, was created by Satoru Sato and Tsutomu Murakami and the screenplay is by Noboru Shiroyama and Minoru Takahashi.

0196 SERIES

SAMURAI GIANTS (*id.*), Eiken, sport, 46 episodes, 10/7/1973 —9/29/1974.

0197 SERIES

CUTIE HONEY (*id.*), Toei Doga, science fiction, 25 episodes, 10/13/1973 — 3/30/1974.

Turning almost solely towards science fiction, Go Nagai created Cutie Honey, a provocative female android involved in the fight against the "claws of the panther," a type of space mafia made up of only women whose goal is to get rid of all earthly women and to secure all men for themselves. The main character attends an all-girl catholic school whose lesbian teachers keep harassing her with obscene propositions. When circumstances require the powers of the android heroine, her costume appears in a "flash," but only after having left her completely naked for a few seconds — to the delight of the male viewers.

The forces Of Evil Were Looking for Trouble.. THEY FOUND HER!

New Cutey Honey ©1995 Go Nagai / Dynamic Planning, Inc. / Toei Video Co., Ltd. This OAV, released in North America by A.D. Vision, Inc. (Cat.# VHSC-001/4), updates the original series.

CHAPTER THIRTEEN: 1974

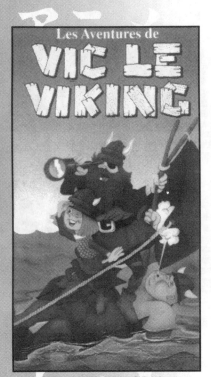

Alps No Shojo Heidi © Zuiyô.

Chiisana Viking Vicke © Zuiyô.

Up to the first half of the 70s, in Italy as well as in the rest of the Western world, Japanese animated productions were completely unknown. Japan's customs and traditions, always tightly bound to the country's past, created an aura of mystery around the ancient land. In 1974, to overcome this perceived distance, the production firm Zuiyo saw the necessity to create a series specifically aimed at the foreign market. They planned to use advanced techniques and skilled artists, both ultimately visible in the excellent screenplay, and researched the particular tastes and prevailing themes of the Western World. Thus, *Alpes no shojo Heidi* was born, an animated transposition of Johanna Spyri's famous novel. It was transmitted in Italy in the summer of 1976, earning immediate success. From the first days, in fact, the public was fascinated by the attention paid to characterization and the fluidity of the animation, something truly surprising for a series of 52 episodes, a series followed with anticipation.

Italy had already opened the door to Japanese animated cartoons with *Barbapapa* and *Chiisana Vicking Vicke*, bought sight unseen, and broadcasts which, in the span of a few years, covered a decade of series. Many of the series contents were originally unknown, and many were not aimed at children or teenagers. They alternated showings on the RAI and on private circuits starting in 1978. The overexposure of the new product surely did not help to garner critical support. The Japanese animated series are rich in technical innovations where the direction is concerned, offering high speed action and total involvement to the audience, as well as the arcing and growing plot lines, contrary to the theatrical style of Disney's cartoons.

Amongst the best series produced this year, *Getter Robot* by Go Nagai marks another innovation in science fiction and the robot genre in particular. Ryo, Hayato and Musashi, the main characters, join their vehicles in three different combinations to create robots capable of fighting, respectively, in the sky, on land and in the sea. The simple but ingenious joining system of the different mechanical parts, created by the now famous Japanese author, was redone and advanced in the following years by many authors of the robot genre. Amongst the many examples present in the Japanese animation panorama, certain series like *Chodenji Machine Voltes V* in 1977 and *Mirai robot Daltanias* in 1979 distinguish themselves, in fact, precisely because of the splendid transformation scenes. The moment of joining produces a decisively impressive effect and is enriched by the rhythmic background music that grasps the attention of the public during the entire scene.

Also by Go Nagai was *Great Mazinger*, the second chapter of the famous trilogy, a series which featured Tetsuya Tsurugi at the control of a new robot against hordes of evil monsters from hell. Very similar to the preceding *Mazinger Z* in its form and contents, *Great Mazinger* appeared decisively more advanced on the technological level. The story line was more mature and the characters more aware of their role. We must remember that certain of Nagai's stories share a common bond. The two Mazinger, Grendinzer and the previously mentioned Geter Robot can in fact confront an enemy monster together, as happens in one famous film, also shown in Italy, because they live in the same universe.

After the success of this cartoon, Reiji Matsumoto, another important name in the Japanese panorama, also decided to enter into the world of animation with the television series *Uchu senkan Yamato*. The author showed great artistic ability, uniting precision and extremely particular technological design with a screenplay rich in pathos and poetry.

The theme of the super hero with a double identity, a constant theme in American comics and cartoons, was finally presented in *Hurricane Polymer,* with an amazing originality which prevents it from falling into cliche. Takeshi, the main character, owes his super power to a powerful helmet that covers his body with an armored suit of amazing power. But the real innovation is in the capacity of his armor to change into powerful ground, air and water vehicles, giving Polymer the ability to fight against the hired killers pursuing him.

Hurricane Polymar ©1996 Nippon Columbia • Tatsunoko Productions. Package Design ©1998 Urban Vision Entertainment. This OAV updates the original series. (Cat.# UV1032)

0198 FILM

KIKANSHA YAEMON D51 NO DAIBOKEN (*The Adventures of Kikansha Yaemon D51*), Toei Doga, science fiction, 62 min., 3/16.

0199 FILM

JACK TO MAME NO KI (*Jack and the Beanstalk*), Group Tack, fairy tale, 98 min., 7/20.

The feature film directed by Gisaburo Sugii in an all new musical interpretation deals with the theme of the popular English fairy tale.

0200 FILM

MAZINGER Z TAI ANKOKU DAISHOGUN (*Mazinger Z Against the Great General Nero*), Toei Doga, robot, 43 min., 7/25.

Third Episode of UFO Robot Against the Space Invaders. Also shown in Italy as a part of a collage made precisely for the Italian big screen, the film features the two Mazinger created by Go Nagai, united in the fight against General Noro's two powerful fighting monsters. The direction is by Nobutaka Nishizawa, who also directed Kotetsu Jeeg in 1975.

0201 SERIES

ALPS NO SHOJO HEIDI (*Heidi, the Little Girl From the Alps*), Zuiyo, classic, 52 episodes, 1/6 — 12/29/1974. [*Heidi*].

Alps No Shojo Heidi © Zuiyô Enterprise / Apollo Films.

Heidi, a young orphan girl, is entrusted to a young aunt who soon decides to unload this responsibility, bringing the little girl to live with her hermit grandfather in the Alps, on a lovely mountain. The encounter isn't one of the best and the girl's exuberance gets on the nerves of the old man but as time goes by, the two become inseparable. One day, the aunt comes back to the mountains to claim the little girl, intending to bring her back to Frankfurt with her where Heidi will have to become a hired companion for Clara, a disabled little girl. The two girls become very close in a short period of time, so much so, that thanks to Heidi and to Peter, the young pastor, Clara recovers the use of her legs. The series, on which Hayao Miyazaki also worked, was directed by Isao Takahata and supervised by Yoichi Kotabe, based on Johanna Spyri's novel. Masahiro Ioka also took part in the project for the screenplay.

0202 SERIES

JUDO SAKA (*The Judo Anthem*), Tokyo Movie, sport, 27 episodes, 4/1 — 9/30/1974.

The young Shinta trains to become a judo champion and this causes him many hardships. The series, like many others dedicated to sport, focuses on the willpower of characters who never seem to get discouraged, in spite of the difficulties in their lives.

0203 SERIES

MAJOKKO MEG CHAN (*Meg, the Little Magician*), Toei Doga, magic, 72 episodes, 4/1/1974 — 9/29/1975.

Meg is a young witch sent to Earth for a period of apprenticeship, together with Non, a young rival colleague. The series also features a clumsy inspector in charge of following the students until the final encounter that will establish which of the two will have the right to rise to the rank of real witch. A high point of the series was its very rich artistic staff, who rotated through the production of every episode. Makiko Narita and Satori Inoue wrote the stories, while Takeo Watanabe was in charge of the background music. It was directed by Isamu Tsuchida, and the character design was by Shingo Araki and Bonjin Nagaki (who also took care of the animation).

0204 SERIES

HOSHI NO KO POLON (*Polon the Little Girl From the Stars*), Nihon Doga for Jihoeigasha, science fiction, 26 episodes, 4/1/1974 —4/4/1975.

0205 SERIES

DAME OYAJI (*Good Morning Dad*), Knack, humor, 26 episodes, 4/2 —10/9/1974.

0206 SERIES

CHIISANA VIKING VICKE (*Vicke, the Little Viking*), Zuiyo, adventure, 78 episodes, 4/3/1974 — 9/24/1975. [*Wickie Le Viking*].

In an antique Northern village lives Vicke, a young viking, son of the village chief. He often finds himself traveling and confronting difficult situations together with his father and the rest of the ship's crew. Gifted with great intelligence and quick wit, the little viking succeeds in saving his companions from difficult situations and hidden traps along the way.

0207 SERIES

GETTER ROBOT (*id.*), Toei Doga, robot, 51 episodes, 4/4/1974 —5/8/1975.

The series, one of many directed by Tomoaru Katsumata and featuring the participation of Kazuo Komatsubara as character designer, is set in the universe of Mazinger and the famous *UFO Robot Grendizer*. Ryo, Hayato and Musashi, at the wheels of the Getter Robot, face the advanced descendants of Earth's dinosaurs. At the end of the series, the monstrous creatures succeed in attaining the upper hand, partially destroying the robot and causing the death of the young Musashi. When all seems lost, the Oni, a race of Orcs that lived before the dinosaurs, take over. They destroy the semi-mechanical reptiles, giving the ground forces some time to recuperate and build Getter Robot G, whose adventures are presented in the series bearing the same name, also by Go Nagai, in 1975. The series was created by Shozo Uchara.

Chiisana Viking Vicke © Zuiyô.

0208 SERIES

SHIN MINASHIGO HUTCH (*Hutch the Orphan — New Series*), Tatsunoko, animal, 26 episodes, 4/5 — 9/27/1974. [*Hutchi*].

Shin Minashigo Hutch © Tatsunoko Pro.

Once he has found his beloved mother, the queen bee, Hutch leaves with his little sister Maya on new adventures in the forest. Life in the hive is too boring for a world traveler such as he, and the fascinating "insect planet" is still full of surprises. The series was lucky enough to have Tatsuo Yoshida for the subject, Seitaru Hara for the general supervision and Yoshitaka Amano for the designs.

0209 SERIES

TONARI NO TAMAGETAKUN (*Tamageta, the Little Neighbor*), Studio Zero for Tohoku Shinsha, humor, 300 episodes, 4/5/1974 — 6/27/1975.

The unpredictable Shotaro Ishimori realizes this new comedy series that features the little Tamageta, a friendly space boy.

0210 SERIES

HOSHI NO KO CHOBIN (*Chobin the Boy From the Stars*), Studio Zero, adventure, 26 episodes, 4/5 — 9/27/1974.

Chobin is a beautiful little alien with two enormous feet, which he uses to jump to incredible heights. He crashes his spaceship on Earth in the middle of the forest, and an old man and his granddaughter offer to help him. Chobin has been followed to our planet by the evil Brunga, who doesn't hesitate to send hired killers against him. Chobin dreams about destroying his very fierce enemy and saving his mother, who is being held prisoner on their homeworld. The task is difficult, but thanks to the animal friends from the forest, his dream comes true and Chobin is reunited with his beautiful mother, revealing that his shape is only temporary and that soon he will go through a wonderful transformation. The story, later turned into a comic by Shotaro Tshimori, was directed, amongst others by Taro Rin, with the drawing supervision by Mitsuo Yazawa.

0211 SERIES

GAN TO GON (*Gan and Gon*), Nihon Doga for Jihoeigasha, humor, 67 episodes, 5/5/1974 — 8/13/1975.

0212 SERIES

GREAT MAZINGER (*id.*), Toei Doga, robot, 56 episodes, 9/8/1974 — 9/28/1975.

Tetsuya Tsurugi is a young man who was raised to be a great warrior by the strict professor Kenzo Kabuto, the father of Koji, pilot of Mazinger Z. Aboard the great Mazinger, an elaboration of the old prototype, the main character combats an ancient underground race, the unholy union of an organic nervous system and a mechanical body. Female robots are also present in this series, with Venus Alpha piloted with little luck by Jun Hono and the clumsy and awkward Boss Borot, who help Tetsuya in his battles. Koji, who moved to America with Sayaka to study, comes back at the end of the series to pilot Mazinger A once again and help his companion out of trouble. Directed by Tohomaru Katsumata, Takeshi Tamiya, Masayuki Akehi, Yasuo Sankichi, Detsuo Imazawa and Nobuo Onuki, the series that was inspired by Go Nagai's manga saw the participation of Susumu Takahisa, Keisuke Fujikawa and Toyohiro Ando as screenplay writers and Keisuke Morishita as character designer.

0213 SERIES

URIKUPEN KYUJOTAI (*Urikupen's Rescue Patrol*), Tatsunoko/Unimax, adventure, 156 episodes, 9/30/1974 — 3/29/1975.

U-RI-KU-PEN is the acronym name given to a team made up of four young animals, Usagi the rabbit, Risu the squirrel, Kuma the bear and Penguin the penguin (they are also helped by a deer, a dog, a wild boar, a rat and lion). Their mission is to save people in danger, strengthened by their great courage.

0214 SERIES

JIM BOTAN (*id.*), Eiken, adventure, 26 episodes, 10/4/1974 —3/28/1975.

0215 SERIES

HURRICANE POLYMER (*id.*), Tatsunoko, super hero, 26 episodes, 10/4/1974 — 3/28/1975.

Urikupen Kyujotai © M.K..

Hurricane Polymer © Tatsunoko Pro.

Takeshi is the son of Tokyo's police chief. Wanting to follow in his father's footsteps but not liking his overly-diplomatic methods, he begins an investigation on a strange group of masked individuals who threaten a well known Japanese scientist. One night, while Takeshi is on guard at the scholar's villa, four lizard-masked men attack him. Takeshi, a karate expert, puts them to flight, but not before one of them has time to injure the old scholar. On death's bed, the professor reveals his secret project to the young man. The Polymer is a fantastic helmet which appears to be very normal, but which has a sophisticated mechanism concealed inside. Whoever wears it sees himself covered with armor made of an impenetrable substance that can, at the sound of Takeshi's voice, change into an airplane, a drill, a tank, a submarine or other powerful machine, giving Takeshi the ability to face his enemies on any field. The young man put the machine to good use, and succeeds in saving his two friends, with whom he works in an investigation firm. Thanks to the countless tricks built into the Polymer, Takeshi is also able to spy on the police investigations. Naturally, as the best tradition in anime would have it, Takeshi is forced to reveal his double identity in the last episode when, captured by some criminals along with his father and companions, he is forced to do one of his wonderful transformations to save their lives. Already at the peak of his career, Tatsuo Yoshida was involved as an author as well as character designer. Together with him were Nagayuki Totyumi as director and Shunsuke Kikuchi for the soundtrack.

0216 SERIES

HAJIME NINGEN GIATRUS (*Giatrus, the Dawning of Mankind*), Tokyo Movie, humor, 77 episodes, 10/5/1974 — 3/27/1976.

This humorous animated series features the adventures of a handful of cave men facing everyday life that, on par with Hanna & Barbera's *Flintstones*, are similar to the situations we live today. Giatrus, the main character of the story, lives with his wife and son Gon in a welcoming cavern in an era characterized by the first rudimentary inventions and discoveries.

0217 SERIES

UCHU SENKAN YAMATO (*Yamato, the Space Cruiser*), Academy Seisaki, science fiction, 26 episodes, 10/6/1974 — 3/30/1975. *Starblazers: The Quest For Iscandar.*

In the year 2199, the Earth is threatened by attacks from the army of the planet Gamilas, and the radioactivity provoked by the nuclear devices that will soon render the planet inhabitable. The spaceship Yamato, a reconstruction of the very famous Japanese battleship from the Second World War, is launched to find Queen Starsha of Iskandar and with her the DNA cosmos, the only mechanism capable of rendering Earth's soil fertile again. The courageous crew has only one year to accomplish the dangerous mission and the voyage reveals itself to be even more dangerous than expected because of the constant attacks by Deslar, an enemy general. After the death of captain Juzo Okita, the commandant of the spaceship goes to the officer Susumu Kodai who, thanks to the help of his companion, completes the mission and restores peace to his native planet.

0218 SERIES

TENTOMUSHI NO UTA (*The Ladybug's Song*), Tatsunoko, soap opera, 104 episodes, 10/6/1974 — 9/26/1976.

Noboru Kawasaki tells of the adventures of seven orphan brothers who live in humble conditions, even though their grandfather is very rich. The main characters, in fact, refuse to ask their generous relative for anything even though the latter keeps offering to support them financially. They work to pay for their expenses, which are always many with such a big family.

0219 SERIES

CALIMERO (*id.*), Toei Doga, animal, 47 episodes, 10/15/1974 —9/30/1975. [*Calimero*].

The friendly black chick created by Nino and Toni Pagot, once the main character of the television carousel of the Mira Lanza, was newly produced in animation by the famous Japanese production firm. The main character, a favorite of many generations of fans, continues to wallow in self-pity and get into trouble, victim of his animal friends' practical jokes.

Star Blazers was previously a registered trademark of Westchester Films, Inc. and distributed by Kidmark. Now it is distributed in the U.S.A. by Voyager Entertainment, Inc. *Star Blazers®* is a registred trademark of Jupiter Films, Inc.

Calimero © Pagot.

CHAPTER FOURTEEN: 1975

1975 was a very important year, as we witnessed the birth of a new style of television series that lasts evento this day. It's possible to define this style as science fiction, but a science fiction marked with elements of insane comedy. *Time Bokan* is one of the better examples of this new style. Sprung from the prolific mind of Tatsuo Yoshida, this cartoon is the first chapter of a long saga, that of the "Time Machine," the first of nine series very much appreciated by the Japanese as well as the Italian public. In these series, the main characters are the "enemies," a trio formed by a disturbing blonde and her two clumsy collaborators, one thin and one dumpy. Although some somatic outlines and names change as the series progresses, the three bad characters are always the same, and the clumsy mechanical means used in their incursions start off with the most different objects. Clearly born to parody the robot series, as they go along, the "Time Machines" come into their own, becoming a genre at the same time as it became a conscious parody of itself.

The year 1975 brought forth two new and important works from Go Nagai: *UFO robot Grendizer* and *Kotetsu Jeeg*, both from the 'robot' genre, that have contributed in giving life, even in Italy, to a phenomenon that didn't go unnoticed. It is necessary to set aside room for a discussion of *UFO robot Grendizer*, as it marked the advent of the robot genre. Immediately welcomed with enthusiasm by a vast public capable of appreciating the style and novelty of the series (up to then — it is important to recall — most aired television cartoons were from the studios of Warner Bros. and Hanna Barbera), *Goldrake* (as it was called in Italy), while it achieved the high ratings of *RAI skyrocket*, it also started violent controversies over the violence present in certain of its scenes.

Where *Kotetsu Jeeg's* television series is concerned, it is important to note an interesting change in the placing of the pilot, who no longer sits in a flight deck to fly the giant robot with a control panel. In fact, the main character, Hiroshi Shiba, thanks to a choreographed transformation, joins the mechanical body of the robot and becomes its head. This symbiosis between man and machine was later proposed again in other 'robot' series, and constitutes a pleasant alternative to the now overused 'pilots in space uniforms.'

In this particular time in Japanese animation, series based on action and technology were not the only ones broadcast. A large number of productions were of a children's genre that found its own place in the 70s: animated stories taken from the classics of Western literature.

Certain series in this trend are definitely part of the fantasy genre, with anthropormorphized animals as the main characters, facing daily problems and everyday difficulties. Others were, instead, made solely for educational purposes. *Mitsubachi Maya no boken*, a series also transmitted in Italy, is a prime example of this latter style, presenting moments in the lives of insects and also touching on fundamental subjects like birth, the struggle to survive and death.

The Western influence was relatively obviously present, and major parts of the series produced in 1975 are linked to European tradition and folklore. The most representative of this genre might be *Flanders no inu*, which arrived in Italy in 1984. It boasts one of the most dramatic and touching finales in Japanese animation. *La Seine no hoshi* is based on the French Revolution as seen through the eyes of the peasants, while *Sogen no shojo Laura* brings us back to the first moments of the American colonization. This last series was inspired by the television movie broadcast many times, even in Italy, entitled *Little House on the Prairie*, originally a book by Laura Ingalls Wilder.

LE MYSTÉRIEUX
VOLEUR
DE FROMAGE

Mitsubachi Maya No Boken © Nippon Animation.

La Petite Sirène was exclusively distributed in French Canada by Prima Film.

0220 FILM

ANDERSEN DOWA — NING YO HOME (*Andersen's Fairy Tale: The Little Mermaid*), Toei Doga, fairy tale, 68 min., 3/21. *The Little Mermaid [La Petite Sirène].*

As was stated many times, the Japanese people are great admirers of Hans Christian Andersen, the Danish writer born in 1805. The success of this film is a confirmation of the popularity of the European fairy tale writer in the Japanese archipelago.

0221 FILM

GREAT MAZINGER TAI GETTER ROBOT (*The Great Mazinger Against Getter Robot*), Toei Doga, robot, 30 min., 3/21.

Sometimes the pilots of the powerful giant robots get carried away with their emotions. A silly rivalry of supremacy and strength threatens the destruction of the Great Mazinger and the Getter Robot at the hands of a cruel monster twice as big as them. The defenders of the Earth save themselves, destroying the enemy, only after understanding the importance of team work and mutual respect.

0222 FILM
GREAT MAZINGER TAI GETTER ROBOT G — KUCHU DAIGE KITOTSU (*The Great Mazinger Against Getter Robot G, the Great Space Encounter*), Toei Doga, robot, 24 min., 7/26.

Bigdron, the light monster, appears in the Japanese sky. The Great Mazinger, the Getter Robot and Venus Alpha run to the help of the endangered population. After a long combat the ground patrol gains the upper hand, but in the course of the battle the young Musashi, pilot of the Jetter Bear, dies, leaving an unfillable void in the hearts of his companions.

0223 FILM
UCHU ENBAN DAISENSO (*The Great Battle of the Flying Saucer*), Toei Doga, robot, 25 min., 7/26.

This is the pilot film that will be followed in October of this year by the very famous robot series *UFO Robot Grendizer* by Go Nagai. Other than the characterization of the main characters and the designs of the weapons used during the conflict, the screenplay is similar to that of the know and loved series.

0224 SERIES
FLANDERS NO INU (*The Dog of the Flanders*), Zuyo/Nippon Animation, classic, 52 episodes, 1/5 — 12/28/1975. [*Le Chien Des Flandres*].

The dramatic series features Nello as main character, an affectionate child and his faithful dog Patrash. It presents the tender friendship that binds them in so many adventures up to their death in a small village of the Flanders. Hayao Miyazaki collaborates to the animation.

0225 SERIES
MONOSHIRI KAN (*The School of Knowledge*), Office Uni, educational, 1560 episodes, 1/1/1975 — 12/31/1979.

0226 SERIES
MANGA NITTON MUKASHI BANASHI (*Ancient Japanese Stories*), Group Tack/AiKikaku Center, fairy tale, 12 episodes, 1/7 — 3/25/1975.

0227 SERIES
MITSUBACHI MAYA NO BOKEN (*The Adventures of Maya the Bee*), Nippon Animation, animal, 52 episodes, 4/1/1975 — 4/20/1976. [*Maya L'Abeille*].

A young and clumsy little bee is the main character of this adventure. Not having to look for her mother this time, nor having to carry out any particular mission, Maya spends her time with her friend Willy as they explore the world around them. During their flights, they do their best to help the weaker insects in danger going as far as to visit the world of humans. The stories, cheerful or sad, follow one another at a rollicking pace that contributes to this series' success, even in Italy. The story, inspired by the tales of Waldemar, is the third Japanese/German production with the publishing firm BasteiVerlag. The other two are *Vicky the Viking* and *Heidi*.

The Dog Of Flanders ©The Dog Of Flanders Production. Pioneer Family Entertainment has recently released this new movie version of the story (Cat.# PINA-0001S)

Mitsubachi Maya No Boken © Nippon Animation.

0228 SERIES

YUSHA RYDEEN (*The Courageous Rydeen*), Soeisha for Tohoku Shinsa, robot, 50 episodes, 4/4/1975 — 3/26/1976.

Akira Hibiki pilots Rydeen the robot, inherited from his ancestors, the inhabitants of the ancient Mo empire. His love for his mother, Queen Lemuria, brings the young man to combat the emperor of Yoma, the fierce enemy of his people. The preliminary sketches for the series were done by Yasuhiku Yoshikaza, now a skillful character designer, who enriches the story with characters whose natural expressions are more suggested than anything by the extremely soft art and the intense dynamics of the forms.

0229 SERIES

LA SEINE NO HOSHI (*The Star of the Seine*), Unimax, adventure, 39 episodes, 4/4 — 12/26/1975.

La Seine No Hoshi © Fuji TV / M.K.

Simone, the natural daughter of the king of Austria and an opera singer, is entrusted to a Parisian florist to be raised far from the royal court. The girl, unaware of her heritage, leads a life like that of any other poor young French girl at the end of the 1700s. The story gets more complicated when the count De Voudrel, friend of the king, recognizes her and adopts her, training her in the use of the sword in order to make her into a partner for his son Robert, who secretly helps the needy under the identity of the Black Tulip. Thus is born the Star of the Seine, heroine of the Revolution, who later joins the ranks of her stepsister Marie Antoinette, after the peasants' rebellion against the noble class. At the end of the Revolution, she and Robert save the queen's children to build a real family. The story by Mitsuru Kaneko was supervised by Masaki Osumi and directed by Yoshiyuki Tomino. The music is by Shunsuke Kikuchi. The production is by Koji Bessho and Ryosuke Nakamura.

0230 SERIES

DON CHUCK MONOGATARI (*Don Chuck's Story*), Knack, animal, 26 episodes, 4/5 — 9/27/1975. [*Le Petit Castor*].

Chuck is a young beaver who lives in the forest with his family. Together with his friends and adventure companions, he finds himself caught up in situations too big for him to get out of by himself. His wise father often has to intervene, offering precious advice. The friendly beaver has since become the mascot of Korakuen, Tokyo's main amusement park. The screenplay is by Osamu Sekita and the preliminary sketches are by Eiji Tanaka.

Don Chuck Monogatari © Knack.

0231 SERIES

GANBA NO BOKEN (*Ganba's adventures*), Tokyo Movie, animal 26 episodes, 4/7 — 9/29/1975.

The main character of the series is a little mouse who fights injustices present in his world.

0232 SERIES

SHONEN TOKUGAWA IEYASU (*The Young Ieyasu Tokugawa*), Toei Doga, historical, 20 episodes, 4/9 — 9/17/1975.

After the Onin rebellion of 1467, Japan entered into a civil war that characterized the premodern era. The three big "daimyo" (feudal lords) Nobunaga Oda, Hideyoshi Toyotomi and Teyasu Tokugawa, succeeded in taking control over the other land owners and thus unified Japan, beginning two different historical moments: the Momoyama period that began in 1573 with the end of the shogun Ashikaga and the unification operated by Oda, and the Edo period that began in 1615 with the fall of the Toyotomi family and the rise to power of the Tokugawa family. The series is an historical commentary on the lives of the famous "daimyo."

0233 SERIES

GETTER ROBOT G (*id.*), Toei Doga, robot, 39 episodes, 5/15/1975 —3/25/1976. *Starvengers*.

After the death of Musashi, third pilot of the Getter Robot, Benkei is trained to replace him. He is a new fighter, assigned to help Ryo and Hayato in their fight to defend the Earth. So, at the controls of the new Getter Robot prototype, they succeed in finally eradicating the threat of the Orcs who, after having destroyed the dinosaurs in the previous conflict, constituted an even worse danger for our planet. The subject, taken from Go Nagai's manga, features the collaboration of four experienced authors: Susumu Takahisa, Shozo Uchara, Yasuo Tamurata and Michiru Torijima. The direction was entrusted to a numerous staff amongst which were Yasuo Yamaguchi, Masamune Ochiai, Takenori Kawada and Akinari Orai. The character design was by Kazuo Komatsubara.

0234 SERIES

UCHU NO KISHI TEKKAMAN (*Tekkaman, the Space Rider*), Tatsunoko, science fiction, 26 episodes, 7/2 — 12/24/1975. *Tekkaman The Space Knight*.

Joji Minami is Tekkaman, a fearless space rider with a shining armor, the end result of a very sophisticated technology, who faces the emissaries of Valdaster, threatening alien invaders. He is brought aboard the Blue Earth, a powerful spaceship, by Andro Umeda ? an extraterrestrial with the capacity to teleport himself, Mutan ? a clever space animal and Hiromi Amachin ? the daughter of the professor who invented the armor. The series finishes with an unexpected and tragic finale. In fact, to defeat the powerful army of Valdaster, the main character has to sacrifice his own life. The concept for the series is by Ippei Kuri and the screenplay by Hiroshi Sasagawa, while Hideo Nishimaki and Eiko Toriumi produced and Masami Suda designed the characters.

0235 SERIES

ARABIAN NIGHT SINBAD NO BOKEN (*Arabian Nights: The Adventures of Sinbad*), Nippon Animation, adventure, 52 episodes, 10/1/1975 — 9/29/1976.

The story of Sinbad is completely changed in this series, and only the name of the main character, a clever child who lives by his wits, is left of the original story. The new situations that are presented have little to do with the *Thousand and One Nights*, a source already exploited in other Japanese animated productions.

0236 SERIES

IRUKA TO SHONEN (*The Dolphin and the Young Boy*), Eiken, adventure, 26 episodes, 7/30 — 8/15/1975. [*Oum Le Dauphin Blanc*].

More known for his appearance in the commercial for a brand of white chocolate, the intelligent dolphin is the main character of a mediocre series. The story is centered on a group of shipwrecked people on a Godforsaken island.

Starvengers ©1992 Peter Pan Industries / Parade Video. All Rights Reserved. (Cat.# 6612).

Tekkaman The Space Knight ©1985 The Congress Video Group. All Rights Reserved. (Cat.# 20020)

Wanpaku Omukashi: Kum Kum © ITC Japan.

Time Bokan © Tatsunoko Pro.

0237 SERIES

WANPAKU OMUKASHI — KUM KUM (*Kum Kum, the Eventful Prehistory*), ITC Japan, children, 26 episodes, 10/3/1975 — 3/26/1976. [*Kum Kum*].

Kum Kum also lives in the prehistoric era, but contrary to the above mentioned Giatrus, he is only a child, closely bonded with ChiruChiru, who is the same age. Together with other children from the village where they live, the characters play and have fun enjoying their carefree childhood in a series entertaining even in its simplicity. The study of characters was done by Yas, pen name of the famous Yasuhiko Yoshikazu.

0238 SERIES

TIME BOKAN (*id.*), Tatsunoko, robot/humor, 65 episodes, 10/4/1975 — 12/25/1976.

This is the first chapter of the saga linked to the time travels that, thanks to the insane humor of the scripts, gained more an more fans in the years to come. Junko and Tamnpei have to find a young girl's grandfather, inventor of the famous time machine who, having left in search of new discoveries through the centuries, has gotten lost in an undetermined historical period. The search for the doctor also interests a strange trio made up of a provocative young woman named Madam Margot and two foolish orderlies Birba and Sgrinfia, whose intention is to find out where the famous "dinamanti" are hidden, treasures which give those who possess them inestimable wealth. Curiously, the trio appears in every series with different features and changed names but nonetheless always recognizable. The ending, as always in this type of series, is very ordinary, as the professor, having found his way back to our days, finds himself barely two steps away from the characters.

0239 SERIES

KOTETSU JEEG (*Iron Jeeg*), Toei Doga, robot, 46 episodes, 10/5/1975 — 8/29/1976.

During some archeological digs, Professor Shiba discovers a little bronze bell belonging to a disappeared civilization. But the professor's life changes when he begins receiving mysterious threats that begin to come true: the ancient Haniwa civilization has come back to life and want to recover the precious find. To prevent that from happening, the professor hides the bell in his son Hiroshi's chest just before he dies at the hands of the hired killers of the evil queen Himika. The young man becomes invincible and, thanks to his father's notes, he transforms himself into the head of a powerful robot to which the rest of the body joins itself, each piece thrown from the space jet by his companion Niwa. The long war once again results in good winning over evil and the enemy civilization destroyed once and for all. Go Nagai obtains yet another success with this series, for the manga (Tatsuya Yoshida contributed to its designs) as well as for the anime adaptation, with a screenplay by Hiroyasu Yamaura, Keisuke Fujikawa and Toyohiro Ando. The series was directed by Yoshio Nitta, Kazuja Miyazaki, Masayuki Akehi, Yugo Serikawa and Masamune Ochiai. The new character designs were by Kazuo Nakamura.

0240 SERIES

UFO ROBOT GRENDIZER (*id.*), Toei Doga, robot, 74 episodes, 10/5/1975 — 2/27/2977. *Force Five: Grandizer* [*Goldorak*].

The system of planets around the far star Fleed is at war. The soldiers of the evil king Vega, driven by their need to survive, attack the unprotected population to submit them to the king's will. The star Vega is dying, and for the thousands of inhabitants, the only hope is to immigrate to another planet. The militaristic society refuses to ask for help, and decides to conquer its new homeland with the use of force. The star system of Fleed is annihilated by the enemy forces, and the only survivor of the massacre is the prince Duke who, aboard the Grendizer, comes to Earth. Adopted by Professor Umon, who is aware of his past, he becomes part of Earth's society, taking the name of Daisuke. The alien threat continues and, the conquered planet now inhabitable, King Vega decides to turn his attention towards our planet. Daisuke prepares himself to defend the earthlings from the serious threat with the help of his companions — Koji Kabuto, pilot of the double spacer, Hikaru Makiba aboard the marine spacer and his sister Maria Grace Fleed, who was thought dead, piloting the Drill Spacer. The battle is harsh but final victory awaits our heroes. Once the war is over, Duke and Maria go back to their native planet that is now rebuilt, to help it flourish. The original story is by Go Nagai and was transposed into animation by Toshio Ketsuta, the designs are by Kazuo Komatsubara and from the 49th episode on, by Shingo Araki. The soundtrack is by Shunsuke Kikuchi while the screenplay is by Shozo Uechera and Keisuke Fujikawa. The direction is by Tomoharu Katsumata, Masamune Ochiai and Masayuki Akemi amongst others.

Grandizer ©1992 Peter Pan Industries / Parade Video. All Rights Reserved. (Cat.# 6613)

0241 SERIES

ANDES SHONEN PEPERO NO BOKEN (*The Adventures of Pepero, the Boy From the Andes*), Wako, adventure, 26 episodes, 10/6/1975 — 3/29/1976.

The young Pepero faces a thousand adventures searching for the mythical Eldorado, legendary city of gold situated in South America where, years before, his father had vanished. Along the way, certain characters join the young character who, having finally found his father, discover the mysterious beauties of the golden city.

0242 SERIES

GANSO — TENSAI BAKABON (*Bakabon the Genius: the Origins*), Tokyo Movie, humor, 103 episodes, 10/6/1975 — 9/26/1977.

Fujio Akatsura still publishes this entertaining comic, in the children's magazine "Comic Bom Bom" edited by the Kodansha. The main characters are once again members of a strange Japanese family, but the episodes mainly concern the clever head of the household.

0243 SERIES

SOGEN NO SHOJO LAURA (*Laura, the Girl of the Prairie*), Nippon Animation, classic, 26 episodes, 10/7/1975 — 3/30/1976.

An animated adaptation of the very famous American television and book series *Little House on the Prairie*, written by Laura Ingalls Wilder. The main character is Laura, a little girl who lives in a wide valley with her family, some of the first American settlers.

0244 SERIES

IKKYUSAN (*id.*), Toei Doga, historical, 298 episodes, 10/15/1975 – 6/28/1982. [*Ikkyû-san*].

Ikkyu is a young boy who is studying to become a buddhist monk. To succeed, he needs a lot of patience and a great willpower. The young boy learns at his own expense the difficulties and sacrifices he must face. Also gifted with a unique cleverness, he resolves

Ikkyusan © TV Asahi / Toei Doga.

complex situations, always adding a touch of humor to the story. Masaki Tsuji and Hiroyasu Yamaura distinguish themselves for the screenplay, Hiroshi Wagatsuma did the preliminary sketches and Kimio Yabuchi took care of the general direction.

CHAPTER FIFTEEN: 1976

The year 1976 heralded the arrival of the great majority of shows and movies dedicated to giant robots. After the success of the genre in previous years, many authors and illustrators were eager to lend their names to the new productions.

Even the Nippon Animation Studio, which had always dedicated itself to sentimental stories and the classics of children's literature, produced *Blocker Gundam IV Machine Blaster*. The series, also seen in Italy, earned some success despite its predictable plot. The protagonists are well characterized, especially Tenpei whose dual Moguru-human heritage leads him to switch allegiances in the name of fairness.

The Tatsunoko, purveyors of many great robot dramas, presented *Go Wapper 5 Goddam*, with the studio's usual blend of classic animation and a touch of humor.

The Toei Doga, reveling in the success of *Mazinger Z* in 1972 and *UFO robot Grendizer* in 1975, proposed three new series: *Daiku maryu Gaiking* that, notwithstanding the solid story, did not appeal to the viewing public, forcing the production firm to cancel the show at the 26th episode; *Magne Robot Gakin*, which didn't enjoy much public favor even in Italy, a vain attempt to remake the basic plotline of *Kotetsu Jeeg*, a series from 1975 which centered on a modular robot held together through electromagnetism. The pilots of the various parts transformed their vehicles into the robot through a process called "sweet cross." The third series from the Toei Co., a coproduction with the studio that eventually became Nippon Sunrise, was *Chodenji robot Combattler V*, the story of a robot that appeared to be a human being, but which broke down into five separate units in order to fight on all types of terrain.

The Tsuburaya, a devoted science-fiction studio, produced one of the first attempts at integrating live action with animation. The result was the series *Kyoryu tankentai Born Free*, in which the animated characters interact with real-world scenery. The monsters and the technological mechanisms are, in reality, small scale models filmed with the cinematography technique known as "step one." The poor results of the experimental technique, notwithstanding the innovative aspect, condemned the series to an ignoble death

Up to the mid-70s the series that were produced for the female public were mostly adaptations of childhood novels or stories of teenagers gifted with magical powers. The series Candy Candy ushered in a new style of animation aimed at girls. It was the beginning of the 'shojo' genre, the soap opera story that features entangled loves, unfaithfulness and intense melodrama, usually focused on small family groups. The stories present, for the most part, a never-ending succession of awful situations that the main character must face, which are resolved with the usual happy ending.

The other productions of this year cannot be easily linked to a particular trend, but one series is remembered for its level of collaboration with an American animation firm. *Little*

Magne Robot Ga-Kin © TV Asahi / Japad / Toei Doga.

Magne Robot Ga-Kin © TV Asahi / Japad / Toei Doga.

Daiku Maryu Gaiking © Fuji TV / Toei Doga.

Lulu was produced by Japanese Nippon Animation for the American ABC, and retold the adventures of the friendly little girl, the charming main character of the famous comic strip created by Marge (Marjorie Anderson Buell) in 1935.

0245 FILM

NAGAGUTSU OHAITA NEKO 80 NICHIKAN SEKAI ISSHU (*The Cat With the Boots: Around the World in 80 Days*), Toei Doga, animal/adventure, 68 min., 3/20.

The third act of the saga of the cat with the boots by Perrault features the feline character in Europe at the beginning of *Around the World in 80 Days*. Naturally the feature film was inspired by the children's literature classic, written by Jules Verne, but the cinematography transposition became, as usual, a completely new version of the original text.

0246 FILM

UFO ROBOT GRENDIZER TAI GREAT MAZINGER (*UFO Robot Grendizer Against the Great Mazinger*), Toei Doga, robot, 27 min., 3/20. [*Goldorak Contre Great Mazinger*].

General Barendos, the first officer of the order of King Vega, kidnaps Koji Kabuto and forces him to reveal the intricacies of the Mazinger, now a historical relic kept at the Museum of Peace. Having seized the earthly robot, the aliens sow death and destruction but they are soon stopped by Duke Fleed at the command of the powerful Grendizer, who reunites the Mazinger with Koji. The two destroy the monster enemy Gubi Gubi and return peace to the Earth.

0247 FILM

GRENDIZER, GETTER ROBOT G, GREAT MAZINGER — KESSEN DAIKAIJU (*Grendizer, Getter Robot G and the Great Mazinger: the Decisive Battle of the Great Monster of the Sea*), Toei Doga, robot, 31 min., 7/18.

This time Nagai's robots face a terrible dragosaurus that appears on the planet. The Great Mazinger, Boss Robot, Venus, Alpha, Grendizer and Getter Robot G's team draw their most powerful weapons to destroy him.

0248 SERIES

HUCKLEBERRY NO BOKEN (*The Adventures of Huckleberry*), Group Tack, classic, 26 episodes, 1/2 — 6/25/1976.

The adventures of young Huck are the source for this series, which has a fresh and young outlook. The main character travels on a raft on the long Mississipi River together with his best friend, a black fugitive named Jim, to help the ex-slave find freedom. The South as described by Mark Twain, pen name of American writer Samuel Clemens, is carefully presented, managing to keep the tone of criticism of the times found in the original text. The general direction was in the care of Mitsunobu Hiroyoshi.

0249 SERIES

MANGA NIHON MUKASHI BANASHI (*Ancient Japanese Tales*), Group Tack, fairy tale, 1/3/1976 — today [was still running when this book was first published in 1991].

This series presents a number of short adaptations of traditional Japanese folktales. Some of the segments include the story of Momotaro, the adventures of the giant

Haha O Tazunete Sanzeri © Nippon Animation.

Gaiking ©1992 Peter Pan Industries / Parade Video. All Rights Reserved. (Cat.# 6614)

samurai, the legend of the long-nosed elves and the oriental ghosts, in episodes of about ten minutes each.

0250 SERIES

HAHA O TAZUNETE SANZERI (*12 000 km in Search of His Mother*), Nippon Animation, classic, 52 episodes, 1/4 — 12/26/1976. [*Marco*].

The theme of the quest to find a missing parent is repeated again, this time offered up by an adaptation of *Cuore*, the famous novel by Edmondo de Amicis. The story features the adventures of little Marco, desperately trying to reach the Andes to join his mother, who immigrated there to work. The series was marked by Hayao Miyazaki for the layout and the original designs of the setting.

0251 SERIES

DAIKU MARYU GAIKING (*Gaiking, the Flying Giant Dragon*), Toei Doga, robot, 44 episodes, 4/1/1976 — 1/27/1977. *Gaiking.*

Sanshiro Tsuwabuki, a young baseball player with a deadly throw, is recruited to pilot a gigantic robot, the Gaiking. Before transforming into the powerful robot, it presents itself as the head of an enormous space dragon that carries a real crew, made up of a variety of characters. The enemies are the once peaceful people of Zela who, because of a natural catastrophe, have been forced to find refuge underground, totally entrusting their lives to machines. As time went by, their society has militarized itself. A war begins between these two factions, and while the ending is predictable it still remains a mystery, as the series was abruptly cancelled partway through. It was directed by Tomoyoshi Katsumada, and the characterization was by Akio Sugino. The original storyline was by Go Nagai and Dynamic Productions, although they don't appear in the credits. For this reason Nagai denounced the company and ceased all collaboration with Toei Doga.

0252 SERIES

MACHINE HAYABUSA (*id.*), Toei Doga, sport, 21 episodes, 4/2 —9/17/1976.

The series, one of many directed by Yugo Serikawa, presents the adventures of Ken Hayabusa, a talented Formula 1 driver, who with his custom car, the Hayabusa Special, blasts across the finish line and into first place an uncountable number of times. His team is made up of other talented pilots who assist him and often sacrifice themselves to help him win the race. The enemy, always present even in sports series, is the terrible Mao Eihabu, whose intentions are to defeat his young rival at all costs. Takao Kasai collaborates on the production for the character design.

0253 SERIES

SHIN DON CHUCK MONOGATARI (*Don Chuck's Story — New Series*), Knack, animal, 73 episodes, 4/7/1976 — 7/30/1977. *Le Petit Castor.*

Given the success earned with a very young public, a second series is produced for Chuck the Beaver that doesn't substantially change the general outline of the previous series. The simple yet important lessons offered by the story are not engraved in an excess of morals, consequently making the viewing of the series pleasant.

0254 SERIES

GO WAPPER 5 GODAM (*id.*), Tatsunoko, robot, 36 episodes, 4/4 —12/26/1976.

A group of children decide, as proof of their courage, to explore an apparently inaccessible island of Tokyo. They discover a space base is buried deep underground, in which they find Godam, a giant robot. Go, Yoko, Daikichi, Norisuke and Godaemon, the main characters, are welcomed by the hologram of Dr. Hoarai, the scientist who built the powerful robot. The emperor Yokohuda, chief of an underground people, wants to take possession of the surface of the Earth. The five, thanks to the robot and help from the doctor, have to confront the enemy and save the planet. The original story is by Tatsuo Yoshida, the character design by Yoshitaka Amano and the direction by Hisayuki Toriumi.

Go Wapper 5 Godam © Tatsunoko Pro.

0255 SERIES

UFO SENSHI DIAPOLON (*Diapolon, UFO Warrior*), Eiken, robot, 47 episodes, 4/4/1976 — 2/10/1977.

Takeshi is a little orphan who forms a rugby team with his school friends. One day, at the end of a game, while the main character is alone on the field, the clouds open and a luminous horse rider appears on a winged horse, pointing his sword at Takeshi's chest. The young boy falls unconscious. At his awakening, a symbol in the shape of a sun appears over his heart, where he was touched. He soon discovers that he is the son of the king of the planet Apolon, brought to Earth to escape death. A terrible war broke out on his planet because of the "heart of energy" discovered by the king, an artifact capable of releasing a great quantity of energy. Before dying, the king hid the key in his son's chest. Thanks to this, the young boy, with his earthly friends, is destined to pilot Diapolon, the powerful robot made up of three different automatons: Edda, Trangu and Legga. After countless confrontations, Takeshi succeeds in freeing his planet from the usurpers and his mother the queen from prison. The story is the work of Tetsu Kariya and Shigeru Tsuchiyama. Directed by Tatsuo Ono, this series' screenplay is by Ohikara Matsumoto, Noboru Shiroyama, Soji Yoshikawa and Seiji Matsuoka. At the drawing board were Takashi Kakuta, Konio Okoto, Isao Kanero, Toshio Kobayashi and Tetsuo Shibuma.

UFO Senshi Diapolon © Kariya Tetsu • Eiken.

0256 SERIES

CHODENJI ROBOT COMBATTLER V (*Combattler V, the Super ElectroMagnetic Robot*), soeisha for Toei Co., robot, 46 episodes, 4/17/1976 — 5/28/1977.

Aoi Hyoma, Naniwa Juzo, Nishikawa Daiseku and little Kita Kosuke are four young earthlings with extraordinary physical and mental abilities who are kidnapped by professor Nanbora to be trained to pilot Combattler V, the electromagnetic robot. Chizuru, the professor's daughter, joins the four young warriors who, after having been initially opposed to the dangerous project, together face the attacks from the armies from the star Cambel. The enemy, General Garuda, initially fights against the Earthly group, but later, motivated by love, he will help the Combattler team to win, finally sacrificing his life.

0257 SERIES

PICCOLINO NO BOKEN (*The Adventures of Piccolino*), Nippon Animation, fairy tale, 52 episodes, 4/27/1976 — 5/16/1977. [*Pinocchio*].

Chodenki Robot Combattler V © Toei.

Piccolino No Boken © Nippon Animation Co., Ltd.

From the very famous children's book *The Adventures of Pinocchio*, written in 1883 by Carlo Lorenzini, better known as Collodi, comes a children's series that moves away from the screenplay by the Italian author. The modifications are evident even in the title, renaming the main character 'Piccolino.'

0258 SERIES

GROIZER X (*id.*), Knack, robot, 36 episodes, 7/1/1976 — 3/31/1977.

The inhabitants of the star Gailer have decided to subdue the people of our planet. To prevent this, the earthly allied forces build a new fighting robot prototype, Groizer X. The main characters of the series written by Go Nagai and Gosaku Ota and directed by Hiroshi Taisenji are Jo and Rita, who fight to defeat the enemy once and for all and to establish the long-awaited peace. The character design is by Norio Suzuki while the animation is entrusted to Shizuko Katsumi.

0259 SERIES

BLOCKER GUNDAM IV MACHINE BLASTER (*The Fourth Battalion Blocker Machine Blaster*), Ashi for Nippon Animation, robot, 38 episodes, 7/5/1976 — 3/28/1977.

This time, the Earth is subject to attacks from the Moguru people. To hinder the terrible threat, Dr. Yuri has a few young people kidnapped: Teppei, Billy, Jinta and Gansuke are all gifted with the Y power and capable, because of this gift, to activate the complex mechanisms of three robots. Yoshida, the doctor's assistant, also gifted with the same power, leads the Blocker team against the evil enemy at the commands of a fourth powerful robot. This is the first show by Ashi Production, founded by Toshihiko Sato after he left Tatsunoko. Sato is also the creator of the series.

0260 SERIES

MANGA FURUSATO MUKASHI BANASHI (*Past Stories of Comic Strips Native Countries*), Dax/Minwasha, fairy tale, 26 episodes, 8/6 —12/24/1976.

0261 SERIES

MAGNE ROBOT GAKIN (*Gakin, Magnetic Robot*), Toei Doga, robot, 39 episodes, 9/5/1976 — 6/26/1977. *Magnos*.

Kazuo Komatsubara, a new collaborator with the Teoi, is the character designer for this new series directed by Tomoyoshi Katsumada. Takeru, a young karate expert, is chosen along with Mai to pilot the magnetic robot Gakin. Gifted with particular powers, the two characters join in one unique being, thanks to a particular position called "sweet cross." They transform themselves into the belt of the powerful robot, to which other elements unite to form a perfect warrior robot. Their enemies are the synthetic monsters sent to Earth by the evil inhabitants of the star Izar, whose intentions are, as usual, to conquer our planet. The story is by Shinobu Urakawa.

0262 SERIES

CANDY CANDY (*id.*), Toei Doga, soap opera, 115 episodes, 10/1/1976 — 2/2/1979. [*Candy*].

On a snowy day, the little Candice is found wrapped in blankets in front of an orphanage run by Miss Pony and sister Maria. Life in the institute is nice, but every child's greatest desire is to find a new family to love them. When Annie, Candy's best friend, is adopted by the Brightons, the only thing she has left is loneliness. Time passes and it seems that it's finally Candy's turn to have a real family. Unfortunately, the young girl's expectations are shattered when she reaches her destination and discovers that she is only the hired companion of a young perfidious daughter of the wealthy Legans. The life of the young girl is not as happy anymore. She must in fact put up with the trials of daily life with the Legan brothers, Iriza and Neal. Alstear and Archibald Cornwell bring a bit of happiness to her life along with their cousin, Anthony Andrew, who immediately falls in love with Candy.

Events lead to Candy being adopted by the austere Andrew family, due to the demands of the three young men, but right on the day of Candy's official presentation, the young Anthony dies, falling from a horse during a fox hunt. Following this, the head of the Andrew family, the antisocial uncle William, decides to send the children to study in England, taking them away from their sad memories. In the college, Candy finds Annie, her long lost friend, and befriends Patty but above all, she meets Terence Grandchester, a rebel and arrogant descendant from a noble English family with whom she falls in love. Iriza and Neal, also in the same college, scheme and eventually manage to have the young man expelled and Candy punished. The girl decides to escape from the college to find Terrence. Some time after, she finds him as an established actor, but with a girlfriend, Susanna Marlowe.

In the meantime, the First World War cuts swathes through the ranks of young Americans who volunteered. Stear is one of the first to die, leaving his fiancee Patty in tears. Time passes and soothes all wounds, the war ends, and a big dinner reunites all the friends near or far on the hill of Pony, a favorite place. Archie and Annie are about to get married and Albert, Candy's dear friend, close to her through every sad episode of her life (and they were countless), reveals himself as the mysterious uncle William. For a long time, there was talk of a second series of the adventures of the unlucky orphan girl. Needless to say it was never considered by the Japanese screenplay writers. Taken from Kyoko Mizuki and Yumido Igarashi's manga, the series was directed, amongst others, by Hiroshi Shidara.

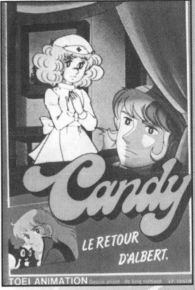

Candy Candy © Mizuki K. / Igarashi Y. / TV Asahi / Toei Doga.

Candy Candy © Mizuki K. / Igarashi Y. / TV Asahi / Toei Doga.

0263 SERIES

KYORYU TANKENTAI BORN FREE (*Born Free, the Group Researches on Dinosaurs*), Sunrise/Tsuburaya, science fiction, 26 episodes, 10/1/1976 — 3/25/1977.

The gigantic dinosaurs from prehistoric times reappear on our planet, generating panic and destruction. A special surveillance group, in order to prevent disasters, manages to bring them to a deserted island on which the enormous animals will live far away from society. The anime was directed by Haruyuki Kawajima, uniting live-action film footage with animated scenes.

0264 SERIES

HOKA HOKA KAZOKU (*The Affectuous Family*), Eiken, humor, 1428 episodes, 10/1/1976 — 3/31/1982.

The five minute episodes that make up the series are rich in humor and feature many in-jokes about common Japanese habits. The main characters are the five members of the Yamano family who, as had happened with Sazaesan, take a poke at the habits of Japanese society.

Intro
-1962
1963
1964
1965
1966
1967
1968
1969
1970
1971
1972
1973
1974
1975
1976
1977
1978
1979
1980
1981
1982
1983
1984
1985
1986
1987
1988
Index

Paul No Miracle Daisakusen © Tatsunoko Pro.

0265 SERIES

PAUL NO MIRACLE DAISAKUSEN (*The Miraculous Battles of Paul*), Tatsunoko, fantasy, 50 episodes, 10/3/1976 — 9/11/1977.

Paul is a young man like so many others, who possesses a magic teddy bear in which lives the spirit of an inhabitant of the enchanted world of Pakkum. Thanks to the magic of the teddy bear, Paul and his friend Nina manage to open a passage to the fantastic place. Their journey in the happy world of fantasy is abruptly interrupted when Belsatan, feeling the presence of human beings, awakens and kidnaps Nina. Paul tries everything to free her from his clutches and bring her back to reality, and he succeeds only after having defeated the evil devil. A series with a brilliant ensemble cast and with good pacing, thanks also to Hiroshi Sasagawa's general supervision and to the character design by Akiko Shimomoto.

0266 SERIES

HANA NO KAKARICHO (*The Rampant Foreman*), Tokyo Movie, comedy, 26 episodes, 10/3/1976 — 3/27/1977.

0267 SERIES

LITTLE LULU TO CHICCHAI NAKAMA (*Little Lulu and her Friends*), Nippon Animation, soap opera, 26 episodes, 10/3/1976 —4/3/1977.

The series uses the elements of the American sitcom to good effect, specifically the rapidity of the dialogue, rich in humor, the pauses and laughtrack, an attentive characterization of the individuals found in Marge's comic strip and the presentation of the ups and downs that characterize any family.

0268 SERIES

DOKABEN (*id.*), Tsuchida for Nippon Animation, sport, 163 episodes, 10/6 — 12/26/1979.

On the trail of *Kyojin no Hoshi*, which opened the door to this type of animation, this series was made which centered on the theme of baseball. The main character is Taro Yamada, a stocky and mild young man with incredible strength who studies in a Japanese school and dreams of becoming a champion. Hiroyoshi Mitsunobu the director and Shinji Mizushima, in charge of the storyline, collaborated on the series giving life to a good production.

0269 SERIES

MANGA SEKAI MUKASHI BANASHI (*Cartoons About the Past*), Dax International, fairy tale, 124 episodes, 10/7/1976 — 3/28/1979.

Every episode of this charming series presents a different fairy tale linked to the oriental or Western traditions. Known and unknown authors were both adapted for the creation of this long-running series directed, naturally, towards a child audience.

0270 SERIES

ROBOKKO VITON (*Viton the Little Robot*), Nippon Sunrise for Tohoku Shinsha, humor, 50 episodes, 10/12/1976 — 9/27/1977.

A third grade student named Ma receives a parcel from America, a gift from his father that contains a peculiar robot. Viton, the little mechanical robot, becomes an inseparable friend for the Japanese child.

CHAPTER SIXTEEN: 1977

1977 was one of the less exciting years in Japanese animation. Lacking any great innovations, this year marked the beginning of many lesser productions that settled for using highly commercial themes to reap success without too much creative effort. Even though this was not always apparent in the quality of the animation itself, where the established studios put their experience and talents to good use, their failure is obvious in the endless repetition of scripts and topics. With the exception of Reiji Matsumoto's *Wakusei robot Danguard Ace*, that earned success with both the film and the television series, the other robot series returned to the usual consolidated standards. The image of the solitary pilot vanished, to be replaced by the standard robot fighting team: groups usually made up of five members, a good-looking one, an introverted antagonist, a young woman, a friendly (often heavy-set) one and a child. The assortment of protagonists didn't always fit this formula, but they always held the bare minimum of the necessary diversity to fulfill the effective requirements of the story.

Wakusei Robot Danguard Ace © Toei Doga.

The melodramatic component was rigorously present in the science fiction series as well as in the soap operas. In this year the trend seemed to take a catastrophic turn, with exterminations and genocide forming the premise of *Gasshin sentai Mekander robot*, in which an alien planet is rendered uninhabitable because of the pollution caused by the evil Edron; *Hyoga senshi Guyslugger*, in which the alien people of Imbem devastate the earthly empire of Solon before the glacier era and *Chogattai majutsu robot Ginguiser*, in which the main characters don't hesitate to send terrible killer monsters to Earth in an attempt to recover the three spheres of the Anderes.

In *Muteki Chojin Zanbot 3*, instead, rather than simply being present in the premise (the surviving members of an alien race are forced to find refuge on Earth after the destruction of their planet) the dramatic elements play a predominant role even in the ending in which viewers witnessed the death of two of the three pilots of the *Zanbot 3*, victims of a suicidal kamikaze. The fate of their families aboard the spaceships was not much better, and the only survivors were the women and the young pilot Kappei.

Where soap operas are concerned, the Japanese tradition of over-the-top storylines for which the cartoons are so criticized, is attentively respected. The merit or demerit of *Wakakusa no Charlotte* is heavily debated, as the show takes great delight in the depiction of tragedy following the disappearance of people dear to the main character. In fact, the story begins with Charlotte orphaned by her mother, to continue with the death of her father and end with the discovery of her mother, still alive. The misunderstandings and the teenage-style dramas that seem to echo those of the more famous *Candy* are present here with the clear intent to manufacture cheap emotion in young women, the major fans of these productions.

Also belonging to the style is *Rittai anime ienaki ko*, that, after the 1970 film *Chibikko Remi to meiken Capi*, tackles Hector Malot's novel *Without Family*. The story of Remi is as dramatic as Charlotte's and, like the previous one, it features the main character involved in the desperate search for his mother. Meanwhile, the list of stories dedicated to time machines continues to grow, with *Time bokan series Yattaman*. The stereotypical charac-

Lupin III: Tales Of The Wolf. Albatross: Wings Of Death ©1977, 1989 Monkey Punch. All Rights Reserved. Packaging ©1993 Streamline Pictures. (Cat.# 90503)

Hakusho No Oji © Toei Doga.

ters are in full force and the enemies are still three: Tonzuro, Boyakki and the chief, Miss Doronjo. The main characters of the story, Aichan and Ganchan, fight to hinder the evil plans of the trio, going to battle with funny animal-like robots capable of destroying enemy robots with the use of independant automatons.

1977 also saw the launch of series made in an attempt to open new styles in an always more closed market. The first is *Cho Supercar Gattizer*, linked to the world of car racing, that also shows some characteristics of a robot story. The five cars of the Gattizer team, driven by Jo, Hiroki, Ken, Kajumi and Sachiyo, can unite into a mechanical construct to form one uniquely powerful race car always involved in strenuous races against the enemy group of Black Demon and his daughter Queen Demon, Jo's grandfather and mother. The second pioneering attempt was made by *Kiyoryu dainsenso AiZenborg*, which followed the lead of the previous *Kyoryu tankentai Born Free*, featuring once again the union of reality and animation. Even in this case the show experienced complete failure and the Japanese production firms abandoned this limited and costly procedure indefinitely.

Lupin Sansei, the only really charismatic and noteworthy product produced this year, featured the second chapter of Lupin's adventures and began to create what would be an indelible mark in Japanese animation, thanks to Tokyo Movie Sinsha, the studio reborn from the old Tokyo Movie.

0271 FILM

HAKUCHO NO OJI (*The Prince of the Swans*), Toei Doga, fairy tale, 62 min., 3/19. [*Les Cygnes Sauvages*].

This story is based on the fairy tale of *The Seven Swans*: in a kingdom live seven young princes and a little princess. An old witch casts a spell at the demand of her granddaughter, and the young men are changed into white swans. To save themselves from their cruel fate, they must collect as many plants of stinging nettle necessary to make sweaters for all of them in the span of seven years. Their sister decides to sacrifice herself and to spin the plants, but to the pain of the barbed plants is added a curse of forced silence: if she lets out even one sound during the long span of time all her efforts will be vain and the little princes will never go back to being human. The old shrew tries to stop her, accusing her of being a witch and proposing to burn her at the stake, but there is a happy ending and the little princess not only saves her brothers, but fulfills her dream of love, marrying a handsome prince. Andersen and Grimm's fairy tales have provided innumerable plotlines for the staff of Toei, and this beautiful piece is no exception. Produced by Chiaki Imada, the design supervision is entrusted to Takashi Abe, the photography is by Tamiyo Hosada and the music by Akihiro Komori. The Italian title, *Heidi Becomes A Princess*, as usual, was purposely chosen to attract more people at the movie theater counting on the similarities between the main character and the Heidi of the Zuiyo's animated series.

0272 FILM

WAKUSEI ROBOT DANGUARD ACE TAI KONCHU ROBOT GUNDAN (*Dangard Ace, the Planetary Robot Against the Army of the Insect Robots*), Toei Doga, robot, 25 min., 7/17.

Four months after the beginning of the television series, Reiji Matsumoto brings to the big screen the characters and the splendid robot, the only movie of his long career. The movie doesn't say much at the narrative level but the level of care in the details and the great expressive strength make it one of the author's best works.

0273 FILM

UCHU SENKAN YAMATO (*Space Cruiser Yamato*), Office Academy, science fiction, 130 min., 8/6. *Yamato: Space Battleship Yamato.*

Even the movie-going public has the chance to enjoy the gorgeous art of the animated series in a movie that utilized the giant screen to its best advantage, enhancing the spectacular scenes and moving the audience.

0274 FILM

CHIISANA JUNBO (*The Little Junbo*), Sanrio, humor, 9/10.

0275 FILM

SHIN KYOJIN NO HOSHI (*The Star of the Kyojin New Series*), Tokyo Movie Sinsha, sport, 12/1.

The most famous stories don't die easily and are remade at almost regular intervals in new and more sophisticated versions. This is the case with the new movie about Hyuma, the star of the Kyojin, enhanced by a screenplay and direction definitely closer to the tastes and needs of the younger generation.

0276 SERIES

TIME BOKAN SERIES YATTAMAN (*The Series of the Time Machines: Yattaman*), Tatsunoko, robot/humor, 108 episodes, 1/1/1977 —1/27/1979.

More entertaining than *Time Bokan*, this series is the sequel to the saga about the time machines and remakes certain classic elements. The main characters are peerless heroes once again, and the enemies remain the standard three: Miss Doronjo, the sexy commander and Boyakki and Fonzuro, the two faithful assistants whose features are almost unchanged from the previous series. The goal of the heroes' travels this time is to recover the Dokurostone, a gem divided into five parts scattered in different historical eras that apparently hide the secret of a mysterious treasure. In reality, the magical treasures form the head of Dokurobei, an extraterrestrial. Once he is joined to his body, thanks to the unfortunate trio, he leaves for his native planet. This series boasts Tatsuo Yoshida as character designer, Hiroshi Sasagawa as general director, Akiyoshi Sakai and Junzo Toriumi wrote the screenplay.

0277 SERIES

ARAIGUMA RASCAL (*Rascal the Raccoon*), Nippon Animation, classic, 52 episodes, 1/2 — 12/25/1977.

This series used the talents of Masaharu Endo for the character design and was animated by Hiroshi Sato and Shigeo Koshi. It presents the adventures of Rascal, a little raccoon who is the faithful adventure companion to young North Sterling, a child who will grow to become a famous American writer. The story is set at the beginning of the century and is enriched by details of life at that time. The design supervision features the collaboration of Michiyo Sakurai. Hayao Miyazaki also takes part in the project.

Time Bokan Series Yattaman © Tatsunoko Pro.

Jetter Malus © Tezuka Production.

0278 SERIES

JETTER MALUS (*id.*), Toei Doga, science-fiction, 27 episodes, 2/3 — 9/15/1977.

A poor copy of *Tetsuwan Atom*, *Jetter Malus* is a little robot that often behaves as a human being and becomes involved in all sorts of adventures together with Miri, his robot friend. Created by Osamy Tezuka as a color remake of *Tetsuwan Atom*, the series didn't receive any attention and ended quietly with the twenty-seventh episode.

0279 SERIES

GASSHIN SENTAI MEKANDER ROBOT (*Mekander Robot: The Fighting Group of the Body Contacts*), Wako, robot, 35 episodes, 3/3 — 12/29/1977.

Because of the pollution created by the monstrous Edron, Queen Medusa, the only survivor from a far-away planet launches a capsule, in which she puts her only son Jimi, into the depths of space. After a long journey, the little one reaches the Earth where he is taken in by Prof. Shikishima. Years go by and the menace of Edron eventually reaches our planet. Jimi, together with the professor's two sons, Ryosuke and Mika, and his friend Kojiro, becomes part of the Mekander team to defend the Earth against the impending doom. One of the enemy generals is, in reality, Medusa, Jimi's mother, who remembers her son only in vague flashbacks. It is during one of these moments that the woman sacrifices her own life to save Jimi and his companions. The soundtrack by Michiyaki Watanabe, the character design by Nobuhiko Okaseko and the design supervision by Tsuneo Ninomiya and Masayuki Hayashi weren't sufficient to bring success to a series with common and predictable premises.

0280 SERIES

WAKUSEI ROBOT DANGUARD ACE (*Danguard Ace, the Planetary Robot*), Toei Doga, robot, 56 episodes, 3/6/1977 — 3/26/1978. *Force Five: Danguard Ace.*

Dangard Ace ©1992 Peter Pan Industries / Parade Video. All Rights Reserved. (Cat.# 6610)

Counselor Doppler declares war on the Earth and leads the conquest of Prometro, the mysterious tenth planet of the solar system. To avoid the danger, the earthlings build Danguard Ace, a giant robot piloted by Takuma Ichimonji that is able to defeat the enemy. Chosen after hard training by captain Dan, a mysterious man with an iron mask (who is, in reality, the father that Takuma thought long dead), the main character begins a long war that, once again, will see the inevitable triumph of good. Certain great artists take part in this series written by Reiji Matsumoto, amongst others, Tomoharo Katsumata as director and the great Shinjo Araki for character design.

0281 SERIES

BARBAPAPA (*id.*), Top Craft, educational, 150 episodes, 4/4/1977 — 3/27/1978. [*Barbapapa*].

The poor animation and the simplicity of the stories didn't halt the growing popularity of this series, especially among the very young, who are fascinated by the incredible transformations of the rubbery characters.

0282 SERIES

ASHITA E ATTACK (*Attack Towards Tomorrow*), Nippon Animation, sport, 23 episodes, 4/4/ — 9/5/1977.

The captain of the female volleyball team of Tachibana High School divides her day between training and her social life. The goal in each of these series is always the same:

to win the championship. The series created by Shiro Jinbo and supervised by Fumio Kurokawa is similar to the previous *Attack Number 1* and features more or less the same themes.

0283 SERIES

CHOGATTAI MAJUTSU ROBOT GINGUISER (*Ginguiser, the Supreme Magical Art Robot of the Fusion of Bodies*), Ashi for Nippon Animation, robot, 26 episodes, 4/9 — 10/22/1972.

The terrible emperor Kaindark of the Suzoriano empire is in search of the three spheres of Anderes that will give a powerful source of energy to the one who possesses them. That is why he sends powerful monsters to Earth to recover the mystical orbs. Confronting them are Dr. Godo and a group of teenagers: Goro Shirogon, leader of the team, Michi Akatsu, Tora and Zanta, gifted with magic powers and skilled at the controls of the robots that make up the powerful Ginguiser robot. The designs are by Tomohatsu Tanaka, the screenplay by Yu Yamamoto and the direction by Masani Anai.

Chogattai Majutsu Robot Ginguiser
© Nippon Animation.

0284 SERIES

HYOGA SENSHI GUYSLUGGER (*Guyslugger, the Ice Warrior*), Tokyo Movie/Oka Studio for Toei Co., science fiction, 20 episodes, 4/12 — 8/30/1977.

The series directed by Noboru Ishiguro features another chapter in Shotaro Ishimori's life. Many decades before the Ice Age, there was only one empire on Earth – the age of Solon. One day, the peaceful inhabitants were attacked by the Imbem, a cruel alien race that devastated the city with its destructive power. The only cyborg warriors that survived, resting within hibernating cells, were Mari, Taro, Riki, Ken and Kaya. The story begins in our days, when the Imbem come back to destroy the earthly city of Tokyo. The five young people, at the controls of the powerful spaceship Guyslugger, must now face both the enemy and their own lust for revenge.

0285 SERIES

CHODENJI MACHINE VOLTES V (*Voltes V, the Super ElectroMagnetic Car*), Nippon Sunrise for Toshi Co., robot 40 episodes, 6/4/1977 — 3/25/1978. *Voltus 5*.

The three brothers Ken'Ichi, Daijiro and Hiyoshi Go, together with Ippei Mine and Megumi Oka, pilot Voltes 5, the gigantic robot, to defeat the army from the planet Boasan, who want to conquer the Earth to increase their galactic dominion. Prince Hainel guides the team of five. He will later reveal himself to be the brother of the three earthly crew members, whose father was an extraterrestrial who had come to our planet years before. The second robot series produced by Toei is directed by Tadao Nagahama. The character design is by Akihiro Kanayama and Nobuyoshi Sasakado.

Voltus 5 ©1983 Modern Programs International, S.A. A 3B Production in association with New Hope Entertainment and Toei Co., Ltd. Distributed by Hi-Tops Video, a division of Heron Communications, Inc (Cat.# HT 0014).

0286 SERIES

SEATON DOBUTSUKI KUMA NO KO JACKY (*The Diary of the Animals From Seaton: Jacky, the Little Bear*). Nippon Animation, classic, 26 episodes, 7/6 – 6/12/1977. [*Bouba Le Petit Ourson*].

The adventures of an orphaned brown bear cub try to move young viewers, alternating tales of joy and sadness. The stories of the animals from Seaton never earned much success and the series ended with the twenty sixth episode.

Intro
-1962
1963
1964
1965
1966
1967
1968
1969
1970
1971
1972
1973
1974
1975
1976
1977
1978
1979
1980
1981
1982
1983
1984
1985
1986
1987
1988
Index

Chojin Sentai Balatack © Toei Doga.

Ippatsu Kantakun © Tatsunoko Pro.

Arrow Emblem Gran Prix No Taka © Toei.

0287 SERIES

CHOJIN SENTAI BALATACK (*Balatack, the Fighting Group of Supermen*), Toei Doga, robot, 31 episodes, 7/3/1977 — 3/26/1978.

Yuji, Tekky, Franco, Yuri and Mack form a group of young men gifted with ESP. With the help of the robot Balatack, they face the Shaizack, inhabitants of the star Y, who had kidnapped Yuji's mother and brother to prevent his father from completing the construction of the time machine. In spite of the absolute stupidity of the aliens, the five young men will have to fight hard to bring peace back to Earth.

0288 SERIES

ORE WA TEPPEI (*I am Teppei*), Shi'ei Doga/ A Productions for Nippon Animation, sport, 28 episodes, 9/12/1977 — 3/27/1978.

What can we expect from Teppei, the son of a mixed-up drunk who, instead of looking for work, spends his time searching for buried treasure? Absolutely nothing. The main character spends his days pulling practical jokes and dares, barely putting up with the time when social services forces him to go to school every day. In spite of the many calls to order, Teppei, true to himself, continues to behave as usual and doesn't study. He demonstrates, however, a particular skill in learning the techniques of Kendo. The story of Tetsuya Chiba is directed for the first part by Tadao Nagahama and by Shigeno Yoshida for the second part.

0289 SERIES

IPPATSU KANTAKUN (*Kanta, the Batter*), Tatsunoko, sport, 53 episodes, 9/18/1977 — 9/24/1978.

After the death of his father, a great baseball champion, the little Kanta forms a team with his many brothers and, thanks to his mother, who becomes coach for the occasion, he wins the students' championship for his father. The general supervision by Hiroshi Sasagawa, the subject by Tatsuo Yoshida, the screenplay by Junzo Toriumi and the character design by Akiko Shimomoto aren't sufficient to make the series stand out.

0290 SERIES

ARROW EMBLEM GRAN PRIX NO TAKA (*The Hawk From the Grand Prix With the Indicator Symbol*), Toei Doga, sport, 44 episodes, 9/22/1977 – 8/31/1978. [*Le Grand Prix*].

The young Takaya Todoroki is determined to become a race car champion. He builds himself a car to participate in a race in which the first prize is a considerable sum of money. The day of the race however, the car he built with his limited abilities and finances does stay on the road and, while facing a dangerous curve, Takaya causes an accident. The main character gets out of it safe and sound, but his vehicle is completely destroyed. A mysterious pilot observes attentively from the stands and, in spite of the accident, he sees in Takaya a great talent. Takaya gets a visit from him in the hospital and, following an attractive offer, decides to become part of the Katori team, owned by a friend of his dead father. Takaya thus has the possibility to drive a wonderful car that will bring him to victory. The mysterious pilot is Nick Ramuda, a character easily identified as racer Niki Lauda. The direction is supervised by Taro Rin in the first part followed by Nobutaka Nishizawa and the graphic characterization is by Takuo Noda.

0291 SERIES

FUSEN SHOJO TEMPLE CHAN (*Little Temple and the Hot Air Balloon*), Tatsunoko, children, 26 episodes, 10/1/1977 — 3/25/1978.

Temple is a little girl with blond hair. Her unfulfilled dream is to become a baton twirler, but her fate changes when she meets Tam Tam, a young musician who travels around the world in a hot air balloon. The little girl goes to one of his shows, after which she agrees to experience the thrill of flying. A gust of wind drags the balloon away; all their efforts to go back towards the village are in vain, and they find themselves on foreign land. Temple and Tam Tam together with a group of animal musicians begin their long journey home.

0292 SERIES

SHIN KYOJIN NO HOSHI (*The Star of the Kyojin — New Series*), Tokyo Movie Shinsha, sport, 52 episodes, 10/1/1977 — 9/30/1978.

After nine years, a sequel was made of the series whose tales had continued in many feature films. Hyuma Hoshi returns to face the best baseball teams with his long lost companions.

0293 SERIES

RITTAI ANIME IENAKI KO (*Animation 3D: Child Without Any Family*), Tokyo Movie Shinsha, classic, 52 episodes, 10/2/1977 — 10/1/1978.

Freely adapted from the novel Without Family by Hector Malot, the animated series produced by Hidekazu Takei and Takayuki Yamasuki and supervised by the famous Osamu Dezaki, follows the 1970 film closely. The search for one's mother is featured again, albeit with an number of more unique plot points. The character design and the design supervision by Akio Sugino as well as the screenplay by Shichiro Kobayashi are excellent and the designs gave the impression that this cartoon was done in 3D, while in reality, the visual effects were made up of many superimpositions of mobile backdrops that give the impression of depth. The soundtrack is by Takeo Watanabe and the shooting by Hirokate Takahashi.

0294 SERIES

LUPIN SANSEI (*Lupin III*), Tokyo Movie Shinsha, police story, 155 episodes, 10/3/1977 — 10/6/1980. *Lupin III: Tales Of The Wolf* [*Edgar, Détective Cambrioleur*].

Noboru Shiroyama, Yutaka Kaneko and a large staff of authors wrote the screenplay for the new amazing adventures of the now famous thief Lupin III and his companions Daisuke Jigen, Goemon Ishikawa and Fujiko Mine, featuring alternating animators —including the now-famous Hayao Miyazaki — under the direction of Takeo Kitahara. In this second series directed by Kyosuke Mikwuija and Yasumi Mikamoto, Lupin's features continue to be quite faithful to the original manga even if, in certain cases, the monkey-like expression is mellowed with a softer stroke. A further evolution is seen in the plots, that present more daring and complex raids, sometimes going beyond the limits of reality. The success of this series was huge. Hajime Hasegawa and Ken'ichi Kobayashi take care of the shooting, while Yuji Ono realized the fabulous soundtrack. The producers are Yasuji and Yoshiaki Takahashi. The general direction is by Kiyonobu Suzuki.

Fusen Shojo Temple Chan © Tatsunoko Pro.

Lupin III: Tales Of The Wolf 2. Aloha, Lupin
©1977, 1989 Monkey Punch. All Rights Reserved. Packaging ©1994 Streamline Enterprises, Inc. (Cat.# 90513)

0295 SERIES

CHO SUPERCAR GATTIGER (*Gattiger the Powerful Super Car*), Wako, sport, 20 episodes, 10/4/1977 — 3/28/1978.

Jo Kabuki is an automobile pilot, son of a scientist and of a mysterious woman who abandoned him at birth. His father dies under strange circumstances, a bomb secretly placed in his car. The people responsible for the attack turn out to be the hired killers of Black Demon, who is none other than Jo's grandfather. Black Demon's daughter, Queen Demon, who collaborates with him, is Jo's long lost mother who stands by the old man in his diabolical intentions, only to save her son disguised as a masked pilot. The staff includes Hitoshi Chiaki who created the original story, Mitsuru Majima and Yukihiro Tomita amongst the screenplay writers, Shiro Murata (under the penname of Shiro Yamaguchi) for character design, all under the supervision of Mitsuru Majima.

0296 SERIES

TOBIDASE! MACHINE HIRYU (*Jump, Dragon Car*), Tatsunoko for Toei Co., sport, 21 episodes, 10/5/1977 — 3/29/1978.

The fame of Tatsunoko Production is linked to their set of series aimed at a teenage audience, that parodies the most famous anime. This series thus satirically features the world of automobile racing, putting next to the team of positive characters a shabby group of rivals, taken in part from the "Time Bokan" series, that get into all sorts of trouble in order to win but who unfailingly lose the various competitions.

Tobidase! Machine Hiryu © Toei.

0297 SERIES

MANGA NIHON EMAKI (*The Japanese Comic Strips on Scrolls*), World TV, historical, 46 episodes, 10/5/1977 — 9/27/1978.

This series presents the major events in the history of Japan, in which the main characters range from courageous leaders to peasants become famous. The scenes, rich in detail, enriched the series, whose episodes show small vignettes of the ancient Japanese world.

0298 SERIES

KYORYU DAISENSO AI-ZENBORG (*Ai Zenborg, the Great Dinosaur War*), Oka Studio for Tsuburaya, science fiction, 39 episodes, 10/7/1977 — 6/30/1978.

The dinosaurs are not extinct, but have survived underground, where they have gone through a genetic evolution. Thus begins this series, enriched by many animated inventions. Now, after a span of thousands of years, the enormous animals claim a planet that was once almost all theirs. The only obstacle they encounter is an Ai-Zenborg giant spaceship piloted by Ai and Zen, two brothers transformed into cyborgs following a deadly accident. The attacks from Ululu, the enemy commander, become more and more violent, so much so that professor Torii prepares an even more powerful weapon: Super AiZen, from the fusion of the mechanical bodies of the characters. Once the threat is gone, Ai and Zen leave the Earth for the deep skies. As in the previous *Kyoryu tankentai Born Free*, also produced by the Tsuburaya, the character design is by Haroyuki Kawajima and Takekatsu Kikuta.

Kyoryu Daisenso Ai-Zenborg © Tsuburaya.

0299 SERIES

MUTEKI CHOJIN ZANBOT 3 (*Zanbot 3, the Invincible Superman*), Nippon Sunrise, robot, 23 episodes, 10/8/1977 — 3/25/1978.

The last descendants of a race of extraterrestrials find refuge on Earth after the destruction of their planet by the perfidious Gaizoku. The same threat follows them to their new planet and the earthlings, furious because of their fear, accuse the alien descendants of being responsible for the attack. The aliens don't get discouraged and, having recovered the spaceships in which their ancestors had come to Earth along with the giant robot Zanbot 3 – made up of three components driven by the little Kappei and by his cousins Uchuta and Keiko – violently crash into Gaizoku's mechanical monsters. The series soon features dramatic twists: the cruel and cynical enemies don't hesitate to place explosive devices inside the bodies of their prisoners. They then free them and make their victims explode whenever they feel like it. The finale is tragic: Uchuta and Keiko die voluntarily, throwing themselves against the enemy when their bombs become activated. The only survivors are Kappei and the alien women, who were put in a safe place before the impact. Thus ends the tragic series directed by Yoshiyuki Tomino. The character designs are by Yasuhiko Yoshikazu.

0300 SERIES

GEKISO! RUBENKAISER (*Run Fast, Rubenkaiser*), Wako for Toei Co., sport, 26 episodes, 10/10/1977 — 2/6/1978.

The dream of a race car driver is to become a champion. The main character of the series faces harsh sacrifices, but at the end, his dream comes true and he becomes an ace in Formula I racing.

0301 SERIES

WAKUSA NO CHARLOTTE (*Charlotte From the Fresh Pastures*), Nippon Animation, classic, 30 episodes, 10/29/1977 — 5/27/1978.

Wakakusa No Charlotte © Nippon Animation.

Charlotte lives with her father on a beautiful ranch not too far from Quebec, in Canada. Her life changes completely when she receives a letter from her mother who up to then was thought dead, that tells her of her mother's arrival to finally come to live with her husband and daughter. The day of the arrival soon comes and Charlotte's father makes his way towards the port to welcome his wife. Adverse fate causes the ship to sink not too far from the dock, and the man drowns trying to save his wife of whom no trace is found. Charlotte, thrown into despair by the events, receives a message from her grandfather, a rich French duke who pretends he only found out about his granddaughter on this tragic occasion. The girl goes to France to meet him and to be educated at a proper level for a girl of her rank. There she finds out the real story about her family. Her father, tired of his life of nobility, had married the young Simone without his parent's consent. His father, the duke of Monford, separated them once he found out and erased all trace of the woman. The furious young heir had then left for Canada with his baby daughter to rebuild his life. After countless hardships, Charlotte finds her mother and with her goes back to the ranch where she was once happy with their father. Nobuya Takahashi takes care of the character design and Eiji Okabe directs the series while Sun'ichi Yukimuro wrote the screenplay.

Intro
-1962
1963
1964
1965
1966
1967
1968
1969
1970
1971
1972
1973
1974
1975
1976
1977
1978
1979
1980
1981
1982
1983
1984
1985
1986
1987
1988
Index

0302 SERIES

MANGA IJIN MONOGATARI (*The Story of the Big Men of Comic Strips*), Group Tack, fairy tale, 46 episodes, 11/18/1977 — 9/29/1978.

The episodes that make up the series were inspired by the works of famous individuals who made important contributions to humanity in the past and present.

0303 SERIES

JOE HEIKA NO PETITE ANGIE (*The Little Angie of Her Majesty*), Ashi for Nippon Animation, adventure, 26 episodes, 12/13/1977 —6/27/1978.

Joe Heika No Petite Angie © Nippan Animation Co., Ltd.

The series, created by Yu Yamamoto and directed by Fumio Kurokawa, features the drawings of Motosuke Takahashi, but it doesn't deserve a positive critic because of the badly-written scripts as well as the poor animation. In the London of the past century, Angie, a young girl gifted with a keen sense of observation, finds herself helping Scotland Yard to resolve a number of complicated cases. The absurdity of the story doesn't stop there – the little girl, in fact, is often a guest of the queen who compliments her for the precious help she gives England.

0304 SPECIAL

YAKYUKYO NO UTA (*The Poem of a Baseball Fan*), Tsuchida Prod. for Nippon Animation, sport, 50 min., 12/23.

The Japanese animation staff makes this first episode of the sports adventures of a female baseball player that inspired the successful television series of 1978.

CHAPTER SEVENTEEN: 1978

The year 1978 is, without contest, the golden year of one of the most prolific authors of the Land of the Rising Sun, Reiji Matsumoto, who produced the majority of his creations in this year and the others closely following it.

Uchu Kaizoku Captain Harlock © Matsumoto R. / TV Asahi / Toei Doga.

Uchu Kaizoku Captain Harlock is renowned as Matsumoto's best piece of work, as well as the most famous. The main character is a space pirate but he is not an anti-hero; on the contrary, he is a man who has chosen freedom, deciding not to submit to a corrupt government that remains indifferent to human sufferings and destiny. The daily routine of the people of earth is troubled, but only for a moment, by the fall of a gigantic sphere that announces Earth's occupation by an alien race. The inhabitants of the Earth put out the fire provoked by the crash and the passage of the sphere through the atmosphere and then go back to their occupations as if nothing had happened and forget about the event. The only free spirit is Harlock who, gathering a handful of courageous individuals aboard the spaceship Arcadia (a ship that contains the spirit and the knowledge of his friend Tochiro) combats the alien invasion of the vegetal people from Mazone but humanity shows no gratitude, and he is considered a fugitive.

One of the major qualities — or faults, depending on who you ask — of Matsumoto is that of setting the stories of his countless characters in a space common to all, so the characters of one series end up meeting characters from some other series or, stories that begin in one series will continue and end in another. Unfortunately, this has no merit for the

Italian fans and the television programmers did not take this particularity into consideration, especially in periods where 90% of the series were bought sight unseen. It is very difficult to reconstruct the exact sequence of events and their time settings even though they can sometimes be guessed at. Harlock for example, appears as a guest star in *Ginga Tetsudo 999*, a series that features a psychological theme that has always fascinated mankind: the search for eternal youth. The only way to obtain it is to replace one's body with a perfect and functional mechanical substitute, but Tetsuro, a poor boy living in a ghetto who follows his dream, discovers after many hardships that he's happier and more "real" remaining the way he is.

Ginga Tetsudo 999 © Matsumoto R. / Fuji TV / Toei Doça.

Another very famous series from the Japanese author also seen in Italy is *Uchu Senkan Yamato*, that returns in 1978, presenting a follow-up to the stories presented in 1974. This time, the Earth is threatened by a mysterious race that travels into space aboard a gigantic white comet.

The common element of these three series is the sharing of the same universe and, most of all, by the depiction of the female characters, who are always ethereal and evanescent and, thanks to their powers, assume a very important role in the story. In *Uchu kaizoku Captain Harlock*, the enemies are the Mazonians, a people of vegetal warrior women; in *Uchu Senkan Yamato* each woman is linked to a role and to a planet: Starsha from Iskandar gives the earthlings a purifier for the Earth, Trelena from Telesar warns them about the people of the comet and Luda is destined to be venerated like a goddess, taking the place of Leda. In *Ginga Tetsudo 999*, finally, the female presence is seen in the character of Maeter, Tetsuo's travel companion, tasked to betray him.

Reiji Matsumoto is also the author of a series completely different from the above mentioned, that came out in 1978 and achieved enough success to ensure its continuation in 1979: *SF Saiyuki Starzinger* was a remake of the famous Chinese legend Saiyuki, set in outer space. The main characters are three cyborgs and a princess escorted by them to a far-away planet.

To the vast robot genre are added *Tosho Daimos*, *Uchu Majin Daikengo* and the very famous *Muteki Kojin Daiturn 3*. This last series was one of the best loved by the public at the time of its release and the story, even in the darkness of its drama, relies on humor and chaos to lighten its tone. Daitarn 3 is one of the first robots to have facial expressions. Before him, few had a similar characterization (Astroganger) and very few (including Daikengo and Trider G7) use it in later productions.

Haikarasan ga Toru, taken from Waki Yamato's manga, is one of the first soap operas for young women to use comedy to form the type of story that it wants to present. This series was not received well in Japan, unlike the success garnered by the manga, because of the time slot it was placed in (it was up against a more popular series, *Uchu Senkan Yamato Z*), thus the Nippon Animation, to limit its losses, decided to end the series once and for all with a quick and poorly-written ending.

Tosho Daimos © Y&K / Toei Doga.

American science fiction has always interested the Japanese people, so much so that countless productions are inspired not only by books considered classics but also by some that are almost unknown. *Mirai Shonen Conan* taken from *The Incredible Tide* by

Alexander Key is one of these. Deeply antimilitaristic, like almost all of Hayao Miyazaki's work, it presents the world of the future after a nuclear holocaust — a theme that the author will use again in *Kaze no Tani no Nausicaa* — in which the few survivors are divided between the pacifists from Hyarbor and the military from Indastria. Finally, even *Captain Future*, taken from the famous novels from the 40s (published in the so-called "Pulp Magazine" by Edmond Hamilton, is adapted for a modern public; the stories' stereotypes remain (the captain, the robot, the android, the scientist in the computer), but they are joined by a beautiful police woman to complicate the adventures. In spite of all that, the results are best described as mediocre.

0305 FILM

OYARO NEZUMI NO FUSHINGINA TABI (*The Wonderful Journey of the Mice Family*), Sanrio, animal, 81 min., 3/11.

A happy mice family experiences extraordinary adventures in the world of animals. Animal stories are very dear to Japanese people who, more often than not, make the characters live situations considered mundane in human society.

0306 FILM

ANDERSEN DOWA — OYAYUBIHIME (*Andersen's Stories: Princess Pollicina*), Toei Doga, fairy tale, 64 min., 3/18. [*Mam'zelle Tom Pouce*].

The very little princess Pollicina lives inside a beautiful flower on the waters of a stream. Flowing with the current, she will meet many of the inhabitants of the stream, even finding, as in all fairy tales, a little Prince Charming just for her.

0307 FILM

KAGAKU NINJATAI GATCHAMAN (*The Ninja Scientific Group Gatchaman*), Tatsunoko, science fiction, 110 min., 7/15.

The adventures of the Gatchaman patrol, after the success of the first series in 1972, carry on in the feature film produced in this year.

0308 FILM

SARABA! UCHU SENKAN YAMATO AI NO SENSHI TACHI (*Good Bye Yamato, Space Cruiser: the Warriors of Love*), Office Academy, science fiction, 150 min., 8/5. *Farewell To Space Cruiser Yamato: In The Name Of Love*.

Returning from a long and difficult war against Deslar and his powerful army, Earth is threatened again by a new alien power: The Empire of the Comet. The film is part of the long saga dedicated to the courageous crew of the spaceship Yamato, and is even presented with a title for exportation, *Arrivederci Yamato*, a fact that shows just how important the Italian market was to Japan.

0309 FILM

LUPIN SANSEI MAMOO NO ICHIHEN (*Lupin III: the First Mamoo Copy*),Tokyo Movie Shinsha, police story, 97 min., 12/16. *Lupin III: The Mystery Of Mamo*.

A nervous inspector Zenigata waits in Transylvania, his car wrecked along impassable mountain roads, while a storm rages in the sky. He is very upset, as he has just received

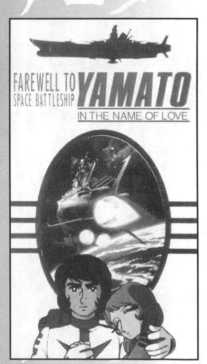

Andersen Dowa: Oyayubihime © Tezuka Production / Toei.

Farewell To Space Battleship Yamato: In The Name Of Love ©1994 Voyager Entertainment, Inc. All Rights Reserved.

news that his eternal enemy Lupin has been executed by the authorities of the country. The inspector rushes to see the body of his antagonist but a surprise awaits him: Lupin, attracted by the news, is there. To their surprise, the man in the coffin appears identical to the thief. The scene moves to Egypt; Inspector Zenigata is sure to capture Lupin who, entering into a pyramid, wants to steal a strange stone from the tomb of a Pharaoh. The inspector's trap fails, as usual, and Lupin can thus return to Japan with the stone. The young and provocative Fujiko, who works for the mysterious Mamoo, recovers the precious stone for him, but the find is a false one and Mamoo decides to capture Lupin to extort the real one. With the help of Fujiko, the deformed Mamoo captures him and has the stone analyzed by his scientists. Meanwhile, Lupin, having escaped from his prison, becomes aware of the real intent of his perfidious adversary: the search for eternal youth.

Mamoo's island is completely inhabited by clones of important historical people, and Mamoo also is a clone of himself, alive for thousands of years. But now, he's looking for eternal youth so that he will no longer have to maintain his body through science. The stone of wisdom is Mamoo's last chance to grasp immortality, and he promises to share the prize with Fujiko and to Lupin in exchange for their help. The thief refuses and Fujiko, to follow Lupin, abandons the project. Mamoo, upset because of the failure of his plan, decides to destroy the Earth so that only he and Fujiko can survive, thus becoming immortal. Fortunately, Lupin succeeds in stopping the plan of the insane character and kills him, only to discover that the real Mamoo is an enormous brain that had survived through the centuries. Seeing all his plans fail, he tells Lupin and Fujiko that he will leave for a far away planet, become immortal and return to Earth to subdue the entire planet. With a clever move, Lupin puts an explosive on the spaceship that, once in space, explodes, killing the menacing Mamoo once and for all. The direction is by Soji Yoshikawa.

Lupin III: The Mystery Of Mamo ©1978, 1989 Monkey Punch. All Rights Reserved. Packaging ©1995 Streamline Enterprises, Inc. (Cat.# 90943).

0310 FILM

CHIRIN NO SUZU (*Chirin's Bell*), Sanrio, adventure, 46 min., 3/11.

0311 FILM

CANDY CANDY HARU NO YOBIGOE (*Candy Candy: the Call of Spring*). Toei Doga, soap opera, 25 min., 3/18.

Candy is confined to the detention room at the college so she can't participate in the "Feast of May," a festival ending with a big masquerade ball and a rose parade. Having received two costumes – of Romeo and Juliet – from her uncle Andrew, the young girl escapes from her prison and alternately wearing the two costumes, she participates in the ball. The film reuses the plot from one of the television series' episode.

0312 FILM

IKKYUSAN TO YANCHA HIME (*Ikkyusan and the Princess Putiferio*), Toei Doga, historical, 15 min., 3/18.

A princess comes to visit the monastery where the young Ikkyu lives, but she is a little pest who is entrusted to the little monk so that he can make her more responsible. The two spend a lot of time together and the young boy succeeds in his mission, thanks to his abilities and Buddhist doctrine.

0313 FILM

WAKUSEI ROBOT DANGUARD ACE UCHU DAI KAISEN (*Danguard Ace, the Planetary Robot: the Great Space War in the Sea*), Toei Doga, robot, 25 min., 18/3.

The second and last animated feature film dedicated to the robot fortress, *Danguard A* marks the end of Takuma Ichimonji's adventures as a talented pilot who defeats the perfidious Doppler.

0314 FILM

CANDY CANDY NO NATSUYASUMI (*The Summer Vacations of Candy Candy*), Toei Doga, soap opera, 19 min., 7/22.

School has ended, and the children are sent to a summer camp, befriending the lonely Terrence. Alone on the shore of the lake, the aspiring actor and Candy finally exchange their first kiss. This film is also taken from the plot of an episode from the television series.

0315 FILM

UCHU KAIZOKU CAPTAIN HARLOCK ARCADIA GO NO NAZO (*Captain Harlock, the Space Pirate: The Mystery of Arcadia*), Toei Doga, science fiction, 151 min., 7/22.

Harlock, the vagabond space pirate, still combats under the banner of liberty to make the entire universe respect the ideals of justice, but on his spaceship Arcadia, faithful ally in every battle, lurks the clues to an obscure mystery.

0316 SERIES

PELINE MONOGATARI (*Peline's Story*), Nippon Animation, soap opera, 52 episodes, 1/1 — 12/31/1978.

Peline Monogatari © Nippon Animation Co., Ltd.

Hector Malot is very liked by Japanese animators. One proof is this soap opera inspired by another one of his novels: Within the Family. Following the death of her father in India, Peline and her mother travel to France where the little girl's grandfather lives. Unfortunately, because of a bad illness, her mother also dies before the end of the journey. Peline remains alone to face life's difficulties. She survives working as a traveling photographer from village to village. After many months, the young girl reaches the house of her grandfather, a blind man who has abandoned his family business, entrusting the management of his company to a greedy grandson and a cynical vice-president. He has done this in reaction to the time when his son Edmond, Peline's father, had left him to go live in the Asian country where he married a Hindu woman. The old man had always refused to meet his daughter-in-law and his granddaughter. For this reason, Peline presents herself under a false name, Olerie, and gets herself hired at the company. Having gained the old man's trust, she becomes his private secretary and reveals her true identity when her grandfather regains his sight and finds in her the features of his son Edmond. The direction is by Hiroshi Saito and Shigeo Koshi and the animation by Hideo Chiba.

0317 SERIES

MAJOKKO CHIKKLE (*Chikkle the Little Witch*), Neomedia/Nippon Sunrise for Teoi Co., magic, 48 episodes, 3/6/1978 — 1/29/1979.

The series is born from Go Nagai's original story, that presents a very different plot than his usual clichés. The main character in fact is the little Chikkle, a witch who came out of an old photo album to study the behavior of human beings.

0318 SERIES

UCHU KAIZOKU CAPTAIN HARLOCK (*Space Pirate Captain Harlock*), Toei Doga, science fiction, 42 episodes, 3/14/1978 — 2/13/1979. *Captain Harlock / Albator.*

Harlock is a pirate from the future, a man who has chosen the way of freedom, preferring space to the planet Earth where values and morals have been lost and forgotten. One day, an enormous spherical object crashes in the center of Tokyo. The enormous sphere bears some mysterious inscriptions on its black and smooth surface, and many scientists begin studying the unknown writing. The renowned professor Daiba succeeds in his attempt to translate the sentence: "Eternal Glory to Mazone." Alarmed by the message indicating the existence of an extraterrestrial civilization, the man tells the authorities who, as their only answer, try to eliminate him.

Tadashi, the professor's son, knowing everything, is attacked by an inhabitant of the alien planet in an attempt to silence him. The inhabitants of Mazone, vegetal women guided by queen Raflesia, have in fact been able to infiltrate the earthly society and even control its government, with the goal of taking possession of the planet. Their only obstacle is Harlock, already aware of their existence, who together with Tadashi, will defeat the alien menace aboard his spaceship, the Arcadia. The original story is by Reiji Matsumoto, the screenplay is by Haruya Yamazaki and Shojzo Uehara. Directed by Taro Rin with the backdrops by Tadao Kubota and Hidenobu Hata. The character design is taken care of by Kazuo Komatsubara and Makoto Kikuchi.

0319 SERIES

TOSHO DAIMOS (*General Daimos*), Nippon Sunrise for Teoi Co., and Toei Agency, robot, 44 episodes, 4/1/1978 — 1/27/1979.

The inhabitants of the planet Baam, searching for a new world suitable for their needs, reach the ends of the solar system and, seeing the Earth, decide to conquer it. In answer to the threat, the robot Daimos is activated, piloted by Kazuya Ryusaka who, during an enemy attack, saves a young woman named Erika who in reality is the princess of the attackers. The young extraterrestrial, having lost her memory, falls in love with the main character and the two live happily together for a brief time. Once healed, Erika decides to go back to her people to prevent the war from going on. Kazuya is considered a traitor and, to demonstrate the uselessness of the conflict, leaves for Giove where the enemy orbital base 4 is stationed. Erika, forced by the emperor Olbam, fires in the direction of her earthly lover who, miraculously spared, decides to avenge himself destroying the alien fortress. The character design is by Akihiro Kaneyama and the general supervision is by Tadao Nagahama.

0320 SERIES

SF SAIYUKI STARZINGER (*The Saiyuki Science Fiction Starzinger*), Toei Doga, science fiction, 64 episodes, 4/2/1978 — 6/24/1979. *Spaceketeers.*

In a distant future, the peoples of the Earth are able to colonize the known parts of the cosmos, thanks to the beneficial radiation emanating from the queen of the Great Planet, at the center of the universe. The lady's old age causes the weakening of her power. In consequence, new hostile forms of life emerge and begin to subdue the various colonies.

Captain Harlock Collector's Video Vol. One ™ & ©1990 New TV. All Rights Reserved. Distributed by Malibu Graphics (ISBN 0-944735-61-4).

Spaceketeers ©1992 Peter Pan Industries / Parade Video. All Rights Reserved. (Cat.# 6611)

The only way to remedy the catastrophe is to replace the old queen with a young and strong one who will be able to reestablish the balance. The choice falls on Aurora, princess of the Moon kingdom. She is helped in her mission by Jan Kogo, a rebel earthly cyborg who has a control ring placed on his head, Jogo from the planet of Water and Akka, defender of the planet of Mud. Together they succeed in reaching the planet and there, with great sadness, they leave their beloved princess. The animated transposition of the series created by Reiji Matsumoto is realized thanks to the good screenplay by Tatsuo Murata and Mitsuru Majima, the designs of Katsumi Suda and the general supervision of Yugo Serikawa.

0321 SERIES

MIRAI SHONEN CONAN (*Conan, the Boy From the Future*), Nippon Animation, adventure, 26 episodes, 4/4 — 10/31/1978. [*Conan, Le Fils Du Futur*].

Men, because of their infinite stupidity, cause the final nuclear conflict, the most disastrous of a number of similar attacks. Millions of people die, the cities are disintegrated, seaquakes and earthquakes succeed one another at a fast pace and only a small group of people save themselves aboard a rocket that reaches a deserted island in the middle of the ocean. Time passes and the survivors die one by one, leaving only Conan, a clever young boy and an old man he calls grandfather. One day, the boy finds young Lana unconscious on the beach. She was trying to escape from the soldiers from Indastria, an island ruled by a military society. Lana is caught and kidnapped, the old man is killed and Conan escapes promising to come back to save her friend. Hyarbor, a second civilization that had developed into a land of peace after the nuclear catastrophe welcomes the young boy after the rescue of Lana and the destruction of Indastria in a seaquake. The series is one of the greatest success of the duo formed by Isao Takahata and Hayao Miyazaki, as his first direction together with Tatsuo Ayakawa. The character design is by Yasuo Otsuka, while the screenplay is written by Koji Yoshikawa, Teruaki Nakano and Tetsu Muramomo.

Mirai Shonen Conan © Nippon Animation Co., Ltd.

0322 SERIES

IKKYUSAN (*id.*), Shien'ei Doga for Nippon Animation, sport, 26 episodes, 4/10 — 10/23/1978.

The young main character follows in the footsteps of his renowned animated predecessors, applying himself with tenacity in the difficult sport of baseball. The *Ikkyusan* series features the elements now constantly exploited in the sport style, without bringing any substantial innovations to the genre.

0323 SERIES

MANGA HAJIMETE MONOGATARI (*The Animated History of the Origins*), Dax, biography, 308 episodes, 5/6/1978 — 3/31/1984.

The animated series presents the biographies of many renowned individuals of history, in the fields of science, art, literature and music. The production has an educational value and confronts in a simple way the historical events that children are forced to learn in school, demonstrating how learning can be fun.

0324 SERIES

YAKYUKYO NO UTA (*The Poem of the Baseball Fan*), Tsushida Prod. for Nippon Animation, sport, 50 episodes, 5/19/1978 — 3/27/1979.

Yuko Mizuhara is a girl who can throw a baseball with rare skill. One day, because of this, she is noticed by the coach of a famous team. She thus becomes the first girl to play professionally in an all men's team. The players on both her own team and others are the main antagonists, always ready to hinder her to assuage their manly pride. But this is only the first episode of a series full of characters, a real collection of stories. The first 24 episodes are centered around Yuko, the others on the rest of the team. The subject is by Shinji Mizushima.

0325 SERIES

MUTEKI KOJIN DAITURN 3 (*Daiturn 3, the Invincible Metallic Man*), Nippon Sunrise, robot, 40 episodes, 6/3/1978 — 3/31/1979.

Professor Haran, a member of an earthly colony on Mars, creates Don Zauser, a powerful mechanical being gifted with its own conscience that soon takes over and transforms the men on the base into the Meganoids, cyborgs under his control. The new soldiers cause death and destruction and the only survivor is Banjo, the son of professor Horan, who escapes to Earth aboard the Daiturn 3 robot. Don Zauser decides to transform the inhabitants of our planet into Meganoids as well, but Banjo with the help of the beautiful Reika and Beauty, of his faithful butler Garrison and his little Toppo, oppose the powerful enemy generals, who are able to transform into gigantic robots.

0326 SERIES

HAIKARASAN GA TORU (*The Girl in Style is Passing*), Nippon Animation, soap opera, 44 episodes, 6/3/1978 — 3/31/1979. [*Marc Et Marie*].

Taken from Waki Yamato's cartoon, the series narrates the story of Benio Hanamura, a young woman who lives in Japan at the beginning of the century. This period is one in which progress and tradition are uneasily mixed, due to frequent contact with the Western world. The wealthy girls attend a school to learn good manners, and even the vivacious Benio must attend the annoying classes, but her father soon decides to give her hand in marriage to the rich Shinobu. The young woman doesn't agree and once in his family's house to be educated in the ways of matrimony, as was the Japanese tradition, she desperately tries to get herself thrown out.

Haikarasan Ga Toru © W. Yamato /
Nippon Animation Co., Ltd.

Eventually Benio returns Shinobu's love, but the war between Russia and Japan forces the young man to leave for the front and not long afterwards, tragic news arrives: Shinobu is declared missing. The young woman becomes a journalist and she is expected to interview a couple of Russian counts visiting Japan. Suprisingly, she recognizes in the man the missing Shinobu who, having lost his memory, was made to believe that he was the noble woman's husband. The finale of the animated cartoon is a great deal less complete and outlined than that of the manga because the television series didn't earn much success in Japan, forcing the screenplay writers to speed up the conclusion. Benio, very upset, gets engaged to Onigima, her boss, but the day of the wedding, Shinobu, having recovered his memory for some time and who had stayed with the countess only out of gratitude since she had only a few months to live, arrives. Free from his ties to the countess, the young man tries to stop the ceremony that instead gets abruptly interrupted by a strong earthquake. Benio and Shinobu find each other through the debris and are finally united.

0327 SERIES

HOSHI NO OJISAMA PETIT PRINCE (*Petit Prince, the Prince of the Stars*), Knack, classic, 39 episodes, 7/4/1978 — 3/27/1979.

Taken from the novel by Antoine de Saint Exupery, a French writer and aviator from the beginning of the 20th century who died in the Second World War during an air raid, the series adapted from the *Little Prince* loses the original descriptive charm. The main character is a young and arrogant prince who reigns on a planet inhabited by only one vain rose. The television adventures don't necessarily reflect those presented in the book.

0328 SERIES

UCHU MAJIN DAIKENGO (*Daikengo, the Cosmic Devil God*), Tori Prod., for Toei Agency, robot, 26 episodes, 7/27/1978 — 2/15/1979.

The story takes place on the recently-conquered planet Emperius. Prince Ryger, the only one to oppose the enemy invaders, runs away from the planet in order to overcome the menace outside the boundaries of his kingdom, so as not to involve the already weakened population. He is helped in the enterprise by Cleo, daughter of the corrupted prime minister, and two friendly robots, Anike and Otoke. Aboard the robot Daikengo they succeed in getting the upper hand over the wicked Lady Baracross, commander of the invasion forces finally regaining the long sought-after peace.

Uchu Majin Daikengo © Tori Production / Toei.

0329 SERIES

GINGA TETSUDO 999 (*Galactic Railway 999*), Toei Doga, science fiction, 113 episodes, 9/14/1978 — 4/9/1981.

The young Tetsudo Hoshino, poor from birth, decides to embark on a long trip on the space train, that will bring him to a distant planet in order to obtain a mechanical body and with it, immortality. He soon meets Maeter, who is also going to that planet and offers to accompany him even giving him one of the very expensive tickets. After a thousand adventures, Tetsudo discovers that Maeter is, in reality, the daughter of the queen, sent into the skies to try to find young courageous men who, transformed into cyborgs, can serve her mother in her conquering cult. Thanks to Tetsuro, Maeter understands she has made a mistake and she rebels against her mother, killing her. Thus ends the series created by Reiji Matsumoto, directed by Nobutaka Nishizawa and characterized in collaboration first with Shingo Araki, then with Tomonori Kogawa under the pen name of Shigeru Kogawa and finally with Kazuo Komatsubara and Kenji Oyama.

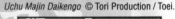

Ginga Tetsudo 999 © Matsumoto R. / Fuji TV / Toei Doga.

0330 SERIES

KAGAKU NINJATAI GATCHAMAN II (*The Ninja Scientific Group Gatchaman II*), Tatsunoko, science fiction, 52 episodes, 10/1/1978 — 9/23/1979. *Eagle Riders*.

After the defeat of the general of the Galactors, General Z runs away into space thanks to the sacrifice of Joe the condor, but he intends not to flee, but to reorganize his offensive against the Earth. He kidnaps a little girl to artificially age her into an adult, names her Gelsadra, and then gives her the command of the army. In the meantime, the Gatchaman aboard their new God Phoenix fight the evil plans of the enemy finding, after some time, their companion Joe, whom they thought dead, but who, in reality, had been transformed into a cyborg by a mysterious professor who had saved him from the explosion of the

Kagaku Ninjatai Gatchaman II © Tatsunoko Pro.

Intro
-1962
1963
1964
1965
1966
1967
1968
1969
1970
1971
1972
1973
1974
1975
1976
1977
1978
1979
1980
1981
1982
1983
1984
1985
1986
1987
1988
Index

previous base of General Z. The general direction is entrusted to Hiroshi Sasagawa in cooperation with Seitaro Hara. The character design is by Ippei Kuri and Yoshitaka Amano.

0331 SERIES
MANGA KODOMO BUNKO (*Comic Strip Books for Children*), Group Tack/Herald Ent., fairy tale, 96 episodes, 10/6/1978 — 9/29/1979.

0332 SERIES
TAKARAJIMA (*Treasure Island*), Tokyo Movie Shinsha, classic/adventure, 26 episodes, 10/8/1978 — 4/1/1979. [*L'Ile Au Trésor*].

The main character, having lost his father, leaves his mother to embark on an English ship as a ship's boy. During the trip, there is a mutiny by the crew and Silver the pirate, takes command by force. The journey then becomes the hunt for a treasure buried on a mysterious island. The series is inspired by Stevenson's novel.

Takarajima © TMS.

0333 SERIES
UCHU SENKAN YAMATO II (*Yamato II the Space Cruiser*), Office Academy, science-fiction, 26 episodes, 10/14/1978 — 4/7/1979. *Starblazers: The Comet Empire*.

Once the threat of radioactivity is taken care of, the warriors from the stars resume their trip to help Trelena from Telesar escape from the Empire of the Comet, a mysterious race that roams the skies aboard a fortress bringing war and destruction. Under the guidance of Susumu Kodai, the army of the Yamato succeeds in defeating the enemy, along with Deslar, who now fights on the side of the earthlings. Worthy of notice is the presence of Yoshikazu Yasuhiko and Noboru Ishiguro amongst the authors of the storyboard. Ishiguro is also the head animator under the direction of Reiji Matsumoto.

Uchu Senkan Yamato II © Westcape Corp.
Star Blazers® is a registered trademark of Jupiter Films, Inc. ©1995 Voyager Entertainment, Inc.

0334 SERIES
SHIN ACE O NERAE! (*Point to the Ace! — New Series*), Tokyo Movie Shinsha, sport, 25 episodes, 10/14/1978 — 3/31/1979.

A sequel to the adventures of Hiromi Oka, the young Japanese tennis player, now at the peak of his career, sees his coach Jin Munakata – a former world champion who won the Davis Cup – die from a serious illness. Todo, always beside him, helps to bring him through this situation.

0335 SERIES
PINK LADY MONOGATARI — EIKO NO TENSHI TACHI (*The Story of the Pink Ladies: the Famous Angels*), T & C for Toei Co., biography, 36 episodes, 10/24/1978 — 6/26/1979.

This series is the story of Mi and Key, the Pink Ladies, a duo that has dominated the Japanese musical scene throughout the 70s and that still today, years after its breakup, is considered a reference point in the history of Japanese pop music.

0336 SERIES
CAPTAIN FUTURE (*id.*), Toei Doga, science fiction, 52 episodes, 11/7/1978 — 10/30/1979. [*Captaine Flam*].

A young scientist, called Captain Future by his men, is always ready to conduct countless investigations throughout the universe to help the space police. He is helped by the robot

Captain Future © Toei Doga.

Greg, whose design resembles that of C3PO in *Star Wars*, the android Otto and professor Simon, whose brain is inserted in a small flying mechanism. Always present as well is Joan, Captain Future's true love. The series produced by Toei Doga features the participation of Tomoharu Katsumata for the general direction and of Tadanao Tsushi for the mecha designs.

0337 SPECIAL

BANDER BOOK (*id.*), Tezuka, adventure, 120 min., 8/27. [*Le Prince Du Soleil*].

Bander, prince of a far away planet, discovers that he was adopted and that he comes from Earth. Aboard a strange time machine, run by the mysterious Black Jack, he searches for truth, eventually discovering that his parents were killed in an attack during a trip into space. In fact, his father, an important scientist, had discovered that the computer that ruled the Earth was condemning him to destruction. Having learned all this, Bander, together with Black Jack who turns out to be his older brother, destroys the terrible computer, giving life back to the planet. The movie constitutes yet another success for Osamu Tezuka.

0338 SPECIAL

DAISETSUZAN NO YOSHA KIBAO (*The Courageous Kinbao From Tall Mountains Covered With Snow*), Nippon Animation, classic, 90 min., 9/23.

0339 SPECIAL

MACHI ICHIBAN NO KECHINBO (*The Number One Miser of the City*), Top Craft, sport, 12/24.

This charming movie is an animated version of *A Christmas Carol* from Dickens.

0340 SPECIAL

CAPTAIN FUTURE KAREINARU TAIYOKEI RACE (*Captain Future: the Great Race in the Solar System*), Toei Doga, science fiction, 45 min., 12/31. [*Capitaine Flam*].

This was presented together with the series as a television special that takes root in the story inspired by the novels of English writer Edmond Hamilton, featuring a new science fiction adventure of the now famous captain.

CHAPTER EIGHTEEN: 1979

Japanese animation is often accused of being a mass production with few expressive capacities and limited basic themes. It is true, however, that certain productions have offered new ideas, revolutionizing the industry's approach to animation and bringing a number of new directorial developments to the forefront, taking animation in a direction that comes to resemble live-action cinematography.

Kido senshi Gundam was a perfect response to the expressed desire for a renewal of that standard, the giant robot genre. Recent shows had been pure imitations of Go Nagai's classics, in consequence beating the same old plots into the ground. *Gundam*, produced by Nippon Sunrise, bears the signature of Yoshikazu Yasuhiko as character designer, of Kunio Okawara for the technical designs and is also inspired, even if in a very superficial way, by Robert Heinlein's novel *The Space Infantry*. The distinctive element in this show is the total realism of the war conflict; no longer taken up by samurais with invincible

Bander Book © Tezuka Production.

Kido Senshi Gundam © Nippon Sunrise.

weapons, war is presented as a technological matter, with the humanoid weapons able to be attacked and even destroyed. Another fundamental element of the saga created by Yoshiyuki Tomino is the appearance of characters with ESP (Extra Sensorial Perception) who, at the controls of robots, use their gift to locate objects in space, abandoning the use of radar.

Always focusing their efforts on the theme of fighting robots, a narrative style Japanese animators have developed as a fusion of the ancient folktales of the Oni giants and Japan's great passion for robotics and the technology pertaining to it, Toei Co. produces *Mirai Robot Daltanias*, a story that centers on the importance of friendship and selflessness. The series presents a group of young people of different ages, members of the same family, all useful to their community. Two of these youths pilot the gigantic Daltanias that, larger than its predecessors, forms a robot and a ferocious mechanical lion named Beralios.

Kido Senshi Gundam © Nippon Sunrise.

Certain animated series were particularly loved by the Italian public, even by the most demanding viewers; amongst the many examples let us note *Versailles no Bara*, taken from Ryoko Ikeda's manga. The complex screenplay that features the main events of the French Revolution in countless detail, gives a perfect account of the feeling of dejection and rebellion of the Parisians, showing the life in the city as opposed to the life at the royal court. To a beautifully intricate plot is added, moreover, designs that are skillfully done — thanks to the presence of Shingo Araki and Michi Himeno, two high class artists — and one of the most popular soundtracks ever recorded. The story of Oscar is one with deep and dramatic tones, that features a denunciation of the aristocratic power and that sees its heroes fall under the gunfire of the king's army. The courageous main character dies July 14th 1789, the day of the taking of the Bastille, after having witnessed the death of her lover Andre, in one of the most tragic finales in Japanese animation.

Versailles No Bara © Riyoko Ikeda / TMS.

Another well known and loved character, even in Italy, is Lupin III. In 1979 TMS comes out with a new film under the direction of Hayao Miyazaki: *Lupin Sansei Cagliostro no shiro*. The element of mystery and suspense is notable and the frequent "coup de theatre" makes it one of the best films of the 70s; moreover, the dynamic animation characterized by sudden changes of perspective contributes to emphasize the excitement and splendor of the incredible situations.

Another incredibly popular release is *Akage no Anne*, taken from the novel Anne of Green Gables by Lucy Maud Montgomery. Once again — as is expected of both Japanese tradition and Western children's literature — the main character is an orphan, Anne, dealing with the problems of daily life in the village where she lives with her adoptive family.

The most famous character on which Miyazaki also worked remains *Conan*, starring in a feature film that features the anti-military spirit of the author in its entirety. Thus we find the characters dealing with the terrifying consequences of the Third World War and with the abuses of the society of Indastria, in a successful remake of the television series.

1979 remains particularly productive for another great author who has fascinated an entire generation with his famous space sagas: Reiji Matsumoto, who, this year, presents television and film viewers with four different productions.

The first is dedicated to the fans of *Ginga Tetsudo 999*, who can finally taste the main events of the television series of 1978 in a feature film enriched with carefully crafted animation and the contribution of a new character designer, skilled in presenting the characters of the story in a similar but very personal interpretation. The adventures of the space train continue with a new special in which the young Tetsuo has his train ticket stolen, running the risk of having to forget about the long trip.

Together with *Ginga Tetsuso 999 Kimi Wa Senshi no Yo Ni Ikirareru Ka*, a television special is also made for a much more popular series: *Uchu Senkan Yamato Aratanaru Tabidachi*, that sees the members of the famous crew united at Gamilas in the desperate attempt to save the planet Iscandar from an army of mysterious aliens. On the trail of the above mentioned *Yamato*, Yoshinobu Nishizaki creates the series *Uchu Kubo Blue Noah*, along lines far too similar to the previous series, showing definitely inferior animation and characterization.

0341 FILM
KURUMIWARI NINGYO (*The Nutcracker*), Sanrio, classic, 97 min., 3/3.

0342 FILM
TATSU NO KO TARO (*Taro the Little Dragon*), Toei Doga, monster, 75 min., 3/17.

In Japan, certain producers of live-action science fiction decide to dabble in the world of animation, making feature films with poor results. Their popularity almost never reaches high levels, and their success is often inconsistent. This is the case of Kikiro Urayama, who created this weak story about a dragon.

0343 FILM
ALPS NO SHOJO HEIDI (*Heidi, the Little Girl From the Alps*), Zuiyo, classic, 107 min., 3/17.

The story of the little Heidi who moved television viewers world wide thanks to the 1974 series is brought to viewers again in this movie that manages to keep the sense of narrative pathos relatively unchanged. The contagious cheerfulness of the little girl once again moves the public, fascinated by the careful representation of the mountain village.

0344 FILM
UMI NO TRITON (*Triton From the Sea*), Office Academy, adventure, 74 min., 7/15.

After the discreet success of the animated series, an attempt is made to present the young boy from the abyss to movie-goers. Triton is once again involved in imaginative adventures from which he always emerges a winner.

0345 FILM
HOKKYOKU NO MUSICA MISICA (*Musica Misica at the North Pole*), Mushi, animals, 80 min., 7/21.

0346 FILM
GINGA TETSUDO 999 (*Galactic Railway 999*), Toei Doga, science fiction, 128 min., 8/4. *Galaxy Express 999*.

The basic theme of the television series of 1978 is retold in a praiseworthy feature film in which some new characters are also featured. The good animation enhances the charming screenplay by Reiji Matsumoto.

Umi No Triton © Westcape Corporation.

Ginga Tetsudo 999 © Leiji Matsumoto / Toei Animation Co., Ltd. Available in English from Viz Video (Cat.# VV GE-001)

0347 FILM

ACE O NERAE! (*Point to the Ace!*) Tokyo Movie Shinsha, sport, 85 min., 9/14.

Made with a graphic technique that to this day is envied by certain recent animated series, *Ace o Nerae!* summarizes the daily events of the series, including some new footage.

0348 FILM

MIRAI SHONEN CONAN (*Conan, the Boy From the Future*), Nippon Animation, Adventure, 123 min., 9/15.

Taken from the television series to be transposed for the big screen, the feature film appears splendid despite the fact that it was made by assembling episodes from the previous version, with a different finale.

0349 FILM

GANBARE!! TABUCHIKUN!! (*Come on!! Tabuchikun!!*), Tokyo Movie Shinsha, humor, 90 min., 11/3.

0351 FILM

LUPIN SANSEI CAGIOSTRO NO SHIRO (*Lupin III: The Castle Of Cagliostro*), Tokyo Movie Shinsha, police story, 100 min., 12/15. *The Castle of Cagliostro.*

Lupin is looking for certain precious matrices that are kept in the castle of the count Cagliostro, an evil man who is keeping the lovely Clarice a prisoner. The kidnapping was intended to force the girl to marry him, but the young woman's heart beats only for the famous thief. Lupin, years before, had been surprised by Clarice while he was stealing from her parents' house. The young girl, fascinated by the thief's kind ways, had kept the secret, sparing him from a certain conviction; now Lupin wants to return the favor. The story turns around two rings with the effigy of the Capricorn that fit together, opening the doors to a precious treasure. One belongs to the count and the other to Clarice, which is the real reason why he is so insistant upon marrying her. At the end of the story, Lupin kills the evil man and, fitting the two rings into the clock of the castle's bell tower, he reveals the mystery: in reality, the treasure is a sunken city that, concealed at the bottom of the lake of the castle, reappears at the stopping of the flow of the water. The thief also recovers the priceless matrix that is, as always, taken from him by Fujiko. The movie is directed by Hayao Miyazaki.

The Castle Of Cagliostro ©1980 Monkey Punch • TMS-K. Package Design ©2000 Manga Entertainment, a Palm Pictures Company LLC. All Rights Reserved. (Cat.# MANG4051-2 WR02)

0352 FILM

TOSHO DAIMOS (*General Daimos*), Nippon Sunrise, robot, 25 min.

0353 SERIES

NOBARA NO JULIE (*Julie of Wild Rose*), Dax, soap opera, 13 episodes, 1/4 — 3/29/1979.

This is yet another soap opera of little importance, with common and predictable stories. Julie, following the death of her parents, moves to her aunt and uncle's house who, although they are in poor financial situation, welcome her as a daughter.

0354 SERIES

AKAGE NO ANNE (*Anne With the Red Hair*), Nippon Animation, soap opera, 50 episodes, 1/7 — 12/30/1979. *Ann Of Green Gables.*

Akage No Ann © Nippon Animation Co., Ltd.

Time Bokan Series: Zendaman © Tatsunoko Pro.

Taken from the very famous novel by Lucy Maud Montgomery entitled *Anne of Green Gables*, the series directed by Isao Takahata had the preliminary sketches done by Hayao Miyazaki. This series narrates the daily life of Anne Shirley, a daydreaming girl with funny-looking red hair. Alone in the world, she spends her days fantasizing about having a house and a family to love her. One day, things seem to change for Anne when Matthew, an old man who runs a farm with his sister, wants to adopt her. Once she reaches her destination, the welcome from the lady isn't too warm. She was, in fact, expecting to see a boy who would help her brother in the hard farm work, and wants to send the girl back to the orphanage. Anne, however, is soon loved by the brother and sister who eventually treat her like their own daughter, sparing no sacrifices to allow her to study. The screenplay is by Chika Shigaki.

0355 SERIES

TIME BOKAN SERIES — ZENDAMAN (*The Time Machine Series: Zendaman*), Tatsunoko, robot/humor, 52 episodes, 2/3/1979 — 1/26/1980.

Time travel is still at the base of this saga that now features Sakura and Tetsu, the Zendaman, combating the enemy trio with the mysterious Miss Mujo as head, along with the robots Zendalion and Zendagorilla. This series, unpublished in Italy, hasn't had the same success as the others.

0356 SERIES

NIHON MEISAKU DOWA SERIES — AKAI TORI NO KOKORO (*The Japanese Series of the Masterpieces: the Heart of the Red Bird*), K & S/Shin'ei Doga. fairy tale, 52 episodes, 2/5/1979 — 7/30/1980.

0357 SERIES

HANA NO KO LUN LUN (*Lun Lun, the Girl From the Flowers*), Teoi Doga, magic, 50 episodes, 2/9/1979 – 2/8/1980. [*Lulu Et Le Mystère De La Fleur Magique / Le Tour Du Monde De Lydie*].

Lun Lun is a special little girl, as she is the only earthly descendant from the kingdom of flowers. This race, who once lived on the earth in peace and harmony with the rest of the human race, had to leave the planet because of the gradual detachment of mankind from nature. Having found refuge on Star of the Flowers, they now need their only descendant. Lun Lun will have to find the marvelous "Flower of seven colors" to allow the young king's son to succeed his father on the throne of the fantastic flowered kingdom.

Lun Lun starts looking for the flower accompanied by Nubo and Cat, a dog and a cat, respectively, the incarnations of two spirits of flowers. Serge also follows them, a mysterious individual always present in the most difficult situations provoked by the main antagonists, Yaboki and Togenisha, two rebels also interested in the flower and intending to usurp the throne. The girl's journey is long and brings her to visit various parts of the globe. In the end, however, she finds the flower in the garden of her own house in France. The mission is finally completed and the king can thus abdicate to his son, who turns out to be Serge, the mysterious stranger. Serge then abdicates in favor of his younger brother, so that he can marry Lun Lun and live with her on Earth bringing the message of flowers everywhere. Part of the staff are Shiro Jinbo, author of the subject and (in certain episodes) screenplay writer, Michi Himeno as the main artist and Hiroshi Shidara, a skillful director.

Hana No Ko Lun Lun © S. Jinbo / Toei Animation.

0358 SERIES

CYBORG 009 (*id.*), Nippon Sunrise for Toei Co., science fiction, 50 episodes, 3/6/1979 — 3/25/1980.

The science fiction series by Shotaro Ishimori is directed and written by Ryosuke Takahashi, while Koichi Sugiyama composed the soundtrack.

0359 SERIES

MIRAI ROBOT DALTANIAS (*Daltanias, the Robot From the Future*), Nippon Sunrise for Toei Co., robot, 47 episodes, 3/21/1979 — 3/5/1980.

In modern-day Japan an alien race attacks the Earth, spreading death and destruction throughout the globe. The cities are razed to the ground and a giant robot is placed to guard the remnants of the populations. The rest of the earthly population lives by their own wits in slums, the children learning young to obtain food by stealing. Kento, Danji, Sanae, Mita, Tanosuke, Jiro and Manabu are part of one of these gangs of children. During a flight in the woods, Kento trips and ends up in a strange cavern. He and his friends discover that it is the entrance to a real space base run by professor Earl, who came to Earth after a conquest of his planet.

The professor entrusts the defense of the Earth to Danji and Kento at the commands of the spaceship Gumper and the robot Atlas, respectively, that are able to unite with the mechanical lion Beralios to form the potent Daltanias. Beralios, dispersed during the landing of Earl on Earth, is called back unexpectedly by Kento when, attacked by the evil Akron, the young man gives off a powerful cross of light. The power of the main character allows the old professor to recognize him as Harlin, descendant of the ancient Helios dynasty dispersed for years. The young man finds his real father and together with him and his companions, he saves the Earth. Toshi Gofumi wrote the screenplay, based on the story by Saburo Yatsude who recovers his role as character designer. The animation by Kojo Akino and Akikiro Kanayama and the series is directed by Norio Nashima, while Tadao Nagahama is in charge of the artistic direction.

0360 SERIES

KUJIRA NO JOSEPHINA (*Josephina the Whale*), Ashi for Kokusai Eigasha, children, 23 episodes, 4/2 — 9/25/1979.

Having an imaginary friend is common to many lonely children. In this case, it's an unusual animal, Josephina the whale, that gives Choppy incredible adventures that will make him grow mentally and spiritually. Once he gains confidence in himself, the main character has no need for the whale so it is thus able to dedicate itself to other insecure children.

0361 SERIES

DORAEMON (*id.*), Shin'ei Doga, humor, 4/2/1979 — today [872 episodes by the end of September 2000].

Doraemon's story is one of the longest running in the Japanese animation panorama. The credit is surely due to the duo Fujiko Fujio who wrote the story, but also, in part, to the designs by Sadayoshi Tominaga, the direction of Yoshiro Owada, the artistic direction of Ken Kawai and the music of Shunsuke Kikuchi.

Doraemon © Fujiko • Shogakukan • TV Asahi.

Intro
-1962
1963
1964
1965
1966
1967
1968
1969
1970
1971
1972
1973
1974
1975
1976
1977
1978
1979
1980
1981
1982
1983
1984
1985
1986
1987
1988
Index

0362 SERIES

THE ULTRAMAN (*id.*), Nippon Sunrise/Tsuburaya, robot, 50 episodes, 4/4/1979 — 3/26/1980.

After the success of the live-action series, broadcast since 1966, the Nippon Sunrise realized the animated version, skillfully remaining faithful to the original premise. The inhabitants of the planet Ultra dedicate themselves to the defense of justice in the universe. One of their operatives is sent to Earth, where, hiding among the people of Japan, he waits in readiness to transform into the gigantic super hero Ultraman.

0363 SERIES

SEATON DOBUTSUKI — RISU NO BANNER (*The Diary of the Animals From Seaton: Banner the Squirrel*), Nippon Animation, animal, 26 episodes, 4/7 — 9/29/1979.

Banner is a little squirrel who, following the premature death of his mother, is raised by a cat. This causes him some difficulties when going back to his world, but his capacity to adapt and his love for a beautiful female squirrel helps him reinsert himself. The captivating series is written by Toshiyuki Hashikura and directed by Akio Kuroda.

0364 SERIES

ANIMATION KIKO — MARCO POLO NO BOKEN (*The Book of Animated Travels: the Adventures of Marco Polo*), M.K./Mad House, classic, 43 episodes, 4/7/1979 — 4/5/1980.

Taken from *Milione,* written by Marco Polo, this series is the animated version of his fantastic adventures in Orient, accompanied with many historical and cultural profiles. In general, it is a very pleasant piece of work.

Kido Senshi Gundam © Nippon Sunrise.

0365 SERIES

KIDO SENSHI GUNDAM (*Gundam, the Warrior With the Mobile Armor*), Nippon Sunrise, robot/science fiction, 43 episodes, 4/7/1979 — 1/26/1980.

For many decades the Earth has been forced to send its exceeding population into space, in special self-sufficient colonies called Side, situated on asteroids orbiting around our planet. The colony Side 3, in the 68th space year, declares itself the principality of Jion, under the duke Degin Zabi, thus proclaiming its own independence. Cassoval Rem and Artasia Som, the sons of the fallen emperor Jion Zum Daiklin, disappear shortly after their father's death.

The earthly government denies political autonomy to the Zabi family. Jion thus moves to the conquest of other colonies, undertaking a war that sees the fall of many territories to the hands of the principality of Degin Zabi. During these years, constant spontaneous mutations are observed that create individuals called "new types," who possess strong ESP powers. In the year 79, a new civil war breaks out between Jion, helped by the subdued colonies and the Earth, allied with the colonies that remained faithful. During an attack on Side 7, a group of teenagers find themselves against its will, replacing the crew of the White Base, a powerful earthly war spaceship. Amuro, the 16 year old son of doctor Tem Ray, finds himself piloting the RX 78 Gundam robot. Fighting against the enemy he discovers he is a "new type." The White Base is run by Bright Noah, a 19 year old official of the earthly union, responsible for the crew, and piloted by Mirai Yashima. Inside the

Kido Senshi Gundam © Nippon Sunrise.

ship are Frau Bow, a fifteen year old girl, close friend of Amuro, who plays the role of nurse and is also assigned to communications, replacing Seira Masu. The latter is in reality Artasia Som, the heir to the past dynasty of Jion.

While the Zabi family intends to make the "New Type" the dominating race, Seira discovers that the most skillful chief commander of Jion is in reality her brother, who is secretly searching to bring the principality back to his house. Fighting alongside Amuro are Kai Shiden, pilot of the Guncannon and Hayato Kobayashi and Ryu Hosei, pilots of the Mobil Suit Guntank. After having moved the conflict to the Earth, the war returns to heaven and both factions suffer enormous losses. After one year of combat that sees the almost total destruction of Jion, the conflict resolves in favor of the Earth, also torn to pieces from the horrors of war.

Kido Senshi Gundam © Nippon Sunrise.

The series produced by Kotoku Nakagawa that consecrates Yoshikazu Yasuhiko amongst the most famous Japanese character designers, features the designs of Okawara Kunio. The direction is by Yoshiyuki Tomino.

0366 SERIES

SHIN KYOJIN NO HOSHI II (*The Star of the Kyojin II — New Series*), Tokyo Movie Shinsha, sport, 23 episodes, 4/4 — 9/29/1979.

Kyojin no hoshi is very liked by both the old and new generation. The first linked to the memories of youth, the second fascinated by a story always current that is based on the most followed sport by the Japanese people, baseball. The new series doesn't disappoint and confirms the success of TMS production but it is stopped after few episodes by the authors of the manga who consider it not respectful of the original plot.

0367 SERIES

PARIS NO ISABELLE (*Isabelle From Paris*), Dax, soap opera, 13 episodes, 4/19 —7/12/1979.

Isabelle is a girl of noble origins, involved in the French Revolution. At the beginning she ranks with the nobles, fleeing from Paris, but she later joins the side of the rebels. The finale is very tragic, with her family massacred and her brother, defender of the weak under the disguise of a masked horseman, killed by the guards while Isabelle watches it all. She is, sadly, the only survivor.

0368 SERIES

SF SAIYUKI STARZINGER II (*The Sayuki, Science Fiction Starzinger II*), Toei Doga, science fiction, 7 episodes, 7/15 — 8/26/1979.

The sequel of Aurora, Kogo Akka and Jogo's adventures is once again given to anxious viewers. Having reached the big planet and restored the galactic energy, the four young people must continue the mission. Girora's solar system, that stayed too long without the galactic energy, doesn't react to the restoration. Aurora and his horsemen must personally intervene to stop the monsters, using the energy emanating from the princess. This task is more difficult but at the end, even the Girara System returns to normal. The farewell to the princess is definitive this time. The three horsemen go back into space, but their hearts will always remain with her – especially that of Jan Kogo.

0369 SERIES

KINPATSU NO JEANY (*Jeany With the Blond Hair*), Dax, soap opera, 13 episodes, 7/19 — 10/18/1979.

Jeany is a girl who lives in the South of the United States at the time of the civil war. Used to luxury, she realizes what the living conditions of the slaves must be. Roger, her childhood friend, in love with her and enrolled in the army of the North, opens her eyes to the reality that surrounds her. The character design is by Masami Abe.

0370 SERIES

KAGAKU BOKENTAI TANSER 5 (*The Adventures of the Scientific Team Tanser 5*), Nippon Sunrise, science fiction, 34 episodes, 7/27/1979 — 3/28/1980.

The temporal patrol Tanser 5, run by Ryu, travels through time equipped with the incredible transforming automobiles. Using their own abilities, the five characters resolve more or less famous enigmas of history, like the mystery of Stonehenge or the Mohai from Easter Island. Mitsuru Suzuki realizes the character design of the series directed by Takao Yotsujin.

0371 SERIES

ENTAKU NO KISHI MONOGATARI MOERO ARTHUR (*The Story of the Knight of the Round Table: Shine Arthur*), Toei Doga, classic, 30 episodes, 9/9/1979 — 3/30/1980.

Masayuki Akehi directs the legendary deeds of Arthur Pendragon, the celtic king who reunited countless warring English kingdoms under his wisdom. The story of the cartoon, however, varies greatly from the original legend: Arthur, son of king Uther and queen Igraine, is entrusted to the care of a servant following the premature death of both his parents, to save him from his father's numerous enemies. Years go by and Arthur is already a man when an edict is proclaimed through the entire kingdom: whoever is able to extract the sword Excalibur from the rock in which it's placed will become the king of England. Arthur, amidst the scorn of the bystanders, gives it a try. To everyone's great surprise, the sacred Excalibur is extracted. The servant thus reveals to everyone, including the stunned Arthur, the truth of the young man's noble origins, showing the amazed crowd the tattoo imprinted on the shoulder of all the blue blooded princes. A handful of courageous men swear their swords to the new king: Lancelot, Passifal, Tristan – the horseman with the harp, Fiene and Guerret. Together they will face countless dangers. Takuo Noda signs the character design of the series.

0372 SERIES

KOGUMA NO MISHA (*Misha the Little Bear Cub*), Nippon Animation, animals, 26 episodes, 10/6/1979 — 3/29/1980.

Misha, the friendly little mascot of the Moscow Olympics of 1980, lives in a quiet animal village with its mother and father and is involved in entertaining experiences with other animal friends. The direction is by Yoshimichi Nitta, while the screenplay is written amongst others by Shun'ichi Yukimuro and Yoshiaki Yoshida.

0373 SERIES

KAGAKU NINJATAI GATCHAMAN F (*The Ninja Scientific Group Gatchaman Fighter*), Tatsunoko, science fiction, 48 episodes, 10/7/1979 —8/31/1980. *Eagle Riders*.

Kagaku Ninjatai Gatchaman F © Tatsunoko Pro.

This is the third and last series that features the five Gatchaman fighters, Ken, Joe, Jun, Jinpei and Ryu. Here, they face the alien Zeta and his Galactors in the final deadly challenge that sees the defeat of the enemy thanks to the extreme sacrifice of the characters who die as heroes. The direction is by Hiroshi Sasagawa, the designs based on an original story by Tatsuo Yoshida, are by Yoshitaka Amano.

0374 SERIES

TOSHI GORDIAN (*Gordian the Fighter*), Tatsunoko, robot, 73 episodes, 10/7/1979 — 2/22/1980. [*Gordian*].

A natural catastrophe is about to occur on our planet and the earthly scientists are busy looking for another planet, capable of satisfying the needs of the human race. The evil empire of Madocter proclaims itself to be the only descendants worthy of surviving the disaster, and initiate a difficult war against the earthly forces, who call upon the triple robot Gordian and his skillful pilot Daigo Otaki. Thus begins the series supervised by Shigeru Yanagigawa and directed by Masamune Ochiai that features the designs of the able Ippei Kuri on a creation by Yu Yamamoto.

0375 SERIES

MANGA — SARUTOBI SASUKE (*The Manga of the Sarutobi Sasuke*), Knack, martial arts, 24 episodes, 10/9/1979 — 4/29/1980.

The little ninja Sasuke, after having learned the secret fighting techniques of the sarutobis, attempts by every possible means to send the silent warriors from the clan of Iga away from the quiet lands in which he lives. Based on fights with magic blasts and strange spells, the series is definitely inferior to that inspired by the manga of Sanpei Shirato, with which it shouldn't be confused.

0376 SERIES

VERSAILLES NO BARA (*The Rose of Versailles*), Tokyo Movie Shinsha, historical, 40 episodes, 10/10/1979 — 9/3/1980. [*Lady Oscar*].

In the pre-revolution France, General De Jarjayes awaits with trepidation the birth of his baby, desperately hoping he will have a heir. Unfortunately however, once again the general's dream is shattered when his wife bears him yet another daughter. De Jarjayes doesn't give up in his quest. He wants a male descendant at all costs who will perpetuate the military tradition of the family. The baby girl is named Oscar, and henceforth is raised as a boy together with her faithful friend Andre Grandier, son of her wet nurse.

Oscar is assigned to the battalion in charge of protecting queen Marie Antoinette and falls in love with the fascinating Swiss count Hans Axel Von Fersel, himself in love with the queen. The situation now seems unbearable for Andre who has always been in love with Oscar and who finally decides to let her know how he feels. To the revelations is also added a tragic incident that deprives Andre of the use of one eye and, in an even more dramatic diagnosis, it is revealed that Andre will progressively lose sight also in the other eye, though he will be unhurt in appearance. Oscar isn't in much better shape – struck with consumption, she only has a few months to live.

Toshi Gordian © Tatsunoko Pro.

Versailles No Bara © Riyoko Ikeda / TMS

The spark is struck with the scandal of the necklace, and the fire of the revolution soon flares up the whole country. Andre is the first to side with the people. The course of events also push Oscar to take the defense of the people. Before leaving, in the woods around Paris, Oscar finally lets Andre know that she has always loved him. The dawn is near and with it, the moment of battle. Andre is the first to be killed, leaving Oscar in deep despair. On July 14th 1789, the people take over the Bastille. Oscar is also present, at the commands of her soldiers. The cannons fire at her command, making her an easy target for the guards of the Bastille. Oscar dies soon after without witnessing the conclusion of the Revolution that sees the beheading of the royal family and the lapidation of count Fersen. The story is taken from Riyoko Ikeda's manga, specialized in historical dramas. The direction is entrusted in the first part to tadao Nagahama and in the second part to Osamu Dezaki, the set designs are by Ken Kawai. Yoshimi Shinozaki worked on the subject and the screenplay. The soundtrack is entrusted to Koji Magahino.

0377 SERIES

UCHU KUBO BLUE NOAH (*Blue Noah, the Space Aircraft Carrier*), Office Academy, science fiction, 24 episodes, 10/13/1979 —3/30/1980.

Following the success of Uchu Senkan Yamato, the producer Yoshinobu Nishizaki made this new series, a clear attempt at imitation of the previous series, in collaboration with Yoshiyuki Hane for the character design and Kazuyori Tanahashi for the direction. The crew of the Blue Noah, a powerful war submarine, is headed towards the Bermuda triangle where there is a base willing to transform the submarine into a spaceship capable of facing the aliens menacing the Earth.

0378 SERIES

SASURAI NO SHOJO NELL (*Nell, the Young Wanderer*), Dax, soap opera, 26 episodes, 10/25/1979 — 4/24/1980.

Little Nell manages an antique store with her grandfather. One day, however, the old man loses all his possessions through gambling and is forced to escape with his granddaughter from the creditor who also wants Nell to marry his grandson. The destination of the two characters is Paradise, the village in which the young woman's brother and mother live. The series directed by Keinosuke Tsuchiya, who belongs to the cycle of Romantic Theater, is produced by Yoshio Kabashima. The music is by Harumi Ibe.

0379 SPECIAL

GANBARE! BOKURA NO HIT & RUN (*Come On! Our Hit & Run*), Nippon Animation, 85 min., 2/18.

0380 SPECIAL

MAEGAMI TARO (*Taro From the Tuft*), Nippon Animation, 70 min., 4/29.

After years of sacrifices and bitterness, an old couple is finally blessed with the arrival of a child they name Taro. The television special features his adventures.

0381 SPECIAL

KAITO LUPIN — 813 NO NAZO (*Lupin the Thief and the Enigma of the 813*), Tatsunoko for Herald Ent., police story, 90 min., 5/5.

Kaito Lupin: 813 No Nazo
© Herald Enterprise • Tatsunoko Pro.

The special is taken from the novel 813, *The Double Life of Arsene Lupin*, written in 1910 by Maurice Leblanc. Here, the gentleman thief dresses as a policeman and is so successful in his double life that he becomes, as Lenormand, head of the Surete.

0382 SPECIAL
TONDEMONEZUMI DAIKATSUYAKU (*The Great Challenge of Tondemonezumi*), Nippon Animation, animals, 90 min., 6/30.

The main character is a mouse in a perennial fight with his scariest enemy, the evil cat of the neighborhood that is desperately seeking to catch him. The breathtaking pursuits and the high-speed sequences of events are at the base of this comedy special.

0383 SPECIAL
ASHITA NO ELEVEN TACHI (*The Eleven of Tomorrow*), Toei Doga, sport, 85 min., 7/1.

In 1979 Japan hosts the soccer world championship. The technical direction of the local national is entrusted to Kantoku Matsumoto. Toei took advantage of this particular moment to feature this sport film directed by Kozo Morishita. The main character is Jiro Ipponji, a horse loving young man who lives on a ranch with his sister. One day, Shin Mizuki and Matsumoto the trainer make him an offer to join the Japanese soccer team. After some thought, he accepts, becoming a talented forward.

0384 SPECIAL
UCHU SENKAN YAMATO: ARATANARU TABIDASHI (*Yamato the Space Cruiser: the New Departure*), Office Academy, science fiction, 120 min., 7/14. *The Space Cruiser Yamato: The New Voyage*.

An army of mysterious aliens cause the explosion of Gamilas to obtain the precious mineral Iskandarium. This causes the blast of the twin planet of Gamilas out of orbit: Iskander. Deslar becomes the ally of the earthly crew of Yamato. Together they defeat the alien threat.

0385 SPECIAL
MARINE EXPRESS (*id.*), Tezuka, science fiction, 120 min., 8/26.

Created by professor Nasenkoff of the Academy of Sciences, the Marine Express is tested in an inaugural trip in which it must travel 25 000 kilometers in 41 hours at the speed of 600 km/h to reach the peninsula of Ki in Japan, leaving from Los Angeles. Three people accompany the professor on this first trip: his son Rock, a train engineer, a funny looking investigator searching for a weapon trafficker and the little Adam, youngest son of Nasenkoff that will later reveal himself as an android. Because of a terrorist attack, the train is thrown through the tunnel at such a high speed that it breaks the sound barrier, catapulting the passengers into ancient times on Easter Island. There, Rock and his friends will have to help the queen maintain her throne against plots by the evil and powerful magician Shalak. This film tracks Tezuka's most famous characters, including the famous Tetsuwan Atom playing Adam, Mitsume Ga Toru, the role of the magician, princess Saphire, the role of the queen who has with her the lion Leo from *Jungle Taitei*. Also present are Don Drakula playing Shalak's assistant and doctor Black Jack who is in every film by the late talented author. The screenplay is obviously by Osamu Tezuka who also takes care of the direction with Osamu Dezaki and the music is by Yuji Ono.

Space Battleship Yamato: The New Voyage

Marine Express © Tezuka Production.

Intro
-1962
1963
1964
1965
1966
1967
1968
1969
1970
1971
1972
1973
1974
1975
1976
1977
1978
1979
1980
1981
1982
1983
1984
1985
1986
1987
1988
Index

Jean Valjean Monogatari © Toei Animation.

0386 SPECIAL

JEAN VALJEAN MONOGATARI (*The Story of Jean Valjean*), Toei Doga, classic, 75 min., 9/15. [*Les Misérables*].

After escaping from jail, Jean Valjean finds refuge with the bishop of Digne, Myriel. Moved by his generosity, the ex-prisoner works on following the right path. So he changes his name to Madeleine and he becomes a mayor, getting involved in helping the needy amongst which are Fantine and the little Cosette whom he takes care of after the death of her mother. When he is forced to reveal his true identity to save a man unjustly accused, Jean Valjean is arrested again. Soon however, he escapes again to save Cosette from the sinister Thenardier. Under the name of Fauchelevent, he begins a new life while Cosette marries the young republican Marius. A nice transposition of Victor Hugo's Les Miserables.

0387 SPECIAL

ANNA FRANK MONOGATARI (*The Story of Anne Frank*), Nippon Animation, biography, 75 min., 9/28.

The young Jewish protagonist is forced to emigrate to Amsterdam with her family to escape the nazi persecution. She finds refuge in a hiding place and, between June 1942 and August 1944, she writes her famous diary. Found by enemy soldiers, the Frank family is deported to the concentration camp of Bergen Belsen where all the members of the family are executed, except for Anne's father. The girl's biography is, in this case, made into a moving film produced by Nippon Animation.

0388 SPECIAL

DAIKYORYU JIDAI (*The Era of the Big Dinosaurs*), Toei Doga, adventure, 90 min., 10/7.

Three young people, nature and animal lovers, are approached by a mysterious UFO that, through a leap in time, brings them into prehistoric times. The main characters thus begin a difficult cohabitation in a strange world filled with ferocious beasts, undisputed rulers of the Earth of the past.

0389 SPECIAL

ASHINAGA OJISAN (*Daddy Longlegs*), Tatsunoko for Herald Ent., musical comedy, 69 min., 10/10.

Enriched by a splendid soundtrack, the special offers the remake of an American film from the 50s, starring the famous actor/dancer Fred Astaire and the fascinating Leslie Caron. The story is that of Judi, a thirteen year old orphan who, thanks to a mysterious and eccentric millionaire, leaves the orphanage to enter into one of the United States' most prestigeous colleges.

Ashinaga Ojisan © Herald Enterprise • Tatsunoko Pro.

0390 SPECIAL

GINGA TETSUDO 999 KIMI WA SENSHI NO YO NI IKIRAREKU KA (*Galactic Railway 999: Can You Live Like a Soldier?*), Toei Doga, science fiction, 120 min., 10/11.

The special is made up of the expansion of two television episodes that make up "The fossilized warriors." The only survivor of a planet whose inhabitants have been changed into rocks steals Tetsuro's pass. The young main character risks having to give up his trip, but as luck would have it, he manages to recover the precious ticket.

0391 SPECIAL

CAPTAIN FUTURE (*id.*), Toei Doga, science fiction, 25 min. [*Capitaine Flam*].

THIRD PART

The Eighties

CHAPTER NINETEEN: 1980

The 80s were not a decade of innovation. Rather, they solidified the strides made in the 70s, with remarkable artistic advances by some of the greater illustrators of the time, including Reiji Matsumoto. His name is linked equally to the two worlds of manga and anime, and 1980 was the year that heralded his enormous success. The space sagas that made him famous were sublime in their attention to technological detail. Matsumoto also made *Marine Snow no densetsu*, an original animated feature film, centered on a denunciation of the uncontrollable technological development. The "adul" themes, which invite both thought and reflection, were enriched with the delicate, poetic elements that make Matsumoto's complex screenplays real works of art.

Ginga Tetsudo 999 was paid a number of tributes during the decade, including *Glass no Clea*, a feature film, and two television specials (*Eien no tabibito Emeraldas* and *Kimi wa haha no yo ni aiseru ka*) expanded from the television episodes. This was also the case for the previous *Kimi wa Senshi no Yoni Ikirareruka*, in which Tetsuro Hoshino continues his space trips with his mysterious companion Maeter. *Uchu senkan Yamato*, Matsumoto's first series transposed into animation, continued in the third season of the series, and is remade into what would be the second last feature film about the courageous crew: *Yamato yo towa ni*.

The robots that captured the imagination of Japanese television viewers are still a very popular genre. Featured as main characters of a large number of series and film productions, 'giant robots' underwent a slow but constant change that began in 1979 with *Kido senshi Gundam*. The unification of classic stories and a new sense of realism continued, albeit to a lesser extent, with *Uchu senshi Baldios*. The Baldios is, in fact, a unique specimen built to defend the Earth from enemy attacks, but he joins the ranks of the normal armies. The authors introduced a rich element of realism to the script, aptly illustrating the dramas and horrors present in any war.

Their focus still firmly within the robot genre, the Nippon Sunrise presented the series *Muteki robot Trider G7*. In this case, the setting and the story are centered around a somewhat less dramatic issue, their focus decisively social – the main character, in fact, is a student who lost his father and who works to support his family – but the humor that is integral to the story makes the series brilliant, even in the constant and recurring fights that take place in each episode.

The sport series conquer new ground in the 80s thanks to *Tsurikichi Sanpei*, that tackled the previously unexplored world of fishing. The repetitive episodes, taken from Takao Yaguchi's manga, offer not only an intriguing depiction of the underwater fauna, with species presented with unique attention and precision, but also introduce the complex skills that the main character learns from his wise grandfather and other experts without the super-powered 'special' skills so prevalent in this kind of anime.

Muteki Robot Trider G7 © Sunrise

Finally, Osamu Tezuka produced a new spectacular film on the legendary *Phoenix*, that takes the character of Gordo through a desperate search for the mythical birds.

0392 FILM

ASHITA NO JOE (*Joe From Tomorrow*), Mushi, sport, 152 min., 3/8.

While waiting for the second series, which features Joe's return to boxing, this very long montage of episodes from the first series is produced with renewed dubbing to bring new fans up to speed with the adventures of the young boxer.

0393 FILM

DORAEMON – NOBITA NO KYORYU (*Doraemon: Nobita's Dinosaur*), Shin'ei Doga, humor, 92 min., 3/15.

Doraemon and Nobita use the time machine once again, to go to prehistoric times with their friends. During the brief visit, Nobita finds a big egg that he brings back with him. Acting as mother, he sits on the egg and when it hatches, he decides to take care of the cute little dinosaur that emerges. The animal grows too quickly, however, generating problems for the two main characters.

0394 FILM

IENAKI KO (*Child Without Family*), Tokyo Movie Shinsha, classic, 95 min., 3/15.

For the cinematic transposition of this latest version of *Without Family*, Tokyo Movie Shinsha uses the splendid sequences of the animated series, designed by Akio Sugino.

0395 FILM

HINO TORI 2772 – AI NO COSMOZONE (*Bird Of Fire 2772: The Cosmic Zone Of Love*), Tezuka, science fiction, 121 min., 3/15. *Phoenix 2772*.

Hino Tori 2772 © Tezuka Production

The saga of the *Phoenix*, by Osamu Tezuka, continues in this majestic science fiction fairy tale. The authorities in control of the world's energy don't care about the concept of ecological balance, putting the Earth on the verge of self-destruction. The young Gordo leaves to search for the mythical bird of fire that makes its nest in deep space, and whose blood seems to have the power to give immortality. When he realizes he won't be able to catch it, Gordo surrenders to the Phoenix, who suggests a trade. If Gordo agrees to sacrifice his life, it will work a wonder and Gordo and the Earth will come back to life to begin a new era. Directed by the skillful Taku Sugiyama, the movie features the animation direction of Noboru Ishiguro and Kazuko Nakamura, weaving together the mythological elements with extremely avant-garde ones. The film owes its success to Iwao Yamaki's photography and Yasuo Higushi's soundtrack.

0396 FILM

MORI WA IKITEIRU (*The Forest that Lives*), Toei Doga, fairy tale, 64 min., 3/15. [*La Forêt Enchantée*].

The young Ania lives with her perfidious godmother and an ugly stepsister in a mountain hut surrounded by luxuriant vegetation. A nice and generous girl, Ania is forced to constantly put up with her family's tortures and she often finds refuge in her day dreams. Her encounter with a young man, who turns out to be the spirit of April and who lives with the other Months in the forest, changes many things...

0397 FILM

TIME BOKAN SERIES – ZENDAMAN (*The Time Machine Series – Zendaman*), Tatsunoko, robot/humor, 25 min., 3/15.

0398 FILM

HANA NO KO LUN LUN KONNICHI WA SAKURA NO KUNI (*Lun Lun, the Girl From the Flowers: Hello Village of the Cherries*), Toei Doga, magic, 25 min., 3/15.

0399 FILM

GINGA TETSUDO 999 GLASS NO CLEA (*Galactic Railway 999: Clea Made of Glass*), Toei Doga, science fiction, 152 min., 3/15.

Clea, a crystalline maid, works in the diner car of the famous space train to earn the money she needs to be returned to human form, after her mother had her placed into a crystal body.

0400 FILM

TERRA E (*Towards the Earth*), Toei Doga, science fiction, 120 min., 4/26. *Toward The Terra*.

Atraxia, a planet 20,000 light years from Earth, is under totalitarian control, a power maintained by an ESP system used to locate and destroy the Mu, a race of mutants with special powers. During a test, 14 year old Tomi discovers that he is a Mu and is saved from extermination by others in the same condition. Embarking on a spaceship, Tomi leaves for the Earth to contribute to the fight against oppression. The film is taken from Keiko Takemiya's original manga.

0401 FILM

GANBARE!! TABUCHIKUN!! GEKITO PENNANT RACE (*Come on Tabuchi!! The Difficult Challenge of the Championship*), Tokyo Movie Shinsha, humor, 90 min., 5/10.

0402 FILM

MAHO SHOJO LALABEL – UMI GA YOBU NATSUYASUMI (*Lalabel, the Magic Girl: Invitation to the Sea for Summer Vacation*), Toei Doga, magic, 25 min., 7/12.

0403 FILM

HAHA O TAZUNETE SANZANRI (*12,000 km in Search of His Mother*), Nippon Animation, classic, 107 min., 7/19.

A montage about the adventures of Marco, taken from the 1976 series.

0404 FILM

JUIPPIKI NO NEKO (*The Eleven Cats*), Group Tack, humor, 83 min., 7/19.

The main characters of the movie are eleven cats involved in the strenuous hunt for an enormous fish that quietly lives in a Japanese lake. The shrewdness of the cats is put to the test in a succession of frenetic attempts and incredible pursuits.

0405 FILM

MAKOTOCHAN (*id.*), Tokyo Movie Shinsha, humor, 90 min., 7/26.

Terra E ©1980 Toei Animation Co., Ltd.

Be Forever Yamato ©1995 Voyager Entertainment, Inc

Cyborg 009 © Toei

0406 FILM

YAMATO UCHU SENKAN TOWA NI (*Forever Yamato*), Academy Seisaku, science fiction, 148 min., 8/2. *Be Forever Yamato.*

The same aliens presented in the 1978 film plant a bomb on Earth to destroy the human race. The courageous Earther crew take off on board the space cruiser Yamato to reach the enemy planet and deactivate the device controlled by the aliens.

0407 FILM

GANBARE!! TABUCHIKUN – A TSUPPARI JINSEI (*Come on Tabuchi!! This is Your Life*), Tokyo Movie Shinsha, humor, 91 min., 12/13.

0408 FILM

CYBORG 009 CHO GINGA NO DENSETSU (*Cyborg 009: The Legend of the Super Galaxy*), Toei Doga, science fiction, 130 min., 12/20. *Cyborg 009: Legend of the Super Galaxy.*

0409 SERIES

KIRIN ASHITA NO CALENDAL (*The Almanac*), Office Uni, 1306 episodes, 1/1/1980 – 10/6/1984.

0410 SERIES

TOM SAWYER NO BOKEN (*The Adventures of Tom Sawyer*), Nippon Animation, classic, 51 episodes, 1/6 – 12/28/1980. [*Tom Sawyer*].

A meticulous adaptation of Mark Twain's *Tom Sawyer*, this animated series features the adventures of the famous American rascal. Between childish pranks and dangerous adventures, Tom and his friends spend eventful and happy days on the Mississippi.

0411 SERIES

MORI NO YOKI WA KOBITOTACHI BELFY TO LILIBIT (*Belfy and Lilibit, the Happy Gnomes of the Forest*), Tatsunoko, children, 26 episodes, 1/7 – 6/30/1980.

Belfy and Lilibit are two tiny elves, the main characters of this "quiet" series for children created by Shigeru Yanagigawa and Tomoyuki Miyata and directed by Masayuki Hayashi. Living in a village inhabited by their own kind, the two young elves learn to coexist with the natural environment through using it and respecting it, building their cultural awareness and wisdom. Akiko Shimomoto is the character designer.

0412 SERIES

NILLS NO FUSHIGINA TABI (*Nill's Marvelous Trip*), Studio Pierrot for Gakken, fairy tale, 52 episodes, 1/8/1980 – 3/17/1981. [*Nils Holgerson*].

Nills Holgerrson, an unyielding rascal, is punished for his bad habit of being mean to animals. Reduced to a height of only a few centimeters, Nills learns to communicate with the animals and he comes to know their joys and fears, finally repenting for the evil he did to them. This is Studio Pierrot's first production.

0413 SERIES

MAETERLINCK NO AOITORI – TILTIL MITYL NO BOKEN RYOKO (*Maeterlinck's The Blue Bird: the Adventurous journey of Tiltil and Mityl*), Academy Seisaku, classic, 26 episodes, 1/9 – 7/9/1980. [*L'Oiseau Bleu*].

The fairy tale of the blue bird that brings happiness, from Maurice Maeterlinck's operetta, relives its most significant moments in this imaginative anime by Yoshinobu Nishizaki. Thrown into a fairy tale world where animals and vegetables can talk, Mityl and Tiltil, a young brother and sister, search for the Blue Bird, who carries a cure for their sick mother. In this cartoon, directed by Hiroshi Sasagawa and written by Keisake Fujikawa, in a departure from the original story, the children return home at the end of each episode.

0414 SERIES
TIME BOKAN SERIES: TIME PATROL TAI OTASUKEMAN (*The Time Machine Series: the Team of Otasukeman's Time Patrol*), Tatsunoko, robot/humor, 53 episodes, 2/2/1980 – 1/31/1981.

As in all the chapters of the time machine saga, the villains are the real main characters of this story, created by Shigeru Yanagigawa, Ippei Kuri and Tomoyuki Miyata and directed by Hiroshi Sasagawa. Atasha, Dovalski and Sekovitch, the members of the new trio, want to change the course of history to bring the mysterious Tommanomanto to power. As usual, two defenders of justice are on their trail: the intrepid story savers Hikaru and Nana, who fight aboard their armed spaceship. The character design is by Yoshitaka Amano and the mecha design is by Kunio Okawara, who was made famous by his work on *Gundam*.

0415 SERIES
MUTEKI ROBOT TRIDER G 7 (*Trider G 7, The Invincible Robot*), Nippon Sunrise, robot, 50 episodes, 2/2/1980 – 1/24/1981.

After the death of his father, Watta Takeo inherits a space transport company, becoming president while he is still in high school. Soon, however, he begins to use his working robot Trider G 7 to hinder the pirate raids of a strange space empire. Torn between his daily life, with the monotony of home and school, and fighting in grand science fiction battles, the hero injects a subtle level of humor into the series. Supervised by Masanori Sasaki, *Robot Trader* is very pleasant to watch. The mecha design is by Kunio Okawara and the character design is by Nobuyoshi Sasakado.

0416 SERIES
FUTAGO NO MONCICCI (*The Moncicci Twins*), Ashi, animals, 2/4 – 8/1/1980. Moncicci.

Known in Italy because of the little stuffed animals, the Moncicis are the 'tender little monkeys,' characters in this overly sentimental and forgettable children series.

0417 SERIES
MAHO SHOJO LALABEL (*Lalabel the Magic Girl*), Toei Doga, magic, 49 episodes, 2/15/1980 – 2/27/1981.

The new series in the "magic" genre is directed by Hiroshi Shidara, famous for Candy Candy, and created by Eiko Fujiwara. Having come to Earth from the land of witches with a magic suitcase stolen from Biscus the magician, Lalabel lives in the house of an old couple and begins her life amongst humans secretly using her magical powers to defend herself against the spells of the magician who wants to take his suitcase back. Life in our world stimulates Lalabel's curiosity, and she writes everything she has learned in her diary. The soundtrack is by Taku Izumi.

Muteki Robot Trider G7 © Sunrise

Uchu Taitei God Sigma © Toei

0418 SERIES

UCHU TAITEI GOD SIGMA (*God Sigma, the Space Emperor*), Academy Seisaku for Toei Co./Toei Agency, robot, 50 episodes, 3/19/1980 – 3/25/1981.

The Earth, having reached an advanced state of technological development, is forced to face problems of overpopulation and an energy crisis. At Trinity City, an immense earthly base, studies are conducted to discover the secret of a potent form of energy able to satisfy the needs of the entire world. Unfortunately. the empire of Elda is determined to steal the formula and launches vicious attacks against our planet. The only defense against the aliens comes from Trinity City in the form of the powerful God Sigma, formed through the bonding of three robots, as in the best tradition of Japanese science fiction. The new series is supervised by Takeyoshi Kanda for the first part, with Katsuhiko Udagawa for character designs.

0419 SERIES

MU NO HAKUGEI (*The White Whale From Mu*), Tokyo Movie Shinsha, science fiction, 26 episodes, 4/4 – 9/26/1980.

In the past, two now-vanished continents, Mu and Atlantis, ruled the seas. The former was inhabited by a just and courageous people, while the latter wanted supremacy at all costs. The people of Mu, unprepared to face a war, put its trust in their wise king RaMu, who sacrificed his own continent to defeat the enemy's army. After 30,000 years, Atlantis returns from its exile outside of space and time. The human race is not defenseless, and the white whale, who has kept the spirit of the wise RaMu, comes to the rescue from the abyss. With the help of Earthly children, reincarnated from certain Mu inhabitants, the immense sea mammal is now ready to face the menace. This brilliant series is created by Motoo Fukuo under the design supervision of Takao Kozai and the direction of the talented Tetsuo Imazawa.

0420 SERIES

SUE CAT (*id.*), Knack, soap opera, 40 episodes, 4/6 – 12/28/1980.

0421 SERIES

MOERO ARTHUR – HAKUBA NO OJI (*Shine Arthur! The Prince With the White Horse*), Toei Doga, classic, 22 episodes, 4/6 – 9/21/1980.

Remade with inevitable changes, the animated story of King Arthur obtained little success in Japan or Italy. Takuo Noda's armor designs are strange in that he makes them similar to those of Japanese samurai. In this second series, directed by Kozo Morishita and Akinori Orai, Arthur – hiding his true identity under the guise of a peasant – undertakes a long and difficult journey to combat a band of evil Vikings who, under the guidance of King Lavik, try to conquer Camelot. During the journey he is joined by two new companions in search of adventure, Bossman and Pete.

0422 SERIES

TSURIKICHI SANPEI (*Sanpei, Passionate Fisherman*), Nippon Animation, sport, 109 episodes, 4/7/1980 – 6/28/1982. [*Paul Le Pêcheur*].

Adapted from Takao Yaguchi's manga, under the direction of Eiji Okabe for the first part and Yoshimichi Nitta for the second, Sanpei Nihira, the fantastic fisher boy, invents all the techniques possible to win a fishing tournament to catch the biggest fish in the most remote Japanese lakes. The moral presented here is the need for reliance on one's skills, not on external factors.

Tsurikichi Sanpei © Nippon Animation Co., Ltd

0423 SERIES

GANBARE! GONBE (*Come On, Gonbe!*), Tsuchida, animals, 112 episodes, 4/14 – 9/30/1980.

0424 SERIES

KUKKOKE KNIGHT DON DE LA MANCHA (*Don de la Mancha, the Crazy Horserider*), Ashi, classic, 23 episodes, 4/15 – 9/23/1980.

Ashi's insane parody of Don Quihote features the already-strange character by Miguel de Cervantes. Set in an undefined era – medieval horse riders and science fiction machines alternate – the visionary character must deal with the whims of a whining Dulcinea who sends him to face the worst dangers to impress her father. Blinded by his love for the young woman, "Don de la Mancha" throws himself head first into the exhilarating adventures, always with a disasterous outcome that leaves the girl's father upset.

0425 SERIES

DENSETSU KYOJIN IDEON (*The Legend of Ideon the Giant God*), Nippon Sunrise, robot, 38 episodes, 5/8/1980 – 1/30/1981.

Ideon, the gigantic god, brings the human race together with the Buff clan, resulting in a terrible war. This spectacular space saga shows the death and the rebirth of the human race in a succession of dramatic turns of events that culminate with the birth of a baby, a symbol of the new union of the two civilizations.

0426 SERIES

UCHU SENSHI BALDIOS (*Baldios the Space Warrior*), Ashi, robot, 39 episodes (only 31 were broadcast), 6/30/1980 – 1/25/1981.

A young man, born on S1, a world demolished by radioactivity, escapes the persecutions of Gattler the dictator and, with a dimensional leap, he reaches the Earth. Marin then becomes the main pilot of the Baldios, a powerful robot built to face the pressing alien attacks. The aliens, incapable of gaining any ground by fighting, make use of strategy and begin a process of thawing out the Earth's glaciers. Only then do they realize that the Earth is no other than the past of S1, as they accidentally traveled through time instead of dimensions. To the final catastrophe is added the awkward love/hate relationship between Marin and Aphrodia, commander of the S1 Army. The screenplay is by Akiyoshi Sakai and Junzo Toriumi amongst others, and the designs are by Osamu Kamijo

0427 SERIES

GANBARE! GENKI (*Come On Genki!*), Toei Doga, sport, 35 episodes, 7/16/1980 – 4/1/1981.

Taken from Yu Koyama's manga and directed by Taro Rin, this dramatic story set in the world of boxing features the little Genki and his father as main characters. A widower, the young child's father decides to become a boxing champion to earn enough to support his son. As destiny would have it, because of his poor health, he takes a powerful punch during a match and dies. From that day, Genki's aim has been to defeat his father's «murderer» in a regular boxing match.

0428 SERIES
KAIBUTSUKUN (*The Little Kaibutsu*), Shin'ei Doga, grotesque, 47 episodes, 9/2/1980 – 9/28/1982.

Fujiko Fujio's little rubbery prince of monsters who first appeared in 1968 makes a comeback. Once again, the little demon and his servant friends Wolf, Frankie and Dracula get into trouble with disturbing regularity. This new series features Ken Kawai for the set design and Masayuki Honda for the design supervision.

0429 SERIES
TONDEMO SENSHI MUTEKING (*Muteking, the Surprising Warrior*), Tatsunoko, science fiction/humor, 56 episodes, 9/7 – 9/27/1980.

Moving slightly away from the «Time Machine» series, the Tatsunoko presents another parody of Japanese action comics. In this case, the Tako band, four funny looking octopuses who want to take possession of the world, try to subdue the human race by accentuating their faults. Takoro, a sheriff, pursues the notorious band on their own planet with the help of Lynn, a young American man who is able to change into Muteking with a magical breath. His particular superhero power is to fight well on roller skates. The character design is taken care of by Ippei Kuri and Ahiko Shimomoto, while the direction is by Shotaro Hara.

Tetsuwan Atom © Tezuka Production

0430 SERIES
OJAMANGA YAMADAKUN (*Little Yamada, the troublemaker of Manga*), Erald, humor, 100 episodes, 9/28/1980 – 10/10/1982.

0431 SERIES
TETSUWAN ATOM (*Iron-Arm Atom*), Tezuka, science fiction, 52 episodes, 10/1/1980 – 12/23/1981. *Astroboy.*

Osamu Tezuka's most famous character comes back in a better version. Once again, the little child-robot with human feelings and an indestructible body, works to resolve mysteries and to hinder the plans of insane scientists and monstrous aliens.

0432 SERIES
TETSUJIN 28 GO (*Man of Steel 28*), Tokyo Movie Shinsha, robot, 46 episodes, 10/3/1980 – 9/25/1981. *New Gigantor.*

Produced by Yutaka Fujioka, this is the remake of the old science fiction series from 1963 that had introduced the theme of the giant fighting robot in animation for the first time, piloted, even by remote control, by a human being. The major cleanup in the designs by Kin'ichiro Suzuki and the renovated design by Minoru Maeda earn points for the series directed by Tetsuo Imazawa, even though the success was minimal. The subject is taken from Mitsutero Yokohama's comic strip, rewritten amongst others by Keisuke Fujisawa, while the backdrops are by Mitsuru Saotome. The soundtrack is by Yasuaki Shimizu.

Tetsujin 28 Go © Hikari Prod. / TMS

0433 SERIES

HOERO! BUN BUN (*Bark, Bun Bun!*), Wako, animal, 39 episodes, 10/9/1980 – 7/9/1981.

Bun Bun is a little dog who's been taken away from its mother. With the help of two older stray dogs, it begins an exhausting search that will bring him to experience various adventures, caused in major part by the difficulties a dog faces as it tries to survive in a world of humans. Once again, a studio of Japanese animation comes up with a series whose main theme is the search for a parent. It seems odd to set it in an animal world, as happened with the most famous series *Konchu monogatari minashigo Hutch*.

0434 SERIES

UCHU SENKAN YAMATO III (*Yamato III, the Space Cruiser*), Office Academy, science fiction, 25 episodes, 10/11/1980 – 4/4/1981. *Starblazers: The Bolar Wars*.

Once again, Susumu Kodai is involved, along with the entire crew of the glorious space battleship Yamato, in saving the world. The threat in this case comes from the sun that, having been hit by a missile, is about to become a supernova. The courageous space travelers must prevent the explosion, which would destroy life as we know it.

0435 SERIES

MANGA KOTOWAJA JITEN (*The Illustrated Encyclopedia of Proverbs*), Tsuchida, documentary, 88 episodes, 10/11/1980 – 6/27/1982.

Each episode is composed of three segments of 10 minutes each, illustrating traditional Japanese proverbs.

0436 SERIES

ASHITA NO JOE II (*Joe From Tomorrow II*), Tokyo Movie Shinsha, sport, 47 episodes, 10/13/1980 – 8/31/1981.

After having caused the death of his great rival Riki in the ring, the young rebel boxer is so distraught that he decides to abandon boxing forever. Drawing on the support of his friends and companions, however, Joe goes back to the ring with new energy. This second series presents a dramatic and unexpected ending: in a final decisive encounter, Joe receives a violent punch that is fatal. The bell rings, the young man sits on his bench in the corner and, smiling, he dies, leaving an incredible void for the numerous fans who faithfully followed the series.

0437 SPECIAL

NODOKAMORI NO DOBUTSU DAISAKUSEN (*The Great Strategy of the Animals in the Woods of Nodoka*), Nippon Animation, 75 min., 2/3.

0438 SPECIAL

CAPTAIN (*id.*), Eiken, sport, 80 min., 4/2.

0439 SPECIAL

HOERO! BUN BUN (*Bark, Bun Bun!*), Wako, Animals, 90 min., 4/2.

Bun Bun is the name of a friendly puppy dog that has been abandoned by its owner, a trainer of fighting dogs, intending to build the dog's strength and endurance. Bun Bun tries everything to get back home and find its mother. This special precedes the animated series by a few months.

Ginga Tetsudo 999 Eien no Tabibito Emeraldas
© Toei Doga

0440 SPECIAL

GINGA TETSUDO 999 EIEN NO TABIBITO EMERALDAS (*Galactic Railway 999: Emeraldas the Eternal Traveler*), Toei Doga, science fiction, 120 min., 4/3.

An expansion of the television episode dedicated to Emeraldas the lonely traveler, this special is a new testament to Reiji Matsumoto's common universe. An android created by the space pirates learns how to transform herself into a new Emeraldas to take the place of the real one, and kidnaps Maeter by hijacking the Galaxy Express on a nearby planet. The android desperately wants to avenge the honor of the real Emeraldas, who hadn't succeeded in beating Tetsuro's companion in a previous encounter.

0441 SPECIAL

WAKAKUSA MONOGATARI (*The Story of the Little Women*), Toei Doga, classic, 90 min., 5/3.

Another animated adaptation of Louisa May Alcott's famous novel *Little Women*.

0442 SPECIAL

MANGA NIHON MUKASHI BANASHI – HI NO KUNI MONOGATARI (*Ancient Japanese Tales: the Story of the Land of Fire*), Tack, fairy tale, 85 min., 5/5.

0443 SPECIAL

MARINE SNOW NO DENSETSU (*The Legend of Marine Snow*), Now Kikkaku, science fiction, 114 min., 8/12.

After having earned success with animated productions featuring a small number of characters, Leiji Matsumoto tries to capture the public's interest with a new project. The degradation of the cultural and environmental conditions of the world, caused by distorted technological development, is the focus once again of this work of social commentary. The film offers a marvelous examination of the conflict between the inhabitants of the Earth and those of the Sea, and warns the young audience against pollution and ecological imbalance.

0444 SPECIAL

YAMI NO TEIO KYUKETSUKI DRACULA (*Dracula the Vampire, the Emperor of Darkness*), Toei Doga, classic, 120 min., 8/19.

Horror stories are, by this point, a standard in Japanese animation. After having opened the road with the ghosts and classic spirits of Japanese mythology, the studios then turned towards the most famous monsters of Western literature. In this case, the Toei Doga produces Dracula, setting the plot in our day and making the famous vampire combat a small group of amateur vampire killers. Presented more like a desperate being persecuted by a hostile populace than the traditionally horrible bloodsucking monster, Dracula redeems himself at the end by saving a number of children from a zombie vampire attack, during which he suicidally wields a cross as a weapon.

0445 SPECIAL

CAPTAIN II (*id.*), Eiken, sport, 8/20.

0446 SPECIAL

IKKYUSAN – OABARE YANCHA HIME (*Ikkyusan, Princess Putiferio*), Toei Doga, historical, 8/25.

0447 SPECIAL

FOOMON (*id.*), Tezuka, science fiction, 120 min., 8/31.

Once again, Tezuka expounds on the themes dear to him, and in Foomon he once again returns to a discussion of the environment. A strange race of monochromatic luminous little beings gifted with extra-sensory powers – the Foomons – wants to build a modern "Noah's Ark" to save the earthly animals from an imminent planetary catastrophe, leaving the "undeserving" humans to fend for themselves. A young Foomon woman named Rococo, having spent time with humans, understands that not all are evil and she tries to save them as well. Failing, and abandoned by her own, she sacrifices herself to save the Earth and all its inhabitants from the disaster. The feature film (produced by Hideko Takei and Takayuki Matsumani and with music by Yuji Ono) is taken from one of Tezuka's first works, *Kitarubekisekai* (*The Next World*).

Foomon © Tezuka Production

0448 SPECIAL

GINGA TETSUDO 999 – KIMI WA HAHA NO YO NI AISERU KA (*Galactic Railway 999: Can You Love as a Mother?*), Toei Doga, science fiction, 120 min., 10/2.

A remake of the episode *Artemis* from *The Transparent Sea* is the basis for this special. The tragedy of the young daughter of an amoeba that wants to become a human being is portrayed with much more sensitivity in this special than in the original television episode.

0449 SPECIAL

NIJUSHI NO HITOMI (*The 24 Teacher's Pets*), Tokyo Movie Shinsha, soap opera, 10/10.

The special presents the day-to-day story of Oishi, a wise school teacher, and the twelve students who live on a small island of the Japanese archipelago.

0450 SPECIAL

BOTCHAN (*id.*), Tokyo Movie Shinsha, humor, 90 min., 6/13.

One day, Botchan, a young teacher, moves to Matsuyama – a little mountain village. Thanks to her wisdom and friendliness she captures the hearts of the inhabitants and her lively pupils. The special is an adaptation of the biography of Soseki Natsume, here given a warm touch of humor.

CHAPTER TWENTY: 1981

1981 was a fundamental year for Japanese animation. *Urusei Yatsura*, taken from Rumiko Takahashi's popular manga, revealed itself as the surprise breakthrough of the year. As in the manga version, the series displays the insane lives of Lamu the beautiful alien and Ataru Moroboshi, a young high school student. The series was a situation comedy of the finest sort, ridiculing the customs and habits of the Japanese people. Boasting a chaotic group of characters and odd situations that constantly bordered on the surreal, Urusei Yatsura was the first and only animated series of its kind. Nothing is spared – the show tackled subjects both religious and profane, and the supporting characters were handed the same twisted psychological bearings as the main protagonists. Interestingly, the show became much more of an ensemble run, as supporting characters were introduced with small parts only to be upgraded to main characters during the course of the show, some even rating entire episodes centered entirely on them.

And while Takahashi's characters acted out their daily lives for an audience of all ages on the television screen, the younger set found themselves addicted to the adventures of *Dr. Slump & Aralechan* by Akira Toriyama. The lives of the inhabitants of Penguin Village (where the doctor and the little robot lived) began to entertain the parents as well, who, during the first few weeks of broadcasting, had wondered about their children's mental health. It must not have been easy for adults to watch an animated cartoon in which the primary occupation of the disheveled doctor Slump is to think up plans to peek under the skirt of the village school teacher, and the erratic behaviour of little Arale wasn't much better. The unusual affection that these funny looking characters inspired from the beginning soon captured a major percentage of the television audience, giving the producers the opportunity to create a merchandising phenomenon. "Aralemania" exploded. Thousands of toys, gadgets, illustrated books, T-shirts and caps were sold on every corner in Japan and the images of the big and strong robot, Arale, winked and smiled on every conceivable surface.

Time Bokan Series: Yattodetaman © Tatsunoko Pro

The production firm Tatsunoko, continuing the never-ending and increasingly insane series *Time Machine*, came out in 1981 with *Time Bokan Series Yattodetaman*, the only one not having the usual trio of *Time Bokan* villans, and *Time Bokan Series Yattaman*. Though the villans in the latter were once again based on the same template as most of the previous movies – the blond gang leader destined to be stripped naked at the final explosion, the thin big nosed scientist and the strong surly bruiser with a monkey face – the main characters of this production are giant humanoid robots, instead of huge toys or strange half robot caterpillars, similar to those of the specific series parodied: the parody and the laid-back satire of popular stories like *Mazinger* can be found in every sequence.

Another science-fiction offering, although with less of a sense of humor, was Reiji Matsumoto's animated mini-series *Sennen Joo*. With *Sennen Joo*, Matsumoto showed that it was possible to tell about the destruction of war without reveling in the explosions and bloody battles, but by describing, with meticulous detail, the prelude to the conflict itself. Focussing on a handful of characters who use any means possible to prevent a terrible catastrophe, their banter and bickering is used as a source of psychological introspection instead of a way to get cheap laughs. This new addition to the genre was expanded by *Sengoku Majin Goshogun* and by *Taiyo no Kiba Dougram*.

Tezuka for his part, doesn't hesitate to flaunt his typical anti-military sensitivity. In the feature film *Bremen 4*, he transforms a donkey, a dog, a cat and a rooster into human beings who help a group of rebels to win a civil war against a tyrannical dictator using only their musical instruments. On the other hand, it is now well known that the Japanese films, comic strips and animated cartoons set in and around various wars are not only a means to present incredible action scenes, but also to say: "We have been through war, and it is ugly. Don't repeat the same mistakes."

0451 FILM
DORAEMON – NOBITA NO UCHUKAITAKUSH (*Doraemon: Nobita's Space Story*), Shin'ei Doga, humor, 91 min., 3/14.

0452 FILM

KAIBUTSUKUN KAIBUTSU LAND E NO SHOTAI (*The Little Kaibutsu: Invitation to the Island of the Monsters*), Shin'ei Doga, humor, 78 min., 14/3.

The little Kaibutsu, prince of the monsters, is involved in a dangerous adventure in his native land to save his faithful little human friend, petrified as punishment by Kaibatsu's father. The only hope for the boy is a flower with magical powers that Kaibutsu and his friends must recover before the deadline imposed by the king.

0453 FILM

KIDO SENSHI GUNDAM (*Gundam, the Warrior With the Mobile Armor*), Nippon Sunrise, robot, 139 min., 3/14. *Mobile Suit Gundam The Movie I.*

A movie remake of the first series of Gundam from 1979. The Archduke of Jion declares war on Earth. The Earth forces take in the young survivors of the destruction of Side 7, and they become a worthy army. Amuro Rey, at the controls of Gundam – a war machine built by his father – does himself honor in numerous battles. The film generated two sequels, in 1981 and 1982.

0454 FILM

TIME BOKAN SERIES TIME PATROL TAI OTASUKEMAN (*The Time Machine Series: the Team of the Otasukeman, the Temporal Patrol*), Tatsunoko, robot/humor, 3/14.

Once again, the time machines and their crazy travelers find success with this film taken from the 1980 animated series. Tommanomanto still has the intention of rewriting history according to his whims, but his henchmen Atasha, Dovalski and Sekovitch lose their duel against the Otasukeman, who bring peace and justice using their strange-looking animal-like machines.

0455 FILM

HAKUCHO NO MIZUMI (*Swan Lake*), Toei Doga, classic, 75 min., 3/14. [*Le Lac Des Cygnes*].

An animated transposition of the very famous classical ballet by Tchaikovski. Odette, a young princess, is held prisoner by an evil wizard. By day, Odette is a splendid swan, by night, she is a beautiful girl. Prince Sigfried is in love with her and does everything in his power to break the spell, thus saving the young girl. The film, also lauded by the Japanese minister of education, won the Moscow Film Festival in 1981 and has had a special recognition in the magazine "Young Artists."

0456 FILM

OJAMANGA YAMADAKUN (*Little Yamada, the troublemaker of cartoons*), Tsuchida for Herald, humor, 30 min., 3/14.

0457 FILM

UNICO (*id.*), Sanrio, fantasy, 90 min., 3/14. Unico the Little Unicorn.

Unico the little white unicorn finds extraordinary adventures sparked by his ability to make people happy, a gift which engenders the envy of the gods. To prevent him from using his powers, Unico is sent into exile on the hill of Oblivion. The wind from the West, however, blows him to a deserted island inhabited by the little devil of loneliness who, having become his friend, accompanies him in his adventures.

Gundam The Movie I ©1981 Sotsu Agency • Sunrise. Package & English adaptation ©1999 Bandai Entertainment, Inc.

0458 FILM
FURITENKUN (*Little Furiten*), Knack, humor, 75 min., 4/11.

0459 FILM
JARINKO CHIE (*Chie the Little Rascal*), Knack, humor, 100 min., 4/11.

Six months were missing at the beginning of the animated series, and the Knack decided to present an explanation of that time.

0460 FILM
ASHITA NO JOE II (*Joe From Tomorrow II*), Tokyo Movie Shinsha, sport, 120 min., 7/4.

An homage in memory of the most loved boxer in Japan (his fans were legion, even though he was just an animated character), the dramatic and passionate feature film ends, as in Tetsuya Chiba and Assao Takamori's marvelous television series, with the death of the main character.

0461 FILM
CAPTAIN (*id.*), Eiken, sport, 90 min., 7/18.

0462 FILM
KIDO SENSHI GUNDAM II – AISENSHI (*Gundam, the Warrior With the Mobile Armor II: the Warriors of the Feeling*), Nippon Sunrise, robot, 134 min., 7/11. *Mobile Suit Gundam The Movie II.*

This film is the second chapter of Amuro Rey's adventures with his companions from White Base. The war continues, bloodier than ever, but the "young soldiers with the mobile armors" don't get discouraged. The final confrontation between Amuro and Char is heavily foreshadowed in this dramatic piece.

0463 FILM
DORAEMON – BOKU MOMOTARO NO NANNA NO SA (*Doraemon: What Am I for Momotaro*), Shin'ei Doga, humor, 8/1.

0464 FILM
NIJUICHIEMON UCHU E IRASHAI (*Nijuichiemon, Welcome To Space*), Shin'ei Doga, humor, 92 min., 8/1.

0465 FILM
SIRIUS NO DENSETSU (*The Legend of Sirius*), Sanrio, science fiction, 108 min., 7/18.

The fights over the water belonging to the family of Prince Sirius and the fire of Princess Malta's family begin a long and harsh war that causes immense problems for the young lovers.

0466 FILM
DR. SLUMP & ARALECHAN HELLO! WONDERLAND (*id.*), Toei Doga, humor, 25 min., 7/18.

0467 FILM
GREEK NO BOKEN (*The Greek Adventures*), Shunmao, animal, 80 min., 7/21.

The astonishing adventures of a young squirrel and of his inseparable animal friends are, once again, the main focus of this story, a film particularly enjoyed by nature lovers.

Gundam The Movie II ©1981/1998 Sotsu Agency • Sunrise. Package & English adaptation ©1998 AnimeVillage.com (Bandai Entertainment, Inc.)

0468 FILM

SAYONARA GINGA TETSUDO 999 – ANDROMEDA SHUCHAKUEKI (*Good Bye, Galactic Railway 999: Andromeda, End of the Line*), Toei Doga, science fiction, 130 min., 8/8. *Adieu, Galaxy Express.*

0469 FILM

YUKI (*id.*), Mushi, fairy tale, 89 min., 8/9.

Taken from the popular Japanese fairy tale, this film tells the sad story of the *Lady of the Snow*, a mythological figure who, through love and gratitude, becomes the companion of a human being. The latter doesn't know that the woman is, in reality, a supernatural creature, and is distraught when he discovers her true origins, breaking the link that bound them.

0470 FILM

NATSU E NO TOBIRA (*The Door To Summer*), Toei Doga, Adventure, 60 min., 8/22.

0471 FILM

AKUMA TO HIMEGIMI (*The Beauty and the Beast*), Toei Doga, fairy tale, 30 min., 8/22.

The very famous fairy tale of Beauty and the Beast is adapted again in this feature film. As in every respectable fairy tale the happy ending is assured, accompanied by the always valid moral "Don't judge according to appearances."

0472 FILM

MANZAI TAIKOKI (*The Funny Story of the Shogun*), Tokyo Movie Shinsha, humor, 98 min., 11/28.

The *Taikoki* is the 16th century book that tells of the life of a very famous shogun, Hideyoshi Toyotomi, one of Japan's unifying forces.

0473 FILM

HANA NO KAKARICHO (*The Rampant Foreman*), Tokyo Movie Shinsha, humor, 11/28.

0474 FILM

SHUNMAO MONOGATARI – TAO TAO (*Tao Tao, the Story of Shunmao*), Shunmao, animals, 90 min., 12/26.

0475 FILM

UCHU SENSHI BALDIOS (*Baldios, The Space Warrior*), Ashi, robot, 120 min., 29/12. *Space Warrior Baldios / Space Warriors: Battle For Earth Station S-1.*

Akiyoshi Sakai's splendid series finds its consecration in this moving film that lingers over its unpredictable and dramatic finale. Following the thawing of the glaciers provoked by the extraterrestrial enemies, the alien spaceship Aldebaran from Gatler and the earthly base Blue Fixer, driven by the commander Tsukikage, initiate the final battle. Marin, aboard the Pulser Burns, travels into the enemy fortress to challenge the alien commander. The duel seems to favor the villan, who offers Aphrodia the possibility to avenge her brother by killing the disarmed hero. The young woman, however, after a moment of hesitation, shoots her commander, who falls lifeless to the floor. Aphrodia then commits suicide, leaving Marin distraught. In the meantime, in space, the bloody battle destroys both factions and their respective armies. Marin, the only survivor, comes back to a devastated Earth bringing with him the body of Aphrodia, the woman he had always loved.

Adieu Galaxy Express 999 ©1981 Toei Animation Co., Ltd. English version ©1997 Orion Home Entertainment Corp. All Rights Reserved. Exclusively licensed throughout the United Stated and Canada by Viz Communications, Inc.

Space Warriors ©1981 Toei Central Film Co., Ltd. Package ©1987 Celebrity Home Entertainment, Inc.

The Adventures Of Swiss Family Robinson
© Nippon Animation

0476 SERIES

KAZOKU ROBINSON – FUSHIGINA SHIMA NO FLONG (*The Shipwrecked Robinson Family on the Marvelous Island of Flone*), Nippon Animation, classic, 50 episodes, 1/4/1981 – 12/27/1982. *The Adventures Of Swiss Family Robinson*.

A family made up of Hernst, Anna and three children, Franz, Jack and Flone, are shipwrecked on a deserted island after a terrible storm. Deprived of any means of survival, the five Robinson family members do what they can to survive in the wild. At the end of the story they make it back to society, as the rule of happy endings commands.

0477 SERIES

SAIKYO ROBOT DIOJA (*Dioja, the Strongest Robot*), Nippon Sunrise, robot, 50 episodes, 1/31/1981 – 1/30/1982.

Prince Mito from Edon fights against a bloodthirsty people who are determined to conquer the Earth, Mito's adoptive planet, with the help of the powerful robot Dioja.

0478 SERIES

TIME BOKAN SERIES YATTODETAMAN (*The Time Machine Series: Yattodetaman*), Tatsunoko, robot/humor, 52 episodes, 2/7/1981 – 2/6/1982.

Tatsunoko's saga of the time machines continues. This time, two women who aspire to be queens travel in the mazes of time. To become queens they must capture the sacred Cosmoparone, a magic changling bird, capable of moving through time. The sweet princess Domenica asks her unaware ancestors for the help of a young man and a young woman from the 80s, giving them the means to travel through time, as well as the help of a centaur robot. The irascible princess Mirenjo has, instead, the collaboration of a shabby little group made up of her younger brother, who wants to become emperor, a scientist as clever as he is ridiculous and a fat brute totally deprived of a brain. For this series Tatsunoko chose Yoshitaka Amano for characterization and the famous Hiroshi Sasagawa for the direction.

0479 SERIES

OGON SENSHI GOLDLIGHTAN (*Goldlightan, the Golden Warrior*), Tatsunoko, robot, 52 episodes, 3/1/1981 – 2/18/1982.

One day, the young Hiroshi Omi finds a gold lighter that leads him to an alien robot that came to Earth to defend our planet from the attacks of the people of Ibalda, an extraterrestrial race ruthlessly ready to conquer. Once again the classic stereotypes of the genre are trotted out for the public, who seem always ready to be thrilled by combat and action over writing and plot.

0480 SERIES

HYAKUJUO GOLION (*Hundred Beast King Golion*), Tokyo Doga for Toei Co./Toei Agency, robot, 52 episodes, 3/4/1981 – 2/24/1982. *Voltron: Defender Of The Universe / Lion Force Voltron*.

The emperor Dai Bagal from planet Garla spreads destruction across half the galaxy and kidnaps the citizens to transform them into horrible combat creatures. In one of these incursions, he arrives on Earth and kidnaps part of the population – including Akira, Takashi,

Tsuyoshi, Isamu and Hiroshi, the five young main characters of the series. Thanks to a lucky break, the young people escape, stealing an enemy aircraft and landing on planet Altea. There, they learn about the legend of the five mechanical lions that join to form the powerful robot Golion. Near the place where they landed is an impressive palace in which princess Fara and her royal counselor live. They tell the young people about the legend of the five lions, and the hologram of the late emperor gives them the keys to activate the powerful mechanisms. Kazuo Nakamura as character designer and Katsuhiko Taguchi, director, are part of the staff.

Voltron © Toei

0481 SERIES

HELLO SANDYBELL (*id.*), Toei Doga, soap opera, 47 episodes, 3/6/1981 – 2/26/1982. [*Sandy Jonquille*].

Sandybell, a lively young girl, lives happily in the green Scottish valleys. At the death of her father, professor Leslie Christie, the young girl discovers a sad secret. Sandybell had been in a shipwreck as a baby, the young professor and a journalist friend had saved her and, because of the absence of her real parents, had decided to take care of her. So, while the journalist had moved to London to pursue her career, Christie had raised the little one in Scotland. Once grown, Sandybell meets the young count Mark Wellington, a talented painter and falls in love. The young man however, is in a bad financial situation, and to avoid being forced to marry a rich and arrogant heiress, decides to run away to live as a wanderer. With Christie dead, and having found out about the existence of her mother, Sandybell moves to London where she begins a promising career as a reporter, which helps her to rediscover Mark who has become a talented painter.

0482 SERIES

OHAYO SPANK (*Good Morning Spank*), Tokyo Movie Shinsha, soap opera/humor, 63 episodes, 3/7/1981 – 5/29/1982. [*Les Aventures De Claire Et Tipoune*].

Produced by Yutaka Fujoka, the series taken from the cartoon written by Shun'ichi Yukimuro and illustrated by Shizie Takanashi is based on the adventures of the funny-looking puppy Spank. After the mysterious ocean disappearance of his father, little Aiko meets the puppy and decides to take care of him. The screenplay of the cartoon was written with the participation of Hiroshi Kanuko, who worked with the original author to maintain the atmosphere of the comic, while Shigetsugu Yoshida supervised the direction and Takao Kozai the drawings. The artistic direction and the backdrops are by Noboru Tatsuike, the photography by Hirokata Takahashi and the music by Koji Magaino.

0483 SERIES

AI NO GAKKO CUORE MONOGATARI (*The Story of Cuore, the School of Love*), Nippon Animation, classic, 26 episodes, 4/3 – 10/2/1981. [*Coeur*].

From Edmondo De Amicis' book, Nippon Animation does the adaptation of the moving adventures of a group of school friends in Italy. Faithfully adapting the original text, the animation often slips into cautious drama, carefully counterbalanced by the tight bonds of friendship that the children share.

0484 SERIES

MECHAKKO DOTAKON (*Dotakon the Little MuddleHead*), Kohusai eigasha, humor, 28 episodes, 4/4 – 10/10/1981.

Dotakon is a funny looking little boy robot built by the young Michiru, an expert in cybernetics, to fulfill her dream to have a brother. The little android soon becomes the hero in every situation that occurs in the villa where Datakon, his creator and the little sister robot Chopiko live. Helped by their faithful butler Kinai and the monster-like timid Capone Gorilla, the peculiar family can always afford the luxury of extravagant adventures, thanks to the millionaire parents of the little scientist. Takeshi Shirato is both director and character designer.

0485 SERIES

MEIKEN JOLY (*The Intelligent Dog Joly*), Visual 80 for Toho Classic, 64 episodes, 4/7/1981 – 6/22/1987. [*Belle & Sebastien*].

Meiken Joly © Visual 80 / MK

In a little mountain village, the young Sebastien lives with his grandfather. One day, he meets an enormous dog named Joly, who becomes his inseparable friend and shares his joys, sorrows and adventures. After having saved a person in trouble, the gentle animal is accused of aggression and is wanted by the police to be put to death. Sebastien decides to take care of him and together, they start searching for the boy's mother, a woman who works in a traveling circus.

0486 SERIES

WAKAKUSA NO YONSHIMAI (*Four Sisters*), Kokusai eigasha, classic, 26 episodes, 4/7 – 9/29/1981.

Taken from the famous classic Little Women by Louisa May Alcott, four sisters, Meg, Jo, Beth and Amy, live through the small and large dramas of daily life during the war, helping their mother keep up the family while their father is at the front. They propose an education model that would influence so many future generations of "little women." In the television series, Beth's premature death is not explored: the young girl in fact is cured by her father's return.

0487 SERIES

DR. SLUMP & ARALECHAN (*id.*), Toei Doga, humor, 243 episodes, 4/8/1981 – 2/19/1986. [*Docteur Slump*].

The insane doctor Slump is a prolific inventor who lives in Penguin Village and who is in love with the beautiful Midori, a school teacher who does not return his love. One day, he decides to use his abilities to build a little robot girl. He names the resulting creation 'Arale,' a naive and irritating child, who radically disturbs the lives of the poor inhabitants of the village. Having soon become friends with some children from her school, including the blond Akane, little Pisuke and sweet Taro, the robot shows her extraordinary strength and uses the strange inventions of her tutor to pass her time in adventures. In one of these, Arale and her friends are thrown into prehistoric times and, after an encounter with gigantic dinosaurs, they come back to the present carrying a mysterious egg that hatches into the sweet Gatchan, a winged baby that follows them around. Created by Akira Toriyama and directed by Minoru Okazaki, the series is so perfect that it has never been equaled even by the later scripts by the same author, and the episodes have kept their charm even over the years. The design supervision is by Minoru Maeda, the backdrops by Mataharu Urata, the production is by Keizo Schichijo and Shunsuke Kikuchi composed the music.

0488 SERIES

FUSEN NO DORATARO (*Dorataro, the Wanderer*), Nippon Animation, adventure, 13 episodes, 4/11 – 8/1/1981.

0489 SERIES

SHIN TAKETORI MONOGATARI – SENNEN JOO (*The New Story of Taketori: the Queen of a Thousand Years*), Toei Doga for Fuji TV, science fiction, 41 episodes, 4/6/1981 – 3/25/1982. *Captain Harlock And The Queen of a Thousand Days.*

Yayoi Yukino is the queen of Lamethal, a planet that goes through a long period of extreme cold and that uses the strength of Earth slaves for the production of energy. Having come to Earth to subdue other people, the queen meets the wise Hajime Amamori and, feeling sorry, she refuses to complete her mission. Lamethal, in the meantime, enters a collision course with the Earth and Yayoi launches the construction of spaceships to save the innocent inhabitants. Lamethal, in the mean time, has instituted a new queen to replace Yayoi, beginning a violent duel between the two. Yayoi eventually wins, but she commits suicide, directing her dying energy against her homeworld, saving the Earth from doom. Yoshinori Kanamori designed the characters, remaining faithful to Reiji Matsumoto's original comic, while the direction of the series, produced by Kenji Yokoyama, was supervised by Nobutaka Nishizawa.

0490 SERIES

TIGER MASK NISEI (*Tiger Mask the Second*), Toei Doga, sport, 31 episodes, 4/20/1981 – 1/18/1982.

After the death of Naoto Date, the first tigerman, Tatsuo, an orphan and great fan of Tiger Mask, decides to follow in his footsteps. He is recruited by the new Tiger Den, who came back to life after Naoto's death to complete his evil plans, and becomes a powerful wrestler. Defender of the weak and oppressed, Tatsuo hides his identity under the disguise of a sports journalist.

0491 SERIES

SENGOKU MAJIN GOSHOGUN (*Goshogun, The God Of War*), Ashi, robot, 26 episodes, 7/3 – 12/28/1981. *Macron-1.*

Goshogun, a marvelous robot piloted by Shingo, Remi and Kiri, fights for justice against the criminal organization Dokuga, led by the handsome Leonardo Medici Bundall. Contrary to normal practice, not only one character designer controlled the production of the animated series, but the entire staff of the Studio Z5. Zunikiko Yuyama, who would later direct Maho no Princess Minky Momo, expertly directs this new production.

0492 SERIES

MANGA MITOKOMON (*Mitokomon in Manga*), Knack, historical, 46 episodes, 9/3/1981 – 7/15/1982.

The story, set in Medieval Japan, features the adventures of Suke, Kaku, Onatsu and the little Sutemaru, a group of courageous youths who form the escort of the viceshogun Mitsukuni Mito in his travels around the village. Together with their lord, the four bring peace and justice back to the places where it has been forgotten. Created by Seiichi Nishino, Kazuyuki Okaseko and Yoshiyuki Nitta direct the series. The soundtrack is by Kentaro Haneda.

Macron-1 ©1986 Saban Productions / Warner - Tamerlane Publishing Corp. All Rights Reserved

0493 SERIES
SHIN DOKONJO GAERU (*The Persistent Frog – New Series*), Tokyo Movie Shinsha, humor, 30 episodes, 9/7 – 3/22/1981.

0494 SERIES
NINJA HATTORIKUN (*Hattori, the Little Ninja*), Shin'ei Doga, humor, 52 episodes, 9/28/1981 – 12/25/1987.

After the success of Kaibutsukun and Doraemon, to mention only a couple, the duo Fujiko Fujio continues to rise with the series dedicated to the ninja Hattori Kun. The plot is similar to that of previous productions, and tells the story of the adventures of Ken'ichi, a Japanese child. The real main character, however, is Kanjo Hattori, the little ninja, inspired by the fighter who lived in Medieval times. The story, set in the present, is rich in humor and with the extravagant comic quality that characterizes the two famous authors.

0495 SERIES
ROKUSHIN GATTAI GOD MARS (*God Mars, Six Gods, United in One Body*), Tokyo Movie Shinsha, robot, 64 episodes, 10/2/1981 –12/24/1982.

Once again, Mitsuteru Yokohama's comics provide ample material for a new animated series, adapted by Keisuke Fujikawa and directed by Tetsuo Imazawa. The characterization is by Hideyuki Motohashi. Takeru is the courageous pilot of the robot God Mars, which he uses to defend the Earth from the attacks of the Gishin emperor, Zul. Takeru however, doesn't know that his real name is Mars and that he originates from the planet Gishin. He eventually discovers his twin brother Marg, brainwashed by the evil Zul. Brotherly love, however, prevails at the end.

0496 SERIES
JARINKO CHIE (*Chie, The Little Girl*), Tokyo Movie Shinsha, humor, 64 episodes, 3/10/1981 – 25/3/1983.

Taken from Etsumi Haruki's comic, the series presents a social comedy, centered on the adventures of a little girl who lost her mother, stuck with the management of a restaurant owned by her father, an alcoholic who is drunk from morning to night.

0497 SERIES
DASH KAPPEI (*id.*), Tatsunoko, sport, 62 episodes, 10/4/1981 –12/26/1982.

Kappei is an incredibly short, but equally incredibly athletic young man. He plays, competes and wins at almost everything, from basketball and ping-pong to fencing and kendo. In love with his lovely landlord, his endless feud with her jealous dog is the breeding ground for endless pranks and practical jokes. This insanely funny series directed by Masayuki Hayashi in the first part and by Seitaro Hara in the second. It is supervised by Shigeru Yanagigawa, and taken from Noboru Rokuta's manga. The design supervision is by Sadao Miyamoto.

0498 SERIES
GINGA SENPO BRIGER (*Briger, the Cyclone From the Galaxy*), Toei Doga (Korea) for Kokusai eigasha, robot, 39 episodes, 10/6/1981 – 6/30/1982.

Rokushin Gattai God Mars © M. Yokoyama / TMS

The asteroid belt hides a secret base, the base of the Cosmos Rangers J9. The heroic Rangers use the transformable Briger in their fight to rid the Earth colonies of the fast-growing criminal element. The Rangers are soon faced with an even greater threat, the much feared Kamen Kamen, the head of colonial organized crime. Monkey Punch's original designs are adapted by Kazuo Komatsubara for animation. The screenplay is by Takao Yotsuji.

0499 SERIES

MAITCHINGU MACHIKOSENSEI (*How Shameful, School Teacher Machiko*), Studio Pierrot for Gakken, humor/erotic, 95 episodes, 10/8/1981 – 10/6/1983.

Machiko is a sweet elementary school teacher who wants to solve all of her little students' problems. Somehow, this always seems to involve her performing an involuntary strip-tease for the delight of her students. One of the first erotic anime for children.

0500 SERIES

WAN WAN SANJUSHI (*The Three Musketeer Dogs*), Nippon Animation, animal, 24 episodes, 10/9/1981 – 3/26/1982. [*Les Trois Mousquetaires*].

Once again Dumas' heroic musketeers are featured characters in an adaptation of his much-loved novel. After countless Western film and television adaptations Japan presents its own version, setting the plot in the world of anthropormorphic animals, playing the story for humor.

Wan Wan Sanjushi © Nippon Animation

0501 SERIES

URUSEI YATSURA (*Those Obnoxious Aliens*), Studio Pierrot for Kitty Film, comedy, 218 episodes, 10/14/1981 – 3/19/1986. *Urusei Yatsura: Lum* [*Lamu*].

The arrival of the alien princess Lamu on the Earth is the spark that begins an epic and unbelievable complicated love "triangle," that eventually widens to include almost every character in this long-running series. Not content with simply playing with the minds of the characters, the plotline also causes catastrophes of biblical dimensions for a small area of Tokyo, called Nerima. Lamu, in fact, falls in love with a high-school student named Ataru and, pretending to be his wife, she moves into his house. Ataru cannot do anything to stop her, as Lamu quickly becomes friends with the boy's mother. Ataru thus learns to live with all the strange things that happen to him. As if it wasn't enough, his friends accuse him of keeping Lamu as a slave, and they do all they can to make sure he "sets her free." The situation works out something like this: Ataru would love to get back together with Shinobu, his first girlfriend, even though his eye constantly wanders to all the other girls in the series. Shinobu doesn't want anything to do with Ataru, and she falls in love with the very wealthy and arrogant Mendo, her classmate. Mendo is particularly interested in Lamu, and tries to get her away from Ataru. Lamu only has eyes for Ataru even though previously, on Uru, she was engaged to Rei, a young man with a terrible curse, which causes him to turn into a colossal alien beast when it takes him by surprise. Rei would love to get back together with Lamu, but this makes Ran, his ex, extremely jealous and very vindictive. Ran conceals a vile temper and maniacal penchant for evil under a sweet smile and her pretty pink outfits. To aggravate the situation, there is the provocative Sakura, granddaughter of Sakurambo exorcist and nurse at Tomobiki high school, Megane,

Urusei Yatsura ©1981 Kitty Films. Licensed to AnimEigo by Compass. English version ©1994 AnimEigo, Inc.

Kakugani, Kibi and Parma, Ataru's school mates who "want" Lamu; Benten, goddess of wealth and good luck, in the form of a frenetic space easyrider and Oyuki, the young girl from the snow, both old school mates of Lamu; Kurama, the princess of the Tengus (little elves with long noses) who had been waiting for a prince to wake her up with a kiss and angry because Ataru did it instead; Lamu's little flame-throwing cousin, Ten; Ryunosuke, a young girl forced by her father to dress and act as a boy... This is one of the most acclaimed Japanese series, rich in humor and incredible situations, overflowing with insane characters and circumstances. The long-running series directed by Kazuo Yamazaki is taken from Rumiko Takahashi's comic, while the character design is by the talented Akemi Takada.

0502 SERIES

ANIME OYAKO GEKIJO (*Animated Parents and Child Theater*), Tatsunoko, sociological, 26 episodes, 10/16/1981 – 3/29/1982. *Superbook*.

0503 SERIES

TAIYO NO KIBA DOUGRAM (*Dougram, the Sun's Fang*), Nippon Sunrise, robot, 10/23/1981 – 3/25/1983.

While, in 1979, *Kido Senshi Gundam* changed the robot genre dramatically, it is only now with *Dougram* that this new style really takes hold. In Dougram, in fact, the robot is considered part of the military presence and is seen in the line of the army. The planet Deroia is invaded by aliens, so seven young people decide to form a resistance group called Peroia 7. At the command of powerful robots, amongst which, of course, is Dougram, the courageous main characters loose their anger against the enemy.

0504 SERIES

HONEY HONEY NO SUTEKINA BOKEN (*The Marvelous Adventures of Honey Honey*), Toei Doga (Korea) for Kokusai eigasha, soap opera, 29 episodes, 10/7/1981 – 5/1/1982.

Honey is a young waitress who works in a restaurant. The young woman's life becomes terribly complicated when her cat eats "the queen of the amazons" by mistake, the famous ring of a very arrogant princess. Honey is thus forced to run away, pursued by princess Florence and her suitors. In fact, Florence promised herself in marriage to whoever would recover the precious gem. Even the gentleman robber Phoenix begins to follow them, attracted by the priceless ring. The end is somewhat absurd, compared to the rest of the story. Honey discovers that she is a phoenix princess, the sister of Florence and separated from her at birth. Phoenix, moreover, will reveal himself as the head of the phoenixes and, as in any happy ending story, marries the young main character. The general direction is by Takeshi Shirato and Yoshiyuki Nitta.

0505 SPECIAL

KAITEI DAISENSO – AI NO NISEN MILES (*20 000 Miles of Love: the Great Navy Battle*), Tatsunoko, science fiction, 139 min., 1/3.

This remake of the famous story of Captain Nemo created by Jules Verne is set in the future. The young Ben and Riki meet the mysterious captain and he uses his submarine to teach them of the marvels of the long-vanished kingdom of Mu.

Superbook © CNB / Tatsunoko Production

Kaitei Daisenso; Ai no Nisen Miles © Tatsunoko Pro

0506 SPECIAL
YASEI NO YOBIGOE HOERO BUCK (*Bark, Buck! the Call of the Forest*), Toei Doga, classic 85 min., 1/3.

The Call of the Forest, the novel written by Jack London in 1906, is the inspiration for this film. The original setting and the dramatic edge of the story remain intact.

0507 SPECIAL
HASHIRE MELOS (*Run Melos*), Toei Doga, historical, 85 min., 2/7.

In a village of Greece, feverish preparations are made for the wedding of the sister of the young Pastor Melos, who wants to make her happy at all costs. He decides, in fact, to buy her a beautiful wedding dress in the nearest city, many kilometers away from their village. When he finally reaches his destination, Melos is arrested when he tries to save a girl who is about to be run over by the royal procession, but he pleads with the king to leave him three days of freedom so that he could be at his sister's wedding. The king accepts but he keeps Melos' friend Selinuntius as hostage – to be killed if Melos doesn't come back. Melos thus begins a race against time that eventually leads him to save his friend's life as well as his own, as the king, moved by so much courage, gives him back his freedom.

0508 SPECIAL
MISTER GIANTS – EIKO NO SEBANGO 3 (*The Glory of Number 3, Mister Giant*), Tsuchida, sport, 90 min., 4/1.

0509 SPECIAL
TOSHI SHUN (*id.*), Dax, biography, 84 min., 4/12.

0510 SPECIAL
MUTSUGORO NO DOBUTSU NIKKI – DONBE MONOGATARI (*The Diary of the Animals of Mutsugoro: the Story of Donbe*), Eiken, animal, 90 min., 4/26.

The life of an orphan and the friendship that he has for the bear of the forest Donbe are the subjects of a sweet and moving show. The feature film is taken from a real story lived by a veterinarian from Hokkaido.

0511 SPECIAL
HELEN KELLER MONOGATARI – AI TO HIKARI NO TENSHI (*Helen Keller, the Angel of Love and Light*), Studio Oka, classic, 84 min., 5/5.

The Keller family calls upon Anne, a skillful teacher, to take care of their little daughter Helen. The little girl is both deaf and blind, and her serious handicap has changed her attitude, giving her a difficult and surly disposition that prevents her from learning the precious lessons given by the patient teacher. In spite of all that, Anne succeeds in tearing the veil that isolates Helen from the outside world, while becoming her best friend. The feature film is inspired by a real story, adapted for the theater by William Gibson in a play called *Miracle Anne*, which also inspired the film, directed by Arthur Penn in 1962 and starring Ann Bancroft.

0512 SPECIAL
LUPIN TAI HOLMES (*Lupin Against Holmes*), Toei Doga, police story, 85 min., 5/5.

The most famous thief of Japanese animation is not the main character of this film – rather, this installment in the series focusses on his famous ancestor. Arsene Lupin, here, faces the even more famous Sherlock Holmes, creation of Arthur Conan Doyle.

0513 SPECIAL

SUGATA SANSHIRO (*id.*), Tokyo Movie Shinsha, historical, 90 min., 6/8.

The young Sanshiro is a judo champion. His teacher, convinced that Sanshiro can become an initiate, tries to remove the boy's almost insane fear of death. Believing in the boy's pure spirit, he imposes the most extreme of all tests: suicide. The young man tries to drown himself but inexplicably survives, and in the meantime he discovers "the Way." Challenged to a dual by his future father-in-law, Sanshiro thinks that he may have found a way to obey his teacher's order, but the teacher makes him understand that the highest level of purity resides in the freedom from the rules imposed by a hypocritical society and invites him to kill his opponent.

0514 SPECIAL

KYOFU DENSETU — KAIKI! FRANKENSTEIN (*The Frightening Legend of Frankenstein*), Toei Doga, classic, 114 min., 7/27.

Baron Frankenstein wants to create life from death, and brings into being a grotesque creature made up of various parts stolen from corpses. The creature is totally out of control, however, and, reacting instinctively, he kills the scientist. Thus begins a violent monster hunt that only ends when the monster sacrifices himself to save the life of a little girl, ending his brief and sad existence. A faithful and moving adaptation of one of the most famous classics of horror literature.

0515 SPECIAL

TOKAIDO YOTSUYA KAIDAN (*Monster Tales to Yotsuya in Tokaido*), Telecom for Tohan kikaku, horror, 8/9.

A young maid is killed by her infuriated boss because she accidentally broke a precious plate. The young woman comes back in the form of a ghost to avenge her death.

0516 SPECIAL

BREMEN 4 – JIGOKU NO NAKA NO TENSHITACHI (*Bremen 4: the Angels From Hell*), Tezuka, science fiction, 120 min., 8/23.

Bremen 4 © Tezuka Production

Four animals, a donkey, a dog, a cat and a hen, decide to leave to seek new adventures away from their mistreatment by humans. Gradually transforming into humans, they become a famous musical group and, thanks to their artistic talent, they bring harmony and hope to the populations. Their contribution to the civil war becomes the decisive blow against the ruling tyrant. Tezuka as usual, deals with peaceful themes. Bremen 4 is no exception, as the animals use their musical instruments to bring a message of peace intended for a young audience.

0517 SPECIAL

BOKURA MANGAKA TOKIWASO MONOGATARI (*We Who Make Manga: The Story of Tokiwaso*), Toei Doga, biography, 84 min., 10/3.

Tokiwaso is the name of the apartment in which, around the year 1953, was the home of Hiroo Terada, the duo Fujiko Fujio, Shotaro Ishimori and Fujio Akatsuka, all of whom are counted amongst Japan's best known mangaka (manga artists) of our times. The movie tells of the group's first years of activity, always stuck with money problems, but motivated by an enthusiasm that enables the five to overcome every difficulty to finally become famous.

0518 SPECIAL

CHISANA LOVE LETTER MARIKO TO NEMU NO KI NO KODOMOTACHI (*Little Love Letter: Mariko and the Orphans*), Now kikaku, biography, 81 min., 12/22.

Mariko is a famous actress particularly interested in the problem of abandoned children. Because of this, she decides to open an orphanage to care for children without parents. The animated special presents the biography of the young actress.

CHAPTER TWENTY ONE: 1982

Amongst the many series that have contributed to make 1982 an important year in the panorama of Japanese animation, *Chojiku yosai Macross* sticks out the most. This series followed the lead of *Kido senshi Gundam*, reinventing the archtype set for the first time by Go Nagai – the combat robot as a solitary fighter, alone against the universe. Macross is a fortress city, a sanctuary where refugees from Earth have rebuilt their now-destroyed home town, Macross City. A trained army watches over the safety of the civilians, their pilots training for combat aboard the fighter robot Valkyrie; no longer was the pilot one man alone with his machine – now they were a group, a team who must work together to achieve a specific goal. In 1986, *Robotech* reached Italy, and immediately became a huge success in both the niche market and the mainstream. This imported version, however, is the unfortunate amalgamation by Harmony Gold America of three separate Japanese series: *Chojiku yosai Macross*, *Chojiku Kidan Southern Cross* and *Kikososeiki*. The different series were combined into one to create a story that is, not surprisingly, horribly uncoordinated and confusing. The original thread of *Macross'* plot (in the first chapter of the *Robotech* saga) and *Mospeada* (third chapter of the same saga) shone through, while *Southern Cross*, sandwiched between two different series, fared the worst.

Robotech ©1985 Harmony Gold U.S.A., Inc / Tatsunoko Production Co., Ltd. All Right Reserved. Licensed to Streamline Pictures for distribution throughout North America

Two very different little witches were introduced in 1982: *Maho no Princess Minky Momo* and *Tokimeki Tonight*. The first series produced by the Ashi gave way, eventually, to others which generated more public attention, but all shared the same plot device: the transformation of a young girl (usually elementary or junior-high age) into a woman with the use of a magic wand. *Tokimeki*, by Toho, distances itself from the other series: the young character Ranze in fact is the daughter of a vampire and a wolfwoman. Having left the infernal kingdom with Satan's permission, the bizarre family decides to live on Earth as a normal family. Ranze has no magical powers, but she has supernatural gifts that derive from her infernal nature.

Another chapter from the "Time Machines" was added to the rich saga: *Gyakuten Ippatsuman*, bringing old and loved characters back for new adventures. The public was appreciative, clamoring for more of the films every year.

Another important series was *Taiyo no ko Esteban*, set in the distant past, another revamp of the plotline used in *Andes shonen Pepero no boken* from 1975 – a young explorer on a journey into a fantastical interpretation of the ancient civilization of the Incas. In this case, however, the young hero ends up tracking down the trail of an ancient alien nation.

Osamu Tezuka chose 1982 to present his version of the classic monster story *Dracula*. His reinterpretation, *Don Dracula*, saw the introduction of a Dracula monstrous only in appearance. The comedy presented a new interpretation of a very old legend, moving the location of the story to modern-day Tokyo.

A curious series that debuted in 1982 is *Tondera House no daiboken*, in which two children travel through the stories of the Judeo-Christian traditions through a dimensional passage opened by a mysterious book (never named, but which is no doubt the Bible). This cartoon must be considered the precursor of what would be the great Tezuka's final work: in 1984, shortly before dying, he began an animated series in collaboration with the Italian Rai, to this day unfinished, based on standard biblical themes.

An important launch in this year was *Pataliro*, not for the story or for the art, which were both mediocre at best, but for what it represents: homosexuality was dealt with for the first time in an animated cartoon. Censorship certainly exists in Japan as in the rest of the world, but every culture defines their own boundaries of what is acceptable, as *Pataliro* proved..

Also worthy of note is *Waga seishun no Arcadia*, which featured the life of an ancestor of Captain Harlock, who was involved in the Second World War. Phantom Harlock is bound by an old friendship to Tochiro, who just happens to be the ancestor of the modern Harlock's sidekick. Harlock tries at all costs to save "My eyes," a large lens that his family has passed down from generation to generation, the same lens that will finally be placed on the bridge of the Arcadia – a ship built by the faithful Tochiro and operated by Harlock himself.

Vengeance Of The Space Pirate ©1980 Toei Co., Ltd / Tokyu Advertising Agency, Inc. Package ©1987 Celebrity Home Entertainment, Inc

0519 FILM

SEROHIKI NO GOSHU (*Goshu the Cello Player*), O Prod., classic, 63 min., 1/23.

The director of the Orchestra «Goldenstar» is not satisfied with the way Goshu, a young musician, plays the cello. There's a concert coming up, and the young man still makes mistakes in certain passages of Beethoven's Pastoral. The depressed Goshu returns home where, in the following days, he meets little animals who knock at his door and, in exchange for little favors, teach him to hold the rhythm, to blend the sound of his instrument with that of the other musicians and to really «feel» the music. This extra help leads Goshu on to success. Taken from a story by Kenji Miyazawa, the film uses the character designs of Yoshio Mamiya and is directed by Isao Takahata. The photography is by Toshiaki Okaseri, while the artistic direction is by Hayao Miyazaki.

0520 FILM

OHAYO SPANK (*Good Morning Spank*), Tokyo Movie Shinsha, soap opera/humor, 40 min., 3/11.

0521 FILM

SHIN DOKONJO GAERU (*The Persistent Frog – New Film*), Tokyo Movie Shinsha, humor, 40 min., 3/13.

0522 FILM

KIDO SENSHI GUNDAM III MEGURIAI SORAHEN (*Gundam the Warrior With the Mobile Armor III: Love Encounter in Space*), Nippon Sunrise, robot, 140 min., 3/13. *Mobile Suit Gundam The Movie III*.

The last act of Yoshiyuki Tomino's saga presents the conclusion of the story, with the final duel between the robot warriors. RX-78 Gundam and the Zak are both destroyed in the conflict that sees the absolute rout of both the Earth forces and those of Jion. The crew from the White Base escapes the catastrophe aboard a rescue module a short time before the final explosion.

0523 FILM

SENNEN JOO (*Queen Millenia*), Toei Doga for Sennen Joo Seisaku Tinkai, science fiction, 120 min., 3/13. [*Princesse Millenium*].

A mysterious planet named Lamethal is on a colision path with the Earth. The crash appears as though it will occur on September 9, 1999 at 9:09 and 9 seconds. In reality, Lamethal hides an obscure mystery: every thousand years, its inhabitants send a queen to Earth, tasked to capture a large number of earthlings to be used as slaves.The film is adapted from the television series by Reiji Matsumoto.

0524 FILM

DORAEMON – NOBITA NO DAIMAKYO (*Doraemon: Nobita's Great Demon*), Shin'ei Doga, humor, 96 min., 3/13.

0525 FILM

MANGA NIHON MUKASHIBANASHI (*Ancient Japanese Tales*), Ai Kikaku, fairy tale, 25 min., 3/13.

0526 FILM

ASARICHAN – AI NO MERUHEN SHOJO (*Little Asari, the Wonderful Love Child*), Toei Doga, soap opera, 25 min., 3/13.

0527 FILM

KAIBUTSUKUN DEMON NO TSURUGI (*The Little Kaibutsu: the Devil's Sword*), Shin'ei Doga, grotesque, 31 min., 3/13.

0528 FILM

NINJA HATTORIKUN NINPOENIKKI NO MAKI (*Hattori the Little Ninja: Chapter From the Diary of Ninnin's Method*), Shin'ei Doga, humor, 30 min., 3/3.

0529 FILM

ALADIN TO MAHO NO LAMP (*Aladdin and the Magic Lamp*), Toei Doga, fairy tale, 65 min., 3/20. *Aladdin and the Magic Lamp*.

Aladdin is a poor Arab street kid, with boundless energy and zest for life. One day, to earn some money, he helps a mysterious individual recover an old lamp in a cavern full of

Gundam The Movie III ©1981, 1998 Sotsu Agency • Sunrise. Package & English adaptation ©1998 AnimeVillage.com (Bandai Entertainment, Inc.)

Aladin To Maho no Lamp © Toei

riches. Upon discovering that the lamp contains a genie capable of granting any three wishes, Aladdin keeps the precious object, a decision that throws him into the middle of trouble again and again. Once again, legends of the Middle East provided inspiration for a Japanese production.

0530 FILM
ZOO NO INAI DOBUTSUEN (*A Zoo Without Elephants*), Group Tack/Herald, animals, 80 min., 3/20.

0531 FILM
SENGOKU MAJIN GOSHOGUN (*Goshogun, the God of War*), Ashi, robot, 60 min., 4/24.

0532 FILM
HAGUREGUMO (*id.*), Toei Doga, humor, 92 min., 4/24.

0533 FILM
SPACE ADVENTURE COBRA (*id.*), Tokyo Movie Shinsha, science fiction, 99 min., 7/3.

0534 FILM
DENSETSU KYOJIN IDEON – SESSIOKUHEN (*The Legendary Giant God Ideon: the Contact*), Nippon Sunrise, robot, 90 min., 7/9.

The «giant god» Ideon, a technologically advanced robot, tries to unite two completely different civilizations. The human race and the Buffs meet and begin a bloody war that changes both societies for the worse. The main character, a young pilot, never gives up his hope for a peaceful future. An interesting space saga with a melancholic tone.

0535 FILM
DR. SLUMP & ARALECHAN (*id.*), Toei Doga, comedy, 90 min., 7/10.

0536 FILM
WAGA SEISHUN NO ARCADIA (*Arcadia of My Youth*), Toei Doga for Tokyu, science fiction, 130 min. 7/28. *Arcadia of My Youth*.

The film is chronologically out of order, set in the legendary captain's younger years. A ruthless race, called Humanoids, represses the people of the colonized planets under an iron fist. A group of rebels led by Captain Harlock is the only answer to the alien threat. Aboard their spaceship Arcadia, built by Tochiro, a very good friend of the Captain, the men embark on a long journey through the galaxy to fight against the evil empire. Their first mission is on planet Tokarga, which is about to be destroyed.

0537 FILM
TECHNOPOLICE 21C (*id.*), Toho, science fiction, 78 min., 7/28. *Technopolice 21C*.

In the 21st century, to overcome organized crime, a special police patrol is formed, composed of android policemen, to minimize risk to the human personnel on the more dangerous missions. These mechanical officers are dubbed technopolice.

0538 FILM
KYOJIN NO HOSHI (*The Star of the Kyojin*), Tokyo Movie Shinsha, sport, 105 min., 8/21.

The year 1982 sees the comeback of certain great characters from the past, like Tetsuwan Atom or Tetsujin 28, who were particularly popular in the sixties. *Kyojin no hoshi* also

My Youth In Arcadia ©1982 Toei Co., Ltd. / Tokyu Agency. English adaptation ©1993 AnimEigo, Inc.

THE ROBOTS ARE THE...
TECHNO POLICE

Technopolice ©1982 Toho International Co., Ltd. All Rights Reserved. Package ©1987 Celebrity Home Entertainment, Inc.

makes an important comeback this year. This film is a compilation of the important events of the series, giving a basic overview of the adventures of the young baseball player. New sequences were added by Magic Bus Studio, featuring champions who were currently playing with the Giants.

0539 FILM

TSUSHIMAMARU SAYONARA OKINAWA (*Tsushimamaru: Good Bye Okinawa*), Agiado for Tushimamaru Seisaku, historical, 10/24.

The tragic images of the historical battle fought during World War Two in Okinawa, an island of the Japanese archipelago, are featured in this animated version of all-too-real events.

0540 FILM

FUTURE WAR 198X NEN (*War of the Future in the Year 198X*), Toei Doga, science fiction 125 min., 10/30.

Birt, an American scientist and designer of military satellites, is kidnapped by Russian spies. The United States destroys the Russians' atomic submarine with a nuclear missile. The Japanese scientist Wataru Migumo vows to avenge the death of his friend, by building a military satellite. In the meantime, notwithstanding the efforts of President Gibson of the United States to maintain peace, armed conflicts break out on the border of the two Germanys and soon escalate into war. This effect is exactly what Bughalin, dictator of the Soviet Military Union (after having assassinated Orlof, the secretary of the PCUS), wants. This hostility divides two young lovers, Shun, of Japanese nationality and Tanya, a young Russian woman. The only way they can be together now is on the battlefield. Shun enlists in the Japanese air force and Tanya in the Soviet battalion. The film is based on Sho Fumimura's manga.

0541 FILM

ROKUSHIN GATTAI GOD MARS (*God Mars, Six-God Combining*), Tokyo Movie Sinsha, robot, 100 min., 12/18. *Godmars.*

The success of the television series *Rokushin Gattai God Mars* leads Tokyo Movie Shinsha to produce a film based on the plot of the first season of the series. The movie manages to keep the storyline intact, but enhances the fraternal love between Mars and Marg, even though the two battled against each other before knowing they were brothers.

0542 SERIES

MINAMI NO NIJI NO LUCY (*Lucy, the Rainbow From the South*), Nippon Animation, classic, 50 episodes, 1/10 – 12/26/1982.

A family of English immigrants comes to Australia in 1836 to participate, despite the high cost and numerous sacrifices they must make, in the colonization of the newly-discovered continent. Lucy May is the youngest daughter of this family and, together with her father, Mr. Popple, her mother and her siblings Ben, Clara, Kate and Tot, she dreams of possessing a big farm near Adelaide. Over the four years of the series, she gets closer to her goal and eventually achieves her lifetime dream at the end of the four-year run.

Godmars ©1982 Hikari Production / TMS, Inc.
Packaging ©1994 The Right Stuf International, Inc.

0543 SERIES

ASARICHAN (*The Little Asari*) Toei Doga, humor, 54 episodes, 1/25/1982 – 2/28/1983.

Mayumi Muroyama, the author of Asarichan, transforms herself into the little character in this series, which describes the day to day problems of a young student. The story is peppered with a huge number of in-joke references to the life of the illustrator.

0544 SERIES

SENTO MECHA XABUNGLE (*Battle Mechanism Xabungle*), Nippon Animation, robot, 50 episodes, 2/6/1982 – 1/29/1983.

Jiron Amos, an inhabitant of Earth, is renamed Zora after the invasion by the Innocents. While trying to steal the new model of worker machine, Xabungle, he encounters Leg, a commander of the crew of the land ship Iron Gear. Jiron, putting aside his strong dislike for Commander Elch, decides to join the crew and begins searching for Timp, his father's murderer.

Sento Mecha Xabungle © Nippon Animation.

0545 SERIES

TIME BOKAN SERIES JYARUTEN IPPATSUMAN (*The Time Machine Series: Ippatsuman the Antihero*), Tatsunoko, robot, humor, 58 episodes, 2/13/1982 – 3/26/1983.

Continuing their immensely popular time machine series, Tatsunoko comes out with Ippstsuman in which the characters are members of a peculiar company of "temporal delivery," the Time Lease. Each time Omuran and Arubo – the managers of the company – want to deliver something to another era, they are hindered by Munmun, Kosuinen and Kiokanshin of the competetor's company Sharecowbellies, that took over the remains of the Clean Aku Trio. But Ippatsuman comes to their aid, saving the day.

0546 SERIES

KIKOKANTAI DAIRUGGER XV (*Armor Fleet Dairugger XV*), Toei Doga for Toshi Co., robot, 52 episodes, 3/3/1982 – 2/23/1983. *Voltron: Legend Of The Universe*.

Our planet has finally reached a period of prosperity because of the mutual-aid agreement formed between Earth and the populations of the stars Mila and Sara. The president of the earth league plans a mission to explore the deep space outside our galaxy, sending the spaceship RuggerGuard, that unexpectedly meets up with a spaceship sent by the Galbeston Empire with the same mission. Attacked, the RuggerGuard defends itself with Dairugger XV, an immensely complex mechanical robot. In Italy, a small part of it was seen at the end of the *Voltron* series; the aim of the American version was to add a conclusion to the series they had created out of *Golion*.

0547 SERIES

MAHO NO PRINCESS MINKY MOMO (*Minky Momo, the Princess of Magic*), Ashi, magic, 63 episodes, 3/18/1982 – 5/26/1983. *Magical Princess Gigi*.

The village of dreams is about to disappear. The king and the queen are preoccupied and think that the cause might be attributed to the fact that human beings are no longer able to dream and fantasize. The king and queen ask their daughter Momo to go down to Earth to discover people's dreams and make them come true with the help of a magic wand that

Maho no Princess Minky Momo © Ashi Production.
Magical Princess Gigi © Harmony Gold U.S.A., Inc.

can transform her into a grown woman. The series presents the typical elements of the "magical girl" type and numbers amongst its collaborators Toyoo Ashida and Noa Misaki for the characterization. The general supervision is by Kunihiko Yuyama.

0548 SERIES

DON DRACULA (*id.*), Tezuka/Sankyo kikaku, humor, 8 episodes, 4/5 – 4/26/1982.

Unperturbed, the famous count has continued to suck blood of innocent victims through the centuries in his palace in Transylvania. One day he decides to move to Japan, bringing his own castle stone by stone. With some difficulty, he tries to adjust to a way of life completely different than anything he had previously known. In a Japanese metropolis there is a lot of life even at nighttime, and the vampire must discover entirely new methods of finding the blood that he craves. His biggest obstacle, however, is Professor Van Helsing, a fearless vampire hunter who has followed the tracks of his worst enemy to his new home. This mediocre comedy series was taken from Osamu Tezuka's comic and directed by Masamune Ochiai; it earned very little critical or commercial success.

Don Dracula © Tezuka Production.

0549 SERIES

TONDERA HOUSE NO DAIBOKEN (*Great Adventure of Amazing House*), Tatsunoko, magic/historical, 52 episodes, 4/5/1982 – 3/28/1983. *The Flying House.*

The young Gen and Kanna find themselves dragged into an amazing adventure, beginning with an amazing creation made by a strange inventor named Time Tokyo. The scientist had built a time machine, the Tindera House, which he uses to take the children through the streams of history. Accompanied by the funny looking robot Kandenchin and by Kanna's brother, Tsukubo, they travel through countless historical eras, having adventures and solving thousands of mysteries from the past.

0550 SERIES

GAME CENTER ARASHI (*id.*), Shin'ei Doga, adventure, 26 episodes, 4/5 – 9/27/1982.

The Flying House © Tatsunoko Pro.

0551 SERIES

PATALIRO – BOKU PATALIRO (*Pataliro, I Pataliro*), Toei Doga, humor, 49 episodes, 4/8/1982 – 5/13/1983.

The adventures of the short and tyrannical monarch Pataliro revolutionize the classic outlines of Japanese series, inserting the theme of homosexuality as a new element. The author Mineo Maya presents a group of characters – all male, even if some don't seem to look like it. Besides the monarch, the not so virile prime minister Bankolan plays an important role in the series, living an ambiguous love story with the fascinating Maraihi.

0552 SERIES

KAGAKU KYUJOTAI TECHNOVOYAGER (*Science Rescue Team Technovoyager*), Jin, science fiction, 18 episodes, 4/17 – 9/11/1982. *Thunderbird 2086.*

The criminal organizations always use sophisticated methods, availing themselves of the most modern technology to complete any kind of criminal undertaking. The only ones who seem to be able to hinder them are the members of the technovoyager, an investigative patrol equally strong on earth, in the sky, on the water or into space. The anime features characters and plots from Jerry Anderson's animated super-marionation series

Thunderbirds, which came from England in the first half of the sixties. The design supervision of the animated series is by Kenzo Koizumi, the design is by Kunio Anoi (first part) and Kazuto Ishizawa (second part), the supervision of the backdrops is by Katsu Amamizu, Mitsuru Ishii and Yasushi Nakamura, the screenplay is by Noboru Ishiguro, Kazuo Yoshioka, Takayuki Kase, Shiro Ishimori, Kiyoshi Kubata; Yao Asegawa is in charge of general supervision and Isao Ikeda is producer. In Italy, T*echnovoyager* has been seen with computer graphic special effects that were added later for the version broadcast in America.

0553 SERIES

ANIME YASEI NO SAKEBI (*The Animation of the Call of the Wild*), Wako, animals, 22 episodes, 5/5 – 12/24/1982.

The series doesn't have any main characters, but each episode features new animal characters in moving adventures.

0554 SERIES

MAKYO DENSETSU ACROBUNCH (*Acrobunch, the Legend of the Magic Country*), Kokusai eigasha (from the 13th episode, TOEI Doga for Kokusai eigasha), robot, 24 episodes, 5/5 – 12/24/1983. [*L'Empire Des Cinq*].

Makyo Densetsu Acrobunch © Movie International.

The four Lando siblings, Jun, Hero, Miki and Reika, along with the wise head of the Tatsuya family and with the help of a powerful robot born from the joining of three super-equipped vehicles, must face a terrible enemy and discover the secret of Quaschika, a long-vanished civilization. The evil emperor Goblin, with the cooperation of the powerful Delos, keeps trying to overpower the earthlings, in order to take possession of mythical buried treasures. The design is entrusted to Yuichi Higuchi, while the production features the collaboration of Yoshyo Nakamura and Shigeo Tsubota. The series is created by Yu Yamamoto.

0555 SERIES

OCHAMEGAMI MONOGATARI COLOCOLO POLON (*Colocolo Polon, the Story of the Joker Goddess*), Kokusai eigasha, humor, 46 episodes, 5/8/1982 – 3/26/1983. [*La Petite Olympe Et Les Dieux*].

Pollon, the youngest daughter of Apollo, lives amongst the gods of Olympus. She has only one wish: to become a goddess. Always ending up in some kind of trouble, along with her friend Eros, Pollon learns from the queen of the goddesses that she will realize her dream only when the piggy bank given to her is filled. To fill it up, she needs special coins which she can only gain by doing specific good deeds for various characters pulled from Greek mythology. This comedy for children also managed to charm older audiences. The entertaining plot is taken from Hideo Azuma's manga; the director Yotsuji Takao directed the animation supervised by Yu Yamamoto. It is the first complete series produced by Kokusai eigasha.

0556 SERIES

TONDEMON PE (*id.*), Tokyo Movie Shinsha, humor, 42 episodes, 6/5/1982 – 4/2/1983.

Monchan, a housewife and Baby Pe, an obnoxious little girl, are the main characters of this comedy series. Their adventures evolve through the classic outlines of modern Japanese society, parodying it as chaotic and unlivable.

0557 SERIES

TAIYO NO KO ESTEBAN (*Esteban, the Young Boy From the Sun*), Studio Pierrot/MK, adventure, 39 episodes, 6/29/1982 – 6/7/1983. [*Les Mystérieuses Cités D'Or*].

Young Lia, a descendant of the ancient Incas, possesses a mysterious gold medallion given her by her father, and which came from the mythical Eldorado. Through perils and a series of difficulties, she finds help in Esteban, a young Spanish boy, and they set off to find the golden city of South America. Some conquistadors, yearning for riches, follow them to take possession of the precious treasures. Moreover, the two young characters are forced to unexpectedly face an alien civilization who also want to control Eldorado. With the help of a giant flying golden bird, who works on solar power, Esteban, Lia and other companions met along the journey, gain the upper hand and outwit the alien threat. An archeological/fantasy series, well written and directed.

0558 SERIES

THE KABOCHA WINE (*The Pumpkin Wine*), Toei Doga, soap opera/humor, 95 episodes, 7/5/1982 – 8/27/1984. [*Mes Tendres Années*].

That which for many would be the dream of a lifetime is nothing but a nightmare for the young Shunsuke. He has spent his entire life surrounded by nothing but women, and now, as a teenager, cannot bear to even look at women of any kind. Without showing homosexual tendencies, the young man rejects any kind of contact with women, and isn't able to even be around them for very long. To re-educate the young man and help him generate normal relationships with women, his family decides to send him to a high school where Shunsuke meets Elle, a full-figured student who falls madly in love with him. The situations he gets into, based entirely on their complicated relationship, are amongst the most entertaining scenes ever created in a series of this type – one that can be included in the soft core-erotica genre. The animated series is taken from the *Kabocha Wine* drawn on paper by Mitsuru Miura.

0559 SERIES

GINGA REPPU BAXINGER (*Baxinger, the Galactic Cyclone*), Kokusai eigasha, robot, 39 episodes, 7/6/1982 – 3/29/1983.

This is the second series that uses the team of Rangers from Cosmos J9 as main characters. In this case, the members of the team are the fearless Don Condor, Billy the Shot, Suke, Laila and Shutekken, the five reckless drivers of the robot Baxinger, a warrior formed by joining their motorcycles.

0560 SERIES

CHOJIKU YOSAI MACROSS (*Super Dimensional Fortress Macross*), Tatsunoko, robot, 36 episodes, 10/3/1982 – 6/26/1983. *Robotech / Macross*.

The year is 1999. An alien spaceship crashes on an Earth devastated by the Third World War. To prevent an alien attack, the nations of Earth form a coalition, a central supergovernment with the goal of restoring the spaceship to use it against the coming aggressors. Ten years later, on the trail of their lost spaceship, the Zentran aliens come to Earth. Immediately intercepted by Macross (the new name given to the spaceship), they begin a conflict which eventually involves the civilian Hikaru Ichijo, whose intervention

Taiyo no Ko Esteban © Studio Pierrot / MK

Robotech ©1995 Tatsunoko Production Co., Ltd. ©1985 Harmony Gold, U.S.A., Inc. / Tatsunoko Production Co., Ltd. Package design ©1995 Streamline Enterprises, Inc.

Robotech ©1985 Harmony Gold, U.S.A., Inc. / Tatsunoko Production Co., Ltd. All Rights Reserved. Package design ©1987 The Art Department. Original Family Home Entertainment release.

Robotech ©1985 Harmony Gold, U.S.A., Inc. / Tatsunoko Production Co., Ltd. All Rights Reserved. Package design ©1993 Live Home Video, Inc. 1993 Family Home Entertainment re-release.

saves the life of Lynn Minmay, a young Chinese girl. In the meantime, Macross makes an uncontrollable leap through space, taking with it Macross City and its civilian inhabitants. Having lost the «folding mechanism,» a space/time travel system, the spaceship and the refugees have to travel back from Pluto to Earth on their own. After forced exile inside the spaceship, the friendship between Hikaru and Minmay becomes stronger, even if the singing career of the young woman continues to separate them. Hikaru meanwhile, decides to enlist. This brings Major Misa Hayase, who is secretly in love with Hikaru, into the picture as the superior of the young man.

During an exploration mission, the two are captured by the Zentrans who discover they are dealing with Micronians (the Zentrans are 15 meters high), who live, as far as they can see, with an absolute lack of morals. The Zentrans are disgusted, simply because 500,000 years before, the Zentrans lived peacefully in a civilization similar to that of the Earth. Genetically more advanced, to protect themselves from external aggressions, they had created a police core formed of gigantic beings reproduced by cloning and thus free of sexual feelings and desires. Soon, however, their natural predisposition to war brought them to revolt first among themselves and then against their creators. Now, the Zentrans want to retrieve the secret of something called "protoculture," which is in reality the essence of humanity: love. While Misa and Hikaru escape back to Macross, the alien spaceships begin to receive Minmay's songs – music that provokes a surprising number of defections. Thanks to Minmay, in fact, the Zentran army is discovering love, their protoculture.

After Macross returns to Earth, they begin negotiations between the two civilizations, but Dolza, their supreme chief, manages to restart the hostilities. The outcome of the fierce battle is his death, along with the complete devastation of the Earth. Two years later the situation seems peaceful again, and the aliens perfectly integrated, but their warlike spirit builds up over the ashes of boredom. The ending is apocalyptic; a series of terrible battles finds Misa and Hikaru the only survivors, happily together after the young man makes his choice between the attractive actress and the courageous soldier.

0561 SERIES
NINJAMAN IPPEI (*Ippei, Ninja Man*), Tokyo Movie Shinsha, historical/humor, 13 episodes, 10/4 – 12/27/1982.

0562 SERIES
CYBOT ROBOTTY (*Id.*), Knack, robot, 39 episodes, 10/7/1982 – 6/29/1983.

Doctor Deko, a cybernetic genius, loves to be surrounded by handyman robots, which is why his house and his garden are completely automated. With the creation of the little Cybot Robotty, however, the professor gives life to a baby robot that behaves exactly like a human being – except for the fact that he's equipped with a holographic projector capable of materializing anything. The little robot makes every effort to get himself and his friends out of the most complicated situations and to win the heart of the young Kurumi, while being sought after by Cybot and the fat Boss. The series is based on Toyohiro Ando and Ken Ishikawa's original script. For the artistic direction, the production firm can count on the collaboration of Noboru Kameyama and Hiroshi Yoshida.

0563 SERIES

SPACE COBRA (*Id.*), Tokyo Movie Shinsha, science fiction, 31 episodes, 10/7/1982 – 5/19/1983. [*Cobra*].

In a distant future, a business man is bored because of lack of adventure in his life. He doesn't have enough money to take even a small vacation, and so he contacts a dream travel agency where it is possible to live the adventure of your dreams – in your dreams! As in the story of Philip Dick, which was the inspiration for the movie *Total Recall*, the strange dream that he is given frightens him, as a program for space adventures doesn't exist! The man discovers, step by step, that he was once a man called Cobra, a solitary pirate hunted by the space Mafia. Years ago, to finally find some peace and rest, he hid his trail by changing both his face and his memories. His desire for adventure is finally fulfilled, and Captain Cobra goes back to action with the android Lady, terrorizing criminal gangs with the psychocannon implanted in his arm.

0564 SERIES

TOKIMEKI TONIGHT (*Night Emotion*), Group Tack for Toho, magic, 34 episodes, 10/7/1982 – 9/22/1983.

It's not that difficult to run into legendary creatures in Japan, especially in the world of animation, and this story, adapted from Koi Ikeno's comic by Toshio Okase and Hiroshi Sasagawa is proof of that. Ranze, a little girl who seems much the same as any other, is the daughter of a vampire and a wolfwoman. The Etos family have left the world of Hell to come to Earth and live a normal life. Things get complicated when Ranze discovers her latent power (she can change into anyone she bites) and when she falls in love with the handsome Shinpeki, her school mate. Unfortunately, a very strict law forbids infernal creatures from marrying human beings. The happy ending however, occurs when the young man reveals himself to be Satan's long lost son.

0565 SERIES

AI NO SENSHI RAINBOWMAN (*Rainbowman, the Love Warriors*), Ai Kikaku, robot, 22 episodes, 10/10/1982 – 3/27/1983.

Takeshi Yamato, having followed the training exercizes of master yogi Daivadattha for years, comes to possess super powers that enable him to transform into different things. He joins the Mecha V Armor, a warrior-mech made up of organic substances that spontaneously assemble, and he can also transform into the seven mega robots RainbowSeven. His duty is to defend Japan against the Shineshinedans (Group diedie).

0566 SERIES

WAGA SEISHUN NO ARCADIA – MUGEN KIDO SSX (*Arcadia of My Youth: Infinite Course SSX*), Toei Doga for Tokyu, science fiction, 22 episodes, 10/13/1982 – 3/30/1983. *Albator '84*.

This series is the sequel to the previous feature film. The space pirate, together with La Mime, his faithful friend Tochiro and the courageous queen Emeraldas, continues his journey in search of freedom. During one of their many stops, Harlock meets a young orphan woman whose parents both died in an attack by the Humanoids. She ends up joining his crew to avenge their deaths.

Space Adventure Cobra ©1982 Buichi Terasawa / Tokyo Movie Shinsha Co. (TMS). All Rights Reserved. Package design ©1998 Urban Vision Entertainment, Inc. Only the movie (#0533), which was released in Japan before the TV series, is available in English.

Albator '84 © L. Matsumoto / Toei Co, Ltd.

Sasuga no Sarutobi
© F. Hosono / Shogakukan / Kyokutsu.

0567 SERIES
HITOTSUBOSHIKE NO ULTRA BASAN (*The Super Grandmother of the Hitotsuboshi Family*), Knack, humor, 13 episodes, 10/16/1982 –1/15/1983.

0568 SERIES
SASUGA NO SARUTOBI (*Sarutobi, True to Himself*), Tsuchida Production for Nas, humor, 69 episodes, 10/17/1982 – 3/11/1984. [*L'Académie Des Ninja*].

0569 SERIES
FUKUCHAN (*Little Fuku*), Shin'ei Doga, humor, 59 episodes, 11/2/1982 – 3/27/1984.

The main character appeared for the first time in 1933, in several newspapers as an ongoing comic strip. It earned so much success that it continued uninterrupted until 1971. Eleven years later, the little Fuku returns in this series, which remains devoutly faithful to the original cartoon.

0570 SERIES
SHIN MITSUBACHI MAYA NO BOKEN (*The Adventures of Maya the Bee – Second Series*), Nippon Animation, animals, 52 episodes, 10/12/1982 – 9/27/1983.

The success of the first series – in Japan as well as in the western world – called for the making of this new set of 52 episodes, centered on the life of insects. Maya and Willy continue to get into trouble while going about their daily lives.

0571 SPECIAL
PENGUIN MURA EIYU NO DENSETU (*The Legend of the Heroes From Penguin Village*), Toei Doga, adventure, 54 min., 1/2.

0572 SPECIAL
SANGOKUSHI (*The Three Kingdoms*), Shin'ei Doga, historical, 93 min., 1/4.

0573 SPECIAL
KAO MEIJIN GEKIJO – NANIWABUSHI DAISUKI (*I Adore Naniwabushi*), Tohankikaku, soap opera, 2/7.

"Naniwabushi" is a famous Japanese lullaby that mothers have known for generations.

0574 SPECIAL
WAGAHAI WA NEKO DE ARU (*I Am a Cat*), Toei Doga, animals, 84 min., 2/17.

0575 SPECIAL
TSUDAN FULL BASE (*Two Strikes With Bases Full*), Group Tack for Toho, sport, 5/5.

0576 SPECIAL
SHIROI KIBA – WHITE FANG MONOGATARI (*The Story of White Fang*), Nippon Sunrise, classic, 85 min., 5/5.

A hunter lives in the North American woods with his faithful companion White Fang, a splendid wolf that follows him in every adventure. The extremely dramatic finale moves the television viewers, especially in the final scene, taken directly from the popular novel. This is only one of the animated versions.

0577 SPECIAL

SONGOKU SICK ROAD O TOBU!! (*Songoku, Flies on the Way of Silk*), Tokyo Movie Shinsha, musical, 73 min., 6/17.

The Legend of Songoku has often been transposed into animation. This time, the musical genre is used by Tokyo Movie Shinsha for this remake of the story, unfortunately one that earned little success.

0578 SPECIAL

OBAKE (*Ghost*), Ai kikaku, humor, 115 min., 8/15.

0579 SPECIAL

ANDROMEDA STORIES (*id.*), Toei Doga, science fiction, 120 min., 8/22.

Based on the story by Ryu Mitsuse and Keiko Takemiya, Masamitsu Sasaki directs this science fiction story that features the music of Yuji Ono. The planet Altair is celebrating a very special event: the wedding of the young King Itaca from Cosmoralia with Queen Lilia. Soon, however, the couple's happiness is darkened by the appearance of a mysterious and evil computer that, with the help of minuscule mechanical insects capable of entering humans' brains, wants to take possession of the planet to create a utopic world of machines. Only the pregnant Lilia survives with her nanny. The twins she bears are treated as a bad omen by the superstitious nanny, and she takes one of the babies away to be raised by a man she trusts. Lilia is forced to escape with her son Gimsa, helped by her brother and by Iru, a female android-warrior, a survivor from the destruction of her native planet Rodon, caused by the same enemy that is now threatening Altair.

The years pass and Gimsa begins to manifest paranormal powers that he uses to reconquer the kingdom with the help of a group of rebels guided by an old scientist. In the meantime, the queen is captured and put into suspended animation by an enormous computer. Gimsa, meanwhile, encounters his twin Alf, raised in a camp of nomads and gifted, like her brother, with strong ESP powers. But, notwithstanding the joining of their forces, the twins don't succeed in getting the upper hand on the enemy. The old scientist, who is in reality the creator of the central computer of which he had lost control, tries to free his friends from the android threat. He reaches a spaceship orbiting around Altair where the Rodonian survivors had found safety. The spaceship crashes on the planet, destroying it. The only survivors, Gimsa and Alf, travel towards a new world aboard a second spaceship, but they also crash, this time on a beautiful blue planet. Their decomposed bodies will create life on Earth.

0580 SPECIAL

AI NO KISEKI DOCTOR NORMAN MONOGATARI (*The Story of Dr. Norman, the Miracle of Love*), Kokusai eigasha, adventure, 84 min., 12/24.

0581 SPECIAL

BOPPEN SENSEI TO KAERAZU NO NUMA (*Boppen the Teacher and the Lake of no Return*), Meruhensha, adventure, 80 min., 4/29.

0582 SPECIAL
JUGO SHONEN HYORYUKI (*Fifteen Young Castaways*), Toei Doga, classic, 75 min., 8/22.

Taken from Jules Verne's novel, this television special directed by Masayuki Akehi tells the adventures of fifteen young people who, because of a shipwreck on a deserted island, are forced to survive in a hostile and primitive world for two years. The different experience helps them to grow into maturity and they return as responsible adults. Hiroshi Wagatsuma realizes the character design, on the screenplay by Aiko Ishimatsu. The soundtrack is by Katsutoshi Nagasawa.

0583 SPECIAL
NYAROME NO OMOSHIROSUGAKU KYOSHITSU (*Nyarome's Math Class*), Studio Zero, humor, 53 min., 8/11.

0584 SPECIAL
SHONEN MIYAMOTO MUSASHI – WANPAPU NITORYU (*The Young Musashi Miyamoto: the Whirling Technique of the Two-Bladed Combat*), Teoi Doga, historical, 84 min., 10/6.

The little Bennosuke Miyamoto is witness to the death of his father, a skilled swordsman, at the hands of Hirata, known for his bravery and his skill. Bennosuke challenges Hirata, but becoming aware of his rival's superiority, he decides to become his disciple instead. Having finally learned the secrets of the use of the katana, Bennosuke kills Hirata. Then, fighting with some of the best warriors of medieval Japan, he acquires the techniques and the shrewdness he needs to become the best swordsman of all time. As an adult, he leaves the name of Bennosuke and assumes the name of Musashi. The book of the five rings that he wrote during his career is an excellent source of psychological preparation for anyone who has to face a trial, even today. Many modern warriors, even traders on the stock exchange, admit to seeking inspiration from the pages of his book and the codes of his life.

0585 SPECIAL
PROGOLFER SARU (*id.*), Shin'ei Doga, sport, 110 min., 10/19.

The prolific pen of the duo Fujiko Fujio once again catches the attention of producers, who finally agreed to do a series dedicated to golf. Basing every episode on incredible tournaments where players use special shots that border on absurdity, the creative duo attempts to step away from their usual themes and concentrate on a series entirely dedicated to one character with a monkey-like face, appropriately enough named "Saru" (monkey).

0586 SPECIAL
THE KABOCHA WINE ORE TO AITSU NO SHINKON RYOKO (*The Pumpkin Wine: She and I On a Honeymoon?!*), Toei Doga, soap opera, 12/27.

CHAPTER TWENTY-TWO: 1983

The year 1983 sees the birth of an important form of animation distribution: the Original Animation Video or OAV.

Dallos: Dallos Hakai Shirei is the first anime to come out directly on video tape without having passed by television or the movie theatre. The convenience of being able to enjoy an animation at any desired time and without commercials brings the anime fans to immediatly adopt this new format, buying video tapes to collect them or rent them. The success is so great that other production firms timidly try OAV. The following years, six come out, three of which continue the saga of *Dallos*: the distributors are still clearly hesitant, not knowing if the success is due to the new format or to the animation itself. In 1985, the OAV producers take the hint and launch such a great quantity of animation on video tapes that there is fear of market saturation. This however doesn't happen and thus, the Original Animation Video becomes one of the main means to distribute animated productions. The television networks, suffering from a drastic drop in ratings, begin signing contracts with OAV production firms for the broadcasting rights of the video tapes after the first months on the videocassette market. The new formula allows the experimentation of a new genre, difficult to broadcast on television, the erotic animation. After appearing as a surrounding ingredient in certain episodes, erotism will take over in series like *Cream Lemon* in which the sexual relationship — whether normal, homosexual or S.& M. — is at the base of the story.

1983 is a year that offers anime TV series of high levels, some of which made history. *Cat's Eyes*, adapted from Tsukasa Hojo's manga, makes its debut. Thanks to the good characterisation and to the theme of "gentleman robber," TMS makes a series in which three sisters endowed with curves in all the right places and gifted with an uncommon astuteness, steal works of art under the nose of policemen to find their disappeared father. Presenting a fluid animation and showing the sensual movements of the three robers in tights, the animated series generates the enthusiasm of mostly adult viewers who await week after week the development of the strange love between one of the sisters and their hunter, an unlucky police lieutenant.

Cat's Eyes © Tsukasa Hôjô / Shûeisha / TMS.

Another revelation of the year is *Maho no Tenshi Creami Mami* , a series belonging to the "magical girl" genre, taken from Yuko Kitagawa and Kazunori Ito's manga. It earns its success because of the songs introduced in the setting of the episodes — sung by the magical character, an eight year old girl capable of changing into a sixteen year old. *Maho no Tenshi Creamy Mami* will give Studio Pierrot the title of Workshop Prince of the "magical girl" animation. In the following years, practically every series of this type will pass through the hands of its skillful illustrators.

On the soap opera front, *Lady Georgie* and *Ai Shite Night* get noticed — both very popular also in Italy — featuring tangled love stories amongst young people, the first set in the Australia and England of the last century, the other in modern Japan amongst the glamour of pop music. In both cases, the sexual aspect is toned down in comparison with the manga from which the series are taken. The "weaker" sex is once again the main character of two entertaining series. The first, *Spoon Obasan,* features with a humorous twist and a

Maho no Tenshi Creami Mami
© Studio Pierrot / NTV.

Super Dimension Century Orguss ©1983, 1992 TMS / Big West. All Rights Reserved. English version ©1992 TMS / Big West / L.A. Hero / U.S. Renditions.

Robotech: The New Generation ©1995 Harmony Gold U.S.A. Inc. / Tatsunoko Prod. Co., Ltd. All Rights Reserved. Package design & art ©1990 Palladium Books, Inc.

European characterisation, the tender adventures of a very old woman from the mountains who often gets into trouble because of the magical spoon she often wears around her neck and which has the power to make her smaller. *Nanako S.O.S.* narrates the funny story of a shy young girl gifted with superpowers, but victim of a terrible form of amnesia that prevents her from remembering who she is and where she comes from. As luck would have it, she meets two young men who offer to help. When the schrewdest of the two discovers Nanako's great capacities, he wants to use her for money, to become the richest man in the world, without however getting any results. A funny parody of the success that certain individuals want to obtain using the capacities of others.

The sports type finds an imitator in *Captain Tsubasa*, a soccer serial featuring young children. If *Captain Tsubasa* has its basis in *Akakichi no Eleven*, featuring endless soccer games in which the use of special shots has become rule, in *Kinnikuman*, the main character is the head of a household, but the series is more explicitly dedicated to the children and filled with insanity more than humour. The duo Fujiko Fujio strikes again using *Paman,* one of its many manga productions, to make a series in which, for once, the heroes are still children. Gifting a group of children with super powers makes it so that the adventures are lived by the children themselves without the help of space cats or of ghosts (like *Doraemon* and *Obake no Qtaro*). A more classical series is *Bem Bem Hunter Kotengu Tenmaru* by Kabuto Mushi (pen-name of Mushitaro Kabuto) who, inspired by *Urusei Yatsura* by Rumiko Takahashi, fetches in popular traditions, elves and demons, making them bring confusion to our days in a series not aimed to young children anymore.

Tatsunoko continues unperturbed with the *Time Machine* series, proposing this time *Itadakiman* whose characters — especially the ennemies — imitate once again the characteristics of the previous series, but using this time the characters of the legend of *Saiyuki*; the parody holds up and, in only twenty episodes, it laughs at the common place of robot series.

Of all the series that feature wars between steel giants as central element, the most innovative in every sense is *Seisenshi Dunbine*. While the robot style, after the dawning of *Gundam*, directs its footsteps towards a more realistic structure in the story and in the technology used — like the excellent *Chojiku Seiki Orguss* and the neglectable *Akudai Sasuken Srungle* — in *Seisenshi Dunbine* we witness a radical change of tendency. The screenplay is fantasy and the fairies are indispensable to the evolution of the story. Amidst court intrigues, betrayals, alliances and indissoluble loves, stand the magical warriors gifted with powers to animate the Aura Battlers, fairy-tale robots which look like insects.

On the contrary, Nagai drives his own productions on a more realistic road making *Psycho Armor Gorborian*, a series in which a curious technological and squared version of his old Mazinger is joined by two robots of the "new generation."

Tatsunoko, other than the *Time Bokan Series Itadakiman*, also proposes *Kikososeiki Mospeada* — later picked up by an american production firm that mixed it with *Macross* and *Southern Cross* into the incomprehensible *Robotech,* which was also seen in Italy — that renew the classic transformations and make the characters' motocycle change into battle armors. *Mirai Keisatsu Urashiman* features the adventures of three policemen of the future in a plausible and not excessively "science-fiction" setting. The character designs unfortunaltly are not really well-done and can be a little annoying to the viewer.

On the movie front, *Crusher Joe* makes his first appearance as a futuristic adventurer, head of a space patrol. The character design is by the much acclaimed Yasuhiko Yoshikazu, already in charge of *Kido Senshi Gundam*.

Finally, from Keiji Nakazawa's original manga, comes *Hadashi no Gen*, a film that brings up once again the terror of the atomic explosion at Hiroshima, seen through the eyes of a child who has lost family and friends in the destruction of the city. Going around in the debris, Gen will come to know numerous personnal dramas and learn to hate war. A touching film and more actual than ever.

0587 FILM

URUSEI YATSURA ONLY YOU (*Those Obnoxious Aliens: Only You*), Kitty Film, comedy, 91 min., 2/21. *Urusei Yatsura: Only You.*

Mendo unexpectedly receives an invitation to Ataru and the extra-terrestrial princess El's wedding, so the young man goes to his friend for explanations. Mendo's illusion to finally have the beautiful Lamu all to himself doesn't last very long. Surprised, Ataru in fact, doesn't know anything about it. Lamu will do anything to defeat her beautiful rival generating chaos, misunderstandings and entertainment. The designs, once again by Akemi Takada, contributes to soften and gives a more adult look to the characters.

0588 FILM

NINJA HATTORIKUN NINNIN FURUSATO DAISAKUSEN NO MAKI (*Hattori, the Little Ninja: the Chapter of the Great Clash in His Native Country*), Shin'ei Doga, humour, 42 min., 3/12.

0589 FILM

PAMAN - BIRDMAN GA YATTEKITA! (*Paman, Here is Birdman!*), Shin'ei Doga, humour, 45 min., 3/2.

Another film-collage made with the best scenes of the television series, originally produced in the 70s by the duo Fujiko Fujio.

0590 FILM

GENMA TAISEN (*The Great War of the Demon of Illusions*), Project Team Argos/Madhouse/Magic Capsul for Haruki Kadokawa, science-fiction, 125 min., 3/12. *Harmagedon.*

Taken from Shotaro Ishimori's manga, with new character designs by Katsushiro Otomo, the film is the first work produced by Haruki Kadokawa, even if the production was effectively done by Madhouse and Magic Bus. Luna, a transilvanian princess comes to know, through her superpowers, that Earth is about to be invaded by Genma (Illusion). So she assembles a great number of espers, whose superpowers are reactivated with the nearing of Genma.

0591 FILM

CRUSHER JOE (*id.*), Nippon Sunrise, science-fiction, 125 min., 3/12.

Urusei Yatsura: Only You ©1983 Kitty Films. English version & Package artwork ©1992 AnimEigo. All Rights Reserved.

Harmagedon ©1983 Kadokawa Shoten Publishing Co., Ltd. English version & Package artwork ©1993 Central Park Media Corporation.

Crusher Joe: The Movie ©1983/1997 Haruka Takachiho & Studio Nue • Sunrise, Inc. Licensed to AnimEigo, Inc. by Sunrise, Inc.

Final Yamato ©1995 Voyager Entertainment, Inc. All Rights Reserved.

Crusher Joe is the captain of a police space patrol, involved in the difficult mission to free a princess, prisonner in hibernation by a group of terrorists. Commanded by the main character, three courageous mercenaries combat by his side: the blond Alfin, the little Ricky and the strong Taros. *Crusher Joe* made by the same staff that worked on the series *Dirty Pair*; the main character even makes an appearance in a movie dedicated to the "lovely angels", when the strong Mugi sees him on a giant screen during a dynamic chase.

0592 FILM

Dr. SLUMP & ARALECHAN HOYO YO! SEKAI ISSHU DAI RACE (*Dr. Slump & Arale Chan: Hoyoyo! the Great Race Around the World*), Toei Doga, humour, 75 min., 3/13.

0593 FILM

MANGA ESOPO MONOGATARI (*The Tales of Esop in Manga*), Toei Doga, fairy-tale, 3/13.

0594 FILM

DORAEMON - NOBITA NO KAITEIKIGANJO (*Doraemon, Nobita's Monstruous Underwater Castle*), Shin'ei Doga, humour, 95 min., 3/13.

0595 FILM

UCHU SENKAN YAMATO: KANKETSU HEN (*Space Cruiser Yamato: Final Chapter*), Toei Doga for Westcape, science-fiction, 160 min., 4/29. *Final Yamato*.

The oceans of Aquarius, a planet near the Earth, are about to cover the few surfaces left and, to save itself, the fortress city that hosts all the inhabitants, detaches itself from the ground, reaching space. Following the lines of a plan to conquer the Earth, the Aquarians divert the waters against our planet that risks to be swept away. Captain Okita, who is believed to be dead, reappears unexpectedly after a period of hibernation and, having evacuated the spaceship, he hurls it against the tide transforming the Yamato in an enormous breakwater. The ring of water undergoes a forced deviation that saves the Earth, while the spaceship sinks in one of the most suggestive scenes of Leiji Matsumoto's production.

0596 FILM

NOEL NO FUSHIGINA BOKEN (*The Marvelous Adventures of Noel*), Iruka Office, fairy-tale, 80 min., 4/29.

0597 FILM

PROYAKYU O JUBAI TANOSHIKU MIRU HOHO (*How to See Baseball in a Way Ten Times More Entertaining*), Tokyo Movie Shinsha for Film Link, humour/sport, 95 min., 4/29.

Takenori Emoto, famous player in the Tigers, a Japanese baseball team, is remembered also today by many regular fans. He is the author of two books that narrate entertaining episodes linked to the baseball world, many of which are transposed in animation and assembled in this movie.

0598 FILM

GOLGO 13 (*id.*), Tokyo Movie Shinsha for Film Link, police story, 94 min., 5/28. *The Professional: Golgo 13*.

The adventures of Golgo 13, a character created by Takao Saito in 1969 as protagonist in a series of police story manga, are transposed into animation by the director Osamu

Dezaki. The main character is once again a negative hero, a ruthless killer who doesn't hesitate to oppose the moral and ethic laws of the society in which he lives. Notwithstanding his cynicism and the cruelty of his actions, Golgo 13 soon earns the favors of an always increasing public, becoming one of the most liked characters of the year.

0599 FILM

XABUNGLE GRAFFITI (*id.*), Nippon Sunrise, robot, 90 min., 7/9.

0600 FILM

DOCUMENT TAIYO NO KIBA DOUGRAM (*The Document of Dougram: the Sun's Fang*), Nippon Sunrise, robot, 90 min., 7/9.

Two years after the television series, Nippon Sunrise proposes a movie remake of the adventures of Peroia 7's fighters, the revolutionnary resistance group from planet Deroia. The young people are supported in their battle against an alien population by strong mechanical robots amongst which the powerful Dougram stands out.

0601 FILM

CHORO Q DOUGRAM (*id.*), Nippon Sunrise, robot, 10 min., 7/9.

0602 FILM

PATALIRO! STARDUST KEIKAKU (*Pataliro! Program Stardust*), Toei Doga, humour, 48 min., 7/16.

The prinicpality of Marinella is all worked-up: the scientists have noticed a meteorite in space that will break-up into hundreds of diamonds because of its friction with the atmosphere. Prince Pataliro prepares a plan to recover the diamonds, but the criminal organization Tarentella, having found out about the project, send Andersen, Jyunia's look-alike, ex-lover of Bancolan, minister of Marinella, to preceed the prince and hinder his plan.

0603 FILM

UNICO - MAHO NO SHIMAI E (*Unico Towards the Magic Island*), Madhouse for Sanrio, fasntasy, 7/16.

0604 FILM

HADASHI NO GEN (*Barefoot Gen*), Madhouse for Gen Prod., sociological, 110 min., 7/21. *Barefoot Gen.*

The tragedy of Hiroshima described with a moving veracity in Keiji Nakazawa's manga is presented in this important film, produced by Yoshimoto Takanori and Yasuieru Iwase, which maintains, unchanged, the narrative pathos. Gen Nakaoka, a second grade student lives in Hiroshima with his family and awaits the birth of a new sibbling. August 6, 1945, the American bomber Enola Gay is forced to deviate from its original destination, the city of Kokura and to launch his atomic bomb on the city where Gen lives. The young boy sees his father and sister trapped under the ruins and his efforts to get them out are vain. His mother, helped by him, prematurely gives birth to the little Tomoko. Obsessively reliving the horrors of war may seem unfair and cruel to Western eyes, but in reality, the memory serves a warning for the future to new and older generations. The direction is by Mamoru Masaki, the backgrounds are by Kazuo Ojika and the character designs are by Kazuo Tomizawa.

The Professional: Golgo 13 ©1983 Saito Productions / ©1993 Streamline Pictures. Package design ©1999 Urban Vision Entertainment.

An eyewitness account of the bombing of Hiroshima

BAREFOOT GEN

Barefoot Gen ©1995 Orion Home Video & Streamline Pictures. All Rights Reserved.

0605 FILM

NINE (*id.*), Group Tack for Toho, sport, 83 min., 9/16.

0606 SERIES

MIRAI KEISATSU URASHIMAN (*Urashiman, The Policeman From The Future*), Tatsunoko, science-fiction, 50 episodes, 1/9 – 12/24/1983. [*Super Durand, Détective De Choc*].

The future has in store for humanity many innovations in daily life derived from technological development. Unfortunatly, criminals have kept-up with the times and with new means available to them, they are able to give violent blows to the law. Only a highly technological police can face the new threat. Ruy Urashima, Claude and the beautiful Sofia are part of the new police corps and, between daredevil pursuits, investigations and a few laughs, they almost always bring back order.

Mirai Keisatsu Urashiman © Tatsunoko.

0607 SERIES

ALPES MONOGATARI: WATASHI NO ANNETTE (*Alpine Story: My Annette*), Nippon Animation, classic, 52 episodes, 1/9 – 12/25/1983. [*Dans Les Alpes Avec Annette*].

Annette's mother dies while giving birth to little Dany. The young girl must take care of her brother like a real homemaker until an aunt moves into their home and becomes part of their family. Lucien, Annette's childhood friend accidentally causes Dany to fall and he looses the use of one of his legs. The little girl, to avenge her brother, destroys the little statue that her companion had sculpted with his own hands to participate in a local contest. From that moment, hatred set-in between them, but it is ironed out when Dany regains the use of his leg. Taking part in the making of the series are Kozo Kusuba for the direction, Kazuo Takematsu for the character design, Taizaburo Abe for the backgrounds and Kenji Yoshida for the screenplay.

Alpes Monogatari: Watashi no Annette
© Nippon Animation Co., Ltd.

0608 SERIES

CAPTAIN (*id.*), Eiken, sport, 26 episodes, 1/10 – 7/4/1983.

0609 SERIES

AKU DAI SAKUSEN SRUNGLE (*Srungle, The Great Orbital War*), Kokusai eigasha, robot, 53 episodes, 1/21/1983 - 1/20/1984. *Macron-1.*

The earthly population has overstepped the frontiers of space and the solar system now hosts many orbital stations. The plague of criminality is always present and is represented by an organisation called "Crimine," headed by the humanoid robot Fork-Rezor. The police can't seem to control the criminals. To come to the police's rescue, Doctor Mandi puts together a flight of courageous soldiers equiped with powerful mecha like the strong Srungle. The series however doesn't bring enthusiasm to anyone; the subject by Juzo Tsubota is common and the character designs, by Yoshitaka Amano, are rather rushed.

0610 SERIES

SEISENSHI DUNBINE (*Aura Battlers Dunbine*), Nippon Sunrise, robot, 49 episodes, 2/5/1983 – 1/21/1984.

During a motocross race, Sho Zama slips on a dimensionnal passage that opens on the world of Byston Well whose people are divided in two factions that are at war. Sho discovers that he possesses the Aura power that gives him the possibility to animate the complicated insect robots and is thus enrolled in the army of the tyrannical Drake Luft. However, having discovered the evil plans of the monarch, the young man decides to join the rebel forces, aboard the bio-mechanical Dunbine. A science-fiction fantasy set amidst court intrigues and technology that makes this series a new and interesting product.

0611 SERIES

AI SHITE NIGHT (*Love Me at Night*), Toei Doga, soap opera, 42 episodes, 3/1/1983 – 1/24/1984. [*Embrasse-Moi Lucille*].

The young Yaeko divides herself between her evening classes and work at her father's restaurant where she usually encounters the young Satomi, who is active in the rock band Beehive. The two young people are linked by mutual affection even if Yaeko's father is against it. The situation changes however, when Yaeko meets the little Hashizo, the brother of the charismatic Go, leader of Beehive. Soon, Yaeko falls in love with Go and has to choose between the two young men who have become rivals to the detriment of the musical group. Taken from Kaoru Tada's manga, the series is very pleasing because of the dynamic screenplay of Mitsuru Majima amongst others and a skillful direction by Osamu Kasai.

0612 SERIES

KOSOKU DENJI ALBGAS (*Albegas, The Electric God With The Speed Of Light*), Toei Doga for Toei Agency, robot, 45 episodes, 3/30/1983 – 2/8/1984.

On a subject by Saburo Yatsude, script by Akyoshi Sakai and Shozo Uehara, character designs by Kageyama Shigenori and mecha designs by Koichi Ohata, Akira Hio and Atsuo Ohara, Toei produces this new robot series directed by Morishita Kozo. Enjoji Daisaku, Jin Tetsuya and Hotaru Mizuki are three young geniuses of robotics who get the first three places at the robot construction exam of their high school. Professor Mizuki, Hotaru's father, decides to make the robot operative and, with certain changes, makes them capable of combining into the powerful robot Albegas, just in time to defend Earth against the attacks of the alien Derinjer.

0613 SERIES

MIYUKI (*id.*), Kitty Film, soap opera, 37 episodes, 3/31/1983 – 4/20/1984.

Mitsuru Adachi's first manga transposed into a television series soon becomes a great success because of the excellent animation totally faithful to the spirit of the manga. Miyuki, a college student, spends her days with her best friend, an exhuberant girl who bears the same name. Other than their names, they share the friendship of Masato, a friendly young man in love with both of them, who will choose one of them only at the end of the story.

0614 SERIES

SOKO KISHI VOTOMS (*Armored Trooper Votoms*), Nippon Sunrise, robot, 52 episodes, 4/1/1983 – 3/23/1984. *Armored Trooper Votoms*.

Kiriko Kyubi is the hero of this series based on the original subject of Ryosuke Takahashi who also directed it. The setting is once again a war and the main character, a mercenary of undisputed fame, finds himself involved in a bloody civil war that makes thousands of victims who died of hunger or fell under powerful mecha. Kiriko, belonging to the special corps of the "perfect soldiers" will thus have to come to understands the harsch reality of a conflict that has been going on for over 100 years. The character design is by Norio Shioyama.

Armored Trooper Votoms ©1983 Sunrise, Inc.. English version & Package ©1996 Central Park Media Corporation. All Rights Reserved.

0615 SERIES

NANAKO S.O.S. (*id.*), Kokusai eigasha, soap opera, 39 episodes, 4/2 – 12/24/1983. [*Super Nana*].

Falling from the deep space in a strong impact on our planet, the young Nanako loses her memory. She is soon helped by a materialistic and insane scientist and his naive assistant that see in her a considerable lucrative benefit. The young woman finds herself forced to manoeuvre between violent admirers who want to marry her and clumsy criminals who have problems with the law, but she always has the upper hand thanks to her super powers. The series, created by Hideo Azuma, is supervised by Yu Yamamoto with designs by the famous Tsuneo Ninomiya. Shiro Murata, Tsumeo Minomiya and Yoshiyuki Kikuchi alternate for the animation under the artistic advice of Hageshi Katsumada. The music is by Ichiro Nitta.

0616 SERIES

TIME BOKAN SERIES ITADAKIMAN (*The Time Machine Series: Itadakiman*), Tatsunoko, science-fiction, 20 episodes, 4/2/1983 – 9/3/1984.

Time Bokan Series Itadakiman © Tatsunoko.

The director of the famous Oshaka school orders three of his students (Hoshi, Sasosen and Hatsuo) to recover the pieces of the Oshakapuzzle, scattered around the world. Three ronins (students who, having failed the entrance exams in a school, attend preparatory courses until they are admitted in an institute) Yan Yan, Dasainen and Tonmentan also want to recover the pieces of the puzzle, hoping to be admitted to the Oshaka school. But the mysterious Itadakiman comes to the help of Hoshi and his friends.

0617 SERIES

KINNIKUMAN (*id.*), Toei Doga, sport, 137 episodes, 4/3/1983 – 8/19/1986. [*Muscleman*].

0618 SERIES

MANGA NIHONSHI (*The History of Japan in Manga*), Tsuchida, historical, 52 episodes, 4/3/1983 – 4/8/1984.

0619 SERIES

MIMU IROIRO YUME NO TABI (*The Thousands of Travels in Mimu's Dreams*), Nippon Animation, adventure, 127 episodes, 4/3/1983 – 2/29/1985.

0620 SERIES

PANMAN (*id.*), Shin'ei Doga, humour, 4/4/1983 – 3/31/1985.

For Mitsuo Suwa, a child like so many others in today's Japan, life changes when a strange costumed character gives him the possibility to become a kind of mini superman. Gifted with an incredible strenght and the power to fly, the young boy gets together with four other children who got the same powers to keep the city under surveillance. Taken from the humorous children's manga by the duo Fujiko Fujio.

0621 SERIES

SPOON OBASAN (*The Little Spoon's Aunt*), Studio Pierrot for Gakken, magic, 26 episodes, 4/4/1983 – 3/9/1984. [*Madame Pepperpote*].

It is the story of a friendly little old lady who possesses a magic gold spoon that she wears around her neck. The curious object can shorten the person who wears it, but the phenomenon can happens at any time. For this reason, the old woman finds herself a few centimeters high in the least appropriate moments. Despite this she has the ability to communicate with animals. The old woman lives in a little house on the edge of the wood together with a few kids and a strange little girl, Liulai, the only one who knows the lady's secret.

0622 SERIES

PASTCON TRAVEL TANTEIDAN (*Pastcon Travels Detective Team*), Tatsunoko, adventure, 26 episodes, 4/4/1983 – 9/26/1984. *Superbook.*

Sho Asuka and Azusa Yamoto, two children very close to one another, come to possess an extraordinary book capable of projecting the reader into the adventures described in the pages. Strangely, the book is a copy of the *Holy Bible* and they find themselves reliving the main events of the history of the christian religion side by side with its protagonists. The executive producer, Kenji Yoshida, entrusted the direction of the series to Masakazu Higuchi and the character designs to Akiko Shimomoto.

Pastcon Travel Tanteidan © Tatsunoko.

0623 SERIES

GINGA SHIPPU SASURIGER (*Sasuriger, the Galactic Wind*), Kokusai eigasha, robot, 43 episodes, 4/5/1983 – 1/31/1984.

The success of the Ranger J9 has given life to another series, based on the same guidelines, featuring the Solar Wind, an amazing train able to change into a battleship robot, the powerful Sasuriger. I.C. Blues, a known boaster in all Asteroid, accepts an incredible challenge by Brady God: in one year he will visit the 50 planets of the New Solar System. Hired Rock, Beat and Birdy begin their trip aboard the transformable train Sasuriger. But the Brady Syndicate tries everything to hinder it.

0624 SERIES

EAGLE SAM (*id.*), Dax, humour, 51 episodes, 4/7/1983 – 3/29/1984.

The mascot of the 1984 Los Angeles Olympics, a friendly eagle dressed with a waistcoat and a top hat with stars and stripes, becomes, in this series, the protagonist of entertaining adventures in which he's involved in spite of himself.

0625 SERIES

LADY GEORGIE (*id.*), Tokyo Movie Shinsha, soap opera, 45 episodes, 4/9/1983 – 2/25/1984. [*Georgie*].

Georgie lives her childhood together with her brothers Abel and Arthur, ignoring that she is the Buttmans' adoptive daughter, a family of Australian farmers. When the two young men fall in love with her and her mother throws her out not to ruin the family's harmony, Georgie leaves for England bringing with her a bracelet that links her to her origins. In London, she encounters Lowell, a young nobleman whom she had met during the inauguration of her country's railway and a love story begins between them. Arthur leaves to search for Georgie, but he discovers a plot by the Duke Dangering to kill Queen Victoria and he is captured and imprisonned in the castle of the evil nobleman. Georgie and Lowell are forced to separate because the young man, sick with consumption, must return to his family. Georgie looks for comfort near Abel, also in London.

Lady Georgie © Y. Igarashi / TMS.

Together they find count Gerald, the girl's father, and Arthur. With the consent of the long lost father, the three young people go back to Australia. Shigetsugu Yoshida skillfully supervises the direction and Junzaburo Takahata, the designs, bringing justice to the moving screenplay by Hiroshi Kaneko and Noboru Shiroyama. The designs are by Noboru Tatsuke and the music by Takeo Watanake. Yumiko Igarashi and Man Izawa's manga moves away from the extremely dilluted version of the animated series and ends with the death of Abel, killed by the duke of Dangering and with the birth of Abel junior by a now adult Georgie. Finally, having gone back to Australia, the young woman finds Arthur, whom was thought dead, and with whom she joins for life.

0626 SERIES

STOP! HIBARIKUN (*id.*), Toei Doga, soap opera, 35 episodes, 5/20/1983 – 1/27/1984.

0627 SERIES

BEM BEM HUNTER — KOTENGU TENMARU (*Tenmaru, the Little Tengu Monster Catcher*), Toei Doga, humour, 19 episodes, 5/26 – 11/3/1983.

It is believed that the Tengu, or long-nosed imp, have taught the ancients martial arts and ninja techniques. Tenmaru, a young representative of this race, opens by mistake a casket where demons and ghosts are locked in. As a punishment, the young Tengu is banned and thus deprived of his long nose until he recovers all the monstruous creatures that are now scattered all over Japan causing trouble whenever they can. Tenmaru's new residence will be the house of Yoko, a young girl that is almost always involved in his adventures. Inspired by *Urusei Yatsura*, this series is taken from Kabuto Mughitaro's manga.

0628 SERIES

PLA RES SANSHIRO (*Plastic Wrestler Sanshiro*), Kaname for Toho, robot/sport, 37 episodes, 6/5/1983 – 2/26/1984.

The young Sanshiro is very skillful in the remote controlled guiding of the robot Juomaru, with which he faces unlickely challenges from other children who have similar robots .

0629 SERIES

SERENDIPITY MONOGATARI PURE TO NO NAKAMATACHI (*The Story of Serendepity: the Friends From the Island of Pure*), Zuiyo, fantasy, 26 episodes, 7/1/1983 - 12/23/1984. [*Biniki Le Dragon Rose*].

A peaceful community lives in the quiet island of Pure in harmony with nature. They solve their daily difficulties under the sign of peace and harmony. Serendipity is a pink dinosaur with big eyes, that protects and wisely gives advices to the population of Pure.

0630 SERIES

MAHO NO TENSHI CREAMY MAMI (*Creamy Mami, the Angel of Magic*), Studio Pierrot, magic, 52 episodes, 7/1/1983 – 6/29/1984. [*Creamy Merveilleuse Creamy*].

The young Yu receives the visit of the elf Pino Pino that gives her a mysterious magic wand with which the girl can change for a year into Creamy Mami , a young music star. Her parents and her childhood friend Toshio, madly in love with Creamy, are completely unaware of Yu's double identity and they'll often hinder the young girl causing her many problems. No one, in fact, must discover her secret or she will lose her magic powers. When, in the middle of the story, Toshio accidentaly sees her friend transform into Creamy, her future is compromised.

For the girl to regain her magical capacity, the two friends get involved in a fantasy adventure that ends with Yu recovering her powers and Toshio losing his memory. Creamy continues her musical tour and at the end of the year, she decides to give a farewell show. During the evening, as she gives her best, singing her entire repertoire, Toshio's memory comes back and Yu loses her powers forever. However, there will be a happy ending. After Creamy's disappearance, the two young people will be closer than ever. Osamu Kobayashi directed the animated series that features Akemi Takada's character designs, drastically different from Yoko Kitagawa and Kazunori Ito's original manga.

0631 SERIES

CHO JIKU SEIKI ORGUSS (*Super Dimension Century Orguss*), Tokyo Movie Shinsha, robot, 35 episodes, 7/3/1983 – 4/8/1984. *Super Dimension Century Orguss*.

Produced by Toshitsuku Mukaitsubu, the science-fiction series features character designs by Haruhiko Mikimoto, famous for the character designs of *Cho Jiku Yosai Macross*. Even though there is the presence of a gigantic mecha, the Orguss Dorifant, reminiscent of ancient prehistoric animals, the story centers primarily on the characters' feelings and on their daily lives. Because of a space-temporal accident, the main character is thrust through time into an alternate world.

Super Dimension Century Orguss ©1983, 1992 TMS / Big West. Exclusively licensed throughout the United States and Canada by L.A. Hero / U.S. Renditions.

0632 SERIES

PSYCHO ARMOUR GORBARIAN (*id.*), Knack, robot, 26 episodes, 7/6 – 12/22/1983.

In an unprecised year of the 21st century, a new menace treathens Earth: the arrival from another dimension of the evil Galadines, gifted with psychic powers. The last defense for the Earth is the fighting robot Psycho Armour Gorbarian piloted by the young Isamu Napoto who is able to move the powerful robot with his strong ESP. Isamu is helped in his battle by his companions Kult Buster and Hans, respectively pilots of the support robots Reido and Garom. The team has been picked-up by the alien Zakoo, whose intentions aren't very clear... A particularity worthy of mention is that *Gorborian* is very similar to the old *Mazinger*. The mystery is soon unveiled: the creator of the series is in fact Go Nagai who has as collaborators Kyoshi Tonosaki and Heita Etsu for the production, Kyomu Fukuda and Yuki Kinoshita for the animation and mechanical designs.

0633 SERIES

CAT'S EYES (*id.*), Tokyo Movie Shinsha, adventure, 36 episodes, 7/11/1983 – 3/26/1984. [*Signé Cat's Eyes*].

Directly taken from Tsukasa Hojo's manga which tells the lives of the three Kisugi sisters who are involved in an entreprise in which they dedicate themselves body and soul. Ai, Rui and Hitomi are the three beautiful owners of the Cat's Eyes coffee shop, but by night, they steal art works: this, to reconstruct the collection assembled by their father, a famous painter who disappeared. Through his works, the young girls hope to find him. The police never catch the skillful thieves that call themselves "Cat's Eyes" (the name of their coffee shop), and puts an unlucky detective on their case full time. Strangely enough, he is no other than Hitomi's fiance and he doesn't have a clue of the three girls' double life. The character designs are by Akio Sugino, the design supervision is by Satoshi Hirayama and Nobuko Tsukada and the direction is by Yoshio Takeuchi.

Robotech: The New Generation ©1995 Harmony Gold U.S.A. Inc. / Tatsunoko Prod. Co., Ltd. All Rights Reserved. Released by Streamline Pictures.

Robotech: The New Generation ©1994 Tatsunoko Production Co., Ltd. ©1995 Harmony Gold U.S.A. Inc. / Tatsunoko Prod. Co., Ltd. Package design ©1994 Streamline Enterprises.

0634 SERIES

KITOSOSEIKI MOSPEADA (*Genesis Climber Mospeada*), Tatsunoko, robot, 25 episodes, 10/2/1983 – 3/25/1984. *Robotech: The New Generation*.

The Invid people are on the verge of extinction because of the continuous genetical experiments done for many generations. Their only hope for survival is to leave their planet in search of a new world to conquer. As usual, Earth is the most attractive planet, forcing its army to defend itself against the umpteenth invasion. This time however, the Earthly defenses don't have the upper hand. The entire fleet is exterminated and the only survivor is Stik Bernard who, in the explosion of his spaceship, has witnessed the death of his fiancee Marlene. Having landed, he finds a conquered world. The only means of transportation left is his Mospeada, a super motocycle with which he plans to reach and destroy the enemy base. During the trip, Stik meets Rei, in difficulty with an Invid patrol. The young man also has a motorcycle, but he isn't able to exploit it to the maximum of its capacities. That motorcycle is in fact, capable of transforming into a Ride Armour, a powerful battle armor. Rei, contrary to Stik, is without ideal, but he let's himself be easily convinced by his new friend to help him in his solitary mission. As time goes by, new characters join them: the first one is Mint Rubble, a lively orphan. The trio is forced to take small nightly trips in order to avoid encounters with the enemy and it is in one of these occasions that a mysterious individual on a Mospeada motorcycle appears and then disappears, leaving them dumbfounded. The road to the enemy headquarters is long. To rest, the young people choose a village along the road where a concert from the very popular singer Yellow Belmont is taking place. A gang of criminals unexpectedly attack the village. Stik and Rei intervene, helped by the mysterious motorcycle rider from a few nights before (who is in reality Fuke Eroze) and by Jim Austin, a skillful mechanic who has put back together a few Armo-Soldiers. To the group is also added Yellow Belmont who we discover to be a boy transvestite, also owner of a Mospeada. In the meantime, the queen Invid Refles, to put down the human rebellion, genitically creates an agent with human female features and makes her infiltrate the group, but the plan fails. Agent Aisha has lost her memory and falls in love with Stik, who loves her too. The days pass and the moment of the final encounter is near: the disparity in means is overwhelming, but the will of the Earthlings will succeed in overturning the fate of the battle. Because of lack of interest by the public, the series was interrupted after the 25th episode.

0635 SERIES

FUSHIGI NO KUNI NO ALICE (*Alice in Wonderland*), Nippon Animation, classic, 24 episodes, 10/3/1983 – 3/26/1984. [*Alice Au Pays Des Merveilles*].

Umpteenth transposition into animation of Lewis Carrol's story. The direction is by Taku Sugiyama, the animation and the screenplay are by Kakuko Nakamura and Marty Murphy. The character designs are by Isamu Kumata and the layout by the veteran Yasugi Mori.

0636 SERIAL

TOKUSO DORVACK (*Dorvack, the Special Soldier*), Ashi, robot, 36 episodes, 10/7/1983 – 6/22/1984.

In an undetermined future, a terrible army from the star Idelia, commanded by general Zeller, invades and subdues a great part of the Earthly population. On the defense side, to respond to the offensive, vehicles called Variable Machines, powerful war machines capable of changing into robots, are prepared. A handful of fighters, the Dorvack group, is trained for combat with these mecha. The pilots are: Masato Mugen, driving a very well equiped desert jeep; Pierre Bonaparte, pilot of the Tulkas, a powerful half caterpillar and Rui Oberon, only young woman in the group, but not less fierce, at the commands of her Gazzette, a helicopter with incredible performances. The character designs are by Osamu Kamijo, the supervision is by Masami Anno.

0637 SERIES

TAO TAO EHONKAN - SEKAI DOBUTSUBANASHI (*Tao Tao's bookshelf, Stories of Animals of the World*), Shunmao , animal, 20 episodes, 10/7/1983 – 3/30/1984.

0638 SERIES

MANGA ESOPO MONOGATARI (*Esop's Tale in Manga*), Nippon Animation, fairy-tale, 58 episodes, 10/10 – 12/22/1983.

0639 SERIES

CAPTAIN TSUBASA (*id.*), Tsuchida, sport, 128 episodes, 10/13/1983 – 3/27/1986. [*Olive & Tom*].

Sport series featuring the lives of Tsubasa Ozora, young Japanese soccer player who will conquer a place amongst the world's greatest champions. Based on Yoichi Takahashi's manga, the character designs are by Yoshihiro Okaseko. The series is directed by Horoyoshi Mitsunobu.

0640 SERIES

IGANO KABAMARU (*id.*), Group Tack, adventure, 24 episodes, 10/20/1983 – 3/29/1984. [Ninja Boy].

This more-than-insane story features Kabamaru, a rough and glutton ninja who wants to conquer at any cost the beautiful Mai, his school companion. With the approval of the girl's grandmother, he moves into her house. The animation isn't of high quality level, but the story is entertaining.

0641 SERIES

GINGA HYORYU VIFAM (*Vifam, the Shipwrecks of the Galaxy*), Nippon Sunrise, robot, 46 episodes, 10/21/1983 – 9/21/1984.

0642 SERIES

KOJIKA MONOGATARI (*The Story of the Fawn*), Kodansha/M. & K., classic, 52 episodes, 11/18/1983 – 1/29/1984.

Taken from Marjorie Rawling's novel, *The Cub*, the series narrates the story of a tender friendship between the little Jody and a fawn. Directed by Masaaki Osumi, under the general supervision of Shun'ichi Yukimuro. The character designs are by Suichi Seki.

0643 SPECIAL

DON MATSUGORO NO SEIKATSU (*The Life of Don Matsugoro*), Toei Doga, humour, 84 min., 2/2.

0644 SPECIAL

UCHU NO HATE MADE BOKENRYOKO (*The Adventurous Voyage at the End of Space*), Tsuburaya, science-fiction, 84 min., 3/3.

Captain Tsubasa © Y. Takahashi / Shûeisha / Tsuchida Production / TV Tokyo.

Prime Rose © Tezuka Production.

Dallos ©1983 Pierrot Project Co., Ltd. Released in North America through Best Film & Video.

0645 SPECIAL
NINE (*id.*), Group Tack, sport, 71 min., 5/4.

0646 SPECIAL
PRIME ROSE (*id.*), Tezuka, science-fiction.

Gai, a member of a temporal control patrol, travels in the past and encounters the story of Primerose, a young girl who has decided to become an expert in the use of weapons to avenge the death of her fiance, cruelly killed by Prince Pirar. The story is by Osamu Tezuka, the direction by Osamu Dezaki, the music by Yuji Ono.

0647 SPECIAL
DOCTOR MANBO TO KAITO ZIVAGO — UCHU YORI AI O KOMETE (*Doctor Manbo and Zivago the Thief: From Space with Love*), Toei Doga, humour, 84 min., 9/12.

0648 SPECIAL
FUJIKO FUJIO SPECIAL — DORAEMON EUROPE TETSUDO NO TABI (*Fujiko Fujio Special — Doraemon, Train Trip Through Europe*), Shin'ei Doga, humour, 111 min., 10/13.

0649 SPECIAL
NINE II KOIBITO SENGEN (*Nine II: Declaration of Love*), Group Tack/Toho, sport, 75 min., 12/18.

0650 OAV
DALLOS: DALLOS HAKAI SHIREI (*Dallos: Order To Destroy Dallos*), Studio Pierrot for Network, science-fiction, 30 min., 12/21. Bandai. *Dallos*.

At the end of the 21st century, the Earth is the victim of overpopulation and the lack of raw material. So much that the colonization of the moon seems to be the only solution. The prosperity of our planet however, is gained at the cost of the sacrifice of the Moon colonies who rebel, forming the anti-government movement guerilla and ask the Skuller, the Office of Supervision, for the independance of their colony. Shun Nonomura, the main character, after the death of his brother at the hand of the earthly government, plans an attack against Alex Riger, commander in chief of the Skuller. Born from the collaboration of Hisauki Toriumi, who is also screenplay writer and Mamoru Oshii, director, this is the first OAV (Original Animation Video) made in Japan.

CHAPTER TWENTY-THREE: 1984

1984 was, for the most part, a year set aside for the refinement and consolidation of already-popular themes, but some spectacular successes emerged from the skills of new artists, like the duo Bronson/Tetsuo Hara and Tsukasa Hojo. The former, already at the pinnacle of their popularity with the manga *Hokuto No Ken*, earned even more success with its anime adaptation, one remarkably faithful to the spirit of the original manga.

Tsukasa Hojo also saw immediate success with his new show. In fact, television viewers tuned in to *Cat's Eyes* with growing enthusiasm, so much that seven months later, TMS produced a second series that set Hojo up for life as one of most popular and best-paid designers in the industry.

Go Nagai's last creation, *God Mazinger*, also came to television in yet another exploitation of the *Mazinger* phenomenon, in a new series that deified the already mythical robot. *God Mazinger* turns out to be, in fact, a God of the Mu empire, at war with the descendants of ferocious dinosaurs.

The collaboration between Japanese production firms and the Western ones became more and more frequent. This year saw Italy jump into the ring, through RAI that, together with TMS, produced *Meitankei Holmes*, about Arthur Conan Doyle's famous detective. The preliminary design sketches that show an anthropormorphic animal characterization of the protagonists, are by the Pagot brothers, while Hayao Miyazaki became personally involved in the animation process. Miyazaki also made *Kaze no Tani no Nausicaa* this year, a feature film destined for the big screen and nigh cult-status in both Japan and the Western World. The fans of the Princess from the Valley of the Wind are still growing in number today, although Miyazaki has made other animated masterpieces, *Nausicaa* is regularly on top of the charts in Japanese entertainment magazines.

Another immensely successful movie was *Urusei Yatsura: Beautiful Dreamer*, the second movie about Lamu and the insane universe she inhabits. The movie featured the new adventures of Ataru, the eternal victim in even more insane situations. *Chojiku Yosai Macross Ai Oboeteimasuka*, sequel to *Chijiku Yosai Macross*, also broke a new gross-profit record, due to the well-written plotline, the unexpected twists and the in-depth, complex characterization present in this spectacular sequel.

The OAV market celebrated its second anniversary by presenting a large number of new titles (though few in comparison to the current number of yearly releases), amongst which was *Mako no Tenshi Creamy Mami Eien no Once More*, which opened with long flashbacks from the old television series. The sequel movie took place after the final concert of the singer and featured an all-new adventure for the main characters.

Kaze no Tani no Nausicâa
© Nibariki / Tokuma Shoten / Hakuhodo / Toei.

0651 FILM
URUSEI YATSURA 2: BEAUTIFUL DREAMER (*Those Obnoxious Aliens: Beautiful Dreamer*), Kitty Film, soap opera, 98 min., 2/11. *Urusei Yatsura: Beautiful Dreamer.*

Under the direction of Junji Shimura and with the screenplay by Mamoru Oshii, this is a new chapter in the lives of the characters of one of the most famous Japanese series of all time. Many misunderstandings derail the group's plans on the day before the great dance at Tomobiki school, but, as always, everything works out in the end.

0652 FILM
WATA NO KUNI BOSHI (*The Planet of the Cotton Country*), Mushi, animals, 90 min., 2/11.

Enriched by a soundtrack by noted pianist Richard Clayderman, known and loved in Japan, the feature film presents the adventures of the little Chibineko (kitten), a cat who aspires to become human for love of its owner.

0653 FILM
BOKENSHATACHI — GANBA TO NANAHIKI NO NAKAMA (*The Adventures of Ganba and his Seven Friends*), Tokyo Movie Shinsha, animal, 80 min., 3/9.

Warriors Of The Wind © 1990 R&G Video L.P.
©1990 Starmaker Entertainment, Inc. A heavily edited version of *Nausicäa*.

Locke The Superpower©1984 Nippon Animation Co., Ltd / Shochiku Co., Ltd. All Rights Reserved. Package design ©1987 Celebrity Home Entertainment, Inc.

It is Ganba the little mouse's turn to appear on the big screen, with a collage of scenes from the television series.

0654 FILM

SHONEN KENYA (*The Young Kenya*), Toei Doga for Haruki Kadokawa, adventure, 110 min., 3/10.

Wataru Murakani is a young Japanese man who lives with his family in Kenya. During a business trip in the capital, Wataru and his father, the owner of a textile business in the capital, are attacked by a ferocious rhinoceros. The two run away separately to try to find refuge, but they lose each other and wander alone in the desert. The young man is welcomed by a Masai tribe, and he befriends the wise warrior Zega and the beautiful Keko, with whom he soon falls in love. The three search for Wataru's father, whom they find after four years of travel.

0655 FILM

KAZE NO TANI NO NAUSICAA (*Nausicaa From the Valley of the Wind*), Top Kraft, fantasy, 118 min., 3/11, *Warriors Of The Wind* [*La Princesse Des Étoiles*].

After having created the successful manga, Hayao Miyazaki decides to transpose the story of *Nausicaa* to a feature film that brings in the collaborative efforts of Kazuo Komatsubara as character designer. The powers of the Earth have destroyed each other and, a thousand years later, an impenetrable toxic jungle generated by the ashes of a nuclear war forces the survivors to live in restricted uncontaminated areas. Nausicaa is the princess of the Valley of the Wind; courageous, faithful and pure of spirit, she lives in harmony with the surrounding world. The rulers of the new cities, however, don't hesitate to use force to quench their thirst for conquest that brings them to look for the "invincible soldier," the thermonuclear weapon so powerful that it had caused the destruction of the old world. Pehite and Tolmekia's armies begin a stupid war that begins to develop into another tragedy, but Nausicaa, who could almost communicate with the enormous insects of the poisonous forest, brings peace back, showing the delicacy and importance of the link between man and nature.

0656 FILM

CHOJIN LOCKE (*Locke the Superman*), Nippon Animation, science fiction, 110 min., 3/11. *Locke the Superman* [*Luc L'Intrépide*].

Young pastor Locke lives in solitude on a distant planet. Gifted with ESP powers, the young man is called upon by Colonel Yamaki to defeat the criminal plans of Lady Khan. Thus begins a war between special humans possessing the ability to use ESP. The movie is one of the first experiments of amalgamation between traditional animation and computer graphics.

0657 FILM

MIRAI SHONEN CONAN — KYODAIKI GIGANT NO FUKKATSU (*Conan, the Young man From the Future: the Return of the Great Plane*), Nippon Animation, science fiction, 47 min., 3/11.

The film is created from delicate editing of the last three episodes (24—26) of the television series, to present the finale of the wonderful story to moviegoers.

0658 FILM

DORAEMON — NOBITA NO MAKAI DAI BOKEN (*Doraemon, Nobita's Great Adventure in the World of Magic*), Shin'ei Doga, humor, 99 min., 3/17.

0659 FILM

ULTRAMEN KIDS (*id.*), Tsuburaya, humor, 25 min., 3/17.

0660 FILM

NINJA HATTORIKUN + PAMAN — CHONORYOKU WARS (*The Little Ninja Hattori + Paman: the Devastating War*), Shin'ei Doga, humor, 3/17.

0661 FILM

OSHIN (*id.*), Sanrio, historical, 120 min., 3/17.

0662 FILM

TOBIUO NO BOYA WA BYOKI DESU (*The Child With the Flying Fish is Sick*), Mushi, classic, 19 min., 3/17.

0663 FILM

PROYAKYU O JUBAI TANOSHIKU MIRU HOHO PART II (*How to See Baseball in a Way Ten Times More Entertaining, Part II*), Magic Bus for Film Link, humor/sport, 95 min., 4/21.

Given the success of the movie in 1982, the producers exploited the same premise with a caricature of the famous Takenori Emoto in a new feature film with the same basic plot as the first.

0664 FILM

PAPA MAMA BYE BYE (*id.*), Toei Doga, drama, 7/6.

0665 FILM

CHOJIKU YOSAI MACROSS AI OBOETEIMASUKA (*Super Dimensional Fortress Macross: Do You Remember Love?*), Tatsunoko, science fiction, 112 min., 7/7. *Macross: The Movie / Clash Of The Bionoids*.

When Macross ended on the Japanese networks on June 26, 1986, Kawamori and Mikimoto were already working on a movie based on the commercially successful series. The movie, however, was notably different than the television series, mostly in the designs of the characters and in the sentimental impact of the plot (with the lives of the characters placed above the events of the war), as well as in the quality of animation down to its smallest details.

Chojiku Yosai Macross: Ai Oboeteimasuka
© Big West.

The story begins with the television series, but then develops along a completely different tangent: from the beginning Macross is in space, Minmay is already a famous singer aboard the spaceship and, contrary to what happened in the series, as well as Misa and Hikaru, the Zentrans also capture Minmay, her cousin Lynn Kaifun and Roy Fokker (who dies during the escape). Arrived on a deserted planet, that they later identify as the Earth, Hikaru and Misa are forced to work together to survive and this close dependency leads them to fall in love with one another. During an exploration, the two discover the ruins of an ancient civilization where an enormous being shows itself to them in the form of a hologram and tells the story of the mysterious Zentrans. Twenty thousand years ago, a

Chojiku Yosai Macross: Ai Oboeteimasuka
© Big West.

Chojiku Yosai Macross: Ai Oboeteimasuka
© Big West.

Lensman ©1990 E.E. "Doc" Smith • MK Co.
Package design ©1992 Lumivision Corporation.
Released by Streamline Pictures.

group of Zentrans and Meltrans (their term for women), tired of having to obey the rules of their society, had found refuge on Earth and begun a new life. Misa finds a piece of metal with strange alien symbols engraved on it in the ruins, and decides to keep it.

In the meantime, Macross, having reached the Earth, rescues the two young people. On the alien ship, meanwhile, a piece of metal, identical to the one found by Misa, is given to Minmay (the aliens consider it the key to a protoculture) with understandable musical notes engraved on it. As soon as the young woman sings those notes, feelings awaken in the Zentrans which had been repressed for thousands of years. Having discovered the secret of the protoculture, the Zentrans want to awaken the same emotions in the Meltrans and to do so, they become allies of the earthlings, who are instructed to write words to the melody; the song will then have to be sung by Minmay.

Misa, studying the metal she found on Earth, discovers that she has in her hands the words to a song and she informs Hikaru of her discovery, but she discovers a bitter surprise: Hikaru is with Minmay. The time has now come for the young man to choose once and for all between the two girls. He chooses Misa, which sends Minmay running away in tears. In the meantime in space, everything is ready for for the final act of the battle, but the singer is nowhere to be found. Hikaru, manages to cure the star's hysteria. Meanwhile, the Zentran emperor who doesn't want to stop the war, launches the final attacks which kills the Meltran emperor. But, announced by a kaleidoscope of colors, Minmay makes an appearance singing Ai Oboeteimasuka. Meltrans and Zentrans, moved by the melody, finally stop fighting. The war is over but it is only a fragile truce. Thousands of Meltran and Zentran fleets still remain scattered through the galaxies.

0666 FILM
SF SHINSEIKI: LENSMAN (*Lensman, the New Science Fiction Era*), Kodansha, science fiction, 108 min., 7/7. *Lensman.*

Lensman is the title of a famous series of science fiction novels written by E.E. "Doc" Smith, published in the 40s in America. Kimball Kinnison, thanks to a magnifying glass inserted on the back of his hand, becomes a superhero gifted with amazing powers. The film was made using a computer graphic for the special effects and scenes with mechanical constructs.

0667 FILM
KINNIKUMAN (*id.*), Toei Doga, sport, 145 min., 7/14.

0668 FILM
THE KABOCHA WINE (*The Pumpkin Wine*), Toei Doga, soap opera/humor, 24 min., 7/14.

Around the same time that the final episodes of the show are being shown in television, this film is shown in movie theaters. It presents innocent situations, and never falls into the realms of bad taste. Shunshuke's phobia towards girls is once again at the center of the story.

0669 FILM
CHIKYU MONOGATARI — TELEPAS 2500 (*The Story of the Earth, Telepas 2500*), Tatsunoko, science fiction, 103 min., 8/4.

0670 FILM

KUROI AME NI UTARETE (*Under the Black Rain*), Tsuchida, war, 8/12.

0671 FILM

KAKKUN COFFEE (*id.*), Ajiado/Tokyo Media Connection for Kakkun seisakudan, humor, 86 min., 8/22.

0672 FILM

MEITANTEI HOLMES — AOI KOGYOKU NO MAKI, KAITEI NO ZAIHO NO MAKI (*Holmes, the Detective: the Episode of the Blue Ruby and the Episode of the Sunken Treasure*), Tokyo Movie Shinsha, animals, 50 min., (two episodes of 25 min. each), 11/3.

0673 FILM

KINNIKUMAN — OABARE! SEIGICHOJIN (*Break Everything, Kinnikuman! The Super Executioner*), Toei Doga, sport, 48 min., 12/22.

0674 FILM

DR. SLUMP & AALECHAN — HOYOYO! NANABAJO NO HI HI (*Dr. Slump & Arale Chan: HOYOYO! The Secret Treasure in the Castle of Nanaba*), Toei Doga, humor, 48 min., 12/22.

The little Arale and her dazed inventor travel through time to Nanaba in 1929 to reach a castle which hides a fabulous treasure. But a group of pirates is waiting for them and the two characters will have to think up a few strategies to gain the upper hand.

0675 SERIES

OKAWARIBOY STARZAN S (*id.*), Tatsunoko, science fiction, 32 episodes, 1/7 — 8/25/1984.

Because of the success earned by the time machine saga, the Tatsunoko comes up with a series that reproduces the content of the previous ones, with ever-more sight gags, but without the defining presence of charismatic characters or any truly unique elements.

0676 SERIES

MAKIBA NO SHOJO KATHY (*Kathy, the Girl From the Factory*), Nippon Animation, classic, 52 episodes, 1/8 — 12/23/1984.

Okawariboy Starzan S © Tatsunoko Pro.

The series is centered on the beautiful Kathy, a humble and sweet girl. Life isn't easy for her, as she is forced to work to help her grandparent, first as a cow girl and then as a babysitter.

0677 SERIES

CHOKOSOKU GALVION (*Galvion, Super Fast Offensive*), Kokusai eigasha, robot, 22 episodes, 2/3 — 6/29/1984.

In the 23rd century the Earth is once again victim of a threat from space. This time, the enemies are the terrible Shadows that engage in endless battles with an action team created for the occasion by the Earth government. The character designs are by Yoshihisa Tagami.

0678 SERIES

HEAVY METAL L GAIM (*id.*), Nippon Sunrise, robot, 54 episodes, 2/4/1984 — 2/23/1985.

On the far off planet Pentagona, the fascinating and enigmatic queen Oldona Poseidal begins a destructive war. A group of young rebels, Kiao, Amu, Leshee and Lilis, make life

Little El Cid no Boken
© Nippon Animation • BRB International.

Tongariboshi no Memol © Toei Animation.

difficult for the scheming tyrant, stealing L Gaim, a perfect combat automaton that is piloted by the leader of their group, Daba Mylord. This series belongs to the now-solid "realistic" robot tradition, begun by the famous *Gundam*.

0679 SERIES
LITTLE EL CID NO BOKEN (*The Adventures of the Little El Cid*), Nippon Animation, classic, 26 episodes, 2/6 — 3/12/1984. [*Rody Le Petit Cyd*].

Young Ruy only has one wish: to become a Cid Campeador like his father. He sets out on a fateful journey to find fame and fortune.

0680 SERIES
SOYA MONOGATARI (*The Story of the Ship Soya*), Kokusai eigasha, documentary, 21 episodes, 2/7 — 6/26/1984.

0681 SERIES
YUME SENSHI WINGMAN (*Wingman the Dream Warrior*), Toei Doga, science fiction. 47 episodes, 2/7/1984 — 2/26/1985. [*Wingman*].

This time, the series is not set on a science-fiction reality, but in a world of dreams. A group of soldiers, capable of transforming themselves into powerful futuristic fighting machines, intervene in the dreams of people in danger. Taken from Masakazu Katsura's manga.

0682 SERIES
TONGARIBOSHI NO MEMOL (*Memol With the Pointy Hat*), Toei Doga, children, 49 episodes, 3/3/1984 — 3/3/1985. [*Crocus*].

Certain inhabitants from the planet Rilulu are forced to make an emergency landing on Earth when their starship's engine fails. On our planet however, their very small height puts them in danger over and over again. Memol, the main character of the series, decides to disobey her parents and explore the new world with a group of friends. On the wings of an old owl, the alien children reach a house all the way at the end of the woods. There they see Mariel, a sick young girl, through the window, with whom they become friends. Their visits become more and more frequent and their bond deepens so much that Mariel begins to feel better. Time passes and a spaceship comes to bring the castaways back to Rilulu. Mariel's condition worsens and Memol and her friends decide not to abandon her in her hour of need and Memol remains on earth. The series, created by Saburo Yokoi, is supervised by Shiun'ichi Yukimuro and directed by Kin'ichiro Suzuki and Osamu Kasai. The designs are by Yasuhiro Nakura.

0683 SERIES
LUPIN SANSEI — PART III (*Lupin III, Part III*), Tokyo Movie Shinsha, adventure, 49 episodes, 3/3/1984 — 9/28/1985.

Although the success of the series has already begun to fade, the adventures of the famous gentleman thief continue with these new episodes. The designs present an unusual and neglected sketching, but are accompanied by a good animation.

0684 SERIES

VIDEO SENSHI LEZARION (*Laserion, the Video Warrior*), Toei Doga for Toei Co., robot, 52 episodes, 3/4/1984 — 2/3/1985.

Once again, robots are the focus of a Japanese series that boasts the talents of Kozo Morishita as director and Hideyaki Motohashi as character designer. In this story, young Takeshi Katori creates a sensational video game about a character named Lezarion, a computerized robot. One day, while he is playing his creation together with an American friend, a short circuit causes Lezarion's data to be transformed into reality. Because of this inexplicable phenomenon, the robot becomes real under the bewildered eyes of the two scientists. Under Takashi's command, the robot becomes the primary weapon used to defeat the evil scientist God Haid.

0685 SERIES

ANIME YASEI NO SAKEBI (*The Animation of Cry of the Wild*), Wako, adventure, 4 episodes, 3/7 — 3/28/1984.

The 1982 series is remade maintaining the graphic and narrative elements almost completely unchanged. Every episode has different main characters, but they are all part of the animal kingdom.

0686 SERIES

GUGU GANMO (*id.*), Toei Doga, humor, 50 episodes, 3/8/1984 —3/17/1985. [*Gugu Ganmo*].

0687 SERIES

OYONEKO BUNYAN (*id.*), Shien'ei Doga, humor, 29 episodes, 4/3 —10/23/1984.

The story is centered on the entertaining adventures of the shrewd cat Bunyan. The character is put on hiatus after this series, and audiences have to wait for *What's Michael*, Makoto Kobayashi's series in 1985 to see another feline with as much potential.

0688 SERIES

KYOJIN GORG (*Gorg, the Giant God*), Nippon Sunrise, robot, 26 episodes, 4/5 — 9/27/1984.

An Australian island hides a mystery, which causes a war between the evil organization Gail and a group of rebels. With the help of powerful robots, the two factions face off against each other, but the most powerful robot is on the side of the rebels. The robot, Gorg, is powered by the young Yuji Tagami, accompanied by his friend, the beautiful Doris Wave.

0689 SERIES

RANPO (*id.*), Tsuchida, adventure, 20 episodes, 4/5 — 9/20/1984.

0690 SERIES

MANGA DOSHITE MONOGATARI (*Animated Stories of "Whys"*), Dax, fantasy, 100 episodes, 4/7/1984 — 3/29/1986.

Naomi Matsui, a famous radio character very popular with young children, guides young television viewers in a fantastic journey through the "Whys." Noemi is always accompanied by a funny looking baby dragon named Robuke.

Gugu Ganmo © F. Hosono / Toei Animation.

Intro
-1962
1963
1964
1965
1966
1967
1968
1969
1970
1971
1972
1973
1974
1975
1976
1977
1978
1979
1980
1981
1982
1983
1984
1985
1986
1987
1988
Index

Attacker You! © Knack.

Palladium Books® Presents

ROBOTECH
Southern Cross

Available for the first time on video tape!

0691 SERIES

CHIKKUN TAKKUN (*id.*), Studio Pierrot for Gakken, humor, 23 episodes, 4/7 — 9/28/1984.

0692 SERIES

GLASS NO KAMEN (*Glass Mask*), Eiken, soap opera, 23 episodes, 4/9 — 9/27/1984.

The world of show business is the setting of this series supervised by Gisaburo Sugii and created by the famous actress Suzue Miuchi. The main character, Maya Kitajima, is a thirteen year-old student. Her dream to become an actress comes true when she meets Chisuga Tsukikage, an artist from the past forced to retire after an accident, who decides to share in her experiences. Maya begins a slow but constant rise to success that soon makes her a rival to Ayumi Himekawa, an actress her own age. Mrs. Tsukikage sees both girls as possible candidates for a very big role, that of "The Scarlet Goddess," whom every actress wants to play.

Masumi Ayami, a young director from a famous production firm, also wants to produce the same play and begins to hinder Mrs. Tsukikage's theater company. Maya's mother's death and a scandal hatched against her make her lose the will to act, but the attentions of a mysterious admirer (who eventually reveals himself to be Masumi Ayami) brings her to new triumphs. Chigusa Tsukikage has another heart attack and doesn't have much time to live, so she finally decides to direct the much awaited "Scarlet Goddess." Maya and Ayumi audition for the lead. The character designs are by the inimitable Shingo Araki.

0693 SERIES

ATTACKER YOU! (*id.*), Knack, sport, 58 episodes, 4/13/1984 —6/21/1985. [*Jeanne Et Serge*].

Yu Hazuki is an enterprising girl who, because of her father's job transfer, must move to another city. She joins the volleyball team on the first day of school and, although she has never played, she beats the school's champion, Nami Hayase. For Yu, this is only the beginning of a brilliant career in the world of volleyball. Taken from Shizuo Koizumi and Jun Makimura's manga, the series is directed by Kazuyuki Okaseko.

0694 SERIES

GOD MAZINGER (*id.*), Tokyo Movie Shinsha, robot, 23 episodes, 4/15 — 9/23/1984.

Returning from its massive success in the 70s, the powerful robot Mazinger is the subject of a remake by its original author, Go Nagai. In the ancient kingdom of Mu, a legend tells of a gigantic being ready to defend the population from any kind of threat. The evil Dorado from the empire of the dinosaurs is determined to conquer Mu, and he attacks the capital with ravenous monsters. King Muraji, aware of the danger, needs the help of a coura- geous young man named Yamato to awake the gigantic statue of the god Mazinger.

0695 SERIES

CHOJIKU KIDAN SOUTHERN CROSS (*Super-Dimensional Cavalry Southern Cross*), Tatsunoko, robot, 23 episodes, 4/15 — 9/30/1984. *Robotech: Southern Cross.*

The Earth is in a desperate situation, as the senseless development of technological re- search has caused the extinction of thousands of plants and animals. The already critical situation is aggravated by the appearance of the alien race of Zors, ready to conquer what is left of our planet. Fortunately, the armored troops Southern Cross are ready to defend the Earth. The main character of the show is Jeanne Francaix, the commander of the 15th earthly battalion, a soldier who prefers music to action. In the course of a battle between the Zors and the earthlings, a soldier named Bowie is taken prisoner.

In the enemy base, Bowie meets an alien, Musika, and it is love at first sight. Held in the prison camp, the young man discovers that the people of Zor don't want the war perpetuated by the supreme commanders of the alien planet. Freed from prison, Bowie promises Musika that he will come back for her. In the meantime, Jeanne falls in love with Seifrietti Weisse, an enemy pilot captured during a battle, who suffers from amnesia because of his injuries. Jeanne decides to take care of him, convinces him that he is an earthling and makes him part of her battalion against her commander's wishes. Time passes and, during an exploratory mission, Jeanne, Bowie and Seifrietti discover something very strange in a large crack blasted open by the fighting: at the bottom of the crack, beautiful uncontaminated flowers grow. The hopes for the planet's salvation are rekindled.

Hearing about the humans' discovery, the commanders from Zor try everything to destroy the flowers, to accelerate the extinction of the human race. Seifrietti, in the meantime, regains his memory and, in an attempt to make things easier for Jeanne, he returns to the Zor base to eliminate the supreme commanders. The final encounter is near, and even Musika is finally convinced of this. She escapes from the base to be with Bowie who, with her help, frees the Zor population while Seifrietti and Jeanne destroy the base. The three commanders, however, escape. Seifrietti rushes to pursue them and, having reached them, sacrifices his own life to kill them. The energy created by the explosion makes the flowers grow and multiply at an incredible rate, creating new hope for humanity.

Robotech: Southern Cross ©1995 Tatsunoko Production Co., Ltd. ©1985 Harmony Gold U.S.A. Inc. / Tatsunoko Production Co., Ltd. Package design ©1995 Streamline Enterprises, Inc.

0696 SERIES

MAHO NO YOSEI PELSHA (*Pelsha, the Magic Fairy*), Studio Pierrot, magic, 48 episodes, 7/6/1984 — 5/31/1985. [*Vanessa Et La Magie Des Rêves*].

Another member of the ranks of the 'magical girls' is Pelsha, a girl born and raised in Africa. During the journey that will eventually bring her back to Japan and her parents, Pelsha receives a gift from three elves. Puri Puri, Gera Gera and Meso Meso give her a magical circlet that enables her to become the dream planet fairy's look-alike, also transforming her into an adult woman. While she travels the dream world, Pelsha finds herself emotionally involved with Garu and Riki, twins who were her childhood friends. The story is taken from Takako Aonuma's manga, the character designs are by Yoshiyuki Kishi while the direction is by Takashi Ano.

0697 SERIES

FUSHIGINA KOALA BLINKY (*Marvelous Koala Blinky*), Nippon Animation, animals, 25 episodes, 7/7 – 31/12/1984.

0698 SERIES

GINGA PATROL P.J. (*Galactic Patrol P.J.*), Eiken, science fiction, 26 episodes, 7/7 — 8/22/1984. [*Il Était Une Fois... L'Espace*].

0699 SERIES

YOROSHIKU MECHADOCK (*Pleased to Meet You Mechadock*), Tatsunoko, sport, 30 episodes, 9/1/1984 — 3/30/1985.

Ginga Patrol P.J. © Procidis.

Yoroshiku Mechadock © Tatsunoko Pro.

The Mechadock is a powerful race car capable of racing on any type of land. This is yet another story set in the very popular world of car racing.

0700 SERIES

FUTARITAKA (*The Two Hawks*), Kokusei eigasha, sport, 33 episodes, 9/20/1984 — 6/21/1985.

This traditionally melodramatic animated story has a distinct dramatic edge, presenting the reckless life of a motorcycle driver. The original manga is by Kaoru Shintani. The series was interrupted halfway because of the production firm's bankruptcy.

0701 SERIES

DOTANBA NO MANNER (*The MuddleHeaded's Behavior*), Eiken, humor, 131 episodes, 10/3/1984 — 4/9/1987.

0702 SERIES

KOALA BOY KOKKI (*id.*), Top Kraft, animals, 26 episodes, 10/4/1984 —3/28/1985.

This story is one of hundreds with animals as the main characters. Kokki, the little Koala, lives with his family in a quiet Australian village inhabited by hat-wearing rabbits and penguins. Kokki, the faithful Lala and some of their friends leave on an adventure to discover the mysterious world of adults.

0703 SERIES

KIKOKAI GALIANT (*Galiant, the Armed Space*), Nippon Sunrise, robot, 26 episodes, 10/5/1984 — 3/29/1985.

The third chapter of the saga created by Ryosuke Takahashi and Hajine Yadachi features the young prince Joldy who, at the controls of the giant robot Galiant, fights the ambitious Madal and his thirst for conquest. The fantasy setting sees the unification of classic and futuristic elements, powerful suits of mechanized armor co-existing with Roman-style soldiers.

0704 SERIES

CHORIKI ROBOT GALATT (*Galatt, the Super Powerful Robot*), Nippon Sunrise, robot, 25 episodes, 10/5/1984 — 4/5/1985.

The humorous series bases itself in part on the archetypes presented in the *Time Machine* saga. The young pilots Michael, Patty and Camille, all three members of the space school JUNB, find themselves having to fight against a team of bizarre characters who want to take possession of our planet. Three robots exhibiting amazing and terrifying powers turn the three inexperienced young people into real heroes.

0705 SERIES

MORI NO TONTOTACHI (*Tonto's Group in the Forest*), Zuiyo, fairy tale, 23 episodes, 10/5/1984 — 4/5/1985.

A group of friendly gnomes lives in a small isolated village of Northern Europe. Day after day, they work at their favorite task, building toys for all the children. Once a year, their wise representative gives the toys to the children who deserve gifts. The story created by Yoshiyako Yoshida is inspired, naturally, by the legend of Santa Claus and features the drawings of Susumu Shiraume. Masakazu Higushi supervises the direction and Koji Kato the designs.

0706 SERIES

ASHITA TENKI NI MARE (*We Hope That Tomorrow Will Be Nice*), Nas, sport, 47 episodes, 10/6/1984 — 9/27/1985.

Taiyo is a short fat boy, whose favorite thing in the world is a good meal. This doesn't prevent him from giving his all when he plays golf, a sport which he discovered completely by chance. He puts his all into rising through the ranks, but his quest to reach professional status keeps him too busy to appreciate the fun in life. Game after game Taiyo continues to amaze both the public and his opponents with shots that seem impossible, focusing his energies and skill with thoughts of food. The cartoon is taken from Tetsuya Chiba's comic strip and the direction is performed by Hiroyoshi Mitsunobu. The screenplay is by Noboru Shiroyama and Ryoichi Atsuki, amongst others.

0707 SERIES

GALACTIC PATROL LENSMAN (*Lensman*), MK for Kodansha, science fiction, 25 episodes, 10/6/1984 — 8/8/1985.

This series was created following the movie's success. It keeps the same general plotline and cast of characters as the successful debut.

0708 SERIES

SEI JUSHI VISMARK (*Vismark the Gunman From the Stars*), Studio Pierrot, robot, 51 episodes, 10/7/1984 — 9/29/1985. *Saber Riders And The Star Sheriffs* [*Sab Rider*].

Three men and one woman from different nations make up a special task force. Commanded by the wise Ruwell, Kikari Shinji from Japan, Bill Wilcox from the United States, Richard Lancelott from England and Marianne, Ruwell's daughter, from France use Vismark, the robot gunman, to defend the earthly confederation from the alien attacks of the extra-dimensional Deskyula.

0709 SERIES

TAO TAO EHOKAN SEKAI DOBUTSU BANASHI (*Tao Tao's Book Shelf, Animal Stories of the World*), Shunmao, animals, 10/9/1984 —4/9/1985.

0710 SERIES

HOKUTO NO KEN (*Fist of the North Star*), Toei Doga, adventure, 109 episodes, 10/11/1984 — 3/5/1987. *Fist of the North Star* [*Ken Le Survivant*].

Kenshiro is a young expert in Hokuto, a martial art based on pressure points which blocks blood flows to make the inside of the body explode. The people of Earth are fighting for survival in a world decimated by the use of nuclear weapons, and two rival schools, the Hokuto and the Nanto, are striving to subdue the populations of the Earth. The young Kenshiro, wandering through the tortured land, spends his time refining his combat techniques and confronting fighters who are trying to destroy the villages of the survivors. The decisive duel happens between the two representatives of the Hokoto school, when Ken and the gigantic Raoh face each other for the command of humanity. In the animated version, Hiroshi Toda and Shozo Uehara, creators and Masami Suda, character designer, have managed to keep intact the feel and plot of the comic series created by Bronson and Tetsuo Hara.

Sei Jushi Vismark © Studio Pierrot.

Fist Of The North Star ©1999 Buronson Tetsuo Hara / Shueisha • Toei Animation. ©1999 Manga Entertainment, Inc. / Palm Pictures, LLC. Package design & summary ©1999 Manga Entertainment Inc. All Rights Reserved.

0711 SERIES

CAT'S EYES (*id.*), Tokyo Movie Shinsha, adventure, 37 episodes, 10/18/1984 — 7/8/1985. [*Signé Cat's Eye*].

After a stint of a few months in the Western World, the Kisugi sisters return to Japan where they continue to steal their father's paintings from exhibitions or private collections in an effort to find him. The character design of this new series is extremely well done, but it lacks the distinctiveness and personality that Tsukasa Hojo, author of the comic, had given his heroines. Although, in the first series, their features were less precise, the art was set apart by a particular tendency towards realism that made Cat's Eyes stand out from other animated productions. Like the previous one, this series is produced by Yutaka Fujioka and the camera work by Hirokata Takahashi.

0712 SERIES

MEITANTEI HOLMES (*Holmes the Investigator*), Tokyo Movie Shinsha, animals, 26 episodes, 11/6/1984 — 5/20/1985. *Sherlock Hound* [*Sherlock Holmes*].

After having abandoned the television scene for a few years, choosing to dedicate himself to film animation, Hayao Miyazaki directs the first four episodes of this series produced by the TMS in collaboration with the RAI and with Marco Pagot's studio. The story is inspired by the adventures of Sir Arthur Conan Doyle's famous detective, and the character designs are by Yoshifumi Kondo.

Meitantei Holmes © TMS / RAI / REVER.

0713 SPECIAL

CHISANA KOI NO MONOGATARI (*The Story of a Little Love*), MK, humor, 84 min., 3/29.

Toshio Hirada directs the adventures of the student Cichi and of her dear friend Sally. This special focuses on the small problems of everyday life.

0714 SPECIAL

KINNIKUMAN (*id.*), Toei Doga, sport, 45 min., 4/7.

0715 SPECIAL

KINNIKUMAN KESSEN! SHICHININ NO CHOJIN VS UCHU NOBUSHI (*Kinnikuman Final Encounter! Seven Supermen Against the Space Warriors*), Toei Doga, sport, 78 min., 4/7.

0716 SPECIAL

BAGI (*id.*), Toei Doga/Sanrio for Tezuka, adventure, 104 min., 8/19.

This film by Osamu Tezuka is a strong condemnation of genetic experiments on animals. Bagi is an artificial creation of doctor Ishigami, who has created a hybrid with a feline body and human cells to give birth to a new creature. Sixteen years later, in a remote area of South America, the young Ryo, who has lived his childhood with the sweet Bagi, sets out to hunt her. The young boy thinks that she is responsible for the death of his mother — the doctor who made the hybrid — who was in fact, killed by men interested in her experiments. The wonderful music by Kentaro Haneda accompanies the splendid animation.

Bagi © Tezuka Production.

0717 SPECIAL

NINE KANKETSUHEN — YATTEKIMASHITA KOSHIEN (*Nine, Final Chapter: Here We Are at Koshien Baseball Stadium*), Group Tack, sport, 84 min., 9/5.

The young Katsuya, a rising star in the baseball world, is finally playing the most important game of his career: the tournament final at the magnificent Koshien Stadium.

0718 OAV

DALLOS II — REMEMBER BARTHOLOMEW (*Id.*), Studio Pierrot for Network, science fiction, 30 min., 1/21, Bandai.

The guerrillas on the moon don't have the strength to attack, and their sabotage of the government's plans is seriously hindered because of the strict controls by the Office of Supervision. On the other hand, even the Office of Supervision can't stop the underground activities of the guerrillas, so the situation seems equally hopeless for both parties. Doug Mac Coy, the leader of the guerrillas, while being chased by the police, meets Shun who helps him to escape. Doug and Shun try to capture the robot police dogs, thinking that they can use them as weapons. In the meantime, Alex Riger, commander of the army, returns to the Office of Supervision as its director and begins to escalate the controls on the guerrillas. Melinda Harst, Alex's fiancee, sets out for the Moon to be with him but she is kidnapped by Doug and his companions before she can reach her destination. In the underground base of the guerrillas, Melinda is surprised to see the suffering of the people in the Moon colonies.

Dallos © Studio Pierrot / Bandai Visual.

0719 OAV

YUKIGESHO SHOJO BAKAREI (*The Snow MakeUp: Young Bakarei*), Wonder Kids, erotic, 30 min., 2/21.

0720 OAV

SEA SIDE ANGEL MIYU (*id.*), Wonder Kids, erotic, 60 min., 5/25.

0721 OAV

CHO NORYOKU BARABANBA (*Super Power Barabanba*), JHV, erotic, 30 min., 6/25, Fairy Dust.

0722 OAV

DALLOS III BOKYO NO UMI NI TATSU (*Dallos III: A Sea of Nostalgia, Act I*), Studio Pierrot for Network, science fiction, 30 min., 4/28, Bandai.

The Lunarians from the first generation refuse to fight against the Earth and, contrary to them, the guerrillas of the third generation want independance. Shun, after having received an invitation from Doug to join them, is undecided as to what to do. The viceconsul, who doesn't like Alex, wants to capture him and Shun, because of the indiscriminate attack against the headquarters finally gets his hands on guns.

0723 OAV

DALLOS III BOKYO NO UMI NI TATSU ACT II (*Dallos III: A Ses of Nostalgia, Act II*), Studio Pierrot for Network, science fiction, 30 min., 7/21, Bandai.

The guerillas gather the people from all the Moon colonies in the mysterious ruins of the venerated Dallos. Alex, personally guiding the federal army, sets out for the decisive battle. While the battle is going on, strange phenomenon start occurring. The ground rises, and the battlefield is filled with light in an instant. When darkness returns, almost no one is left alive. Shun, who survived, takes his grandfather Taizo and sets out for the Sea of Nostalgia where the Lunarians now rest. Shun looks out at the cemetery that arises from the Sea of Nostalgia, and finds the answer that he's been looking for.

0724 OAV
KONEKOCHAN NO IRU MISE (*The Kitten's Store*), Wonder Kids, erotic, 25 min., 7/21.

0725 OAV
MACHIKADO NO MERUCHEN (*Stories on the Way*), Kitty Film, Comedy, 52 min., 7/21.

Hiroshi is a student at Shinjuku High School who dreams about writing children's books one day. To do so, however, he needs money so he is forced to work to scrape together the funds. The romantic experience he has with Hiroko, whom he meets in an underpass, sets him on the path to making his dream come true.

0726 OAV
CREAM LEMON SERIES PART I — KOBI IMOTO BABY (*Cream Lemon Series Part I: the Fascination of the Little Sister*), Soeishinsha, erotic, 25 min., 8/10. Fairy Dust.

At her father's second wedding, Ami sees her brother Hiroshi again — the brother with whom she once had an incestuous relationship. When her mother had gone to work one night, the two siblings had discovered that they shared an attraction for one another, and had given in to their desires.

0727 OAV
BIRTH (*id.*), Kaname, fantasy/science fiction, 80 min., 9/5. Victor. *Planet Busters.*

The inorganic androids and the inhabitants of the planet Aquaroid begin a long and terrifying space war. The main characters of the OAV are the courageous Namu Shurugi and the sweet Rasa Yupiter, descendants of the Zacs, who were destroyed without pity by the Aquaroid army.

0728 OAV
CREAM LEMON SERIES PART II ESCALATION (*id.*), Soeishinsha, erotic, 25 min., 9/10. Fairy Dust.

After having caught her mother in bed with the piano teacher, Rie is sent to a strict catholic boarding school. There, she meets the beautiful Naomi who drags her into a homosexual relationship to which a third girl will be added, the perverted Midori. The triangle that is formed in the school room lasts until morning, becoming progressively more perverse. Rie becomes nothing more than a pleasure object for her two companions.

0729 OAV
SHINING MEI (*id.*), All Production, erotic, 26 min., 10/15.

0730 OAV
MAHO NO TENSHI CREAMY MAMI — EIEN NO ONCE MORE (*Creamy Mami, the Magic Angel: Still Eternity*), Studio Pierrot, magic, 92 min., 10/28. Bandai.

The famous singer Creamy Mami has been out of the spotlight for one year now: Yu in fact, had to give the magic wand back to Pino Pino. Suddenly, however, a big publicity campaign announces the return of Creamy on stage. Yu and her friends investigate, discovering that it is a setup by Shingo to fool the singer's many fans.

Planet Busters © 1986 Idol Co., Ltd / Harmony Gold U.S.A., Inc. Package design ©1992 Streamline Pictures.

0731 OAV

FRUITS VIRGIN (*id.*), Showa, erotic, 25 min., 11/25.

0732 OAV

CREAM LEMON SERIES PART 3 — SF CHOJIGEN DENSETSU RAU (*Cream Lemon Series Part 3: the Science fiction Legend of the Superdimensional Rall*), Soeishinsha, erotic, 25 min., 12/3, Fairy Dust.

King Lamoru plans to conquer the Universe, but prophecies foretell that his plans will be hindered by an armed warrior carrying the sword of Rivers. A highly sexual film with a mediocre plot.

0733 OAV

HENSOKYOKU (*Variations*), Wonder Kids, erotic 25 min., 12/20.

0734 OAV

CUTIE LEMON VIRGIN ROAD (*id.*), Five Star, erotic, 25 min., 12/22.

CHAPTER TWENTY-FOUR: 1985

The year 1985 witnesses the debut of two shows that became notorious — and highly censored — in Italy. The first was the feature film *Lupin sansei: Babilon no ogon densetsu*, starring the shapely Fujiko and an entire planet of half-dressed alien women. A large number of scenes were deemed too risqué and were cut, but unfortunately the movie loses a lot of coherence from this act of censorship. It is difficult to reconstruct the plot, the events are out of chronological order and certain characters appear with no introduction, confusing the viewer. The same thing happened with *Hono no Alpen Rose*, the second work in question. Here, more than ever, the intervention of the Italian distributor made a mess of what had been a solid show. The series is a soap opera, narrating the life of the little Alicia (going under the name of Jeudi to hide from her pursuers), who has to face a number of hardships in a Europe torn to pieces by the Second World War. There is no sexual content in the show, but everything about the Nazis has been cut out, and of the original 25 minute episode, only ten are left. It is difficult to reconcile a story in that particular setting without mentioning the Nazis, especially since young Jeudi is being chased by them.

Japanese audiences have always supported stories inspired by children's literature classics. *Shokojo Sarah* is one of these, and it received a warm welcome from viewers. Freely adapted from *Sarah Grewe* by F.H. Burnett, it tells the story of a rich girl who, having become poor, searches her soul and finds the strength to continue.

Another important trend, that of the "magical girls" genre, was enlarged with another new entry, *Maho no Star Magical Emi*. The basis of the plot is the same as all series of this genre, as Mai also uses a magic wand to change into an entertainer — Emi, the singing witch. Along with this new series, two new chapters of the adventures of two famous witches, Creamy Mami and Minky Momo, were released solely for the videocassette market. Creamy Mami makes her stage comeback, while Minky Momo lives a fantastic adventure on Peter Pan's island. Mitsuru Adachi, an illustrator who specialized in sports soap operas, realized one of his biggest successes in 1985 with the release of his successful animated series *Touch*, set in the world of baseball. The main characters are two twin

Maho no Star Magical Emi © Studio Pierrot.

brothers and a young girl. Following the death of his brother Kazuya, a baseball player and model student, Tatsuya tries to imitate his brother's accomplishments and conquer Minami's heart.

The year 1985 also marks the debut of a new collaboration between Japan and the United States in the show *Transformers*. The Japanese animation is good, but it was not enough to bring the show up to Japan's standards, as the American scripts were aimed at a young audience and contained a huge number of very obvious 'moral lessons.' Japan has since collaborated with the USA on a number of shows, the best-known among them being G.I. Joe and Jem, the latter one — an almost prototypical magical girl show — without contest the better of the two.

The still young OAV market was strengthened during the year with the release of new and popular titles, most notably the beginning of the *Megazone 23* saga. Along with a complex and twisting plot, the director and the style of drawing were changed for every chapter, sometimes making the characters completely unrecognizable. Another important series which debuted was *Tatakae! Iczer One*, 30 minutes of science fiction and gore, which soon caught the public eye.

The prolific Rumiko Takahashi introduced another vastly popular series with *Hono Tripper*, the episode which marked the beginning of *Rumic World*, while the always loved "rough copy" draws the crowds with a very good OAV entitled *Dirty Pair — Nolandia no nazo*.

0735 FILM

URUSEI YATSURA: REMEMBER MY LOVE (*Those Obnoxious Aliens: Remember My Love*), Kitty Film, comedy, 90 min., 1/26. *Urusei Yatsura: Remember My Love.*

Kasuo Yamasaki, director of the animated scenes, proves his talent once again with this feature film that distinguishes itself by its unprecedented levels of non-sequeter insanity. Lu, trying to kidnap Lamu, changes Ataru into a pink hippopotamus. Even in this predicament, the unfortunate young man manages to ruin the plans of his rival.

0736 FILM

NINPU KAMUI NO KEN (*Ninja Wind Dagger Of Kamui*), Project Team Argos/Madhouse for Kadokawa, historical, 132 min., 3/16. *The Dagger Of Kamui.*

This movie is considered the masterpiece of the year, primarily because of the screenplay taken from Tetsuo Yano's story, along with the direction of the very talented Taro Rin. The movie follows the adventures of a ninja, Jiro, wrongly accused of murder, who runs from his executioners and searches for final proof of his own innocence.

0737 FILM

BOBBY NI KUBITTAKE (*In Love With Bobby*), Team Madhouse for Haruchi Kadokawa, soap opera, 44 min., 3/16.

0738 FILM

KINNIKUMAN — SEIGICHOJIN VS KODAICHOJIN (*Kinnikuman, the Super Executioner Against the Superman of the Past*), Toei Doga, sport, 45 min., 3/16.

Urusei Yatsura: Remember My Love ©1985 Kitty Films. English version & package artwork ©1992 AnimEigo. Licensed to AnimEigo by Compass, Ltd. All Rights Reserved

The Dagger Of Kamui ©1985 Haruki Kadokawa Films Inc. Licensed to AnimEigo by Toei Co., Ltd. English version ©1993 AnimEigo, Inc.

0739 FILM

GUGU GANMO (*id.*), Toei Doga, humor, 25 min., 3/16.

0740 FILM

TONGARIBOSHI NO MEMOL (*Memol With the Pointy Hat*), Toei Doga, children, 30 min., 3/16.

0741 FILM

DORAEMON — NOBITA NO LITTLE STAR WARS (*Doraemon: Nobita's Little "Star Wars"*), Shin'ei Doga, humor, 3/16.

This short film is a parody of George Lucas' famous saga, starring Fujiko Fujio's most entertaining characters forced to play the parts of Luke Skywalker and Darth Vader.

0742 FILM

NINJA HATTORIKUN + PAMAN — NINJA KAIJU JEEP VS MIRACLE TAMAGO (*Hattori the Little Ninja + Paman: the Jeep Monster Against the Miracle Egg*), Shin'ei Doga, humor, 53 min., 3/16.

0743 FILM

GON GITSUNE (*Gon, the Fox*), Ai Kikaku Center, fairy tale, 3/16.

The film, featuring a clever fox as the main character, is produced to celebrate the tenth anniversary of the television series *Manga Nihon Mukashi Banashi*.

0744 FILM

HALLEY NO KAGAMI (*Halley's Mirror*), Toei Doga for Kagaku Hakuran Kay Kyokai, science fiction, 25 min., 3/16.

The search for a new world to escape the overpopulation of Earth is the basis for this enchanting production. The film, created by the great Reiji Matsumoto, was designed to be shown only at the Tsukuba museum of science. It features the characters of Meguru, Mayu and the android Zero, who search for an access way into unexplored space.

0745 FILM

PENGUIN'S MEMORY — SHIAWASE MONOGATARI (*Penguin's Memory: a Happy Story*), Animation Staff Room, documentary, 101 min., 5/25.

The feature film was inspired by a famous Suntori beer commercial and uses the same characters.

0746 FILM

GINGA TETSUDO NO YORU (*One Night on the Galactic Railway*), Group Tack for Herald, animals, 107 min., 7/13. *Night On The Galactic Railroad*.

To help his invalid mother, Giovanni, a tender kitten, splits his time between work in a print shop and his studies. He never gives up hope that one day, his father will return from the fishing area of the Northern Ocean. One night, during the festivities of the Alpha Centurion star, the young cat goes out to get some milk for his mother, but wanders off towards a hill in the outskirts of town and is amazed by the sight of a steam locomotive. He recognizes his friend, Campanella, on the train, and joins him on his journey. The magical train leaves for space, following the Milky Way. During the trip, the two cats have the opportunity to

Night On The Galactic Railroad ©1985 Asahi Group / Herald Group / TAC. English version & package artwork ©1995 Central Park Media Corporation.

see places they never dreamed of and meet extraordinary characters. The film, produced by Masato Hara and Atsumi Tashiro, is taken in part from Kenji Miyazawa's novel and is directed by Gisaburo Sugii. The story's screenplay is by Minoru Betsuyaku and animated by Marinosuke Eguchi and Jiro Saruyama.

0747 FILM

CAPTAIN TSUBASA — EUROPE DAIKESSEN (*Captain Tsubasa: the Great European Final Challenge*), Tsuchida, sport, 41 min., 7/13.

The stories of the young captain of the Japanese national junior soccer team continue, as Ozora Tsubasa, together with his unbeatable team, plays against the major teams of Europe.

0748 FILM

DR. SLUMP & ARALE CHAN — HOYOYO! YUME NO MIYAKO MECHAPOLIS (*Dr. Slump and Arale: the Dream Capital*), Toei Doga, humor, 38 min., 7/13.

0749 FILM

KINNIKUMAN — GYAKUSHU! UCHUKAKURE CHOJIN (*Kinnikuman Counter Attacks! The Hidden Space Superman*), Toei Doga, sport, 39 min., 7/13.

This is the most demanding challenge ever for Kinnikuman, as the hero risks defeat by a terrible superman from space. As usual, justice wins over evil and the film has a happy ending.

0750 FILM

LUPIN SANSEI — BABILON NO OGON DENSETSU (*Lupin III: The Legend of the Babylonian Gold*), Tokyo Movie Shinsha, police story, 100 min., 7/13. *Lupin III: Legend Of The Gold Of Babylon*.

"If you go to Babylon, three dark wells you will find. The Candelabra I will bring, so I can find my love..." Singing this strange song, the old, drunk Rosetta turns up in Lupin's hotel room and tells him of an ancient legend. In the year 500 B.C., the capital of Mesopotamia had fallen into the hands of Persian gods. Before the city was destroyed, a god had come from heaven and had put all the Mesopotamian gold in a secret hiding place. Just before the old woman could finish her story, goons under orders from a man named Marciano, a Mafia boss, barge into the room. They are also looking for the gold, and they try to shoot poor Lupin. By the time that Lupin gets the upper hand however, Rosetta has left, leaving behind a mysterious candelabra.

Marciano's father had found some ancient tablets in New York, under Madison Square Gardens, and had left for the Middle East to look for the treasure. His efforts had led to nothing, however, so Marciano decided to continue his search along with the provocative Fujiko. Lupin, possessing some of the tablets, decides to leave for Babylon. The tenacious inspector Zenigata is on his trail, this time with five sexy police women. The main character arrives at the excavation site, overcomes the first two dark wells, and finally, in the third, sees a holographic projection of a woman who, sent to Earth in the far-off past, wakes up every 76 years to try to find the gold. The god in fact, will come to our planet with Haley's comet to recover the ancient treasure, thus allowing the woman to return to

Lupin Sansei: Babilon no Ogon densetsu
© Monkey Punch / TMS.

Intro
-1962
1963
1964
1965
1966
1967
1968
1969
1970
1971
1972
1973
1974
1975
1976
1977
1978
1979
1980
1981
1982
1983
1984
1985
1986
1987
1988
Index

her native planet. For this to happen, Lupin must position the candelabra on the sparkling tower of Babel.

After some incredible adventures, the scene returns to New York; it is there, in fact, that the famed tower is kept. When the god had come back to take what men had built in his honor, he had failed and, during the journey home, the tower had fallen on a deserted beach in what is now Manhattan. Lupin and his companions prepare for action. The candelabra, unfortunately, doesn't call a *god* back from space, but an alien spaceship that attacks the tower in the hope of recovering the gold. The old Rosetta transforms herself into the girl of the third well, but looks aren't enough to corrupt Lupin who decides to avenge himself by giving the treasure back to the earthlings to whom it rightfully belongs.

0751 FILM

ODIN — KOSHI HANSEN STARLIGHT (*Odin: Photon Sailor Starlight*), Westcape, science fiction, 139 min., 8/10. *Odin: Photon Space Sailor Starlight.*

This incredible space odyssey tells the story of a sailing ship activated by light energy. After having recovered the pilot Akira Tsukuba, adrift in space and Sara, the only survivor of the Alford spaceship (although currently suffering from amnesia), Captain Nara comes across an enormous mechanical fortress programmed to destroy mechanical creations — including starships! During the escape, the Starlight runs into a spacial-temporal distortion that throws them towards Uranus, two billion kilometers away. The discovery of an alien flying saucer on one of the satellites of the frozen planet reveals the existence of distortion points in space, shortcuts which make it easy to contact other civilizations.

Akira and the members of the crew take possession of the Starlight and go back into the distortion point which they found, but they end up in the gravitational field of the three interacting stars, at the mercy of attacks from unidentified war machines. The men escape from a closed space called the 'Ginnungagap' with great difficulty. Followed by the mechanical army, the Starlight is forced to fight against troops which turn out to be the army of the people of Cyborg. Sara, regaining her memory, remembers that she is a descendant of the queen of Odin, whose people, after having collectively decided to become biomechanical, had become unwitting victims of their robotic parts. Destroying the computer that controls the mechanisms, the Starlight crew ensures their survival and can thus continue their search for Odin. The movie, directed by Takeshi Shirato and Eichi Yamamoto, is written by Yoshinobu Mishizaki, who also produced the film.

0752 FILM

YOSEI FLORENCE (*Florence the Fairy*), Sanrio, fairy tale, 10/19.

0753 FILM

JUIPPIKI NO NEKO TO AHODORI (*Eleven Cats and An Albatross*), Group Tack for Herald, animals, 91 min., 12/15.

0754 FILM

KINNIKUMAN — HARESUGATA! SEIGICHOJIN (*Kinnikuman, How Nice! The Super Executioner*), Toei Doga, sport, 60 min., 12/21.

0755 FILM

CAPTAIN TSUBASA — AYAUSHI! ZENNIHON JR. (*Captain Tsubasa: Danger! Japanese Juvenile Championship*), Tsuchida, sport, 60 min., 12/21.

0756 FILM

GEGEGE NO KITARO (*Kitaro Gegege*), Toei Doga, horror, 39 min., 12/21.

0757 SERIES

SHOKOJO SARAH (*Little Miss Sarah*), Nippon Animation, classic, 46 episodes, 1/6 — 12/29/1985. [*Princesse Sarah*].

Shokojo Sarah © Nippon Animation Co., Ltd

Taken from the famous novel *Sarah Grewe* by F.H. Burnett, this series tells the sad story of little Sarah. Her father, a rich businessman, puts her in a luxurious private school where she is treated like a little princess and taught the rules of high society. Her father dies unexpectedly, and it is discovered that he had squandered all his money, and left poor Sarah with nothing. The director of the school forces Sarah to perform the worst of the chores to earn enough money for food and board, and she transfers her to the miserable attic of the school. The screenplay is entrusted to Toshitsugu Saitu.

0758 SERIES

KIDO SENSHI Z GUNDAM (*Gundam Z, The Warrior With the Mobile Armor*), Nippon Sunrise, robot, 50 episodes, 3/2/1985 — 2/22/1986.

A large number of people have died over the years of the war between the Earth and the principality of Jion. To prevent another rebellion, the Earth government (known as Union), decides to spend their energies and money on rebuilding the planet to the detriment of the colonies, considered only as source of raw materials. Senator Blex Forra rebels against the situation and, having reached Side 2, he founds an antigovernment movement, the AEUG (Anti Earth Union Government). His ideal of freedom spreads from the colonies to the Earth, where the private industry that has invested enormous capital for the colonization of space doesn't support the Union's anticolonial policy.

To prevent the AEUG from getting too much power from the financing coming from Earth, the Union creates a special branch of the army, known as the Titans. When the new soldiers repress a AEUG demonstration with poisonous gas, causing the death of 30,000 people, a movement of sympathy is formed on Earth, known as Kalaba, headed by Hayato Kobayashi. Amuro Rei also becomes an active collaborator of the Kalaba. Because of his hatred of violence and his space-phobia caused by his memories of the past war he had kept himself away from current events, but he now returns at the commands of the Dijeh.

The real main character of the story, however, is Camille Vidan, a powerful Newtype born on Side 7, who pilots the Z Gundam, the technologically more advanced version of the old RX 78 which was destroyed on Jion during the final encounter between Amuro and Char. Blex Forra dies at the hands of the Titans, and the control of the antigovernment movement ends up in the hands of Quatro Bagina, in reality Char Aznable, who supported the final attack on Jion in the first chapter of the saga. In Z Gundam, we also catch up with other characters from the preceding series such as Bright Noah, who is now married to Mirai Yashima with two children. The new conflict brings an escalation in the levels of death and violence in the series, to culminate in ZZ Gundam, the third series produced in 1986.

0759 SERIES

HAI! STEP JUN (*Here I am, Step Jun!*), Toei Doga, soap-opera, 45 episodes, 3/10/1985 — 1/12/1986. [*Va-y Julie!*].

Jun is a little girl gifted with an exceptional intelligence that allows her to build some spectacular inventions. When she falls in love, however, Jun proves that she is just like every other girl, and she decides that she will do anything to conquer the heart of the handsome Zero. The story is by Yasuichi Oshima, the character designs are by Kazuo Komatsubara and the direction by Hiroshi Shidara.

0760 SERIES

TOUCH (*id.*), Group Tack/Toho, sport/soap opera, 101 episodes, 3/24/1985 — 3/22/1987.

Taken from a manga by Mitsuru Adachi, the story is about the lives of three great friends: the twins Katzuya and Tatsuya Uesugi, and the young Minami whom both twins are in love with. The harmony of the group is shaken when Kazuya, a baseball champion, dies in a car accident. His brother does everything he can to replace him in the team, keeping the memory of Kayuza alive and winning the heart of Minami. The series is based on a project by Ren Usami and produced by Masamichi Fujiwara.

0761 SERIES

OBAKEN NO QTARO (*Qtaro the Ghost*), Shin'ei Doga, humor, 92 episodes, 4/1/1985 — 3/29/1987.

Once again, the duo Fujiko Fujio takes one of its old characters and features it in an animated series. This series is another story about Qtaro, the household ghost, the faithful and inseparable companion of little Shota.

0762 SERIES

PROGOLFER SARU (*id.*), Shin'ei Doga, sport, 147 episodes, 4/2/1985 — 3/23/1988.

0763 SERIES

ONEGAI! SAMIADON (*Please Samiadon!*), Tokyo Movie Shinsha, humor, 78 episodes, 4/2/1985 — 2/4/1986.

Samiadon is an elf who, like many famous predecessors, has been found by an earthly boy who takes care of him. After his stormy landing on a beach of the Japanese coast, the elf decides to stay on our planet.

0764 SERIES

CHOJU KISHIN DANCOUGAR (*Super-Bestial God-Machine Dancougar*), Ashi, robot, 33 episodes, 4/5 — 12/27/1985. *Dancougar*.

Shinobu Fujiwara, Sara Yuki, Masato Shikibu and Ryo Shiba fight at the commands of the powerful Dancougar robot, battling the alien Muge Zibaldos and General Shapiro, Sara's ex-boyfriend, who is now on the side of the alien invaders. The robot, one of the most elaborate in a television series, is the combination of four other robots, who are capable of transforming into animal androids (eagle, lion, panther and elephant).

Hai! Step Jun © Toei Animation.

Hono no Alpen Rose © Tatsunoko Pro.

0765 SERIES

HONO NO ALPEN ROSE (*The Fire Alpine Rose*), Tatsunoko, classic, 49 episodes, 4/8/1985 — 4/3/1986. [*Julie Et Stéphane*].

The action is set during the Second World War, when the Brendell family is forced to leave Austria to seek refuge in Switzerland. During the flight, the airplane is hit and crashes on German soil. When little Alicia regains consciousness, she is alone and doesn't remember anything from her past. A little boy named Lundi finds her and decides to treat her like his sister, renaming her Jeudi. Time goes by and, once grown, the girl decides to leave with Lundi to search for her roots. She meets the young composer Leonard Aschenbach, who recognizes her as his childhood friend Alicia Brendell, and she is finally able to reunite with her father, who is dying in a hospital. The girl then decides to go to her grandparents' house where her mother, almost blind, and Matilda, a perfidious girl passing herself off as Alicia, live.

Alicia's grandparents know the truth but they can't intervene because Matilda is the daughter of a powerful crime boss. Alicia and Lundi however, succeed in chasing the impostors away, and Alicia is finally able to live with her mother. When everything seems to be resolved, Count Gulmont steps in. He had tried to hinder her search before, because he is in love with the young Miss Brendell, but she doesn't love him back. The Count hires JeanJacques to kidnap Alicia. The young man, however, discovers that he is Lundi's older brother from whom he was separated at birth so he rebels against the Count's orders. Count Gulmont then attempts vengeance by himself, kidnapping Alicia. JeanJacques saves the girl, but dies with the Count who has remained trapped on the boat. The end of the story sees Alicia and Lundi grow up to become nurse and doctor, united in work as in life.

0766 SERIES

HEI! BUNBU (*id.*), Nippon Animation, humor, 130 episodes, 4/8/1985 — 4/3/1986.

Bunbu is a friendly living automobile, lovingly looked after by young Ken. The car's liveliness however, exasperates the young man's mother, always preoccupied with her son's safety.

0767 SERIES

MUSASHI NO KEN (*Musashi's Sword*), Eiken, sport, 72 episodes, 4/18/1985 — 9/26/1986.

One of the most popular sports in Japan is kendo, a sword-based martial art that is a popular gimmick to draw the attention of the viewing public. Musashi is a young fan of this noble discipline who dreams, along with many other animated characters, to become a champion.

0768 SERIES

KONPORA KID (*id.*), Toei Doga, humor, 26 episodes, 6/3 —12/23/1985.

0769 SERIES

MAHO NO STAR MAGICAL EMI (*Magical Emi, the Star of Magic*), Studio Pierrot, magic, 38 episodes, 6/7/1985 — 2/28/1986. [*Emi Magique*].

Little Mai Kazuki is playing in her attic when she finds a magical mirror. It emits a ray of light, that makes a stuffed flying squirrel come to life. The entity presents itself to Mai as a spirit capable of giving her magical powers, thanks to a special bracelet. It gives the bracelet to the little girl, telling her that with magic, she'll be able to make her biggest dream come true — to become a famous magician like Emily Lowell. So Mai transforms into an older girl, and she changes her name to Emi and becomes part of Magic Art, run by her grandparents, two friendly and very skilled magicians. Emi earns instant success, reminding everyone of the ancient splendor of magicians. At the end of the year, Mai is forced to decide if she wants to keep her powers forever or give them back. She opts for the latter, preferring to reach her dream with her own strength. She thus says good-bye to the little spirit that she had affectionately named Topo. Created on the trail of the incredible success obtained by the "magical girls," the series presents the character designs of Hiroshi Yamamoto and Yoshiyuki Kishi and the direction of Takeshi Ano.

0770 SERIES

TATAKE! CHOROBOT SEIMEITAI TRANSFORMER (*Combat! Super Live Robots Transformer*), Toei Doga/Marvel Hasbro, robot, 100 episodes, 7/6/1985 — 11/7/1986. *Transformers*.

At the ends of the galaxy there is a planet that has developed life based entirely on technology. The planet is called Cybertron, and its people are intelligent robots capable of transforming into the most disparate forms. Two opposed factions have been competing for thousands of years for supremacy of the planet: the perfidious Destrons, headed by the evil Galvatron, and the courageous Cybertrons, headed by Convoy. The energy that keeps the Cybertrons alive is almost depleted, and the forces of good build the Ark, a great spaceship, to find new sources of energy in space. Discovering this, the Destrons follow the Cybertrons to destroy them. Both lose control of their respective spaceships, crashing on the Earth of 4 million years ago, and the robots develop the ability to transform into earthly motor vehicles. The war relentlessly continues, unfortunately involving the innocent human population.

0771 SERIES

DIRTY PAIR (*id.*), Nippon Sunrise, science fiction, 24 episodes, 7/15 — 12/26/1985. [*Dan Et Danny*].

In 2141, mankind's dream to colonize the stars has come true but the problems that afflicted human beings on Earth haven't disappeared. The police can't control organized crime and the illegal activities that spring up regardless of controls and punishments. Private agencies that cooperate with the police are created as a possible solution, and one of these (the World Welfare Work Agency), employs the two main characters, Yuri and Kei. As talented as they are clever and ruthless, they are known with terror as the "Dirty Pair" even though their code name is actually "Lovely Angels." During the missions, Yuri and Kei are accompanied by MUGHI (Military Utility Genetic Higher Intelligence), a mild beast and by Nammo, a little robot with a conscience. The Dirty Pair were presented for the first time in a Japanese science fiction magazine and, later on, because of the great success they earned, Nippon Sunrise turns it into animation under the supervision of Haruka Takachiko, already famous for the movie *Crusher Joe*. The series, directed by Toshibumi Takisawa, is produced by Takayuki Yoshi and is written, amongst others, by Toshiki Inoue, Mitsuri Shimada and Yasushi Hirano.

Dirty Pair © H. Takachiho • Studio Nue / Sunrise / NTV.

0772 SERIES

AOKI RYUSEI SPT LAYZNER (*SPT Layzner, the Blue Comet*), Nippon Sunrise, robot, 38 episodes, 10/3/1985 — 6/26/1986.

Eiji Asuka, the pilot of an amazing robot whose design recalls that of the Mobile Suits in Gundam, is a young man who is half alien, with an earthling for a father and a mother who came from the star Glados. The movie, based around interplanetary war between the Earth and Glados, is an excuse to treat the problems of racism that Eigi must face because of his mixed blood. The series has been highly rated by most, due mostly to its high-quality animation and a deeply emotional plot.

0773 SERIES

NINJA SENSHI TOBIKAGE (*Tobikage, The Ninja Warrior*), Studio Pierrot, robot, 41 episodes, 10/6/1985 — 7/14/1986.

An alien spaceship, while it is fighting a flight of Samurai robots, lands on the planet Shuma. The planet's army, taken by surprise, can't contain the devastation brought by the battle and are soon forced to retreat. The sixteen year old Joe Maya, to save himself from a robot's attack, sneaks into the spaceship, where he discovers the existence of enormous robots whose movements repeat the movements of the pilot inside it. Thanks to Kurojishi (the name of the robot), Joe routs the opposing army. To develop his skills and power level he adds Tobikage, a real ninja robot, who seems impervious to weapons. As a curious note, the designs of the female characters is entrusted to Toshihiro Hirano, known for the sensual designs of *Tatakai! Iczer!* and *Dangaio*.

0774 SERIES

SHOWA AHOZOSHI AKANUKE ICHIBAN (*The Stupid Agenda Of The Elegant Showa*), Tatsunoko, science fiction, 22 episodes, 10/7/1985 — 3/24/1986.

Yu Atsuki, a newcomer in the field, comes out with this new series, famous in Japan for the most part because of the manga from which it originated. This series sees Tanne Kojiro become a super hero at the service of justice.

Showa Ahozoshi Akanuke Ichiban © Tatsunoko Pro.

0775 SERIES

GEGEGE NO KITARO (*Kitaro Gegege*), Toei Doga, horror, 108 episodes, 10/2/1985 — 3/21/1988.

The success of Kitaro's previous series taken from Shigeru Mizuki's comic drove the producers to make one more, in tune with the modern television viewers' tastes. While maintaining a balance of humorous and horrific tones, the situations are changed so that this does not fall into the list of simple remakes. The character designs have also been changed, in certain cases making them so good-looking that they completely change the intent of the original.

0776 SERIES

HIGH SCHOOL KIMENGUMI (*id.*), NAS humor, 84 episodes, 10/20/1985 — 10/3/1987. [*Le Collège Fou Fou Fou*].

The series is taken from Moto Nuzawa's disturbing comic, published in the magazine *Shukan Shonen Jump*. The main characters are five strange young high school students who are part of the Kimenguimi circle, all madly in love with their teacher.

High School Kimengumi
© M. Shinzawa / Shueisha / Fuji TV / NAS.

0777 SERIES

YUME NO HOSHI NO BOTANNOZU (*Bottanozu's Dream Star*), Sanrio, humor, 26 episodes, 10/21/1985 — 4/12/1986.

0778 SPECIAL

SANGOKUSHI (*The Three Kingdoms*), Shin'ei Doga, historical, 93 min., 3/20.

An epic story set in China in 265 A.D, towards the end of the Han dynasty, *Sangokishi* tells of the incredible impact of Liu Pi who, uniting with the fat Chan Fei and Wan Fu, wins a war against the ruthless Cho Sho. Using tactics and trickery before weapons, the three bring freedom and justice to the population. Taken from *Sang Huo*, one of the first poems of the Chinese literary tradition, *Sangokushi* is based on history, but is told as a fantastic legend and enriched with many elements of fantasy.

0779 SPECIAL

KONPORA KID — UCHU E TOBIDASE! KONPORA FAMILY NO WAKUWAKU BOKEN DAIRYOKO (*Konpora Kid: Jump Towards Space!*), Toei Doga, adventure, 7/29.

0780 SPECIAL

AKUMATO NO PRINCE MITSUME GA TORU (*The Three Eyed Prince From the Island of Demons*), Toei Doga, historical, 85 min., 8/25.

0781 OAV

NORA (*id.*), Film Link, action, 56 min., 1/21, Pony/Canyon.

During the second half of the 21st century, the space colony Frontier arises in the "Great Point 5," far away from our planet. The main character of the story is Nora, a girl who, with the help of doctor Zakaiasen and Professor Dohati, tries to solve the problems that arise from their nuclear missiles and the ongoing war.

0782 OAV

GREED (*id.*), Vivo for Film Link, action, 57 min., 1/21, Pony/Canyon.

Vai, the king of evil, is the uncontested lord of Greed, a planet subdivided into six distinct areas. Rid Kairu, the main character, leaves Hyunu to fight the perfidious king and reestablish peace. Rid's father had also tried to kill Vai when he was young, but his efforts were in vain. The young man feels it's his duty to save the family's honor. Along the road, Rid meets five companions who decide to follow him, proving themselves indispensable in the final fight.

0783 OAV

AREA 88 ACT I — URAGIRI NO OZORA (*Area 88, Act I: the Skies of Deceit*), Studio Pierrot, war, 50 min., 2/5, King Record. *Area 88 Act I: The Blue Sky Of Betrayal.*

After having received his diploma from the YAL (Yamato Airlines) pilot school, Shin Kazama is dragged by his friend Satoru Kanzaki to a bar to celebrate. After forcing him to drink, Kanzaki makes Shin sign a three-year service contract in the air force of the little kingdom of Asran. Kanzaki is desperate to win Satoru's girlfriend for himself, and take his place in the airline company. Working as a mercenary pilot for Area 88, Shin must bring down a huge number of enemy planes to earn enough money to buy back his contract and leave.

Area 88 ©1985 Project 88. English version ©1992 Central Park Media Corporation. All Rights Reserved.

On the verge of destroying the last plane he needs to make his quota, the unfortunate pilot runs out of ammunition and is hit, forcing him to an emergency landing. The money he has earned is needed to buy another plane and new weapons, and Shin remains a prisoner of the Area 88.

0784 OAV
SAFE DREAMING (*id.*), Wonder Kids, erotic, 30 min., 2/21.

0785 OAV
GINGA HYORYU VIFAM — KIETA JUNININ (*Vifam, the Shipwrecks of the Galaxy: the Twelve Who Disappeared*), Nippon Sunrise, robot, 50 min., 2/25, Warner/Pioneer.

The spaceship Geinas, with 12 shipwrecked people traveling on board, is about to go back to planet Taut but during the trip, it is forced to go through dangerous enemy territory. The group harmony is put to the test, and it is only through sharing a few happy moments — including the party for Scott's birthday, the young pilot of the Vifam robot— that the characters don't lose hope.

0786 OAV
GENMUSENKI LEDA (*Leda's Dream War*), Kanama Production, fantasy, 72 min., 3/1, Toho Video. *Leda: The Fantastic Adventure Of Yohko.*

Yoko is a 17 year old girl who, like many girls her age, feels insecure, especially now that she has decided to confess her feelings to the boy she loves. To find the courage to do so, the young woman composes a melody that will give her courage at the right moment. A couple of days later, while Yoko is walking down the street with her headset on, she spots the young man. As soon as she turns on her walkman, however, the ground sucks her in and the young girl finds herself alone in a mysterious unknown world. There, she meets a talking dog and a fierce little girl, the only one remaining to guard the Temple of Leda. With the help of a robot and her new friends, Yoko defeats the perfidious ex-priest of Leda whose intention is to expand his dominion onto Earth, thanks to Yoko's music — music capable of opening the dimensional passage between two worlds.

0787 OAV
MEGAZONE 23 (*id.*), Artland/Artmic, science fiction, 80 min., 3/5, Victor. *Megazone 23 Part I.*

Divided in three parts, the story that is inspired by *Universe* by Robert A. Heinlein, begins in what appears to be the Tokyo of the 90s. The main character is Shogo Yasagi, a young man who works in a fast-food restaurant. One night he is called by his friend Shinji, a test driver who wants to show him something exceptional, a strange and powerful motorcycle called Garland. Shinji has "borrowed" the motorcycle from the organization he works for, that soon discovers the missing machine and wants it back. In fact, one night, certain men circle the garage where the two young men stay and they burst in shooting. Taking advantage of the blackout caused by the shooting, Shogo escapes with the motorcycle while his friend is killed. The following day, Shogo decides to ask for help from the "Eve Information Show," a television program run by the famous singer Eve Tokimatsuri. Shogo doesn't reveal his name on the air, but as soon as he says the name of the motorcycle, the show is interrupted and he is made to talk so he can be identified.

Leda ©1985 Toho Co. Ltd / Kaname Productions. All Rights Reserved. English version ©1997 Toho Co., Ltd. Synopsis & packaging ©1997 The Right Stuf International, Inc..

Megazone 23 ©1985 Idol / Artmic.

Seeing the men who killed Shinji get closer, he escapes once again with the Garland, that automatically changes into a robot to protect him. The young man moves in with three of his friends, Yui Tanataka, a ballerina, Mai Yumekanou, a rock singer and Tomomi Murashita, an aspiring film director. With the three girls, he discovers an underground city ruled by the gigantic computer Bahamod. It is there that Shogo learns the truth from B. D., the head of a group of rebels who are trying to free themselves from the computer: five hundred years before, an alien attack had destroyed human civilization, and the survivors had saved themselves aboard a gigantic spaceship which contained the Megazone 23, where time had stopped in the 20th century.

Shogo decides to go to Eve Tokimatsuri to make his findings public, but once in the television studios, he finds out that the singer is only a hologram created by Bahamood, one of the many means it created to hold the population under its control. Forced to abandon the motorcycle, there is nothing left for Shogo to do, except to return to Yui. The first part is certainly the most complex where plot is concerned, and is entrusted, for the designs, to Toshihiro Hirano, who created all the characters except for Eve, who was created from the beginning by Haruhiko Mikimoto, adapting his distinctive style to mesh with that of the other authors.

Megazone 23 ©1985 Idol / Artmic. Package design ©1995 Orion Home Video and Streamline Pictures. All Rights Reserved.

0788 OAV

CREAM LEMON SERIES PART IV — POP CHASER (*id.*), Soeishinsha, erotic, 25 min., 3/13, Fairy Dust.

Lia travels the world on her powerful motorcycle in search of adventure. Her wandering brings her to an unknown city run by a man named Zack, head of a group of threatening hooligans. There, Lia meets the beautiful Mai and falls in love with her. During a raid by the criminals, Mai is kidnapped and Lia intervenes to free her. Nonstop action mixed with a good dose of sex.

0789 OAV

CREAM LEMON SERIES PART V — AMI AGAIN (*id.*), Soeishinsha, erotic, 25 min., 4/10, Fairy Dust.

Ami can't seem to have healthy relationships with boys her age because of the memory of her sexual relationship with her now-vanished older brother. Her friends try to get her out of the abyss of misery she's placed herself in, and drag her to a disco where she meets another young man with whom she dances all night. The young man, "Don Juan," takes her to his place to have his way with her. Ami's big awakening is something of a tragedy, as she realizes that she has made love with the stranger from the disco and not with her brother, as she has been dreaming all night.

0790 OAV

CUTIE LEMON II — GRADUATION (*id.*), Five Star, erotic, 25 min., 4/17.

0791 OAV

SENGOKU MAJIN GOSHOGUN TOKI NO IHÔJIN (*Warring-States Machine Goshogun: The Time Stranger*), Ashi, adventure, 80 min., 5/10, Tokuma Shoten. *Goshogun: The Time Étranger.*

The story begins in a deserted city where the Goshogun team members receive six letters which foretell the destiny of one of the members of the team: the beautiful Remi has been

GoShogun: The Time Étranger ©1985 Tokuma Shoten / Ashi Productions Co., Ltd. English version & package ©1995 Central Park Media Corporation.

predicted to die within two days. The story then continues forty years later, when we find Remi alive and ready to go to one of the team's meetings. An unexpected illness strikes her, and she is immediately brought to the hospital in critical condition. Her companions rush to her side with the intention to help her. They then relive Remi's adventures for the past 40 years, and learn how she escaped death in the deserted city. The film is taken from a story by Kunihiko Yuyama and the music is by Tachio Akano. Even though the characters have the same designs as the television series, the subject and the setting have been renewed.

0792 OAV

CREAM LEMON SERIES PART VI — ESCALATION II KINDAN NO SONATA (*Cream Lemon Series Part VI — Escalation II, Prohibited Sonata*), Soeishinsha, erotic, 25 min., 5/21, Fairy Dust.

For Naomi, her graduation, the day she's been waiting for, finally comes. She worked for a long time, and earned her diploma from the all-girl school where she spent her teenage years. To celebrate, she organizes a party to which she invites her friends Rei and Midori. During the evening, the passion that was prohibited at school is rekindled and the girls once again give in to their lust.

0793 OAV

DREAM HUNTER REM (*id.*), Orange Video house, erotic, 30 min., 6/10.

0794 OAV

MAHO NO TENSHI CREAMY MAMI — LONG GOODBYE (*Creamy Mami, the Angel of Magic: the Long Goodbye*), Studio Pierrot, magic, 50 min., 6/15, Bandai. The Enchanting Creamy Mami: the Long Goodbye.

A few years after she gave back the magic wand, Yu starts suffering from a strange form of metamorphosis: during the day she turns into Creamy, while at night she becomes Yu again. She finds it impossible to hide her secret any longer, and she is seen by Shingo Tachibana who forces her to make a science fiction movie with Megumi Ayase. Before the end of the movie, however, she is "cured" by Pino Pino and mister Tachibana must use Toshio as substitute for the last scenes. Creamy vanishes forever, while Megumi finally takes her loving Shingo to the altar.

0795 OAV

KARUIZAWA SYNDROME (*id.*), Kitty Film, soap opera, 90 min., 7/5, Pony/Canyon/Five Ace.

Yoshihisha Tagami, famous in the Western World for his Grey and Horobi manga, gives another proof of his great talent. Science fiction and horror are not the basis for this romantic story set at Karuizawa, a vacation spot in the center of Japan, although they do bring the story to where it needs to begin. Kohei the photographer, Sumio the young illustrator and Kaoru, her older sister (and madly in love with the young man), are the main characters of the anime.

0796 OAV

MAHO NO ROUGE LIPSTICK (*The Magic Red Lipstick*), Akushinsha, erotic, 25 min., 7/10, Fairy Dust.

Little Yuma receives a magic lipstick as a gift from a space salesman and when she puts it on, she changes into an adult woman. With her new shape, Yuma decides to seduce her brother who responds to her charm and who finds himself involved in an incestuous relationship without knowing it.

0797 OAV

CREAM LEMON SERIES PART VII: IKENAI MAKOCHAN — MAKO SEXY SYMPHONY (*Cream Lemon Series Part VII: Don't Do It Little Mako — Mako's Sexy Symphony*), Soeishinsha, erotic, 25 min., 9/10, Fairy Dust.

Mako is very shy and she doesn't really feel at ease with boys even though she has a boyfriend whom she doesn't love. Coming home from school she meets a mysterious girl who persistently tries to provoke her. The stranger is the one to unlock Mako's sense of modesty when, turning up unexpectedly at her house, she teaches Mako many secrets of the erotic arts, revealing herself to be a supernatural spirit.

0798 OAV

MAHO NO PRINCESS MINKI MOMO — LA RONDE IN MY DREAM (*Minky Momo, the Princess of Magic: The Circle of My Dream*), Ashi, 80 min., 7/25, Bandai. *Magical Princess Gigi.*

The earthly parents of little Momo —in reality the princess of Fantasy Kingdom — win a trip on an island but the plane that is carrying them mysteriously disappears. Learning the news from television, Momo gets to the place where they vanished aboard her helicopter, where she discovers that her parents were kidnapped by a group of children who live on the top of a mountain in a tropical island. The children want to adopt the couple, to make them the "parents" of the community. Using her magical powers, which she's had from birth, the little girl clears up the situation, even meeting Peter Pan himself.

Maho no Princess Minki Momo © Ashi / Network.

0799 OAV

AREA 88 ACT II — OKAMITACHI NO JOKEN (*Area 88, Act II: The Wolves' Request*), Studio Pierrot, war, 57 min., 8/5, King Record. *Area 88 Act II: The Requirements Of Wolves.*

While in Japan, Ryoko begins to find information about Shin Kazama, her disappeared fiancé. At the same time, at Area 88, winds of war are blowing. All are alarmed by the destruction of Area 81 by a squadron of flying mercenaries, the flight of the wolves.

0800 OAV

JUSTY (*id.*), Studio Pierrot, science fiction, 44 min., 8/5, King Record.

The young Justy becomes part of the galactic patrol with his sister Jerna. Justy, accompanied by Lieutenant Trevor, leaves on a mission aimed to combat crime in the universe. His mission brings him to face unexplainable paranormal events. The movie is taken from Tsuguo Okazaki's famous manga.

0801 OAV

DALLOS SPECIAL (*id.*), Studio Pierrot, science fiction, 90 min., 8/5, Bandai.

The videotape presents a compact edition of Shun Nonomura's story and his fight against the Government Supervision Unit. This is a faithful and dutiful homage to the series that inaugurated the OAV market.

0802 OAV

SOKO KISHI VOTOMS — THE LAST RED SHOULDER (*Armored Troopers Votoms: The Last Red Shoulder*), Nippon Sunrise, robot, 60 min., 8/21, Toshiba Soft.

Kiriko Kuyubi, who escaped from Udo, starts looking for Fiana, his best friend. Along the journey, he meets three former companions who are going to Red Shoulder to kill Perzen the dictator. Kiriko, thinking this may be linked to the girl's disappearance, decides to follow them. Fiana is actually a prisoner of the evil Perzen, who wounds Kiriko and then dies along with Kiriko's three unfortunate companions. The young man saves himself, helped by the young woman, who continues her trip leaving her companion alone once again.

0803 OAV

CREAM LEMON SERIES PART VIII — SUPER VIRGIN (*id.*), Soeishinsha, erotic, 25 min., 9/10, Fairy Dust.

Young Mako sees a few young girls, who reject the opposite sex, gifted with incredible ESP powers get upset with the unfortunate Tamachi. Mako falls in love with the young man but when the two get together, Mako is immediately taken by the young women, and tied naked to a tree. Tamachiku and his friends, also gifted with psychic powers, save her.

0804 OAV

THE CHOCOLATE PANIC PICTURE SHOW (*id.*), Kaname, humor, 33 min., 9/21, SVI (will become CBS Sony Group).

Mambo, Chimbo and Chombo give birth to an overwhelming madcap musical, irreverently and hysterically funny.

The Chocolate Panic Picture Show © Kaname.

0805 OAV

MUJIGEN HUNTER FANDORA — REM FIGHT HEN (*Fandora, the Hunter From the Dream Dimension: the Chapter of the REM Fight*), fantasy/science fiction, Kaname, 33 min., 9/21, Nippon/Columbia.

An ancient legend says that when the red and blue rock will fit together, peace will finally be a reality. Fandora, a young warrior, possesses the first gem and to obtain the second she leaves for the kingdom of Rem. The evil Kadas lives in Rem, and, under the guidance of the cunning Geruzu Berg tries to forcefully gain control over the population. Geruzu, in possession of the blue gem, finds himself confronting the fury of Fandora. The story which evolves over three chapters, is by Go Nagai.

Mujigen Hunter Fandora © Dynamic Kikaku / Kaname / Nihon AVC / Nippon Colombia.

0806 OAV

GINGA HYORYU VIFAM: KATE NO KIOKU — NAMIDA DAKKAI SAKUSEN! (*Vifam, the Castaways From the Galaxy: "Kate's Recollection," the Strategy of the Touching Blackmail*), Nippon Sunrise, science fiction, 60 min., 9/25, Warner/Pioneer.

To celebrate the peace between the Earth and the planet Kukutonian, Rodi and his thirteen companions are invited to Myura's ceremony. There, she gives them the good news on Kate. The young girl who was thought dead is in fact alive and well on Kukutonian, even though she is suffering from a bad form of temporary amnesia.

0807 OAV

CREAM LEMON SERIES PART IX — HAPPENING SUMMER (*id.*), Soeishinsha, erotic, 25 min., 10/7, Fairy Dust.

The beautiful Yuki lives her teenage years observing her sister Keiko, who is going through an intense love story with her boyfriend Akira. The young man, however, turns out to be a perverted pedophile who abuses Yuki when her sister's away. When Keiko comes home, hearing the shouts, she goes up to her sister's room and finds Yuki in bed with Akira. The young man is immediately thrown out and Yuki, who had liked it, satisfies her needs with Miyuki, a boy her own age.

0808 OAV

TATAKAE! ICZER ONE (*Fight! Iczer One*), AIC, horror/science fiction, 25 min., 10/19, Kubo Shoten. *Iczer-One Act I.*

The alien people of Cthulhu (an outer space race completely made up of females) intend to use the Earth as their new home, and, having come close to it in a gigantic pyramid-shaped spaceship, they secretly launch an attack. Sending the Bedem, monstrous creatures capable of taking possession of the humans' bodies, to Earth, the Cthulhu try to attain their goal without fighting. Fortunately the female android Iczer I is aware of their plans and knows that the only person on Earth capable of helping her defeat the aliens is Nagisa Kano, a Japanese high school student unaware of her abilities to activate the Iczer robot piloted by Iczer I. The Cthulhu do everything to prevent the encounter between the two, but Iczer I convinces Nagisa to help her save the Earth and avenge her parents who were killed by the Bedems. The two get the upper hand in the first encounter but the real war is yet to begin. A science fiction/horror show enriched by a few erotic scenes. The character designs are by Toshihiro Hirano.

0809 OAV

CHUHAI LEMON — LOVE 30 S (*Lemon Cocktail — Love 30 S*), Tsuchido, police story, 45 min., 10/19, Wonder Kids.

The muscular Goro Tatsumi is a skillful and clever police detective, even though he looks unintelligent and unmannered. Seventeen year old Maki is a modern and uninhibited high school student who will do anything to be with her beloved detective, not concerned by the 20 years difference in age between the two. They're a curious couple whose differences are kept consistently ironic, even in moments of great tension, especially when Tatsumi is forced to use his monstrous strength to save himself and the young woman from the most complicated of plots. Some spicy scenes give this anime all the ingredients to make it as successful as Tsutomi Shinohara and Sho Shimura's manga.

0810 OAV

CREAM LEMON SERIES PART X — STAR TRAP (*id.*), Soeishinsha, erotic, 25 min., 11/10, Fairy Dust.

The story, a parody of *Star Trek*, features the adventures of Lan and Kanaka, the two lesbian commanders of a renewed Enterprise, dealing with a mysterious gigantic plant they find on their travels. When escape seems impossible, the two are always willing to open fire. The show doesn't lack for sex scenes, as we always see the two women in bed in between combat sequences.

Iczer-One ©1985/86, 1992 Kubo Shoten / A.I.C. All Rights Reserved. English version ©1992 U.S. Renditions. All Rights Reserved.

0811 OAV

TWINKLE NORA ROCK ME! (*id.*), Film Link, adventure, 57 min, 11/21, Pony.

Nora Skora lands on Space Ball to follow a criminal and arrest him, with the help of her powers. The local police chief happens to witness this and calls the girl to entrust her with a special mission. A dangerous wanted man named Fuchero lives in the city of Dazzul, gifted with the same psychic powers as Nora. She, therefore, is the only one who can stop him. Helped by Max, a young man she meets in a bar, the young woman completes her mission.

0812 OAV

WHAT'S MICHAEL? (*id.*), Kitten Film, humor, 60 min., 11/25 Kitty Enterprise.

Michael the cat, the main character of Makoto Kobayashi's cartoon doesn't try to be ironic or funny (as in the case of Isodoro or Garfield), and yet, his adventures are irresistible. This animated version adds a certain cachet to the narrative, and this OAV, following in the footsteps of the series, succeeds in making its mark.

0813 OAV

DREAM HUNTER REM. SANMU YOMIGAERU SHINIGAMI HAKASE (*id.*), Project Team for Fikyn Kikan, adventures, 45 min., 12/15, King Record.

Rem is a young woman who can't dream, but who has the extraordinary ability to enter into other people's dreams. She decides to use her powers to become a private investigator. Soon, however, Sakaki, a clever police lieutenant,arrives in her life.

0814 OAV

TENSHI NO TAMAGO (*The Angel's Egg*), Studio Dream, fantastic, 80 min., 12/15, Tokuma Shoten.

Through the centuries, birds are on the path to extinction; in the world of the future they are only a memory. A young soldier sees a young girl run along the road; he comes down from his tank to give her a mysterious egg. The two travel together to the place where the egg was found and, thinking that it will hatch, she falls asleep next to it. The young man breaks the egg while the young girl is sleeping and when she awakes she commits suicide out of pain. A dream-like story that borders on the absurd.

0815 OAV

RUMIC WORLD — HONO TRIPPER (*Rumic's World: Fire Tripper*), Studio Pierrot, fantastic, 48 min., 12/16, Shogakukan. *Rumik World: Fire Tripper.*

Suzuko, who was adopted as an infant, is a victim of an explosion along with little Shuhei, her neighbor. Traveling through time back to the 16th century, the young woman finds herself alone in the middle of a guerrilla attack where she meets Shukumaru and his little sister Suzu. In a tragic accident, Suzu is buried when a burning house collapses on top of her. Before she is killed, the young girl vanishes into thin air. Suzuko, protecting the young warrior from a burning beam, comes back to our time with him a few hours before the explosion that occurred at the beginning of the story. Taking care of Shukumaru, Suzuko discovers that he is none other than Shuhei, who was catapulted back in time several years before her and is now grown up. She also finally remembers that she is Suzu, the little girl who disappeared in the fire, born in the Middle Ages in Japan. Choosing to live with the young man she has now fallen in love with, Suzuko decides to consciously use her gift — to travel through time

Fire Tripper © Takahashi Rumiko / Shogakukan.
English version & package artwork ©1992 Central
Park Media Corporation. All Rights Reserved.

through fire — for the first time. She takes the young man near a tank she knows is going to explode. Taken from Rumiko Takahashi's series, *Rumik World*.

0816 OAV

LOVE POSITION — HALEY NO DENSETSU (*Love Position: Haley's Legend*), Tezuka, science fiction, 93 min., 12/16, Packing Video.

An entity coming from Haley's comet takes possession of the body of Zamba, an American criminal and, controlling his mind, pushes him to look for a certain girl and kill her. In the meantime, young Subaru brings the beautiful Lamina to Japan, a woman whom his father his father had fallen in love with during the Vietnam war, so that the two may finally be together. Zamba also comes to Japan, killing everyone who gets in the way of his mission. The woman he intends to to kill is, in fact, Lamina.

0817 OAV

BAVISTOCKI — HATESHINAKI TARGET (*Bavi Stock: Infinite Target*), Kaname, science fiction, 45 min., 12/20, Nikkatsu Video Film.

Muma, a dumb girl, is kept hostage on the third planet of the Bentika kingdom. The space police, whose base is on planet GPP, decides to send agent Kate to save her. Once her dangerous mission is completed, the agent returns to free Bavi.

0818 OAV

VAMPIRE HUNTER "D" (*id.*), Ashi, horror, 80 min., 12/21, Epic, Sony. *Vampire Hunter D.*

On the Earth of the future, the human race is forced to live under the control of vampires and mutants. Doris, however, doesn't want to give in to them and decides to ask for the help of the mysterious "D" to fight them, promising him her own body. The vampire count, Lee, wants to marry the young woman and he sends the mutant Reigin and his daughter Ramika to kidnap her. Their mission fails, when "D" turns out to be a "danpiru" with human and vampire blood and makes them flee. The count's army finally captures Doris, but the young woman is soon freed by "D." Doris' father, a vampire hunter, was killed by the count and the young woman is afraid that the same thing will happen to her companion. This, of course, does not happen and "D," the son of Dracula, defeats his enemy, who dies along with all the inhabitants of the castle.

0819 OAV

DIRTY PAIR — NOLANDIA NO NAZO (*Dirty Pair: Nolandia's Mystery*), Nippon Sunrise, science fiction, 55 min., 12/21. Bandai. *Dirty Pair: Affair On Nolandia.*

Yuri and Kei, special agents of the WWWA, are called up during their vacation for a mission in a strange land called Nolandia. The country, suspended in midair, is populated by fantastic creatures and emanates an unexplainable source of ESP powers. The two must deal with the disconcerting visions sent to them by the little Misuni, a creature born from genetic experiments. Beside themselves, often unable to distinguish dream from reality, the two try to reestablish order. The evil is uprooted, and the organizers as well as the scientists in charge of the diabolical experiments suffer the fury of the two most uncontrollable private detectives in the universe. This particular character design makes Yuri and Kei more true to life than usual, also giving them a more mature style.

Vampire Hunter D ©1985 Epic / Sony, Inc. / MOVIC, Inc. / CBS/Sony Group, Inc. Package design ©1999 Urban Vision Entertainment.

Dirty Pair: Affair On Nolandia ©1985 Haruka Takachiho / Studio Nue / Sunrise / NTV. Packaging ©1992 Streamline Pictures.

Megazone 23 Part II ©1987 Idol / Artmic.

Tenko no Shiro Laputa © Nibariki / Tokuma Shoten.

CHAPTER TWENTY FIVE: 1986

Despite the continued popularity of television series, by 1986 OAVs were the format of choice for new releases, surpassing the number of new shows by a full 100%. Television producers began to feel the crunch brought on by the swift march of direct-to-video releases and the unique content they could provide. This pressure was brought to bear on both private and public television stations, who reacted in different ways to try to stem the tide. Some gave carte blanche to authors and directors to produce new and innovative series with far more visual impact, increasing the levels of violence, sex and fast-paced, frenzied stories. Their ultimate goal was to hook the viewer after one episode, to keep audiences watching throughout the run of the show. Trying to move away from direct competition, other stations began to make deals with OAV producers for the rights to transmit the shows on their network after the commercial release of the tape. Yet another group of networks tried to fight fire with fire and produce their own OAVs, broadcasting them (after some time) on their channels.

Older productions and favorite characters were dug out and remade for a more modern public, including Princess Arimatsu in the comedy *Robotan*, and the omnipresent *Gundam* in the new *Double Z*. The world outside of Japan offered fresh ideas, some from already existing manga, novels, or even video games, as is the case with *Super Mario Bros*. A recent survey revealed that the game's main character, Mario, was the most known amongst children under 14 years old across the world. *The Wizard of Oz* and *Pollyanna's Secret* debuted on series television, while Holmes, the famous detective, attracted mystery-lovers to the movie theatres. The plotlines became richer, drawing on mythologies from around the world, with the most attention paid to the styles of Western and Pan-Asian screenplays. This movement produced the movie *Arion*, a colossal project by Yoshikazu Yasuhiko, based mostly upon Greek mythology, although many of the references were partially changed to fit the story. Toei Doga played its winning card, launching Masami Kurumada's television series *Saint Seiya*, based along the same lines as *Arion*, but with more emphasis on the combat scenes and with supplementary characters primarily designed to become toys, which were very successfully realized by Bandai.

Inspired by Anglo-Saxon literature, and a success in its own right, was the wonderful *Tenku no shiro Laputa*, from the master of animation, Hayao Miyazaki. Combining a bit of Jules Verne with a little bit of Jonathan Swift, *Laputa* offered up a new vision of a technologically advanced Northern Europe which had kept the culture and styles of the last century. Shakespeare himself is credited for creating the magical setting mined as the source for the screenplay and characters of the romantic OAV *Windaria*.

As for co-productions with other countries, America took the lion's share, most notably in the form of Marvel Comic's contributions to the series (of questionable quality) *G.I. Joe*, which boasted a troop of personality-less, ultra-patriotic commandos. In the meantime, the rising popularity of the *Transformers* continued to bring in fans for Marvel and Toei Doga who, adapting their releases to changing merchandising laws, continued to produce dozens of new collectable, transforming robots.

Fortunately intelligent discourse was not left by the wayside as *Maison Ikkoku*, Rumiko Takahashi's already famous comic, was brought to the screen. The story, while structured like a soap-opera, told stories of regular people with healthy doses of irony and humor. This can be considered the year's second great release, just behind *Dragonball*, by the always-eclectic Akira Toriyama, who, after a long absence from television screens, brought this poetically-inspired series (based on the *Legend of the Stone Monkey*) to the attention of audiences everywhere.

0820 FILM

URUSEI YATSURA LAMU FOREVER (*Those Obnoxious Aliens! Lamu Forever*), Kitty Film, humor, 94 min., 2/22. *Urusei Yatsura: Lum The Forever.*

To leave something of himself for posterity, Mendo decides to make a movie with the help of Mezane and his enemies and friends from school. They decide to make a movie about an ancient legend passed down through the generations of Mendo's family. Lamu, the lead actress, must play a monstrous princess. Everything seems to go well until a curse, linked to a cherry tree cut down during the filming, strikes Lamu, and their plans take a turn for the worse.

Urusei Yatsura © Takahashi Rumiko / Shogakukan / Kitty / Fuji TV.

0821 FILM

HOKUTO NO KEN (*The Fist of the North Star*), Toei Doga, martial arts/post-holocaust, 90 min., 3/8. *Fist Of The North Star* [*Ken Le Survivant*].

This high-quality film is a remake of the first series, and takes particular care to keep the storyline intact. The art and animation by Toei Doga add a new level of interest to the film, bringing Japanese fans of the young master of the seven stars to the movie theaters in droves.

0822 FILM

DORAEMON: NOBITA TO TETSUJIN HEIDAN (*Doraemon: Nobita and the Platoon of the Ironmen*), Shin'ei Doga, humor, 97 min., 3/15.

In this adventure, Doraemon has to battle a deadly robot that wants to take over the planet. The cat prepares for the final deadly encounter, flying a second giant robot with his friend and owner Nobita.

0823 FILM

PROGOLFER SARU SUPERGOLF WORLD E NO CHOSEN (*Progolfer Saru: Challenge at the Super Golf World*), Shien'ei Doga, sport, 45 min., 3/15.

The movies about Saru the golf player continue. This time, Mister X invites the main character to the professional World Tournament. Saru must use all of the resources and abilities at his disposal during his struggles with the greatest champions of this sport.

Fist Of The North Star ©1986 Toei Animation Co., Ltd. Package design ©1991 Streamline Pictures.

0824 FILM

OBAKE NO QTARO TOBIDASE! BAKEBAKE DAI SAKUSEN (*Jump, Ghost Qtaro! Bake Bake's Great Strategy*), Shin'ei Doga, humor, 13 min., 3/15.

Fujiko Fujio experiments with a new type of animation in this feature film, testing a new technique for portraying three dimensions. Qtaro and his group of crazy and kind-hearted friends get into another set of impossibly strange situations, dragging in innocent by-standers by the dozen.

0825 FILM

CAPTAIN TSUBASA: ASU NI MUKATTE HASHIRE! (*Captain Tsubasa: Run Towards Tomorrow*), Tsuchida, sport, 41 min., 3/15.

0826 FILM

KINNIKUMAN: NEW YORK KIKI IPPATSU! (*Kinnikuman: Imminent Crisis in New York*), Toei Doga, sport/humor, 45 min., 3/15.

Wrestling is a very popular sport in Japan, and a number of films and series feature the stories of real or imaginary wrestlers. Here, the main character is Kinnikuman, battling the evil General in a series of fights in New York City.

0827 FILM

GEGEGE NO KITARO YOKAI DAISENSO (*Kitaro Gegege: the Great Spectral War*), Toei Doga, horror, 39 min., 3/15.

A group of cruel Western ghosts want to take over Japan. Kitaro gathers his friends together to face the attack of the spectral creatures.

0828 FILM

ARION (*id.*), Nippon Sunrise, mythological, 120 min., 3/16. [*Arion*].

Arion, son of Poseidon and Demeter, is forced to fight the gods to bring peace back to Olympia and to avenge the death of his mother, innocent victim of the war between Zeus and the God of the sea. The movie is designed by Yoshikazu Yasuhiko, who shows immense talent with the character designs and in the screenplay, based on his original manga. The wonderful animation adds to the easy feel of the feature film that became one of the year's major successes.

0829 FILM

TOUCH: SEBANGO NO NAI ACE (*Touch: Ace Without a Number*), Group Tack for Toho, sport/soap opera, 93 min., 4/12.

The movie covers the main events of the television series and ends with the tragic death of Kazuya.

0830 FILM

HADASHI NO GEN II (*Barefoot Gen II*), A.P.P.P., drama, 85 min., 5/15.

Three years after Hiroshima, Gen is in the fourth grade. Together with his adoptive brother Ryuta, he works hard to take care of his sick mother and to provide for his family, along with Masa, Katsuko and Katchin, a group of orphans who live nearby. A terrible typhoon destroys the little ones' house and they find themselves homeless. Gen puts himself at their disposal to rebuild it. A new staff has been hired on to create this second chapter of Gen's life, including Mori Masaki as director, Keiji Nakazawa as screenplay writer, Kazuo Tomizawa for the animation and Kazuo Ojika for artistic direction. The author of the original manga, like his character, survived the blast of August 6, 1945 and, also like

Touch: Sebango no Nai Ace © Adachi / Shogakukan / Toho / Asatsu.

him, lost part of his family when he was still a child in a brawl between drunken members of rival gangs. The manga came out in "Shonen Jump" and earned the public and the critics' favor very quickly, so much so that it has since been translated into eight different languages.

0831 FILM
TABIDACHI AMISHUSHO (*The Final Chapter of Ami the Traveler*), Sueishinsha, adventure, 6/21.

0832 FILM
PROJECT A-KO (*id.*), Sueishinsha, humor/science fiction, 80 min., 6/21. *Project A-ko.*

An alien spaceship crashes in the center of Graviton City, creating a crater around which, years later, the city is rebuilt. It is there that the redhaired A-Ko lives in eternal conflict with the very rich and powerful B-Ko because of her friendship with the ever-bubbly C-Ko. C-Ko eventually turns out to be the lost princess of the aliens of the spaceship sixteen years before. The tranquillity of the school in which the three girls study, and soon the entire city, is disturbed by little street wars and by alien invasions that no one can seem to stop. Yuji Moriyama, who takes care of the character designs, seems to have learned a lot from the *Urusei Yatsura* movies, and gives his best for this production, creating spectacular and entertaining action scenes.

0833 FILM
KOULDRON (*id.*), Toho, fantasy, 7/12.

0834 FILM
HIGH SCHOOL KIMENGUNI (*id.*), Nas, insane, 51 min., 7/12.

0835 FILM
GEGEGE NO KITARO SAIKYO YOKAI GUNDAN! NIHONJORIKU (*Kitaro Gegege: The Devastating Monsters' Army Arrives In Japan*), Toei Doga, horror, 49 min., 7/12.

Kitaro, Nezumi and their friends must solve a dense and dangerous mystery. Some of their ghost friends seem to have vanished without a trace. The diabolic team finds itself fighting against ghostly demons from distant China.

0836 FILM
CAPTAIN TSUBASA: SEKAIDAI KESSEN!! JUNIOR WORLD CUP (*Captain Tsubasa: the Great World Challenge!! Juniors World Cup*), Tsuchida, sport, 41 min., 7/12.

0837 FILM
MAPLE TOWN MONOGATARI (*The Adventures of Maple Town*), Toei Doga, animals, 24 min., 7/12.

0838 FILM
RUNNING BOY STAR SOLDIER NO HIMITSU (*The Secret of the Stellar Soldier Running Boy*), Film Link, science fiction, 49 min., 7/20.

At this point it's become common to see anime or manga characters transformed into toys, gadgets, stickers and various other merchandise aimed at children, especially video games. This movie for the very young is peculiar, not so much for the plot or for the style of animation, but because, for the first time, a character born for the video game market

has been reversed, and turned into animation for the big screen. The skillful marketing operation has as its center the video game produced by Hudson for the Famicon console in 1988, featuring the adventures of the young Genta Shinoyama, a video game fan who finds himself flying a real spaceship to defeat the galactic pirates.

0839 FILM
SUPER MARIO BROS.: PEACH HIME KYUSHUTSU DAISAKUSEN (*Super Mario Bros.: the Great Strategy for the Liberation of Princess Peach*), Nintendo, humor, 60 min., 7/20.

Around the same time as the above mentioned Running Boy, Nintendo also proposes a anime based on one of their own video games. Mario had his first major appearance in *Donkey Kong*, the video game in which a player maneuvering the Italian hero must save a beautiful girl who has been kidnapped by a giant gorilla. Mario has starred in a sucession of other games, one of the most famous of which is *Mario Bros.*, where the carpenter (or plumber, or mechanic or perhaps all of the above) is partnered with his brother Luigi to disinfect his factory from an invasion. The idea for the film was taken from that game.

0840 FILM
AI CITY (*id.*), Toho for Movick/Ashi, science fiction, 90 min., 7/26. *Ai City (Love City)*.

Taken from Shuho Itabashi's famous science fiction manga, the feature film narrates the story of young Ai, a girl gifted with E.S.P., who runs away from F.R.A.U.D., the organization that was holding her prisoner. Once free, she tries anything she can to stop the perfidious Kei, a criminal who experiments on psychics himself.

0841 FILM
MEITANTEI HOLMES (*Holmes the Detective*), Tokyo Movie Shinsha, animals/detective, 50 min., 8/9.

0842 FILM
TENKU NO SHIRO LAPUTA (*Laputa, the Castle in the Sky*), TokumaShoten, fantasy, 195 min., 8/9.

Young Sheeta is held prisoner by the secret police aboard a hot air balloon. Taking advantage of the chaos provoked by a pirate attack, the young woman tries to escape but she falls from the balloon. Suddenly, the pendant she wears lights up, allowing her to glide softly into the arms of the astounded Pazu, a young miner who offers her a place to stay. The army and the pirates don't give up, however, as they are interested in her pendant, a precious jewel that indicates the road to Laputa, a floating island in the sky, the last fragment of an ancient civilization possessing the secret of levitation, great treasures and terrible weapons. The long series of pursuits, escapes and forced alliances culminate in the final encounter on Laputa. The movie presents another step in the evolution of Hayao Miyazaki's style, one transitions perfectly smoothly between situations of humor and tension, perfectly reflecting the moods of the characters. Another fascinating point drawn out by Miyazaki is the use of a technology similar to that described by Jules Verne in his novels, a wonderful nineteenth century fresco capable of pulling the spectators into a magical world, transcending time itself.

0843 FILM
TOBIRA O AKETE (*Opening the Door*), Kitty Film, fantasy, 83 min., 11/1.

Ai City ©1986 Toho Co., Ltd / KK Movic / Ashi Productions. English version ©1995 Toho Co., Ltd / KK Movic / Ashi Productions. Released by The Right Stuf International Inc.

Motoko Arai, a popular Japanese fantasy author, releases one of her great successes for the big screen. Miyako Negishi, appearing to be a perfectly normal young student, is in reality gifted with ESP powers. This unusual situation brings her to face some unexpected situations that end up involving her closest and most faithful friend.

0844 FILM

JUICHININ IRU! (*We Are Eleven!*), science fiction, 91 min., 11/1. *They Were 11.*

This science fiction story, set in a military academy in space, written by famous manga author Moto Hagio, is transposed into animation. Ten cadets from the academy are sent in mission into the cosmos for their final exam. However, they discover the presence of a stowaway.

0845 FILM

TOUCH II: SAYONARA NO OKURIMONO (*Touch II: A Goodbye Gift*), Group Tack for Toho, sport/soap opera, 80 min., 12/13.

The second chapter of the movie adventures of *Touch* opens one year after the death of young Kazuya, and closes on the students championship victory over the team of the Meisei.

0846 FILM

DRAGONBALL: JINRYU NO DENSETSU (*Dragonball: the Legend of the Divine Dragon*), Toei, martial arts/humor, 12/20.

0848 FILM

HI NO TORI HOO HEN (*Bird of Fire: the Chapter of Hoo*), Toho, classic, 50 min., 12/20.

0849 FILM

TOKI NO TABIBI TO TIME STRANGER (*The Time Travelers: Time Stranger*), Project Team, Argos/Madhouse for Haruki Kadokawa, historical/time travel, 90 min., 12/20.

Science fiction and fantasy are the basis for this movie taken from Mayumura Taku's original concept. Hayasaka Tetsuko, a seventeen year old university student, finds herself traveling through time with Jiro Agino after a mysterious accident. In spite of themselves, they find themselves thrown into feudal Japan.

0850 FILM

KINNIKUMAN SEIGI CHOJIN VS SENSHI CHOJIN (*Kinnikuman the Executioner Against the Superman Warrior*), Toei Doga, humor, 12/20.

0851 SERIES

ROBOTAN (*id.*), Tokyo Movie Shinsha, humor, 1/6 – 9/20/1986.

A remake of the highly successful 1966 animated cartoon, *Robotan* is better made this time around. The animation techniques used in the Eighties are mostly focused on creating visual impact, which is why a humor series like this reaps the end rewards. The scripts remain much the same as they were in the previous incarnation, with a few modifications and updated costumes.

They Were 11 ©1986 Kitty Enterprises, Inc / Victor Company Of Japan, Ltd. English version and package artwork ©1992 Central Park Media Corporation. All Rights Reserved.

0852 SERIES

AI SHOJO POLLYANNA MONOGATARI (*The Adventures of the Adorable Little Pollyanna*), Nippon Animation, classic/ soap opera, 51 episodes, 1/12 – 12/28/1986. [*Pollyanna*].

The little and lively Pollyanna, who managed to stay cheerful even after the death of her mother, is sent to live with her aunt, the stern Polly Harrington, after the death of her father. Pollyanna begins her new life with spirit and energy, making many new friends, including the irrepressible Jimmy. Her constant smiles eventually soften even the hard heart of her aunt, who grows to love her young niece.

0853 SERIES

UCHU SEN SAGITTARIUS (*Spaceship Sagittarius*), Nippon Animation, science fiction/animals, 77 episodes, 1/10/1086 – 10/9/1987.

Taken from the Italian comic *Mouse, Giraffe and Frog* by Andrea Romoli, the series earns the public's favor and is considered one of the ten best in 1987. The characters of the story are a group of friendly, human-like animals that leave for space to look for a famous teacher who disappeared mysteriously. As often happens, the character design is somewhat distorted, but all in all, the series is dynamic and the animation well done.

0854 SERIES

MAPLE TOWN MONOGATARI (*The Adventures of Maple Town*), Toei Doga, animals, 52 episodes, 1/19/1986 – 1/11/1987. [*Les Petits Malins*].

The concept for this childrens' series is simply that of the daily life of a family of rabbits in a village populated with beautiful animals. Taken from a story by Chifude Asakura, the series is directed by Junichi Sato, with music is by Akiro Kosaka.

0855 SERIES

DRAGONBALL (*id.*), Toei Doga, martial arts/humor, 153 episodes, 2/26/1986 – 4/12/1989. *Dragonball*.

Another version of the popular *Legend Of The Stone Monkey*, *Dragonball* details the ups and downs of life for Goku, the nephew of the famous monkey and a little boy gifted with incredible strength. Like his grandfather, he has a magical pole that has the power to change his size, with which Goku combats the countless opponents who hinder his search for the "dragon balls" that can make any wish come true. Young Goku however, only wants it to recover the fourth ball that was left to him by his grandfather. The author of the series is the unpredictable Akira Toriyama, author of the frantic manga, already made famous by *Dr. Slump and Arale-chan*. The character designs are by Minoru Maeda and Mitsuo Shinto, scenes are by Inoue Toshiki and Mitsuru Shimada. The production is by Keizo Shichijo.

0856 SERIES

KIDO SENSHI ZZ GUNDAM (*Mobile Suit ZZ Gundam*), Nippon Sunrise, science fiction, robot, 47 episodes, 3/7/1986 – 1/31/1987.

After the defeat of the Titans, the antigovernment movement AEUG sees its power slowly weakening. In the meantime, aboard the asteroid Axis, some survivors from Jion who still

Dragonball ©1986 Bird Studio / Shueisha • Toei Animation. English version ©1995 Toei Animation. Released by FUNimation Productions, Inc.

want to conquer the Earth under the guidance of the clever Haman Kan, send soldiers to every colonies, but they fail miserably in their first attack. Haman, then, to put pressure on the Earth Federation Government, lands on Earth to impose her will at the federal congress in Dakar. The Earthly rulers ask for an armistice, offering Side 3 instead, but Haman refuses and shows her strength by destroying the city of Dublin in Ireland. Axis' soldiers, having absorbed the expatriates from Jion and the Titan fugitives, build the Neo-Jion empire.

After having subdued the Earth, Haman secretly embarks on a civil spaceship to reach the AEUG's Near Ahgama flagship and to destroy it using her Mobile Suit. Having failed in her mission, however, the woman is forced to find refuge on Side 3. In the meantime, the vice-ruler of Neo-Jion, Gremi Toto, the first from the Zabi family to be born in a test-tube, rebels to rebuild the old empire. Haman, who sees in him her worst enemy, attacks with her army of Mobile Suits and surrounds Gremi, onboard the asteroid Axis. The result of the war is disastrous for both sides, and Haman dies after having defeated her rival. The AEUG federal fleet can thus subdue the survivors from Neo-Jion thanks to Judo Ashita, the true main character of the series, who finally brings peace back to the universe with his powerful ZZ Gundam.

0857 SERIES

MAHO NO IDOL PASTEL YUMI (*Pastel Yumi, the Star of Magic*), Studio Pierrot, magic, 26 episodes, 3/7 – 8/29/1986. [*Suzy Aux Fleurs Magiques*].

One day, Yumi Hanazono, a little girl who lives in the city of flowers with her family, prevents a flower from being cut down and for this, she receives the visit from two elves, Keshimaru and Kazimaru, who are touched by her love for nature. To reward her, the two decide to give her a pendant and a magic wand, which can make the drawings she traces in the air come to life. This is the third series made by Studio Pierrot to feature the adventures of girls gifted with magical powers.

0858 SERIES

MAISON IKKOKU (*id.*), Kitty Film, soap opera/humor, 96 episodes, 3/26/1986 – 3/2/1988. *Maison Ikkoku* [*Juliette Je T'Aime*].

Rumiko Takahashi, author of the very famous series *Urusei Yatsura*, shows us a slice of Japanese society of the 80s. Maison Ikkoku is a boarding house smoothly run by the young widow Kyoko Otonashi, who still nurtures a deep link with her dead husband Soishiro. One of her boarders, the young student Yusaku Godai, cannot declare his love because of that husband, and because of the age difference between them. The difficult situation is made worse by the other tenants, who can never resist the opportunity for a cruel joke, especially Yotsuya (a mysterious individual whom we know nothing about). The mysterious young man snoops through Godai's room, sometimes accompanied by the drunk Mrs. Ichinose and by Akemi, a young girl who goes around the house half naked disturbing both Godai's studying and his romantic thoughts. The two young people eventually crown their dream of love in a happy ending that will not only see them married, but also the parents of a beautiful little girl. The direction is by Takashi Anno, supervised by Ronosuke Onbu and Nobuko Nakajima. The scenes are by Kazunori Ito, Mitsuru Shimada, Yu Kaneko and Hiroshi Konichikawa.

Maison Ikkoku ©1997 Rumiko Takahashi / Shogakukan • Kitty Film • Fuji TV. Exclusively licensed throughout the United States and Canada by Viz Communications, Inc. All Rights Reserved.

0859 SERIES

SEKAI MAISAKU AMIME DOWA (*Animated Fairy Tales of the World's Masterpieces*), Mushi/Rankin Bass, 4/3 – 5/1/1986.

0860 SERIES

MANGA NARUHODO MONOGATARI (*Manga Stories to Understand Things*), Dax, fairy tale, 102 episodes, 4/5/1986 – 3/26/1988.

After the great successes obtained with the series *Manga Hajimete Monogatari* and *Manga Doshite Monogatari*, a new series debuts on TV screens, the third chapter of the set of animated fairy tales. This time the main character is Atsumi who, accompanied by a strange little dragon, travels in a marvelous dream world along with fantastic characters. The character is inspired by a very famous radio character adored by children, Atsumi Kurasawa.

0861 SERIES

GINGA NAGAREBUSHI GIN (*Gin, the Four Legged Comet*), Toei Doga, animals/adventure, 21 episodes, 4/7 – 9/29/1986.

Yoshihiro Takahashi's manga, published for many years in the pages of "Shonen Jump," is the starting point of this series with very similar designs. Gin, a beautiful dog with silver fur, sees his master die while they're hunting, victim of the claws of a powerful bear. Forced to take care of himself in a hostile world, the animal finds refuge on a nearby mountain, but there he has the bad surprise of running into Guma, the ferocious bear, uncontested leader of that territory. The fight sees Gin wounded and only the stray dog Kabuto's intervention saves him and allows him to kill the strong enemy. The two then become inseparable.

0862 SERIES

GOQCHOJI IKKIMAN (*Ikkiman, the Super Pitcher*), Toei Doga, science fiction/sport, 36 episodes, 4/13 – 11/23/1986. [*Ricky Star*].

Toei Doga comes out with a sport series rich in humor and with a science fiction twist, taken from Yasuo Tanami and Kazuo Takahashi's original manga published in the weekly "Shunan Shonen Magazine." In a near future, the whole world is fascinated by "battle ball," a mixture of baseball and American football. The Blue Planets and the Satan's Blackers, the two contending teams for the World title, add a deep and abiding hatred for each other to the formerly healthy competition. But when the Blue Planets' new player arrives from Hokkaido, the outcome of the clashes turns in their favour. The new acquisition is Ikkiman, a young man as shy and clumsy with the girls as he is good on the field.

Goqchoji Ikkiman
© Y. Tanami / K. Takahashi / Toei Animation.

0863 SERIES

WONDER BEAT SCRAMBLE (*id.*), Tsuburaya, science fiction, 26 episodes, 4/11 – 11/19/1986.

The hero of the story is the young Susumu who, after the mysterious disappearance of his father, decides to investigate the incident with his companions from the space team, the White Pegasus. He discovers that his father, whom he thought dead, is in reality in the hands of the Visuals, powerful extraterrestrials who hold the Earth under their power. Susamu then begins a tiring fight to find his father and kill the enemy.

0864 SERIES

ULTRAMEN KIDS NO KOTOZAWA MONOGATARI (*The Proverbs of the Ultramen Kids*), Mushi, humor, 4/16 – 11/19/1986.

Following the success obtained by the live-action series produced in the 70s, this show is a sarcastic realization of an Ultramen's family adventures. The characters are purposefully warped, in a style known as 'super-deformed,' drawn with small bodies and big heads. This series, with its reliance on visual humor, is one of the most entertaining of the year 1986.

0865 SERIES

SEISHUN ANIME ZENSHU (*Young People's Animated Masterpieces*), Nippon Animation, biography, 35 episodes, 4/25 – 12/26/1986. *Animated Classics Of Japanese Literature*.

Created by the staff at Nippon Animation, the animated series features the best of the Japanese classical literature. Every episode is taken from operas by some of the Land of the Rising Sun's greatest authors, such as Soseki Natsume, Ogai Mori, Osamu Dazai, Yukio Mishima, Eiko Tanaka and Yasunari Kawabata.

0866 SERIES

HIKARI NO DENSETSU (*Hikari's Legend*), Tatsunoko, soapopera/sport, 18 episodes, 5/3 – 9/20/1986.

Japanese animators tend to be very fond of the world of sports, and series set in that genre are countless. Hikari no Densetsu, a brilliant soap opera, is a grand example of a sports series, and it features the sentimental adventures of a young gymnast who must deal with a tormented love story and keep the perspective to enter into the group of the best Japanese athletes. The author of the original manga is the famous Izumi Asao.

0867 SERIES

MACHINE ROBOT CRONOS NO DAIGY AKUSHU (*Machine Robot: Cronos Great Counter Attack*), Ashi robot, 44 episodes, 7/3/1986 – 5/7/1987. *Machine Robo: Revenge Of Chronos*.

On the far away planet of Kronos a population of intelligent robots is fighting for survival. Because of attacks brought about by beings similar to them but with profoundly evil motives, the war seems to take a bad turn. Unexpected help comes to the defense of Kronos in the form of two human beings, Rom and Leina Stool, who escaped from their captors to fight for the reconquest of the planet Kronos.

0868 SERIES

CHIJO SAIKYO NO EXPERT TEAM G.I. JOE (*The World's Strongest Expert Team G.I. Joe*), Toei Doga for Takada/Astro/Marvel, action, 33 episodes, 7/24/1986 – 3/27/1987. *G.I. Joe*.

A special division of the American army fights against the evil secret organization Cobra. Made in Japan and based on a screenplay and characterization by Marvel Comics, this series is part of the countless co-productions between America and Japan, which are often characterized by a particular lack of interest and an over-emphasis on ethics and morals.

Animated Classics Of Japanese Literature ©1986 Nippon Animation. English version and package ©1995 Central Park Media Corporation. All Rights Reserved.

Machine Robo ©1986 Ashi Productions Co., Ltd. Licensed through IDO International Co., Ltd. English version and package ©1997 Software Sculptors Ltd. All Rights Reserved.

0869 SERIES

BUGTTE HONEY (*id.*), Tokyo Movie Shinsha, humor, 51 episodes, 9/25/1986 – 9/25/1987.

The popular Hudson video games company is once again the source of an animated series, this time centered on the adventures of Genjin Takahashi, a young video game champion who existed in reality, and who was very popular amongst young Japanese people. The young man usually finds himself involved in tiring challenges against the great Kyura, his most feared rival, but he can count on the support of many friends, including the friendly Honey.

0870 SERIES

HEART COCKTAIL (*id.*), Marchensha for Kodensha, soap opera, 77 episodes, 10/3/1986 – 3/26/1988.

Taken from Seizo Watase's manga, *Heart Cocktail* is an intelligent parody of the contradictions often inherent to couples. Takeshi and Keiko are continuously looking for the modus vivendi that will allow them to join their lives together. The greatest particularity of the series is however, the graphic design obtained by a mediation between the normal animated productions and that of the original manga designed in a "straight line" style with a face characterization intentionally naive.

0871 SERIES

ANMITSUHIME (*Princess Anmitsu*), Studio Pierrot, sociological/humor, 51 episodes, 10/5/1986 – 9/27/1987.

In 1955, Shosuke Kuragane wrote the story of a young princess not accustomed to royal life and, six years later, she tried to transform it into animation. However, the high cost and the lack of experience forced the production firm to abandon the project. Twenty-five years from its bankruptcy, Studio Pierrot decides to try again with this dynamic, funny and extremely popular television series. During the Japanese Middle Ages, a princess named Anmitsu lives in the Amakara castle, the royal daughter of a local lord and sole heir to her father's enormous fortune. The little girl loves to joke, play, and have fun all day long instead of studying and learning to behave as a girl of her social rank. For this reason, her parents assign her a tutor, young Tanemaru, with whom the little girl falls madly in love.

0872 SERIES

BOSCO ADVENTURE (*id.*), Nippon Animation, fantasy, 26 episodes, 10/6/1986 – 3/30/1987. [*Les Aventures De Bosco*].

0873 SERIES

OH! FAMILY (*id.*), Knack, comedy, 26 episodes, 10/6/1986 – 10/5/1987.

The daily life of the Andersons, representing the classical stereotype of the American family, constitutes the plot of this brilliant situation comedy produced by Takashi Hisaoka and created by Nishino Seichi. The main characters are Wilfrid, Sharon and their three children, Tracy, Fea and Key. The latter, a boy with clear homosexual tendencies, is often at the center of little misunderstandings that provoke the embarrassment of the entire family. In Italy, the episode "Los Angeles: a Meeting With Destiny" has been omitted because of a concrete reference to the character's sexual preference who, in love with his sister

Bosco Adventure © Nippon Animation / Yomiuri TV.

Fea's boyfriend, doesn't hesitate to kiss him. The screenplay is a collaboration between Shunichi Yukimuro, Yoshi Yoshida and Tsuneyuki Ito. The character designs are entrusted to Fumio Sasaki.

0874 SERIES

OZ NO MAHOTSUKAI (*The Wizard of Oz*), Panmedia, fairy tale, 52 episodes, 10/6/1986 – 10/5/1987.

L.F. Baum's *Wizard of Oz* contains certain themes very dear to Japanese authors and public. Based on a screenplay by Akira Negoro and Akira Miyazaki, with a style that makes the animation almost palpable, the animated cartoon is one of the remakes that is closest to the original story, despite the many Western interpretations which have distorted it and even changed the ending. The direction is by Masaru Endo and Hiroshi Seito, the character designs are by Shinobuya Takahashi on designs by Suichi Seki. The music is by Takeo Watanake.

0875 SERIES

SAINT SEIYA (*Id.*), Toei Doga, martial arts/science fiction/mythology, 114 episodes, 10/11/1986 – 4/1/1989. [*Les Cheveliers Du Zodiaque*].

There are times in history where the forces of evil begin to move to take over. It is in these moments that the "Saints" manifest themselves, warriors gifted with transcendent energy and outer space weapons inspired by the constellations and blessed by the Goddess Athena, and ready to do anything to defend peace and justice. Saori, the modern incarnation of Athena, surrounds herself with the "Bronze Saints" represented by Pegasus Seiya, Dragon Shiryu, Cygnus Hyoga, Phoenix Ikki and Andromeda Shun, who defend her from the hired killers of Ares from the Great Temple in Greece, who passes himself off as the Goddess's high priest. Subsequently, the Bronze Saints find themselves facing the Gold Saints, Oriental zodiac signs, Odin's God Warriors and Poseidon's Marine Generals. Taken from Masami Kurumada's manga, the animated version has been directed by Kozo Morishita, Masayuki Arehi and Tomoharu Katsumata. The character designs have been entrusted to Shingo Araki and Michi Himeno. The scenario and plot are by Takaota Koyama.

Doteraman © Tatsunoko Pro.

0876 SERIES

DOTERAMAN (*id.*), Tatsunoko, humor/science fiction, 10/14/1986 – 2/24/1987.

Tatsunoko is once again riding high with this new completely insane series created by the talented Ippei Kuri, who was also character designer in *Gordian*. One night, young Shigeru witnesses an amazing event, as the wise Inchiki appears to him from another dimension. A good demon, Inchiki gives the young man the Iperdotera, an extraordinary power that allows him to transform into the warrior Doteraman. Accompanied by the sweet Dotera Pink, the young man combats the monsters that live in Inchiki's dimension.

0877 SERIES

GANBARE! KICKERS (*Come On, Soccer Player*), Studio Pierrot, sport, 23 episodes, 10/15/1986 – 3/25/1987. [*But Pour Rudy*].

With Akira Sajino's direction, we witness the adventures of a promising soccer player whose ambition is to become champion. Taken from Noriaki Nagai's manga and produced

Ganbare! Kickers © N. Nagai / NTV / Studio Pierrot.

by Yuji Nunokawa, the series is designed by Takeshi Ozaka and the screenplay by Yu Kanebo and Isao Shizutani.

0878 SERIES

DORIMOGU DAA! (*I Am Dorimogu*), Japconmart, animals, 49 episodes, 10/15/1986 – 10/4/1987.

Wars can also be entertaining, if fought with eagerness by an army of friendly moles! In this original debut, the Japaconmart launches an entertaining series for children based around the surprising and fierce Dorimogu.

0879 SERIES

TATAKAE! CHOROBOT SEIMEITAI TRANSFORMER 2010 (*Combat! Super Live Robots Transformers 2010*), Toei Doga/Marvel, robot, 35 episodes, 11/14/1986 – 6/26/1987. *Transformers*.

The second season of the series set in the year 2010, *Transformers* features robots from the planet Cybertron, led by Rodimus Convoy, still at war with Galvatron and the army of Deltrons. This time as well, the screenplay is by Marvel Comics and the animation is entrusted to Toei Doga.

0880 SPECIAL

SEITO SHOKUN (*High School Friends*), Ashi, soap opera, 70 min., 2/23.

The friendship that started at school between Nakki, Konishi, Satsukino, Tamura, Okita and Iwasaki grows stronger as years go by and, having become adults, the friends help each other through the day to day problems of life. Seito Shokun saw the day as a manga in the magazine "Shojo Friend," and Yoko Shoji, the author, has created a full 23 issues for a mostly female audience. Given its great success, in 1984 a made for television movie is released based on the original comic strip.

0881 SPECIAL

SANGOSHO DENSETSU AOI UMI NO ELFY (*The Legend of the Corals: the Elves from the Blue Sea*), Nippon Animation, fairy tale, 84 min., 5/19/1986. [*Elfie*].

The scene is set in the twenty-first century: from beneath the waters of our planet mysterious lands resurface with a thundering roar, inhabited by strange beings that break the natural balance and put the human race in danger. The earthly and underwater creatures unite to face their common enemy.

0882 SPECIAL

SANGOKUSHI II AMAKEKERU EIYUTASHI (*The Three Kingdoms II: the Heroes That Run in the Sky*), Shin'ei Doga, historical/classic, 95 min., 8/22/1986.

Given the enormous enthusiasm shown when the first chapter came out, the adventures of young Liu Pi continue in this second special, produced, like the first, by Shinei.

0883 SPECIAL

GINGA TANSA 2100 BORDER PLANET (*Galactic Investigations 2100 Frontier Planet*), Tezuka, science fiction, 120 min., 8/24.

Transformers The Movie ©1987 Sunbow Production Inc / Hasbro Inc. All Rights Reserved. Packaging ©1999 Rhino Entertainment Co. This movie is made of a compilation of episodes.

Under the direction of Osamu Tezuka, the special presents the sad story of Subaru, who sees his son Prokyon die because of a mysterious space virus. His daughter, also victim of the same virus, is about to die and Subaru decides to embark on a long journey to look for an antidote.

0884 SPECIAL

BUNNA YO KI KARA ORITEIKOI (*Bunna, Come Down From the Tree*), Dax, humor, 50 min., 12/20.

0885 SPECIAL

MISTER PENPEN (*id.*), Shin'ei Doga, humor, 12/29.

0886 OAV

COOL COOL BYE (*id.*), adventure, Cream Land, 45 min., 1/21. Pony.

Reck and Frene, belonging to a famous warrior family, are forced to go to the base of the Penguins, an organization that kidnaps women from their villages. Entering the Penguin Base, and battling the mysterious young woman named Kuri, Reck and his companions save all the hostages and even convert Tanguin, one of the leaders of the organization.

0887 OAV

CREAM LEMON SERIES PART XI: KURONEKORAN (*The Black Cat's Room*), Soeishinsha, erotic, 25 min., 1/25, Fairy Dust.

0888 OAV

CREAM LEMON SERIES PART XII IKENAI MAKO CHAN, MAKO SEXY SYMPHONY II (*Cream Lemon Series Part XII: Don't Do it Little Mako, the Sexy Symphony of Mako II*), Soeishinsha, erotic, 25 min., 2/25, Fairy Dust.

0889 OAV

THE HUMANOID: AI NO WAKUSEI LEZERIA (*The Humanoids: Lezeria, Planet of Sadness*), Kaname for Heromedia, science fiction, 45 min., 3/5, Toshiba/Emi. *The Humanoid*.

The female robots that made the now famous illustrator Hajime Sorayama a success, now become the main characters of this special-effect heavy OAV.

0890 OAV

MIJIGEN HUNTER FANDORA II DEADLANDER HEN (*Fandora, the Hunter From the Dream Dimension II): Deadlander Chapter*), Kaname for Meromedia, fantasy/science fiction, 43 min., 3/10, Nippon Columbia.

The mythical Yogu Sogos rises and wakes the beautiful Fantine from her sleep. During the trip to Deadlander, Fandora, Kue and young Soto are attacked by pirates and Soto is injured. Delerious in his dream, the young man sees Yogu Sogos and Fantine invoking the blue stone. Later, Fandora opens up the stone's power, turning Soto into an adult and revealing his true identity: Yogu Sogos.

0891 OAV

GEBAGEBA SHO TIME! (*It's Time to Laugh Geba Geba!*), Cream Land, humor, 25 min., 3/21, Pony.

MYSTICAL, STYLISH, ACTION-PACKED

The Humanoid ©1986 Hiro Media / Kaname Productions / Toshiba-EMI Ltd. English version and package artwork ©1991 Central Park Media Corporation. All Rights Reserved.

Intro
-1962
1963
1964
1965
1966
1967
1968
1969
1970
1971
1972
1973
1974
1975
1976
1977
1978
1979
1980
1981
1982
1983
1984
1985
1986
1987
1988
Index

Mister Geba Geba is the main character of this entertaining movie taken from a successful made for television movie. The animator Renzo Kinoshita lost the original film in a fire, which is why, in this OAV, there are only new episodes.

0892 OAV

OKUBYO NA VENUS (*Shy Venus*), Toei Doga, soap opera, 20 min., 3/21, CicVictor.

Yumiko Kiritawa is about to make her dream to become a great singer come true in the United States. After having learned to dance and sing in New York, she comes back to Japan for her first concert. This OAV featured four songs composed especially by Ami Osaki. The designs are supervised by Michi Himeno.

0893 OAV

ADESUGATA MAHO NO SANNIN MUSUME (*Animated Show of the Three Little Witches*), Studio Pierrot, magic, 30 min., 3/28, Network.

Yu, Mai and Pelsha find themselves together to celebrate the new year and relive together the magic that follows them in their television series. The wonderful video ends with a show that sees the three characters with their magic counterparts, Creamy, Emi and Pelsha as adults.

0894 OAV

KENRITSU CHIKYU BOEIGUN (*The Body Guard of the Body From the Earthly Province*), Studio Gallopp, adventure, 45 min., 4/1, Toshiba Soft.

The provincial council of Kyushu is looking for a way to organize their defense. The secret society Denjugumi is in fact, ready to fight for the conquest of the quiet land.

0895 OAV

CHOJU KISHIN DANCOUGAR: USHINA WARETA MONOGATACHI E NO REQUIEM (*Super-Bestial God-Machine Dancougar: Requiem for the Victims*), Ashi, science fiction, 90 min., 4/21, Bandai.

Following the Zorbados, Shinobu Fujiwara and his mechanical aides enter into another dimension in which they confront enormous robots controlled by Desguyer, but a worse enemy awaits Shinobu, Ryo, Masato and Sara at the end of the tiring battle, the powerful Muge Zorbados.

0896 OAV

GOGO TORAEMON (*id.*), Studio Pierrot, humor, 30 min., 4/25, Warner Pioneer.

In this commemoration of the victory of the Hanshin Tigers in the professional baseball championship, the real players, trainer and leaders are used as the basis for the animated characters.

0897 OAV

BARIBARI DENSETSU PART I TSUKUBAHEN (*The Legend of the Strident Wheels Part I: Tsukuba's Chapter*), Studio Pierrot, sport, 30 min., 5/10, Kodansha.

The rise to success of a young motorcycle rider named Gun begins at the precise moment when Miyuki Ichinose, daughter of the leader of a motorcycle team sees him pass a mo-

torcycle with 750 cc with one with less than a tenth of the power. The trials that await the young man are many, but the rivalry with Hideyoshi, an already confirmed racer, contribute to make his life even harder.

0898 OAV

SOKIHEI M.D. GEIST (*The Armor of the Demon M.D. Geist*), Production Wave for Heromedia, horror, 45 min., 5/21, Nippon Columbia. *M.D. Geist*.

During the post nuclear holocaust, powerful armored warriors fight for survival in a hostile environment.

0899 OAV

RUMIC WORLD PART II THE CHOJO (*Rumic's World Part II: Super Gal*), Studio Pierrot, science fiction, 45 min., 5/21, Shogakukan. *Rumik World: Maris The Chojo* (*Supergal*).

Maris, a wild redheaded girl from the future, is one of the members of the Space Police, a vigilant group that ensures order on Earth and in the universe. The power that makes her a super policewoman is controlled and channeled by an armored bikini that helps her use her incredible psychic powers. But during one of her most eventful missions, Maris finds out that she's not the only one that can be considered "super." Taken from one of the episodes of *Rumik World* by Rumiko Takahashi.

0900 OAV

MEGAZONE 23 PART II HIMITSU KUDASAI (*Megazone 23 Part II: Please Tell Me the Secret*), AIC/Artland/Artmic, science fiction, 80 min., 5/30, Victor.

In the second part of the series, we find Shogo officially wanted for the homicide of Tomomi and Yui. Having assembled many friends he launches an attack against the military to take back the Garland and get in contact with Eve. Meanwhile, the mysterious aliens, who are never shown, stop every attack coming from Megazone 23. In fact, during a battle, they succeed in introducing probes with deadly tentacles into the gigantic spaceship, which causes a lot of damage and numerous losses amongst the earthly troops.

Having recuperated the motorcycle clumsily used as bait to capture them, Shogo and his band set out to battle with the police and the army to reach Bahamood. Many of them die in the attempt, but the survivors are destined to repopulate the Earth. In fact, Shogo learns from a reactivated Eve that Bahamood, which is also a capsule programmed to bring back on the planet a group of people to start new civilization, is now coming back to life. It is for this reason that Adam was programmed as a defense system that, given the impossibility to save Megazone 23, would use it as bait to attract the enemy spaceship in a deadly trap.

Even B.D. philosophically accepts the situation, allowing Shogo to save himself and choosing to leave with a few faithful followers towards the unknown, abandoning the spaceship with a few robots aboard. So, while the operation is successful and the destruction of five centuries-worth of a branch of the human race is finished, Shogo, Yui and their companions are launched towards the Earth. When they come out of the capsule, they find an uncontaminated world, entirely at their disposal. The very realistic drawings are by Yasuomi Umetsu.

MD Geist ©1986 Nippon Columbia Co. English version and package artwork ©1994 Central Park Media Corporation. All Rights Reserved.

Maris The Chojo (The Supergal) © Takahashi Rumiko / Shogakukan. English version and package artwork ©1992 Central Park Media Corporation.

Violence Jack

0901 OAV

VIOLENCE JACK BANGAIHEN VOL. I: HARLEM BOMBER (*Violence Jack Extra Episode, Vol. 1: Harlem Bomber*), Ashi, post-holocaust, 40 min., 6/5, Soeishinsha. *Violence Jack Part 2: Hell's Wind.*

A catastrophe of gigantic proportions, caused by meteorites falling to the Earth, almost completely destroys the civilization of our planet. The disaster provokes the inevitable degradation of the survivors, who close themselves in wretched villages forming bands of tyrants. The need to regain order pushes Violence Jack, a gigantic individual more animal-like than human, to cut the throat of anyone who even thinks about being evil, helped by the questionable power to regenerate the parts of his body lost in battle by having himself hit by lightning. The excessive violence and sexual violence presented makes this OAV one of Nagai's productions with the most impact, even if, unfortunately, the animation is weak in technique and the screenplay mirrors the more degrading tones of the manga from which it is taken.

0902 OAV

CREAM LEMON SERIES PART XIII AMI III IMA YORETE AMI (*Cream Lemon Series Part XIII: Ami III, Now I'll Hug You Ami*), Soeishinsha, erotic, 25 min., 6/10, Fairy Dust.

0903 OAV

PELIKAN ROAD CLUB CULTURE (*id.*), Studio World, sport, 55 min., 6/21, Nippon Columbia.

Kenichi Watanabe is a high school student whose greatest passion is his MBX 50 motorcycle. For this reason, he organizes a motorcycle club called Culture with his friends Shigeru and Tomomitsu. Only after a broken heart does Kenichi become an adult.

0904 OAV

CHOJIKU ROMANESQUE SAMY: MISSING 99 (*Super Dimension, Romanesque Samy: Missing 99*), Project team/Eikyu kikan, science fiction, 60 min., 7/15, TDK KOA.

A legend tells about a war in the ancient past between God and the Devil, which God won, to obtain the right to create the Galaxy. Now, the same circumstances impose a new conflict to establish if good or evil will rule in this universe this time around. The main character is Sami, an ordinary girl, and her companions Tokio, Silver and Dews, battling against the evil Noa.

0905 OAV

SOKOKISHI VOTOMS BIG BATTLE (*Armored Troopers Votoms: The Big Battle*), Nippon Sunrise, science fiction, 55 min., 7/5, Toshiba Soft.

Kiriko and his friends find themselves in the city of the Koba, where there is an experimental garage created by Bararant. To save Fiana, held hostage by Bararant, Kiriko and his companions must face the robot Niva, who was created in the same garage. After the battle, Kiriko destroys the document of Red Shoulder.

0906 OAV

KIZUOIBITO (*The Daredevil*), Madhouse, adventure/erotic, 40 min., 7/5, Bandai.

As it often happens, when a manga gains a measure of success it is taken apart to be used as the basis for an animated series. This was exactly what happened to Ryoichi Ikegami, known for his earlier successes in *Mai* and *Crying Freeman*. The main characters of Kizuoibito are Keisuke Ibaraki, a gold digger nicknamed Baraki, and Yuko, a fascinating television journalist. A love story develops between the two, and the young woman decides to follow her companion in his travels.

0907 OAV

LYON DENSETSU FREIJA (*Freija, the Legend of Lyon*), Uchu Doga, erotic, 25 min., 7/7. *Legend Of Lyon: Flare.*

0908 OAV

CALIFORNIA CRISIS TSUIGEKI NOHIBANDA (*California Crisis: The Closer Attacks*), Studio Unicorn for Heromedia, adventure, 45 min., 7/21, CBS/Fox Video.

During a business trip to Los Angeles, Noera finds himself involved in the battle between Convoy's band and that of Van. Escaping with Masha, a girl he met by accident, the young man finds a mysterious sphere and discovers, looking inside of it, that it is possible to see the panorama of Death Valley. So the two young people decide to get to the bottom of things by personally going to the valley.

Lyon Densetsu Freija © Uchu Doga.

0909 OAV

COSMOS PINK SHOCK (*id.*), AIC, science fiction, 40 min., 7/21, Nippon Victor.

The rocket flown by the fascinating sixteen year old Mitsuko lands on an unknown planet and the young astronaut is arrested. Only one soldier investigates her life, and shortly before she is to be put to death, Mitsuko escapes into space with a few of her companions.

0910 OAV

ITOSHI NO BETTY MAMONOGATARI (*My Dear Betty! Diabolical Stories*), Big ban for Toei Video, horror/erotic, 53 min., 7/21, Toei Video.

Taken from Kazuo Koike and Seisaku Kano's original manga, this animation describes the afflicted life of the maladjusted Tanpei and Betty the witch who, to solve their household problems, don't hesitate to call upon infernal demons and dragons, or to ask the witch's terrible friends and family for help. Notwithstanding the dark and menacing atmosphere that surrounds them, the two always seem to get through in unexpected, entertaining and often titillating ways.

0911 OAV

AMON SAGA (*id.*), Center Studio, fantasy, 75 min., 7/21, Toei Video. [*Amon Saga*].

One day, Amon came to the city of Sarahan, chosen by a rich merchant as the place to save his daughter Licya, held hostage in return for a plant from a golden valley. After having rescued the young woman, Amon goes to the valley to combat the evil emperor.

0912 OAV

TATAKAE! ICZER ONE ACT II ICZER SIGMA NO CHOSEN (*Combat! Iczer One Act II: the Challenge of Iczer Sigma*), AIC, science fiction/horror, 29 min., 7/23, Kubo Shoten. *Iczer-One Act 2.*

After having seen Iczer I and Nagisa win aboard the Iczer Robot, Big Gold, ruler of the Cthulhu, decides to play his ace card: Iczer 2 and the robot Iczer Sigma. Nagisa Kano, who intends to protect the Earth from the evil that has slowly taken over, must face certain

Amon Saga © Baku Yumemakura • Amano Pro • Tokuma Shoten • T & M.

monstrous creatures alone, while Iczer I looks for a way out from the dimensional labyrinth in which she was projected by the aliens. Once reunited, Iczer I and Nagisa find themselves confronting a new, terrible adversary, whose robot is energized by Cepia, the pilot's lover, whose robot was destroyed in the previous episode. The battle is an equal one, with two gigantic robots, two alien androids and two girls both animated by a need for vengeance.

0913 OAV

GALL FORCE ETERNAL STORY (*id.*), Artmic/AIC, science fiction, 86 min., 7/26, CBS/Sony. *Gall Force: Eternal Story*.

Elsa, Rabby, Catty, Pony, Lufy, Patty and Rumy are part of the crew on the Starleaf spaceship, seven representatives of the solenoid race, a people composed only of females who reproduce themselves by cloning and who are at war with the paranoid metamorphics. Trapped because of a breakdown, the Starleaf remains at the mercy of a gelatinous paranoid being that places a "contact device" in Elsa and Patty, a compound generated by the union of the energy from light and DNA solenoids that kills the former but functions on the latter. Forced to abandon the Starleaf because of the danger of worsening the damage to the reactor, the young women embark on the starship Blossom without Catty, who turns out to be an android, and Pony, who dies in the explosion.

The young solenoids remove the contact device from Patty, which then, after a quick metamorphosis, presents herself as a male-clone of her host. The discovery of the Plan of Unification of the Species, a secret project whose objective is the fusion of the solenoids and the paranoid races, motivates Rabby to send Rumy and the new clone-being to Earth, while she and Patty make the chaos satellite explode to destroy all the combat forces that are on the surfaces and nearby. Freely taken from Hideki Kakinuma's manga, the film features character designs by Kenichi Sonoda and the direction of the already famous Katsuhito Akiyama.

Gall Force: Eternal Story ©1986 MOVIC • Sony Video Software International Corporation. English version and package artwork ©1992 Central Park Media Corporation. All Rights Reserved.

0914 OAV

CALL ME TONIGHT (*id.*), AIC, comedy, 30 min., 7/28, Bandai.

The high school student Lumi Natsumi runs a telephone club during the night. One night she receives a phone call by a certain Ryo Sugiura who says he can become horrible every time he gets excited. Lumi takes the situation seriously and, to get him used to stimuli, she brings the young man to the amusement park where he transforms himself again. The young woman, however, makes him change again and Ryo finally turns back to a normal state.

0915 OAV

NAYUTA (*id.*), Circus Production, science fiction, 80 min., 7/31, Toshiba EMI.

Coming home from school, Nayuta saves a woman and her son from a certain death and brings them to a hospital. Unexpectedly, the woman is kidnapped and Nayuta begins to get interested in her son Kiro, who is gifted with ESP powers and who wears a peculiar metallic circle on his head. Without realizing it, Nayuta ends up in a conflict between the Jarna group and the Hazado aliens.

0916 OAV

KIKOKAI GALIANT TETSU NO MONSHO (*Armored Mechanism Galiant: Iron Emblem*), Nippon Sunrise, robot/fantasy, 55 min., 8/5, Toshiba Soft.

Madar wants to unify the lands of Asto using the strength of warrior robots, and he keeps believing in the legend that announces the coming of an avenger called the Iron Giant, who will destroy all the armies. Hai Shartat, one of the sons of Madar, is extremely ambitious and his yearning for power brings him to kill his father and to attack his brother Jordi and his little sister Chururu. During the encounter the two siblings are saved by a mysterious ray of light and the evil Hai will find himself in front of the mythical Iron Giant.

0917 OVA

WINDARIA (*Id.*), Kaname, fantasy, 101 min., 12/8, Victor. *Windaria*.

This film, clearly of Shakespearian inspiration, tells the love story of a prince and a princess from two rival countries. Their love is thwarted by a war created by an agreement between a traitor and the enemy. Silent witness of this story, Windaria, an age-old tree, watches, from the top of a hill, the course of the events. Character designs by Mutsumi Inomata.

0918 OAV

AREA 88 ACT III MOERU SHINKIRO (*Area 88, Act III: the Ardent Mirage*), Studio Pierrot, adventure, 88 min., 8/15, King record. *Area 88 Act III: Burning Mirage*.

This is the conclusion of the *Area 88* saga. After countless battles, Saki, commander of the area, declares all the mercenary contracts ended, and invites them to leave. Shin Kazama, practically a prisoner of the barracks in which he served for a long time, realizes that he has become accustomed to all the combat and the friends he made in the force. Only his need to reunite with his beloved Ryoko, who is still waiting for him in Japan, interferes with his desire to go back to Area 88.

0919 OAV

MAJO DEMOSTEADY (*Fiancee Even If A Witch*), Tokyo Media Connection/Ajiado, magic, 42 min., 9/5, Herald Pony.

Hirashi Seki lives alone in an old apartment. When he wakes up one morning, he finds a beautiful, naked young woman in bed next to him, and he immediately falls in love. The two begin living together, until the young woman mysteriously disappears. Following this, Hirashi is victim of a car accident that throws him into another dimension populated by ideal partners for common folk. It is there that the young man finds Maml and together they return to the real world.

0920 OAV

DREAM HUNTER REM II SEIBISHINJOGAKUEN NO YOMU (*Dream Hunter Rem II: Spiritualist Dream of the Seibishin School*), Project Team/Eikyu kikan, fantasy, 60 min., 9/5, King record.

The students from the Seibishin all-girl school die under mysterious circumstances and Rem, the Dream Hunter, is called in to investigate. Yoko Takamiya informs them that the cause of death can be attributed to Kyoko's sister's ghost, a girl who died after having been kept prisoner in the clock tower by a group of young men.

Windaria ©1986 Idol Co., Ltd / Harmony Gold U.S.A., Inc. Package design ©1992 Streamline Pictures.

Area 88 ©1986 Project 88. English version ©1992 Central Park Media Corporation. All Rights Reserved.

SOMETHING DEADLY IS ON THEIR MINDS!

ROOTS SEARCH

Original Japanese dialogue with English subtitles.

Root Search ©1986 Nippon Columbia Co., Ltd.
English version and package artwork ©1992 Central
Park Media Corporation. All Rights Reserved.

SHONAN BAKUSOZOKU
BOMBER BIKERS OF SHONAN

Shonan Bakusozoku ©1986 Toei Co., Ltd.
Licensed to AnimEigo, Inc. by Toei Co., Ltd.
English version ©1993 AnimEigo, Inc.

0921 OAV

ROOTS SEARCH SHOKUSHIN BUTTAI X (*In Search of the Roots: The Soul Eater*), Production Wave, science fiction, 45 min., 9/10, Nippon Columbia. *Roots Search.*

Moira, a young girl from planet Torumekusu, has a strange premonition during an ESP experiment: an extraterrestrial is getting closer to her planet, intending to exterminate the human race. The first to face the alien threat are the members of the experimental center.

0922 OAV

SHONAN BAKUSOZOKU: NOKOSARETA HASHIRLY ATACHI (*Shonan's Hooligans: Surviving Motocycle Rider*), Toei Doga, adventure, 55 min., 9/10, Toei Video. *Shonan Bakusozoku: Bomber Bikers Of Shonan.*

Easy riders, rockabilly bands, mods and punks are the characters in this video series with a high level of entertainment and a certain level of nostalgia for certain values of the past. The group of high school motorcycle riders, "Shonan Bakusozoku" or "Shobaku," as they are commonly called, is a type of club of "good hooligans" who always look for fights with the neo-nazi groups who disturb the public peace. The young men who form the team want to pass themselves off as tough, but they always reveal a tender heart and personal interests that go beyond the usual "fights and motors." The shiny-haired Yosuke Eguchi, the big and strong Yoshimi Harazawa, the mysterious Shinji Sakurai and the hardheaded Kakuji Marukawa are led by the "supercombed" Noboru Ishikawa and make up the team. This animation is interesting above all for the characterization of the "young rebels" fad that hit Japan during this time. The school uniforms were worn with certain changes: the jacket worn over the white sweater almost reached the knees, and the pants were extremely big; the way of walking round-shouldered with the hands in the pockets and the peaked forelock over the eyes gave the young people a look close to an ork.

0923 OAV

MAHO NO STAR MAGICAL EMI SEMISHIGURE (*Magical Emi, the Star of Magic: Little Rain*), Studio Pierrot, magic, 60 min., 9/21, Bandai.

This OAV presents the life of young Mai in a flashback style. We find her at the beginning of the story a little older and looking at a photo album. In it are photos of the most important moments of her career as Magical Emi, magic and singing superstar.

0924 OAV

AOKI RYUSEI SPT LEYZNER ACT III: KOKUIN 2000 (*SPT Leyzner, the Blue Comet III: the Journey Towards 2000*), Nippon Sunrise, science fiction, 55 min., 10/21, Toshiba Soft.

To prevent a war against our planet, even though a space ring covers the entire planet of Grados, the evil Kain prepares to launch a powerful attack. His plan is hindered, however, by his son Lu, who doesn't hesitate to kill him to take the control of the planet. The young man thus finds himself facing the earthly Eiji, brother of Julia, but the young woman succeeds in separating them before irreparable damage is done. Julia remains with Lu while Eiji returns to Earth where his beloved Anna awaits.

0925 OAV

MUJIGEN HUNTER FANDORA III: PHANTOSHEN (*Fandora, the Dream Dimension Hunter III: Chapter Phantom*), Kaname, fantasy, 45 min., 11/21, Nippon Columbia.

The two stones, Luria and Endoran, were kept by the young Kue in a temple to establish the limits of the universe, until the dimensional wall was destroyed. Knowing that Yogu Sogos is about to become a god through a particular magic ritual, Fandora and her companions prepare themselves to attack Yogu. Kue, whom Fandora is in love with and who dies at the end of the combat, also helps them.

0926 OAV

CREAM LEMON SERIES PART XIV NARIS SCRAMBLE (*id.*), Soeishinsha, erotic, 25 min., 11/21, Fairy Dust.

Naris, the University rector's daughter, must solve the existing problems in the school until one day Lami, the leader of a group of hooligans, is challenged.

0927 OAV

CREAM LEMON SERIES PART XV SF CHOJIGEN DENSETSU RALL II LAMORU NO GYAKUSHU (*Cream Lemon Series Part XV: the Science fiction Legend of the Rall II Superdimension Lamoru's Counterattack*), Soeishinsha, erotic, 25 min., 11/21, Fairy Dust.

The perverse Lamoru is risen and continues to bother princesses and common women to satisfy his base instincts. With the help of the Rivers sword, Carol fights for her freedom against the obscure tyrant.

0928 OAV

BAVI STOCK II EYES MAN AI NO KODO NO KANATANI (*Bavi Stock II: Eyes Man, Beyond the Heartbeat of love*), Studio Unicorn, science fiction, 45 min., 11/25, Nikkatsu Video Film.

0929 OAV

KATSUGEKI SHOJO TANTEIDAN (*Scenes of Investigators*), Tokyo Movie Shinsha, adventure, 30 min., 11/25, Japan Home Video.

0930 OAV

URBAN SQUARE KOHAKUN NO TSUIGEKI (*Urban Square: The Pursuit of Ambra*), Network, police story, 55 min., 11/28, Bandai.

Ryo Matsumoto, a screenplay writer with little talent, finds himself witness to a strange murder, but the police don't believe his story because there is no sign of a dead body. To protect himself from the killers who are after him and to shed light on the case, the writer decides to hire Mochizuki. The beautiful Yuki Tamura is involved in the homicide and is taken hostage with Ryo. The young woman escapes and notifies the detective. Once the young man is free, they face down the criminals.

0931 OAV

KYOSHOKU SOKO GUYVER (*Bio-Booster Armor Guyver*), Studio Live, science fiction/horror, 55 min., 12/13, Bandai. *The Guyver: Out Of Control*.

Young Akira Fukamachi accidentally gets his hands on the armor Unit Guyver, taken from the criminal organization Cronos, that transforms him into a ruthless, monstrous superhero.

ORIGINAL VIDEO ANIMATION • ENGLISH SUBTITLED VIDEO

Guyver: Out Of Control ©1987, 1993 Yoshiki Takaya / Tokuma Shoten / G.P. All Rights Reserved. Exclusively licensed throughout the United States and Canada by L.A. Hero / Nippan.

Outlanders ©1986, 1993 Johji Manabe / Hakusensha • Tatsunoko Production • Victor. English version ©1993 Dark Image Entertainment. All Rights Reserved. Exclusively licensed throughout the United States and Canada by Nippan.

HILARIOUS, ACTION-PACKED & TOTALLY UNEXPECTED ANIMATION

WANNA★BE'S

Wanna Be's ©1986 & 1992 MOVIC / Sony Video Entertainment (Japan) Inc. Package artwork ©1992 Central Park Media Corporation. All Rights Reserved.

To recover the precious device, the hired killers murder some friends of Akira and kidnap Mizuki, his girlfriend. The story is taken from Yoshiki Takaya's original manga.

0932 OAV

BARIBARI DENSETSU II SUZUKACHEN (*The Legend of the Strident Wheels II: Chapter of Suzuka*), Studio Pierrot, sport, 50 min., 12/16, Kodansha.

Gun, Mi and Hiro decide to accept Hideyoshi's offer to join the team to participate in the motorcycle championship. They manage to bring their team to victory, but Hideyoshi's career is soon interrupted by of a deadly car crash.

0933 OAV

OUTLANDERS (*id.*), Tatsunoko, science fiction, 45 min., 12/16, Victor. *Outlanders*.

During the invasion of the Earth, carried out by the Santovask empire, photographer Tetsuya Wakatsuki meets the alien princess Kam, who saves his life during the total destruction of Japan. That action begins a disconcerting love story rich in humor that brings the provocative alien to decide to marry the earthling, trying all the while to save the Earth from the catastrophe and earning the hatred of her own race because of it. Characterized by a humorous design "a la Takahashi," this cartoon is based on Joji Manabe's manga and the help of the studio Katsudon.

0934 OAV

DELPOWER X BAKUHATSU MIRACLE GENKI (*Delpower X: The Explosion of Miraculous Strength*), Big Ban, adventure, 40 min., 12/21, Nippon Columbia.

Manami Hanemoto, a high school student, is the niece of the old scientist Tatsuemon, inventor of the high-powered robot Delpower X. The young girl has to pilot the robot against the Germanoid soldiers of Getzeru, who want to destroy the robot.

0935 OAV

TWINKLE HEART: GINGAKEI MADE TODOKANAI (*Twinkle Heart: We Don't Get to the Galaxy*), Project Team, science fiction, 45 min., 12/21, Krown Record.

On a far away planet, Cherry Lemon and Barry leave to look for the treasure of Love following the order of the old Ogod. Having arrived on Earth, they decide to stay, changing the spaceship into a diner. When they learn certain information concerning the treasure, the three don't hesitate to intensify their search.

0936 OAV

WANNA BEES (*id.*), Artmic Animate Film, sport, 45 min., 12/25, SVI. *Wanna-Be's*.

After the success obtained with *Gall Force*, the same staff gets back to work, creating this new film for the home video market. Professional wrestling is a sport comedy that is incredibly popular in Japan, attracting as many fans as baseball, the national sport. Wanna Bees is the name of a team of two female wrestlers, Eri and Miki, who are bound and determined to win. In fact, after having lost many times in the ring to the rival team of the Foxy Ladies, they get back to fighting after some very harsh training sessions, inciting them to give the best of themselves at the cost of long periods of sacrifice.

CHAPTER TWENTY SIX: 1987

This year, Nippon Sunrise finally managed to bring one of the most popular duos in animation history to the big screen: *Dirty Pair* hit theatres in 1987, and garnered incredible popularity. The catastrophic duo raged on the big screen for an hour and twenty minutes of action, music and madcap, non-stop entertainment.

The famous gentleman robber Lupin III is once again the star of a feature film made for the big screen, *Fuma Ichizoku no Inbo*, an entertaining and lively treasure hunt. Director Yasuo Otsuka, recognized as a master since his work on *Miyaki*, showed his skill once again with a thrilling sequence of car chases. Another visually stunning movie was *Honneamise no Tsubasa Oritsu Uchu Gun*, a science fiction offering with a classical flavor, which eschewed the typical Japanese stereotypes in favor of new characters with curiously animated facial expressions.

On television, audiences waited for the introduction of *Anime Sanjushi*, a very simple remake of the story of the three musketeers, which remained relatively faithful to the original story, expcept for the fact that the character of Aramis was turned into a woman. *Hokuto no Ken* runs again in a second season about the man with the seven stars, in which Ken, the taciturn and solitary warrior, faces new hordes of very powerful criminals who, as always, try to opress the weak and the poor. Unfortunately, the stressing of certain themes becomes excessive, and the combat scenes that constituted the main part of the previous season are now only barely present, the show suffering for the change. The flashbacks are too numerous and badly inconsistent with what had been shown before. The flashback memories showed events yanked out of their proper chronological sequence, and the confusion this engenders ranks *Hokuto no Ken II* much lower than the first series which it tried to emulate.

The Wings Of Honneamise ©1987/1995 Bandai Visual. English version ©1995 Bandai Visual. Package design & summary ©2000 Manga Entertainment, Inc. All Rights Reserved.

Nippon Sunrise stole star Tsukasa Hojo from the TMS, the creator who became a star after *Cat's Eyes* turning to *City Hunter*, in which a brilliant Ryo Saeba deftly maneuvers between neck breaking missions and romancing beautiful young women. It goes without saying that such a series was an open invitation for comedy! And it did become a success, so much so that in the years to come, *City Hunter* gains more than one sequel and the loose living young "city hunter" continues to satisfy his admirers for a long time.

Soap operas were also revived, with *Kimagure Orange Road* leading the pack. The touching series, chronicling the adventures of Madoka, an emancipated, energetic and (naturally) good-looking high school student with a heart of gold, drives the public wild. The passion for this series generated a push for a sequel, which went straight to OAV.

After audiences sat through some re-warmed offerings such as the new production of the Group Tack inspired by the comic *Hyatari Ryoko* by Mitsuru Adachi, and the second chapter of the tender (but over-the-top) animal stories of *Maple Town* in the new *Palm Town*, arrived the unpredictable *Mister Ajikko*. This is an insanely funny series about a young boy who wants to become a great chef. Imitating the feel and the conventions of the sports series, the kitchen was turned into a battlefield in which the chefs compete through the meals they cook, which battle each other to the 'death'.

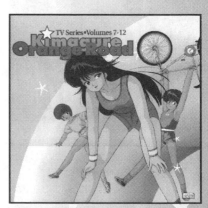

Kimagure Orange Road ©1987 Toho • Studio Pierrot. Character designs ™ & © Matsumoto Izumi / Shueisha • NTV • Toho. Subtitled and released by AnimEigo. Licensed by Toho International Co., Ltd. English version ©1998 Toho International Co., Ltd. All Rights Reserved.

Akai Kodan Zillion and *Kiko Senki Dragonar* showed us two "real" wars. In the first, a show made primarily to market a toy gun with photoelectric cells by Sega, portrayed the difficult conquest of a planet by the people of Earth, hindered by a peculiar race of insectoids with human features, whose design and characterization recall the masks and carnivals of the Carnival of Venice. The second show was an undisguised, even if well done, imitation of *Kido Senshi Gundam*, with even the title remaining strangely similar. Here also, as in *Gundam*, the overpowering presence of a handsome blond opponent and amazingly true-to-life robots and machinery created an unmistakeable atmosphere.

The most important OAV to come out this year was the now-famous *Grey Digital Target*, a fantasy adventure with touches of reality that dealt with hard issues such as social conditions and power games. The movie earned a great deal of success, but the manga fans protested against the inevitable differences between the animation and the printed form. Had the movie followed the plot of the manga exactly, however, the mass market would have complained about the lack of originality in simply replaying old, tired plots. This is a major factor in most adaptations, and differences can be found between the source material and the animated end products in almost every production.

The year 1987 closed with the success of *Genji Monogatari*, a show popular with the female viewing audience. The movie was taken from Murasaki Shikibu's original eleventh century novel. A love story with a historical setting, *Genji Monogatari* fascinated watchers with the hypnotic flow of the story, which followed the intricate rules of Japanese romantic literature.

0937 FILM

ONEAMISE NO TSUBASA: ORITSU UCHU GUN (*Wings of Honneamise: Royal Space Force*), Gainax, science fiction, 120 min., 3/7. *The Wings of Honneamise*.

Set in the 50s in an alternative world, the movie meticulously describes the empire's preparations to launch their first spacecraft. The main character is Shirotsug Lhadatt, a member of the Royal Space Force, a group which has recently sunk in the public opinion because of repeated failures. It is up to the RSF, however, to send the first man into space even though willing candidates are almost impossible to find, due to the risk involved. When Shirotsug volunteers, he is immediately accepted. The cold war with the Republic, the opposing power, is bringing the country to famine. When the launch base is moved to the border of the other country, the latter sabotages the project and begins a harsh war. The shuttle is launched into space, however, and the movie ends on a meditative Shirotsug pondering on the future of humanity. *Honneamise* is based on *Royal Space Force*, a short film by Hiroyuki Yamaga and Yoshiyuki Sadamoto, founders of the production firm which created the full feature film. The former took charge of the screenplay and direction, while Sadamoto designed the animation and the characters, inspired by the characters created by famous American actors like Treat Williams and Harisson Ford. Internationally known Ryuichi Sakamoto was hired to compose the soundtrack, based on his work on the soundtracks of *Furyo*, *The Last Emperor* and *Tea in the Desert*.

0938 FILM

BUTS & TERRY (*id.*), Nippon Sunrise, soap opera, 80 min., 3/14.

Buts and Terry are two young members of a good men's baseball team, the first is a pitcher and the second a catcher. Gifted with strong personalities and a love of bike racing, the young men find themselves involved in a challenge between rival gangs and befriend a young woman who is grieving her boyfriend's death in a motorcycle accident. There is no lack of the standard genre fights that bring life to this feature film.

0939 FILM
DORAEMON: NOBITA TO RYU NO KISHI (*Doraemon: Nobita and the Dragon Rider*), Shin'ei Doga, humor, 43 min., 3/14.

0940 FILM
DIRTY PAIR (*id.*), Nippon Sunrise, science fiction, 80 min., 3/14.*Dirty Pair: Project Eden*.

Yuri and Kei, WWWA agents, are involved in a suicide mission on the mining planet Agana. The planet is ruled by two empires, headed by the capitalist Edia and the socialist Urdas, who are locked in a perpetual conflict. Urdas becomes the target of mysterious nightly attacks, and Edia is immediately suspected. Edia then hires the "Lovely Angels" to exonerate herself and to prevent a war of power. What the two agents get into however, is a far more complicated and dangerous.

They discover "Project Eden," run by the mysterious Professor Watsman, a desperate attempt to create a new human race from a rocky nucleus that can assimilate genetic codes from the planet's fertile soil. Hidden in an abandoned industrial complex and surrounded by monstrous native creatures which help him with his experiments, the Professor also possesses a very expensive bottle of wine that the thief Carson D Carson is desperately trying to steal. The thief runs into Yuri and Kei, and joins them in their mission. The screenplay by Hiriyuki Hoshuyama, the general supervision by Koichi Mashimo and the direction by Katsuyoshi Yatabe make this movie one of the most popular of its kind. Tsukasa Dokite, the character designer, worked on the original drawings of Haruka Takachiho, who originally created the dynamic duo.

0941 FILM
PROGOLFER SARU KOGA HIKYO KAGE NO NINPO GOLFER SANJO (*Progolfer Saru: Secret Zone of Koga: Here is the Ninja Player From the Shadow*), Shin'ei Doga, sports, 40 min., 3/14.

0942 FILM
SHIN MAPLE TOWN MONOGATARI PALM TOWN HEN (*The Story of Maple Town New Series: Chapter Palm Town*), Toei Doga, animals, 30 min., 3/14.

0943 FILM
MANATSU NO YO YUME (*Dream of a Summer Night*), Tokyo Hall, classic, 75 min., 3/14.

0944 FILM
OBAKE NO QTARO SUSUME! HYAKUBUN NO ICHIDAI SAKUSEN (*Go Qtaro the Ghost Strategy of 1/100*), Shin'ei Doga, humor, 3/14.

0945 FILM
KIN NO TORI (*The Golden Bird*), Toei Doga, fairy tale, 52 min., 3/14.

Dirty Pair: Project Eden ©1987, 1994 Haruka Takachiho & A.A. • Sunrise, Inc • NTV. Package design How Studio ©1994 Streamline Enterprises, Inc.

0946 FILM

TOUCH III: KIMI GA TORISUGITA ATO NI (*Touch III: Since When Have You Gone*), Group Tack for Toho, sport, 85 min., 4/11.

The last of the three movies summing up Mitsuru Adachi's series ends with the departure of Tatsuya, and the bold baseball players have to play for the national title.

0947 FILM

TAKARAJIMA (*Treasure Island*), Tokyo Movie Shinsha, Classical/Adventure, 90min., 5/9

Before dying, an old sailor gives a yellowed map to young Jim. The precious map shows the way to a buried treasure. Jim decides to leave on a long journey in search of the mysterious island marked on the map, finding himself in a battle with a crew of pirates led by an impostor who fakes friendship to obtain the map and the clues to the treasure. This is one of the adaptations closest to the original text of Stevenson's novel.

0948 FILM

S.O.S. KOCHIRA CHIKYA (*S.O.S. This Is The Earth*), Tokyo Hall, Science fiction, 15 min., 6/15.

0949 FILM

URUSEI YATSURA: LAMU NO MIRAI WA DONARUCCHA (*Those Obnoxious Aliens: What Future For Lamu?*) Kitty Film, science fiction, 7/18. *Urusei Yatsura OVA 1: Inaba The Dreamer.*

0950 FILM

SAINT SEIYA (*Id.*) Toei Dvga, fantasy, 45 min., 7/18. [*Saint Seiya 2: La Légende De La Pomme D'Or*].

Saint Seiya © M. Kurumada / Shueisha / Toei Animation.

The story begins when the young kindergarten teacher Eris sees a luminous body falling from the sky. Curious and attracted by the object, she decides to look for it. Soon, however, the object reveals itself to be a golden apple which contains the spirit of the evil goddess of vengeance who, strangely enough, has the same name as the girl. Landing on a Greek island, the apple uses his power to awaken the remains of an ancient Greek city and with it, a group of warriors, faithful to the evil goddess of the Ghost Fire.

Intending to wreak vengeance and conquer all that stands before her, the goddess possesses the body of Eris and captures the unaware Saori. Tied to a cross made of rock, Saori is half conscious when the evil power of the apple slowly sucks the life out of her body to transfer it to the spirit of the goddess who, after the sun sets, will come back to life. Immediately, the Bronze Saints run to help and face their enemies in combat. After a series of encounters the Saints seem to be losing, but, thanks to the intervention of Ikki and to the golden armor of the Sagittarius, our heroes emerge victorious.

0951 FILM

DRAGONBALL: MAJINJO NEMURIHIME (*Dragonball: The Princess Asleep In The Castle Of The Gods*), Toei Doga, adventure, 45 min., 7/18. [*Dragonball 2: Le Château Du Démon*].

0952 FILM

BUGTTE HONEY: MEGALOM SHOJO RONDO 4622 (*Bugtte Honey: The Dance 4622 Of Young Magalom*), Tokyo Movie Shinsha, Humor, 48 min., 7/21.

Dragonball: Majinjo Nemuri Hime © Bird Studio / Shueisha / Toei Animation.

0953 FILM

KAZE GA FUKU TOKI (*When The Wind Blows*), Nippon Herald, drama, 85 min., 7/25.

An old English couple are living peacefully in their quiet country village when a nuclear bomb explodes nearby. The two old people continue their daily life scrupulously following the government directives, despite their total isolation and deprivation. The two only begin to slowly comprehend the fact that they are dying from the radiation that surrounds them. This dark film is taken from Raymond Briggs' comic strip and directed by Tommy Murakami, who uses, for the most part, real backdrops — miniature versions of the house interiors. The soundtrack is, in part, by David Bowle.

0954 FILM

AITSU TO LULLABY SUI YOBI NO CINDERELLA (*Lullaby with him: Wednesday Cinderella*), Studio Pierrot, 52 min., 8/1.

0955 FILM

GOKIBURI TACHI NO TASAGARE (*The Face Of The Cockroaches*), TYO/Kitty film, 100 min., 11/21. *Twilight Of The Cockroaches.*

0956 FILM

LUPIN SANSEI FUMA ICHIZOKU NO INBO (*Lupin III: The Scheme Of The Fuma Family*), Tokyo Movie Shinsha, adventure, 75 min., 12/26. *Lupin III (Rupan III): The Fuma Conspiracy.*

After having decided to get his head straight, Goemon Ishikawa announces his intentions to marry the sweet Murasaki Suminawa, and prepares himself for the wedding ceremony. When the two are about to say yes, the emissaries from the mysterious Fuma criminal organization suddenly interrupt the ceremony and, in the chaos, kidnap the girl. Their target is, in reality, a precious vase belonging to the Suminawa family which contains an ancient key that opens the door to a temple made of gold. Lupin, Jigen and Goemon intervene, proving their great investigative skills, and after a series of breathless pursuits, they free Murasaki and find the treasure although, as usual, they don't keep it for long. Finally reunited with his future bride, Goemon decides to let her go because his adventurous life would be too dangerous for her. The movie reaches new heights of quality, thanks to the expert animation by Masayuki Oseki and the direction of Yasuo Otsuka.

0957 FILM

GENJI MONOGATARI (*Genji's Story*), Group Tack for Herald, classical/historical, 120 min., 12/19. *The Tale Of Genji.*

The story, set in ancient Japan, is about Genji, the son of the emperor, who is in love with his father's second wife. When she realizes that she is pregnant with Genji's baby, she locks herself up in a convent. The young prince has no other alternative than to console himself with other courtesans. The story is also available as a manga by Waki Yamato.

0958 SERIES

AI NO WAKAKUSA MONOGATARI (*The Romantic Story Of The Little Women*), Nippon animation, classical, 48 episodes, 1/11/1987 – 12/27/1988. [*Les Quatres Filles Du Dr March*].

Rupan III: The Fuma Conspiracy ©1987 Toho Co., Ltd / Tokyo Movie Shinsha. Licensed to AnimEigo, Inc. by Toho Co., Ltd. English version ©1994 AnimEigo, Inc. All Rights Reserved.

Original Japanese dialogue with English subtitles

The Tale Of Genji ©1987 Asahi Group / Herald Group / TAC. English version and package ©1995 Central Park Media Corporation. All Rights Reserved.

Ai no Wakakusa Monogatari Nippon Animation Co., Ltd.

Another interpretation of Louisa May Alcott's novel, directed by Fumio Kurokawa, makes a drastic change to the ending and keeps little Beth alive. The screenplay doesn't add anything to the path laid out by previous versions, presenting a rather flat adaptation. Yoshifumi Kondo's designs, on the other hand, are captivating and very well done. The series is produced by Junzo Nakajima, the screenplay by Masato Takamichi and the supervision of the designs is by Nobushiki Yamazaki.

0959 SERIES

SHIN MAPLE TOWN MONOGATARI PALM TOWN (*The New Story of Maple Town; Palm Town*), Toei Doga, animals, 44 episodes, 1/18/1987 – 12/27/1988.

Patty, the little rabbit, moves with her family from Maple Town to the not so quiet Palm Town where they soon find new friends and adventure. The direction is entrusted to Hiroshi Shidara. Amongst the illustrators are Tomoko Arikawa and Tsuneo Ninomiya. The artistic supervision is by Kazuo Komatsubara, and the list of screenwriters includes Chifude Asakura, Tomoko Kaneharu and Shigeru Yananigawa, while Akiko Kosaka wrote the brilliant soundtrack.

0960 SERIES

KIKO SENKI DRAGONAR (*Chronicals of a War of the Dragonar Armored Mechanism*), Nippon Sunrise, robot, 48 episodes, 2/7/1987 – 1/30/1988.

In the year 2087, the European Economic community and China become the major industrial powers on Earth. The colonization of space, initiated peacefully, degenerates as time goes on and deep disagreements form concerning the exploitation of raw materials. The Moon colonies decide to unite in one great military force called Giganos, pooling their advanced scientific knowledge. Under the rule of the minister Giltor, Giganos decides to declare war on the Earth and all the other colonies.

The series begins with the theft of three Giganos robots, the Metal Armor Dragonars, who are brought to the headquarters of the earthly allies aboard the Idaho spaceship. During the trip, however, the spaceship intercepts the enemy cruiser Humbolt and is forced to land on the Arkahdo colony, which holds a famous astronaut academy. Kain Wakaba, Light Newman and Tap Oceano, three cadets, find the diskettes needed to activate the three powerful robots and, having reached Idaho and unaware of the danger, they activate the Dragonars. The Metal Armors, programmed to analyze the characteristics of the voice that activates them for the first time, identify the three young men, and they become the only possible pilots for the robots. The Giganos blow up the colony and the survivors go back to Earth aboard the Idaho. Amongst the survivors is Linda Plato, daughter of a scientist from Giganos and sister of the commander of the enemy forces; Rose Pattenton, a sixteen year old Moon native; and their friend Diane Lance, a young American teacher. The long conflict finishes again in Earth's favor. The science fiction series is by Takayuki Kanda, who supervised the designs, Kenichi Onuki who supervised the character designs, and Kunio Okawara.

0961 SERIES

HOKUTO NO KEN II (*Fist Of The North Star II*), Toei Doga, martial arts/post holocaust, 43 episodes, 3/13/1987 – 2/18/1988.

After having beaten Raoh, Ken decides to retire with his beloved Julia, who is dying. In the meantime, a new aristocratic class rises up who enjoy oppressing the poorer people. Only Kenshiro, now alone and more mature, can reestablish order by helping the remaining rebels to free themselves from their oppressors. But when everything seems to be going well, certain events bring Kenshiro to take a long trip through the Valley of the Demons. According to legend, not even the greatest martial artists in the world can survive on this continent. It has also been said that the Hokuto Genmi was born for this fight alone.

0962 SERIES

HYATARI RYOKO (*A Beautiful Sun Ray*), Group Tack, sport/soap opera, 48 episodes, 3/29/1987 3/20/1988. [*Une Vie Nouvelle*].

This is a new chapter taken from Mitsuru Adachi's original manga, and another success for the author, who takes particular care with the characterization. Young Kasumi moves in with her aunt, a landlady who owns a little rooming house for students. Kasumi soon befriends the other boarders, including Yusaku. Love soon grows between the two even though the young woman is engaged to marry the strong Kazuhiko, who is currently in America for his studies. The episodes present a succession of misunderstandings, innocent loves and entertaining moments that give a certain charm to the series produced by Masato Fujiwara and written by a large staff, including Mitsuru Shimada and Higashi Shimizu. The character designs are by Minoru Maeda. The backdrop supervision is by Yoshihiro Kawamura, Kazuya Takeda and Nobuairo Okaseko.

0963 SERIES

ULTRA B (*id.*), Shin'ei Doga, humor, 51 episodes, 4/5/1987 – 3/27/2988.

0964 SERIES

CITY HUNTER (*id.*), Nippon Sunrise, police story, 52 episodes, 4/6/1987 – 3/28/1988. *City Hunter* [*Nicky Larson*].

Ryo Saeba is the main character of this second series inspired by the manga by Tsukasa Hojo, a young Japanese author loved by both the public and the critics. The story plays on the public's taste for police stories, the same taste that brought success to *Cat's Eyes*, even if it doesn't skimp on the humorous and erotic scenes. It is possible to contact Ryo Saeba, a very unorthodox private investigator, by writing the letters XYZ on the notice board of the Shinjuku station in Tokyo. The services offered by the fascinating detective range from gunman to teacher, from bodyguard to anything "else" desired. His favorite clients are the beautiful women of the Japanese capital, notwithstanding the threats from his jealous partner Kaori Makimura. He never gives up the hope that he will be paid well... as nature intended.

0965 SERIES

KIMAGURE ORANGE ROAD (*The Capricious Orange Road*), Studio Pierrot for Toho, soap opera, 48 episodes, 4/6/1987 – 3/7/1988. *Kimagure Orange Road* [*Max & Compagnie*].

The story is taken from a comic strip by Izumi Matsumoto and presents a different kind of love triangle: Kyosuke is in love with Madoka, while Hikaru is in love with him. Madoka, whose feelings are ambiguous, is torn between the friendship she shares with Hikaru and

City Hunter © Tsukasa Hojo / Shueisha • YTV • Sunrise. Packaging design ©2000 A.D. Vision, Inc. Released in North America by A.D.V. fansubs.

Kimagure Orange Road ©1987 Toho • Studio Pierrot. Character designs ™ & © Matsumoto Izumi / Shueisha • NTV • Toho. Subtitled and released by AnimEigo. Licensed by Toho International Co., Ltd. English version ©1998 Toho International Co., Ltd. All Rights Reserved.

the love that she is starting to feel for Kyosuke. Moreover, the young man has inherited extrasensory powers from his maternal grandparents, that he often uses to reach none-too-noble ends. The skillful direction is by Osamu Kobayashi and the character designs by Akemi Takada, with the design supervision by Masako Goto and the backdrops by Shichiro Kobayashi. The soundtrack is entrusted to Shiro Sagisu and the main screenplays are by Kenji Terada.

0966 SERIES
GERAGERA BUS MONOGATARI (*The Story of Geragera Bus*), Telescreen, humor, 52 episodes, 4/7/1987 – 3/29/1988. [*Bof*].

0967 SERIES
ESPER MAMI (*id.*), Shin'ei Doga, magic, 119 episodes, 4/7/1987 – 10/26/1988. [*Malicieuse Kiki*].

This story adds another page, albeit a small one, to the "magical girl" genre. In fact, the red headed Mami receives certain extrasensory powers that she uses to perform good deeds. A slightly humorous series, *Esper Mami* is taken from Fujiko Fujio's manga.

0968 SERIES
AKAI GODAN ZILLION (*Zillion, the Red Ray*), Tatsunoko, science fiction, 31 episodes, 4/12 – 12/13/1987. *Zillion*.

Zillion ©1991 Tatsunoko Production Co., Ltd / Streamline Pictures.

In the year 2250, an earthly spaceship lands on Malice, a planet destined to become a colony of our world. Everything goes well until 2387, the year that marks the destruction of the Earth fleet around Malice by an alien population with overpopulation problems. The earthlings, defenseless against the aliens from Noza, discover a substance previously unknown until then that, unlike other weapons, is fatal to the invaders. They then create an limited number of rifles which they then give to the White Nuts team, composed of two young men and one young woman: named, respectively, Champ, J.J. and Apple. Strangely enough, this animation has followed the usual pattern in reverse: the characters and spaceships were toys first, before they were turned into characters in a TV show.

0969 SERIES
MACHINE ROBOT BUCCHIGIRI BATTLE HACKERS (*Machine Robot, the First Breach Combats*), Ashi, robot, 35 episodes, 6/3 – 12301987.

0970 SERIES
TRANSFORMER THE HEAD MASTERS (*id.*), Toei Doga for Takara, robot, 35 episodes, 7/3/1987 – 3/28/1988. *Transformers*.

After Convoy's death and the abandonment of the commandos, the powerful Fortress Maximus becomes the head of the Cybertron troops. The war now continues in space to defend new forms of energy from the Destron army. After the two first series written by the American company Marvel Comics, Toei Doga continues the adventures of the transforming robots by itself, and kept drawing crowds in Japan.

0971 SERIES
MIDNIGHT ANIME LEMON ANGEL (*id.*), Aichi, erotic, 47 episodes, 10/1/1987 – 9/28/1988.

In Italy, it would have been unthinkable to produce an animated series on the erotic adventures of three disturbing teenagers, but not in Japan, and *Lemon Angel* is a clear proof of this. Up to now, cartoons for adults were only available on videotape, but with this series, they make their debut on Japanese television screens. For obvious reasons, the show was scheduled only after midnight, a time in which Erika, Mike and Tomo could freely express their erotic dreams for the delight of "Los Amigis de las Noches." Under the motto "the one that is left is love," the beautiful young women are the proof that cartoons can keep adult interest, and that they can be successfully broadcast at time slots where they are obviously not intended for children.

0972 SERIES

NORAKUROKUN (*Little Norakuro*), Studio Pierrot, soap opera, 48 episodes, 10/4/1987 – 10/2/1988.

Created in 1931 and immediately published in "Shonen Club," *Norakurokun* began with a violent heart. The main character, a clever dog, is one of the longest running characters in the history of Japan. It is still presented today in the monthly Kodansha magazine "Comic Bom Bom." The author, Suiho Tagawa, now works with An Ken, the story has changed with time and the grandson of the original hero has become the main character. Like the new manga, the television series also features Norakuro with a young Japanese boy as his companion.

0973 SERIES

MISTER AJIKKO (*id.*), Nippon Sunrise, humor, 99 episodes, 10/8/1987 – 9/20/1988. [*Le Petit Chef*].

Initially made for "Shonen Magazine," Daisuke Tarasawa's manga is immediately transformed into this animated series, the first of its kind, that presents the struggles of Yoichi, a young Japanese cook. The complex gastronomical art is presented in a careful way, and with respect for Japanese tradition: the young protagonist finds himself confronted by expert colleagues in the kitchen in the hope of satisfying the demanding and expert judges. Yoichi doesn't stop at making typical meals; rather, he experiments. He takes out some ingredients or aromas to better the classic recipes, and pays careful, personal attention to the freshness of the meat, the fish and the vegetables. Yohiko is always with him, helping the young man with gentle advice and ideas for experimenting with new dishes. The preparation of the recipes occupies a vital place in the manga as well as in the television series, and the recipes are taught very carefully, for the delight of the viewers who tend to be cooking lovers.

0974 SERIES

ANIME SANJUSHI (*The Animated Three Musketeers*), Gakken, classic, 52 episodes, 10/9/1987 – 2/17/1988. [*Sous Le Signe Des Mousquetaires*].

The adventures of the famous three musketeers go through some changes in this version, produced by Yasuo Kaneko: D'Artagnan is now a country boy who will do anything to become a musketeer, while Aramis is a beautiful woman who hides her secret under the clothes of a man to avenge the death of her lover. The other characters are the same as in Dumas' original novel. In fact, we find Constance, the Queen's lady-in-waiting, the pernicious Mylady, ready to come up with the most diabolical plans to get the Queen in trouble. Written by Yasuo Tanami, the series is supervised by Kunihiko Yuyama and designed by Shingo Ozaki, who re-worked the original designs by Monkey Punch.

Anime Sanjushi © NHK / Gakken.

0975 SERIES

ANIME HACHIJUNICHIKAN SEKAI ISSHU (*Around the World in 80 days — The Anime*), Nippon Animation, animals/adventure, 25 episodes, 10/10/1987 – 3/26/1988.

The unpredictable Mr. Fogg always knows what to do in difficult situations, and to win a bet he decides to take a trip around the world in only eighty days. The faithful Passepartout travels with him and proves himself to be extremely useful in many circumstances. The characters of Verne's novel are given new designs here, presented as anthropomorphic animals.

0976 SERIES

BIKKURIMAN (*id.*), Toei Doga, humor, 75 episodes, 10/11/1987 – 4/2/1988.

0977 SERIES

ORA GUZURA DADO (*Hey, I Am Guzura!*), Tatsunoko, humor, 44 episodes, 10/2/1987 – 9/20/1988.

0978 SERIES

KAMEN NO NINJA AKAKAGE (*Akakage, The Masked Ninja*), Toei Doga, adventure, 23 episodes, 10/13/1987 – 3/22/1988.

The evil Gen Yosai is the head of the Kanamekyo clan, and he surrounds himself with the most powerful warriors in the land to maintain his power and supremacy. Akakage the ninja, sworn enemy of Gen, styles himself as the defender of the weak. He doesn't sell out to the powerful clan, and begins to fight with his companions Sokage and Shirokage to bring peace back to the region.

0979 SERIES

MANGA NIHON KEIZAI NYUMON (*Introduction to Japanese Economy*), Knack, documentary, 25 episodes, 10/13/1987 – 3/29/1988.

0980 SERIES

TSUIDE NI TONCHINKAN (*Anyway, it Doesn't Matter*), Nas, humor, 43 episodes, 10/17/1987 – 10/1/1988.

0981 SERIES

GRIMM MEISAKU GEKIJO (*Grimm's Theater Masterpieces*), Nippon Animation, fairy tale, 25 episodes, 10/21/1987 – 3/20/1988.

0982 SERIES

LADY LADY (*id.*), Toei Doga, soap opera, 21 episodes, 10/21/1987 – 3/23/1988.

The series is the first chapter of the story of Lady Lyn, the sweet little girl with blond hair, born from the magical pen of Yoko Hanabusa. Daughter of a rich English count who remarried a Japanese woman, Lyn moves from Japan to London after her mother's death, to live with her father and her stepsister. Not too welcomed at the beginning, she gains the friendship and the sympathy of those who surround her, becoming a perfect English lady. The series is produced by Kazuo Yokoyama and by the young Hiromi Seki. Hiroshi Shidara is director.

0983 SPECIAL

TETSUKAMEN O OE D'ARTAGNAN MONOGATARI (*The Adventures of D'Artagnan: Hunted Iron Mask*), Toei Doga, classic, 5/5.

D'Artagnan and the king's musketeers, who, with the underhanded Milady, come up with a plan against King Louis.

0984 SPECIAL

JUGOSHONEN HYORYUKI (*Fifteen Young Castaways*), Nippon Animation, classic, 54 min., 10/19.

0985 SPECIAL

KITERETSU DAIHY AKKA (*The Encyclopedic Kiteretsu*), Staff 21, humor, 54 min., 11/2.

Once again, a cartoon from Fujiko Fujio sparks off an irresistible animated production.

0986 SPECIAL

SAINT ELMO HIKARI NO HOMONSHA (*Saint Elmo, the Visitor From the Light*), Toei Doga for Mainichi Eigasha, science fiction, 12/31.

0987 OAV

DIRTY PAIR LOVELY ANGELS YORI AI O KOMETE (*Dirty Pair: With Love From the Lovely Angels*), Nippon Sunrise, science fiction, 47 min., 1/1, Vap Video.

This time the "Lovely Angels" are on the trail of a skillful counterfeiter. Yuri, however, is busy with her boyfriend, so Kei is assisted by the bankrupt Kyariko. An unbeliveable number of difficulties are thrown in their path, to culminate with the discovery that Mack's son, the number one suspect, is a cyborg, Terminator style. In the second episode, also on the tape, the WWWA sees its experimental weapons laboratory invaded by the head of the organization Markas, who holds Gulu, the director, hostage. Yuri and Kei come up with a plan to solve the problem.

0988 OAV

ELF 17 (*id.*), Agent 21, science fiction, 30 min., 1/14, Toei Video.

Prince Maskato Taila decides to take a trip through the Milky Way and, to chose the guide who will accompany him, he organizes a contest. The finalists are a young woman named Lu and K.K., a big brute, both chosen for their fighting skills.

0989 OAV

HELL TARGET (*id.*), Nakamura, science fiction/horror, 50 min., 1/21, Victor.

An exploratory spaceship has disappeared on the mysterious planet Inferno II. A few years later, a second spaceship lands there with a crew of nine people, who discover the existence of a monstrous creature that kills people by bringing to life their darkest hidden fears. Kitazato Makuro, the only survivor, fights the monster but he loses, thus leaving a third spaceship at the mercy of the monstrous being.

0990 OAV

CHOJIN DENSETSU UROTSUKIDOJI (*The Legend of the Super Divinity: the Wandering Boy*), Javn, science fiction, 40 min., 1/21, Javn. *Urostukidoji: Legend Of The Overfiend. Birth Of The Overfiend.*

There are three races living in the universe: the humans, the demons and the human-beasts. Every three thousand years, the Chojin rises to unite the three races in one world called the "Kingdom of Eternity." At the Myojin High School, the beautiful Akemi is everyone's dream girl, including the introverted Nagumo who, caught by the idolized Ozaki spying on the girls in the dressing room, is injured and bleeds. To mock him in front of everybody, Ozaki decides to stop the bleeding by licking the little cut. Following Akemi, Nagumo sees her while she is dragged to the infirmary by the enigmatic Yoki, who transforms into a demon, showing violence with no restraint. Fortunately, Amano, a new student with strange powers, comes to her aid and saves Akemi. Thinking that Amano saved her, Akemi falls in love with him.

In reality, Amano is a demon who, with Megumi, his nymphomaniac sister, and Kuroku, a little elf, is looking for Chojin to destroy him. Using their sense of smell to track him down, the three think that Ozaki who transformed when attacked by killer demons, holds the power of the ultrademon. Notwithstanding all this, Ozaki is easily beaten by Amano, who suddenly remembers the legend. Whoever drinks the blood or the semen of the ultrademon acquires some of his powers. Amano then realizes that Chojin is incarnated in Nagumo, who dies in a car accident. During the night, Nagumo comes back to life and after having sexually assaulted a nurse, he transforms into the final stage of Chojin, a huge being that completely devastates the hospital and triumphantly rises above the world of the living. Taken from Toshio Maeda's disturbing manga, the movie produced by Yasuhito Yamaki is directed by Hideki Takayama and written by Noboru Aikawa. The soundtrack is by Misamichi Amano.

0991 OAV

GREY DIGITAL TARGET (*id.*), Ashi, science fiction, 80 min., 1/25, Tokuma Japan. *Grey: Digital Target.*

In the 26th century AD, the human race is subdivided into in Common People, Fighters and City Dwellers. Only the City Dwellers can live in luxury, contrary to the Common People who live in suburban ghettos and who work daily to be able to survive. Some of them want to become Fighters to better their condition. They automatically start at the F level and battle to reach the A level, which gives them the permission to ask for citizenship. Only three percent succeed, while the others die in cruel battles against an unidentified "enemy." Grey Death attempts the social climb following the death of his girlfriend who became a Fighter before him. Having become a skillful warrior, the young man realizes that the higher the level, the higher the difficulty, because powerful androids begin to appear amongst his adversaries. Only the death of human soldiers can earn one the credits to go to a higher level, and the fact that he is being pitted against androids means that his desired goal seems farther and farther away. Beyond all that is Toy's strong will, the first computer with a conscience that, based on deviated logical principles, wants to exterminate the human race, thinking it is fulfilling their greatest wish. The concept is taken from Yoshihisa Tagami's manga and is directed by Tetsu Dezaki, who also supervises the weak screenplay with Yasuki Hirano and Kazumi Koide. The soundtrack is by Goro Ohmi.

0992 OAV

GAKUEN TOKUSO HIKARUON (*Hikaruon, the School Private Investigator*), AIC, science fiction/horror, 30 min., 1/28, Bandai.

This very well done OAV is a tribute to the success of the series about the Space Sheriffs, a group of heroes in armor who fight for what's right. From that origin rises Hikaruon, the school investigator, who deals with the mysteries that occur inside a Japanese high school.

0993 OAV

BODY JACK (*id.*), Ross, erotic, 30 min., 1/28, Bandai.

The beautiful Nakano and Komaba are the most admired girls in their high school. Asagedani is physically attracted to Komaba, who doesn't seem to know he exists. Doctor Toyama has invented an apparatus that allows one to possess other people's bodies, and the young man, after having bought the apparatus for 50 yen, takes control of Komaba's body, forcing her to touch herself in provocative ways. He/she is caught by Nakano in this state who, thinking that the erotic provocation is for her benefit, gives herself to Komaba, giving way to a strange triangle... with only two sides.

0994 OAV

YUME KARA SAMENAI (*Remaining in the Dream*), Shaft, soap opera, 40 min., 2/21, RVC.

0995 OAV

CREAM LEMON SERIES PART XVI ESCALATION III TENSHITACHI EPILOGUE (*Cream Lemon Series part XVI: Escalation III, the Angel's Epilogue*), Soeishinsha, erotic, 25 min., 2/21, Fairy Dust.

Rie and Midori are about to graduate and, before they leave the school, they decide to initiate Arisa and other new students to the sapphic cult, so as to maintain the "tradition" inside the austere catholic walls.

0996 OAV

MUGEN SHISHSHI BOKEN KATSUGEKI HEN (*The Dreamy Gentleman, Chapter of the Stormy Adventures*), Studio Gallopp, adventure, 49 min., 2/12, Picture.

The techniques that the young investigators are forced to come up with to face down criminals are many. Having found out about five recent kidnappings, and the last victim, the beautiful ballerina Atsuko Fukuin, Mamiya decides to dress up as the pianist Sakurako Satomi, the next intended victim of the criminal organization, so that she can gain entry to the Lion's Den. There, Mamiya discovers the existence of a mechanism capable of bringing the dead back to life. The goal of the kidnapping is, in fact, to obtain energy from the young lives.

0997 OAV

BUBBLEGUM CRISIS (*id.*), AIC, science fiction/adventure, 53 min., 2/25, Toshiba EMI. *Bubblegum Crisis*.

Mega Tokyo 2032: because of the frequent terrorist attacks by the biomechanical soldiers from the Buma organization, a new outlaw defense group is formed to fight crime under the code name Knight Sabers. The members of this team are four ruthless and sensual

BUBBLEGUM CRISIS
The Japanese Animated Cyberpunk Classic
Episode 1 of 8 • Subtitled in English

Bubblegum Crisis ©1987 by Artmic, Inc & Youmex, Inc. English version ©1991 by AnimEigo, Inc. All Rights Reserved.

young women: Priss, Linna, Celia and Nene, all armed and equipped with the powerful armor Hard Suits. Directed by Musani Akiyama and based on a story by Toshimutsu Suzuki, the OAV is followed by a number of sequels. The character designs are by Kenichi Sonoda.

0998 OAV

DREAM HUNTER III MUINKUBINASHI MUSHA DENSETSU (*The Dream Hunter III: the Fantastic Legend of the Headless Warrior*), Project Team, fantasy, 60 min., King Record.

An ancient legend has been passed down through the years in the little village of Muimura: once, the samurais from the Heige family secretly came into the village, after having lost a battle at Dannoura. Tomomori Taira also came with them, but he was immediately beheaded and he is now a headless ghost who seeks vengeance. To rid the village of the head-hunter ghost, the people had made a doll that resembled Tomomori's girlfriend and had offered it to the divinity of the temple. The ghost had thus stopped appearing until Katsuhiko Mitsu took the doll away, provoking the ghost's anger once more and forcing Rem to deal with the problem.

0999 OAV

TWILIGHT Q TOKI NO MUSUBIME REFLECTION (*Twilight Q: the Reflection of the Temporal Knot*), Asia Do, adventure, 30 min., 2/28, Bandai.

The student Mayumi Takizawa and her friend Kiwado find a photographic camera near a beach and once the negatives are developed, they see the pictures of a very handsome young man. The girls ask Uemura, Kidawo's brother, to try to find the owner of the camera and he discovers that the camera is a prototype that won't be distributed until a few years from now. All of a sudden the camera disappears, and Mayumi rushes to the beach to try to find some clues. There, the young woman is thrown into the future where she sees her tomb and meets Hirata, the young man from the picture, who is destined to become her husband.

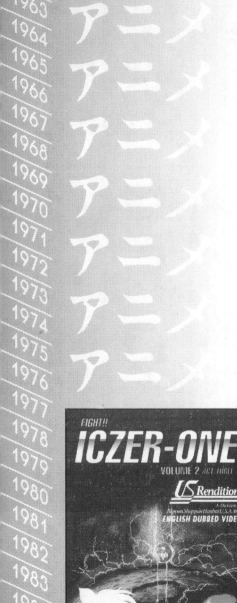

Iczer-One ©1987, 1992 Kubo Shoten / A.I.C. English version ©1992 U.S. Renditions. All Rights Reserved.

1000 OAV

TATAKAE! ICZER ONE, ACT III: KANKETSU HEN (*Fight Iczer One! Act III, Final Chapter*), AIC, science fiction/horror, 46 min., 3/4, Kubo Shoten. *Iczer-One Act 3*.

The duel between Iczer 1 and Iczer 2, battling with the vital energies of Nagisa in Iczer Robot and Sepia in Iczer Sigma, is terrifying in its intensity. After their initial defeat, however, the champion android of the Cthulhu comes back and takes possession of Nagisa's mind. When Iczer 1 furiously penetrates into the alien headquarters, she is spotted by her earthly friend and with much sadness, Iczer 1 hits her with her mortal beam. Nothing stops the blond alien in the Cthulhu base. Iczer 1, fighting hundreds of monstrous creatures, as well as the antagonistic Iczer 2, puts an end to the threat of the demonic Big Gold. to save her friend from oblivion, Iczer 1 decides to distort time and space bringing Nagisa back to the day in which everything had begun, erasing everything from her memory. She then goes back into space, sad and alone.

1001 OAV

MARYU SENKI (*Demonic War Annals*), AIC, horror, 30 min., 3/5, Bandai.

The head of a group mandated to help the time controllers is brutally killed by the 'formers,' who behead him so that he won't be reborn. Years pass and the descendants of the survivors of the group decide to seek vengeance and get ready to attack.

1002 OAV

SHIN CREAM LEMON GOJIKANME NO VENUS (*Cream Lemon New Series: Venus From the Fifth Hour*), Soeishinsha, erotic, 25 min., 3/21, Fairy dust.

1003 OAV

RUMIC WORLD WARAU HYOTECHI (*Rumik's World: the Laughing Target*), Studio Pierrot, horror, 50 min., 3/21, Shogakukan. *Rumik World: Laughing Target.*

Azusa, a girl of the upper class, is promised in marriage at a tender age to Yuzuru, following laws of etiquette that demand that the upper class not mix with commoners. Having reached their teens, Asuza and Yuzuru realize that things have changed. Yuzuru likes a school companion who follows him everywhere, while Azusa really loves the young man. The difficult situation is aggravated by the curse that hovers over the young woman: possessed by infernal "famished ghosts," she is pushed to kill anyone she believes to be an enemy, Azusa attacks Yuzuru and his girlfriend and is finally killed by an arrow from the young man. The video is taken from an episode of *Rumik's World*, a series of brief stories created and illustrated by Rumiko Takahashi.

Rumik World: The Laughing Target © Rumiko Takahashi / Shogakukan / Kitty / Pony.

1004 OAV

DIGITAL DEVIL MONOGATARI MEGAMI TENSEI (*The Story of the Digital Demon: the Reborn Goddess*), Animate Film, horror, 45 min., 3/25, Tokuma Shoten.

Akemi is a brilliant high school student, skilled with computers, whom Yumiko, a new school companion, falls immediately in love with. The young man is too busy with his computer, however, with which he creates Loki, a digital demon who follows Akemi's orders. Akemi begins using this powerful weapon for personal vendettas against local hooligans and his teachers, but the demon escapes the young man's control and attacks whoever gets in his way. When Loki turns against Akemi himself, the young man decides to do something to stop him and save the beautiful Yumiko.

1005 OAV

MINNA AGECHAU (*I'll Give You Everything*), Animate Film, erotic comedy, 45 min., 3/28, CBS Sony.

Yuno is a girl from a wealthy family who, one day, peeping into a neighboring house with some of her friends, sees a young man pleasuring himself in front of a pornographic magazine. Having pity for the young man's loneliness, Yuno goes to his house, determined to become his sexual 'good fairy.' Even after the official engagement, problems continue to arise that the skillful amateur sex therapist will almost always solve. The fast-paced comedy is inspired by Hikaru Yuzuki's manga.

1006 OAV

HEAVY METAL L GAIM III FULL METAL SOLDIERS (*Id.*), Sunrise, science fiction, 55 min., 3/28, Bandai.

Daba My Lord and his group of renegades continue their fight against the evil Oldona Poseidal with the help of the powerful robot L Gaim. In this new chapter of their adventures, however, the war is harsher. Daba in fact, is forced to choose between saving his companion Leshi from the hands of the enemy or finally killing Oldona.

1007 OAV

SHONAN BAKUSOZOKU II 1/5 LONELY NIGHT (*Shonan's Hooligans II: 1/5 of a Lonely Night*), Toei Doga, adventure, 50 min., 4/10, Toei Doga, Toei Video.

Even tough guys have a tender heart. After a thousand misunderstandings and proud gestures wrongly interpreted, the rough Yoshimi decides to declare his love to the sweet Nagisa, but to do so, the entire motorcycle band "Shobaku," to which Yoshimi belongs, must be there. Thanks to an amazing pursuit of the train that she is on, Yoshimi finally expresses his feelings and discovers that they are shared.

1008 OAV

CHOJU KISHIN DANCOUGAR: GOD BLESS DANCOUGAR (*Dancougar, The Super Bestial Machine-God: God Bless Dancougar*), Ashi, robot, 80 min., 4/15, Toho. *Dancougar*.

One year after the combat against Muge Zobaldos, the Earth slowly rebuilds the areas destroyed by the war. The main characters spend their time as they always do: Shinobu rehearses for his upcoming concert, Sara works as a model and Ryo coaches the soldiers from the base. One day, Lora, Masato's beautiful girlfriend, has a premonition of a new threat in a dream. The four pilots will have to face a powerful robot that will explode in the middle of the city.

1009 OAV

SHIN CREAM LEMON WHITE SHADOW (*Cream Lemon New Series: White Shadow*) Soeishinsha, erotic, 25 min., 4/15, Fairy Dust.

After having had a crazy erotic dream, a beautiful gymnast, particularly skillful in the use of the ball and ribbon, decides to involve her boyfriend in an embarrassing sexual encounter.

1010 OAV

YOJU TOSHI (*The City of Monsters*), Madhouse, horror, 80 min., 4/25, Japan Home Video. *Wicked City*.

When organized crime transcends the threshold of reality and becomes an infernal power in the real sense of the word, then even the police must find help beyond the conventional. In order to fight against the demons in human form that infest the city with their corruption, a police detective seeks the help of a mysterious woman with an unknown past who has the power to make her nails grow as long as daggers and make her hair move like tentacles. The morale of the detective is really put to the test because of the uncertainty around the pattern of the demon attacks, and the incredible disguises of the demons themselves.

1011 OAV

SHIN CREAM LEMON MANINGYO (*Cream Lemon New Series: Magic Doll*), Soeishinsha, erotic, 25 min., 5/1, Fairy Dust.

1012 OAV

SHIN CREAM LEMON ETUDE YUKI NO KODO (*Cream Lemon New Series: Etude, Beat of Snow*), Soeishinsha, erotic, 25 min., 5/21, Fairy Dust.

The beautiful Yukari lives free of any constraints and her parents give her anything she wants. The young girl often stays home alone, but her strong will isn't enough to save her from the sexual violence that surrounds her.

1013 OAV

PROJECT AKO II DAI TOKUJIZAIBATSU NO INBO (*Project A-Ko II: the Conspiracy of the Rich Daitokuji*), APPP, science fiction, 50 min., 5/21, Soeishinsha. *Project A-ko 2: Plot Of The Daitokuji Financial Group.*

A-Ko and C-Ko were invited on board a spaceship while Teru Daitokuji, father of B-Ko, plots to take it over. In a story that involves the army, spies from various countries and governments, as well as aliens, A-Ko will do everything in her power to destroy the entire spaceship.

1014 OAV

CIRCUIT ANGEL KETSUI NO STARTING GRID (*The Circuit Angel: the Starting Gate*), Studio Unicorn, sport, 45 min., 5/21, TDK Core.

Sho who wants to become a famous motorcycle rider, injures Mariko's boyfriend during an encounter and offends Nagasa, the trainer to whom the young girl is very attached. Mariko decides to seek vengeance and challenges the opponent to a motorcycle race. With the help of Nagasa, the girl begins an intense training to win the race.

1015 OAV

BATTLE KAN (*id.*), Nikatsu Video, erotic, 30 min., 5/25, Fairy Dust. *Battle Can Can.*

1016 OAV

SHIN KABUKICHO STORY HANA NO ASUKAGUMI (*Kabukicho's New Story: Asuka's brilliant Group*), Toei Doga, adventure, 48 min., 6/12, Toei.

Asuka Kuraku is forced to face the arrogant Kurenai, a boy linked to a motorcycle gang that holds a strong grudge towards Asuka. When Asuka wins the encounter, the gang of the Onizoku Ladies confront him to avenge their companion, but the police stop them in time.

1017 OAV

CHOJIKU YOSAI MACROSS: FLASHBACK 2012 (*Macross The Superdimensional Fortress: Flashback 2012*), Tatsunoko, musical, 30 min., 6/21, Bandai.

Three years after the release of the movie *Ai Oboeteimasuka*, a 30 minute OAV is launched into the market, consecrating once and for all the phenomenal success of Lynn Minmay. The movie, edited like a video clip, contains the Chinese singer's most famous songs, mixed with scenes from the television series and the movie and with a few minutes of new animation created especially by Haruiko Mikimoto and Shoji Kawamori, in which the future destiny of the characters after the war is shown through flashbacks. Minmay, now in her thirties, continues her singing career while Hikaru continues his rise in the earthly military hierarchy but the most amazing destiny is the one of Misa Hayase, promoted to commanding officer of the Megaroad 01 spaceship, Kawamori's first project for *Macross* (nothing is ever thrown away!). The movie *Flashback 2012* also contains large sections made from the ending for the 1984 movie and a huge concert by Lynn Minmay. All the designs of this OAV have been collected in a beautiful book: *Chojiku Yosai Macross Gold Book.*

Project A-ko 2 ©1987 Soeishinsha/Final-Nishijima/ Pony. English version & package ©1993 Central Park Media Corporation. All Rights Reserved.

Battle Can Can ©1987 Nikkatsu Corporation. All Rights Reserved. English version released under license by Kitty.

Flash Back 2012 © Big West.

1018 OAV

SPACE FANTASIA NISENNICHIYA MONOGATARI (*Space Fantasy: the Story of the Two Thousand and One Nights*), Tokyo Movie Shinsha, science fiction, 58 min., 6/21, Victor Music.

In the year 2085, after having colonized space, the colonists set up a program to repopulate the human race: an ovule and a sample of sperm from the Robinsons are sent by spaceship to the planet Ozma. After 375 years, the spaceship lands, bringing the people born during the long trip, and life goes on calmly until a second spaceship lands on Ozma. The captain, a descendant of the Robinson family, seeks the help of the population to face an unforeseen lack of the human species in the rest of space. Taken from Yukinobu Hoshino's manga.

1019 OAV

CREAM LEMON SPECIAL DARK (*id.*), JHV, erotic, 47 min., 6/25, Fairy Dust.

1020 OAV

SENGOKU KITAN YOTODEN AGOKU NO SHO (*War Stories From the Legend of the Mysterious Sword: Act of Escape*), Minami Machi, adventure, 43 min., 6/26, Bugyosho Cic Picture Video. *Yotoden I.*

The story is set in 1582, in one of the darkest and most violent times of Japanese history, during the many alternating civil wars. The tragedy of the people, victims of the perfidious lords and the fights between samurais or ninjas, lose in importance in face of what is about to occur. Demons arise, made strong by the evil that lurks in the souls of Japanese people, and they foresee the creation of the kingdom of the dark. The only way to defeat them is to use the three blades of goodness: the dagger, the enchanted sword and the spade. The young Ayame from the Kasumi ninja clan possesses the first weapon, Sakon from the Hyuga family has the second one and Ryoma from the Hagakure clan, the third. United in the fight, they will defeat the demonic threat once and for all.

1021 OAV

BLACK MAGIC MARIO 66 (*id.*), Animate Film, science fiction, 48 min., 6/28, Bandai. *Black Magic M-66.*

The enterprising video reporter Sybel unexpectedly falls on what will become the scoop of a lifetime: following a plane crash, two deadly robots with female features have been lost in the woods. The army is frantically looking for them, trying to find them before anyone discovers their existence, or worse, before anyone is killed by them. After a violent encounter the M66 F6 model escapes, and rages out of control. Only a few people know that this model, following the orders given it as control test, is seeking Ferris, the granddaughter of the robot's creator, to kill her. A race against time begins where the reporters cross paths with the army, in a succession of difficulties and small conflicts. The OAV follows Masamune Shirow's manga.

1022 OAV

SHIN CREAM LEMON YUMEIRO BUNNY (*Cream Lemon New Series; Dreaming About Bunny*), Soeishinsha, erotic, 25 min., 7/10, Fairy Dust.

1023 OAV

TWD EXPRESS ROLLING TAKE OFF (*id.*), Gakken, science fiction, 55 min., 7/21, Shockiku Home Video.

Ken, Duke and Ivan work as space carriers with their astrocargo Slider 7. One day, Duke rescues a girl, Rina, who really an android created by count Godum who wants to use his robots for personal gain. Ken and his companions thus go the planet Light County, to shed light on the situation.

1024 OAV

ROBOT CARNIVAL (*id.*), APPP, fantastic, 90 min., 7/21, Victor. *Robot Carnival*.

Robot Carnival ©1987 A.P.P.P.
Package design ©1991 Streamline Pictures.

This is a movie in a few parts, divided as though for episodes of a television show. In the first, made by Katsuhiro Otomo and Atsuko Fukushima, we witness the destruction of a quiet village by the Robot Carnival, following a type of "Frankenstein's Monster" in a science fiction version by Koji Morimoto. The third episode by Hidetoshi Omori tells of the rescue, by a robot of his owner, the prisoner of mechanized troops. The fourth episode, by Yasuomi Umetsu, shows a reversal of the so-far similar plots — this time, it is the creator of a female robot who falls in love with his creation. After the *Starlight Angel* episode by Hiroyuki Kitazume, it is Hiroyuki Kitakubo's turn, with the strange fight between two nineteenth century inventors aboard robots built with the technology of that time. *Cloud*, by Mao Lambo, narrates in a dreamlike way the humanization of machines, the artistic techniques bringing the art closer to illustration than animation. In Takashi Nakamura's episode we see combat technology in action. The conclusion is also entrusted to Otomo and shows the epilogue of the opening episode, in which, at the place where Robot Carnival has been, a man finds a deadly musical box and unfortunately decides to keep it.

1025 OAV

MAPS SAMAYOERU DENSETSU NO SEIJINT ACHI (*Maps: the Shipwreck of the Legendary Aliens*), Gakken, science fiction, 53 min., 7/21, Nippon Columbia.

Gen, a college student, and his girlfriend Oshimi are kidnapped by the crew of the spaceship Lipumira. Twenty thousand years before, in fact, some aliens had hidden an ancient map on Earth and Gen has the precise directions to find it.

1026 OAV

KINDAN NO INOKU SHIROKU CRISTAL TRIANGLE (*The Prohibited Apocalypse: the Crystal Triangle*), Animate Film, science fiction, 80 min., 7/22, CBS Sony. *Crystal Triangle*.

Crystal Triangle ©1987 MOVIC / Sony Video Software International Corp. English version and package artwork ©1992 Central Park Media Corporation. All Rights Reserved

The search for the Urajukkai, a mythical book of prophecy, pushes Koichiro Jindai to travel the world. One day, Koichiro solves a puzzle cube that leads him to find the mirror of Yata, that can bring him to the ancient book. The young man seems to have fulfilled his dream when the U.S.S.R., the United States and a Buddhist monk intervene to find the book, provoking its destruction instead.

1027 OAV

MAJOKKO CLUB YUNINGUMI A KUKAN KARA NO ALIEN X (*The Four From the "Little Witches" Club: Alien X from the A Space*), Studio Pierrot, magic/science fiction, 45 min., 7/28, Bandai.

An alien race is about to launch an attack against the Earth: to face the threat, Yu, Mai, Pelsha and Yumi, each the main character of their own television show, reacquire their magical powers. Yumi transforms into Creamy, Mai turns into Emi, Pelshe becomes an adult and Yumi, with the help of the magic wand, creates the space costumes for the group. Together, the four witches succeed in destroying the aliens. All this however, doesn't happen in real life, but in a movie that the four are filming. Coming out of the movie studio, the four are attacked by a horrible monster but, without their magic powers, they have to run away.

1028 OAV

SHIN CREAM LEMON SUMMER WINDOW (*Cream Lemon New Series: a Window on Summer*), Soeishinsha, erotic, 25 min., 7/30, Fairy Dust.

Yo, a motorcycle rider, meets the beautiful Mina on a beach and he falls in love with her. After having spent a passionate night with Mina, the young man is extremely surprised when he discovers that the mysterious young girl has disappeared.

Hi no Tori: Yamato Hen © Tezuka Production / Kadokawa Shoten / Tohokushinsha.

1029 OAV

HI NO TORI YAMATO HEN (*The Bird of Fire: Yamato's Chapter*), Madhouse, historical, 48 min., 8/1, Cic Victor.

The Phoenix, the mythical bird who rises from its own ashes, is seen by people of all civilizations as a symbol of power and immortality, but no one has ever been able to capture it. When Oguma plays his flute, giving life to crystal melodies from ancient eras, the Phoenix comes close to him, inviting him to play some more. In exchange, the mythical bird, the creature that personifies the essence of life, gives the young man some of its blood, and he gains the chance to achieve immortality by drinking it.

1030 OAV

DEAD HEAT (*id.*), Nippon Sunrise, adventure, 29 min., 8/7, Cic Victor.

Japan, a country always ready to follow trends, is tempted at the beginning of the 21st century by the moto-robot races. The main character of the anime is in fact the class D pilot Makoto who, to raise his competition level, races against his rival Natsuo. Contrary to what usually happens in animated cartoons, Makoto doesn't succeed and is forced to abandon the race when his engine catches fire.

1031 OAV

PUTSUN MAKE LOVE OMIAI SCRAMBLE (*Suddenly Make Love Arranged Marriage Scramble*) Agent 21, erotic/humorous, 25 min., 8/14, Toei Video.

Through a matrimonial agency, Saori Hagigawa, a college student, is forced to meet with a skirt chasing casanova. The two are just about to end up in bed together when the clever girl is replaced by her boyfriend Yugi Sakazaki, skillfully dressed as a woman.

1032 OAV

TWILIGHT Q MEIKYU BUKKEN FILE 538 (*Twilight Q: the Case of the Labyrinth, File 538*), Studio Dean, adventure, 30 min., 8/28, Bandai.

For some time now, all the planes that fly over Tokyo have been mysteriously disappearing without a trace. A private investigator begins to investigate a strange couple that he considers guilty, but he can't find any proof.

1033 OAV

KIZUOIBITO ACT II OGON NO FUKUSHUSHA (*The Daredevil Act II: The Golden Avenger*), Madhouse, adventure, 45 min., 8/28, Bandai.

Keisuke Ibaraki, also known as "White Haired Demon Baraki," penetrates into the jungle with Yuko. Keisuke saves an old tribe leader during an attack by a puma, and the leader thanks him by informing him of the location of a treasure. After having found the treasure "Baraki" escapes with Peggy, a carpenter on the ship, thanks to Yuko's sacrifice.

1034 OAV

LILY CAT (*id.*), Studio Pierrot, adventure, 60 min., 9/1, Victor Music. *Lily-C.A.T.*

Seven investigators travel to L.A.O.3. planet aboard the Salude spaceship, unaware of the threat that is about to fall upon them. Certain characters actually die because of a virus brought on the spaceship by Lily, the cat of the computer operator.

1035 OAV

PANTS NO ANA (*The Hole in the Underwear*), AIC, erotic, 9/5, Gakken.

This OAV was based on a compilation of experiences lived by readers of the "Bombi" magazine. *Yoiko no Nikki* (Diary of a Good Boy), *Tesina no Ossan* (The Boor of the Conjuring Trip), *Kaguashiki First Kiss* (First Kiss Fragrances), *Sayonara wa Shiroi Namida ni Nosete* (GoodBye With White Tears), *Meniko no Fuko* (The Unlucky Beniko), *Mambo de Ganbo* (id.) and *Occult no Shojotachi* (The Occult Girls) make up this OAV.

1036 OAV

PUTSUN MAKE LOVE VOLUME II JOSHIBU SENNYU! GUCCHON FOCUS (*The Funny Loves Vol. II: Infiltration in the All Girl Boarding School! Sexual Objective*), Agent 21, erotic/humor, 25 min., 9/11, Toei Video.

Yuji decides to dress up as a girl to photograph naked girls. He secretly enters the all girl school, but he is caught by Akimoto, a teacher, the camera breaks and the film is exposed, rendering the entire adventure in vain.

1037 OAV

BUBBLEGUM CRISIS II: BORN TO KILL (*id.*), AIC/ARTMIC, science fiction/adventure, 30 min., 9/5, Toshiba Emi. *Bubblegum Crisis 2: Born To Kill.*

This time around, the Knight Sabers find themselves confronting some of the most powerful armies of the Buma organization. The Super Boomer is the most advanced robot ever built, but to operate it, the criminals need Cynthia, an android girl, whose body lies at the bottom of the sea of the Mega Tokyo Bay in a black metal container.

1038 OAV

TATAKAE!! ICZER ONE TOKUBETSU HEN (*Fight Iczer I!! Special Chapter*), AIC, science fiction, 100 min., 9/25, Kubo Shoten. *The Complete Iczer-One.*

Lily C.A.T. ©1987 Victor Music Co., Ltd.
Package design ©1994 Streamline Enterprises,
Inc. All Rights Reserved

Bubblegum Crisis ©1987 by Artmic, Inc &
Youmex, Inc. English version ©1991 by
AnimEigo, Inc. All Rights Reserved.

Dangaio ©1990 A.I.C. / Emotion. Released by U.S. Renditions.

Neo-Tokyo ©1986 Haruki Kadokawa Films, Inc. All Rights Reserved. Package Design HOW Studios ©1993 Streamline Enterprises, Inc.

This is a collection on one videotape of the already shown episodes of the story of Iczer One, released theoretically for the joy of the fans, but mostly for the profits of the production firm. The OAV also presents the making of the series, including appearances by the singer who worked on the soundtrack.

1039 OAV

MAHO NO YOSEI PELSHA (*Pelsha the Fairy of Magic*), Studio Pierrot, magic, 45 min., 9/25, Pierrot Project.

The television adventures of Pelsha are collected in this OAV, that also features new animated scenes based on the original songs and the soundtrack with new music videos.

1040 OAV

HAJA TAISEI DANGAIO (*Great-Planet Evil-Destroyer Dangaio*), AIC, science fiction, 45 min., 9/28, Bandai. *Dangaio 1.*

Mia Alis, Pai Thunder, Lamba Nom and Roll Kulan, all possessing extraordinary powers, are kidnapped by the cynical professor Tarsan to be sold as weapons. The four girls soon rebel against their kidnapper and the evil chief of the Galimos pirates. In homage to the glorious robots of the 70s the fighters can unite, giving life to the powerful Dangaio, and the team wins the fight against the enemy robot Blood D1, piloted by Gill Berg. The splendid animated characterization is by Toshihiro Hirano.

1041 OAV

TO-Y (*id.*), Studio Gallopp, soap opera, 60 min., 10/1, Shogakudan/CBS Sony.

During a concert Toy, leader of the musical group Gasp, gives a powerful insult to Yoji Aikawa a popular singer who came to the show to look for a new musician for his group. Deeply affected by what happened, the man tries to prevent Gasp from playing at the next concert.

1042 OAV

MEIKYU MONOGATARI (*Labyrinth Tales*, a.k.a. *Manie Manie*), Project Team Argos, adventure, 50 min., 10/10, Kadokawa Shoten. *Neo-Tokyo.*

Little Sachi, forced to stay home alone during evenings, always invents new games to pass the time. Playing hide and seek with a cat, the little girl ends up with the cat in the world of mirrors in which anything can happen. A friendly Pierrot and Sachi, invited by her, go to an amusement park. The character design is by Taro Rin.

1043 OAV

CREAM LEMON MEI BAMEN SOTSUGYO ALBUM (*Cream Lemon: Year Book*), Soeishinsha, erotic, 60 min., 10/21, Fairy Dust.

1044 OAV

THE SAMURAI (*id.*), Suna Kobo, soap opera, 45 min., 11/1, CBS Sony.

Samurai stories are here placed in a modern setting. In fact, the main character, Takashi Chimatsuri, is a young fighter of our days, who possesses a powerful sword that was captured by his father during a duel against the skillful Kagemaru Akari. One day, the young man runs into the twins Toki and Kagedi Akari, who returned to regain the sword and to avenge the death of their father. The character designs are by Yamazaki Kazuo.

1045 OAV

DEVILMAN TANJO HEN (*Devilman: The Genesis*), O Prod., horror, 51 min., 11/1, Kodansha King Record. *Devilman Vol. 1: The Birth*.

In this first OAV the story is told once more of the demon young man to whom an entire animated series was dedicated, produced by Toei. This time the plot and designs are more faithful to Go Nagai's original manga. Akira, a good and sensible young man, meets Ryo, an ambiguous individual who warns him about the Earth's future: a population of demons is about to come out of hiding to invade the world.

Ryo then proposes an experiment to Akira: they must both put on a gigantic mask that, according to Ryo, allows the bearer to transform into a demon. Only like this, fighting the infernal beings with their own weapons, will they have the ability to defeat them. Nothing happens when they try the mask, so the two young men go to a disco in the hope of awaking the demons inside them. Only Akira, trying to save Ryo when he is attacked by people already possessed by demons, changes into Devilman, a hairy and beastlike being with bat wings who, with unthinkable violence, massacres the infernal creatures. The direction is entrusted to Tsutomu Ida, while the character designs are by Kazuo Komatsubara. The sequel of this first episode launched on February 25, 1990, in what will be the central chapter of a foreseen trilogy.

Devilman ©1987/1995 Dynamic Planning / Kodansha / Bandai Visual. Package design & summary ©2000 Manga Entertainment, Inc. Devilman is a registered trademark of Go Nagai and Dynamic Planning.

1046 OAV

X DENSHA DEIKO (*We Leave With the X Train*), Argos, adventure, 50 min., 11/6, Konami Kogyo.

Toru Nishihara is a young employee of a publicity firm. One day, at the subway station, he sees a ghost train pass by. While he witnesses this in astonishment, someone drags him away and informs him of the train's next appearance, in the province of Shizuoka. The army is also present and begins a battle with a horde of ghosts. After the defeat of the army the only hope is Toru, who gets ready to exterminate the ghosts once and for all by himself.

1047 OAV

KAZE TO KI NO UTA SEINARU KANA (*The Poem of the Wind and the Trees: Sanctus*), Konami Kogyo/Herald, drama, 60 min., 11/6, Shogakukan.

It is the beginning of a new school year in an all boys school in England at the end of the 1800s. Young Serge is put in the same room as Gilbert, a handsome blond boy who in no way tries to hide his homosexual tendencies. Serge's initial discomfort soon changes into love even if their relationship is often put to the trial, because of Gilbert's unfaithfulness and Serge's scruples. The OAV presents an animated version of the first three volumes of Keigo Takemiya's manga for girls. The story boards are designed with taste and skill by Yasuhiko Yoshikazu.

1048 OAV

SHONAN BAKUSOZOKU III JUONSU NO KIZUNA (*The Hooligans of Shonan III: the Ten Ounce Link*), Toei Doga, adventure, 52 min., 11/13, Toei Video.

Intro
-1962
1963
1964
1965
1966
1967
1968
1969
1970
1971
1972
1973
1974
1975
1976
1977
1978
1979
1980
1981
1982
1983
1984
1985
1986
1987
1988
Index

Even tough motorcycle riders possess hidden qualities, showing that they too have a heart and brains. Konda, once the arch enemy of the Shobaku gang, decides to take up boxing to prove to himself and to the world that he can face an opponent without the use of tricks, and also to please his old trainer who is about to retire.

1049 OAV

GALL FORCE II: DESTRUCTION (*Id.*), Animation/Artmic/AIC, science fiction, 50 min., 11/21, CBS Sony. *Gall Force 2: Destruction*.

Lufy, the Solnoid fighter from the Starleaf crew, is found in a state of suspended animation by the members of the Lorelei spaceship, including Shildy and Spea, who try to reanimate her. The blond fighter discovers that the major part of the Solnoid troops are now cyborgs, and, finding a girl identical to Catty from the Starleaf, she learns that there are many others like her. The young woman explains to Lufy that she is one of the many copies of Catty Nebulart, commander of the Elite Intelligence Agency, who secretly works for the Plan of Unification of the Species. The present mission consists of reaching the ninth solar system, where it seems that the Plan has had a partial success. In that quadrant space, in fact, a new species has been generated. The young man born of Patty through the Contact Point and Rumy, the youngest girl of the former crew of the Starleaf, are slowly repopulating the planet. A threatening security system called Damia, however, threatens the entire group of planets that form the ninth solar system.

1050 OAV

TAIMAN BLUES SHIMIZU NAOTO HEN (*Lazy Blues: Naoto Shimizu's Chapter*), Premier International, soap opera, 30 min.,11/25, Keibunsha.

Naoto Shimizu, a member of the MND motorcycle gang wins a fight against Yokota, chief of the Laku rival gang. Thus begins a rivalry between the two for the control of the MND gang.

1051 OAV

RELIC ARMOUR LEGACIAN (*id.*), Atrie Giga, science fiction, 50 min., 11/28, Bandai.

The inhabitants of the planet Libatia, where Arushya Grace, the main character, lives, are mentally controlled by the evil Daats. Professor Grace, however, having discovered the threat, slightly modifies the robot legaciam and because of this, she is kidnapped by the enemy. Arushya escapes with the powerful fighting device, but soon runs out of gas. She is soon rescued by her friends Dorothy and Bric, and by Zeno Mosesti, an inhabitant of Saribari.

1052 OAV

MAKYO GAIDEN LE DEUS (*The Legend of the Demon's Border: Le Deus*), Ashi, science fiction, 48 min., 12/1, Toho Video. [*Deus*].

Riot is searching for the Eye of Zaren, the key to the "lido," a mineral capable of releasing unlimited energy. Spika and Seneka leave on the mission with Riot, and during the trip, the beautiful Yuta joins them. She helps her companions find the mysterious "lido." The Demusta group is also very interested in the mineral, and it kidnaps Yuta to obtain it. Riot, Spika and Seneka, piloting the robot Le Deus, prepare to attack the enemy.

1053 OAV

BUBBLEGUM CRISIS III: BLOW UP (*id.*), AIC, science fiction, adventure, 30 min., 12/5, Toshiba Emi. *Bubblegum Crisis 3: Blow Up.*

The criminal organization Genom orchestrates a plan to exploit the area where Celia and Priss live. In the meantime, Masson discovers that Celia, daughter of the deceased doctor Stingray is a member of the Knight Sabers. The young woman thus goes to the tower of Genom to face Masson and avenge the death of her father.

1054 OAV

BOKU NO OLDIES WA ALL COLOR (*My Old Songs Are All in Color*), Tatsunoko, soap opera, 27 min., 12/10, Nippon Columbia.

1055 OAV

DAIMAJU GEKITO HAGANE NO ONI (*The Violent Encounter of the Steel Demons*), AIC, robot/horror, 60 min., 12/10, Tokuma Shoten.

Takuya and Haruka, scientists living on a small island, risk their lives attempting to re-cover a sample of an unidentified object generated by the explosion caused by the tests of a larger weapon. After three years of study, Hakura discovers that some particles that are only found on the island are capable of opening dimensional doors. When Takuya tries to find out more, however, an entity comes from another dimension and possesses Haruka, transforming him into the ferocious and gigantic biomechanical robot Doki. To save his friend and colleague from the monstrous being, and the world from his catastrophic deeds, Takuya decides to let himself be possessed by the Absolute Power and also becomes a monstrous and unstoppable demon.

1056 OAV

SHINMA JINDEN BATTLE ROYAL HIGH SCHOOL (*True-Magic God-Legend : Battle Royal High School*), Dast, horror, 60 min., 12/10, Tokuma Japan. *Battle Royal High School.*

Byodo the magician controls the mind of the young karate-ka Riky Hyodo from another planet. Zankan, a space inspector, and the young Yuki Toshihiro discover that fact and go to try to help him, but Yuki becomes the instrument of Kain, a rival of Byodo. The face-off sees Hyodo victorious and with him, Byodo.

1057 OAV

SHORI TOSHU (*The Winning Pitcher*), Toei Doga, sport, 72 min., 12/11, Toei Video.

Hoshi, a baseball coach, gives a spot to Katsumi, a member of a school baseball team that won the summer tournament. Having become a professional, the young man begins a glorious ascension as a pitcher. The following year, Hoshi becomes president of the team and he and his players win the national championship.

1058 OAV

PUTSUN MAKE LOVE VOL. III ACHI WO! KOCHI MO! PUTSUN SANKARU KANKEI (*The Funny Loves Vol. III: Here and There! Triangular Relationships*), Agent 21, erotic/humor, 25 min., 12/11, Toei Video.

Bubblegum Crisis ©1987 by Artmic, Inc & Youmex, Inc. English version ©1991 by AnimEigo, Inc. All Rights Reserved.

Battle Royal High School ©1987 Tokoma Japan Communications Co., Ltd. Licensed to AnimEigo, Inc. by Tokoma Japan Communications Co., Ltd. All Rights Reserved.

Intro
-1962
1963
1964
1965
1966
1967
1968
1969
1970
1971
1972
1973
1974
1975
1976
1977
1978
1979
1980
1981
1982
1983
1984
1985
1986
1987
1988
Index

MADOX-01 © Pony Canyon, Inc. English version ©1995 AnimEigo, Inc. All Rights Reserved.

Junk Boy © Yasuyuki Kunitomo / Futabasha Co. • Victor Entert., Inc. English version & Package ©1996 Manga Entertainment, Inc. All Rights Reserved.

After having experienced the theft of a compromising film, Yuji rushes to the house of her teacher Akimoto to recover it. The beautiful Saori, however, wrongly interprets the gesture of her companion and, fearing that he will betray her, she decides to throw herself into the arms of her ex-boyfriend.

1059 OAV

GOOD MORNING ALTHEA (*id.*), Animate Film, science fiction, 50 min., 12/16, Bandai.

During the war between the Earth army and the people of Stemma, the Automaton armor built by the humans to defend themselves against the enemy is lost. Althea, a girl from Stemma, tells the story of the armor to Garolii and Nikolai, two surviving earthlings, and together they decide to look for it to destroy it.

1060 OAV

METAL SKIN PANIC MADOX 01 (*id.*), AIC, science fiction, 50 min., 12/16, Pony Canyon. *Madox-01: Metal Skin Panic.*

Madox, an amazing new weapon, is developed to replace the ancient armored tanks, but the representatives of the Kirugoa group are strongly opposed to its use. All traces of the Madox are lost until Koji finds it and decides to bring it home. But when Koji goes out to meet his girlfriend Shori, Kirugoa's men begin the attacks aimed at recovering the weapon.

1061 OAV

JUNK BOY (*id.*), Madhouse, erotic, 52 min., 12/16, Victor MP. *Junk Boy.*

Ryohe Yamazaki works in the publishing firm that edits the pornographic magazine "Potato Boy." One day, Aki Sawamoto, a girl he had met at a Turkish Bath and who had offended him by telling him that he didn't know how to make love, comes to the firm. Ryohe convinces her he is very capable, but she seems to be more interested in the editor in chief Yuki Oda.

1062 OAV

KIZUOIBITO ACT III HAKUKA TSUKI (*The Daredevil Act III: the Devil With the White Hair*), Madhouse, adventure, 30 min., 12/16, Bandai.

GPX is an organization that sells pornographic videos based on famous people. Peggy, taken hostage, is forced to perform in erotic scenes with Keisuke. After an initial moment of confusion, the two try to escape.

1063 OAV

SENGOKU KITAN YOTODEN II KIKOKU NOSHO (*Stories of War From the Legend of the Mysterious Sword: Act of the Satanic Roar*), Minami Machi, adventure, 40 min., 12/18, Bugyosho Cic Victor. *Yotoden II.*

1064 OAV

HI NO TORI UCHU HEN (*The Bird of Fire: Space Chapter*), Madhouse, science fiction, 48 min., 12/21, Cic Victor.

Yotoden ©1988 JVC. English version and package ©1997 Central Park Media Corporation. All Rights Reserved

1065 OAV

DIRTY PAIR I (*id.*), Nippon Sunrise, science fiction, 50 min., 12/21, Vap Video. *Dirty Pair Original 1.*

Some prisoners serving a life sentence have started a rebellion on the planet Karos and Yuri and Kei are trying to save the director of the prison, who has been taken hostage. Once freed, to avenge himself, the director enters the control room to kill the prisoners with weapons and poison gas. The Dirty Pair are kept out by the locked door, but they soon overcome the obstacle, breaking down the door with Yuri's powerful ring. They enter and stop the director from killing the prisoners, finally restoring order.

The second episode presented on the videotape is set on Halloween night, and sees Yuri and Kei on a mission to recuperate the plan of the roboticized weapons, taken from the experimental center. After having made an emergency landing in the city of Eleonoa, involuntarily awakening powerful robots, the girls encounter a gang of kidnappers who had infiltrated the city. The fight ended, Yuri and Kei find themselves involved in a new battle, this time against the robots.

1066 OAV

KATTE NI SHIRO KUMA (*Do What You Want, Little Bear Shiro*), AIC/Artmic, animal, 30 min., 12/21, CBS Sony.

Shiro is a clumsy and absentminded white bear that lives with his mother and brother Daichan. The family decides to visit a modern city with Shiro's friend Uripo, but they soon come back when they discover that humans' meals are not as appetizing as those the bears are used to.

1067 OAV

SHIN CREAM LEMON FUTARI NO HEART BREAK LIVE (*Cream Lemon New Series: Two Broken Hearts*), Soeishinsha, erotic, 25 min., 12/26, Fairy Dust.

Ruri is in love with Koji, who in turn has a crush on the famous singer Saito Konami. When Ruri takes possession of a magical power given to her by some aliens, she can transform herself into her rival and thus win Koji over. Their relationship could last, if it wasn't for the fact that they argue more often than not.

Original Dirty Pair © Takachiho & Studio Nue • Sunrise. Released in North America by A.D.V. Films. Packaging design ©1998 A.D. Vision, Inc.

CHAPTER TWENTY SEVEN: 1988

Directly from Katsuhiro Otomo's manga came the feature film *Akira*, designed and released even before the manga reached its conclusion. The animation and detailed designs were very well done, but it was met with disappointment from Japanese fans, who saw the movie as too synthetic compared to the original manga. Fortunately for Kodansha and for Otomo, *Akira* was still successful, reaching cult status in some areas. It was as popular abroad as at home, perhaps even more so, and some American producers expressed interest in a live-action adaptation.

The year 1988 is the year in which audiences saw the conclusion of the long-running series *Urusei Yatsura*. In February the feature film *Last Movie Boy Meets Girl* was released, in which the sentimental adventures of the beautiful alien and of the lunatic earth-

ling finally found a happy ending. The public, glad to see the characters find their dreams, found their joy mixed with sadness at the end of the show that had been so popular so so long. Lum's fan club convinced the producers to come out with two more stories for *Urusei Yatsura*, taken from the original comic strip, that were chosen by members of the fan club to be part of a summer special: *Ikari no Sharbet* and *Nagisa no fiancés* were the titles given to the short pieces. Around the same time as the release of *Boy Meets Girl*, Takahashi's body of work spawned another important film: *Maison Ikkoku Last Movie*, the conclusion of another fascinating and saccharinely sentimental story, in which Kyoko and Godai finally get married.

In April the great author Hayao Miyazaki gave another sweet and innocent film to his countless fans, the magical *Tonari no Totoro*. The film had that "Miyazaki touch", that dreamlike and magical atmosphere which lends all his works a touch of whimsy. The "magical girl" stories were more popular than ever, with the releases of *Esper Mami*, *Himitsu no Akkochan* — a remake of the 1969 series — and finally, a 50 minute OAV called *Harbour Light monogatari Fashion Lala Yori*.

Following the immense success earned by the television series *Saint Seiya*, begun in 1986, two movies were released in march and July, intended for the big screen: *Kamigami no atsuki tatakai* and *Shinku no shonen densetsu*. Both featured stories set in different times and places than the series, turning the same base concept into independent stories. Another great release, not from Toei Doga this time but from Nippon Sunrise, came out in April. Riding on the waves of the success enjoyed by 1987's *City Hunter*, a sequel was released, called *City Hunter II*. The show disappointed, however, placing much more emphasis on the slapstick comedy than on the bittersweet relationship between the main characters which so delicately marked the last episodes of the first series.

Two OAVs, both taken from Masamune Shirow's manga, were produced by AIC/Bandai and for Agent 21/Toshiba Eizo Soft, respectively. *Appleseed* and *Dominion* became more popular abroad than at home, following the American publication of the manga by Eclipse. The first OAV was limited to one single release while the second, even though less interesting, came out in two acts.

The home video market continued to grow, saw a new release in 1988 that was destined for enormous success. *Kido keisatsu Patlabor* was released in a set of five OAVs in 1988, making it a true miniseries, with its 30-minute episodes and arcing plotline. The twist that placed *Patlabor* apart from other robot stories to date was the vision of the future it presented: the robots are seen as mere mechanisms at the service of public order, within a real and true urban police team. This kind of utopian future saw machines as a tool in the hands of justice.

1068 FILM
GINGA HEIYU DENSETSU WAGAYUKU WA HOSHI NO OUMI (*The Legend of the Heroes From the Galaxy: Towards the Ocean of Stars*), Madhouse, science fiction, 59 min., 2/6.

Reinhart Von Musel, the youngest captain in the Galactic Empire, is a skillful and courageous commander who has earned the respect of his crew. In the surroundings of the imperial army, however, someone like him is subject to envy from his peers and superiors. In fact, during the voyage to the fortress of Izerloan, Reinhart is faced with an assassination attempt. Yan Wang-Lee is another very young captain in the Alliance army of the Free Planets who must deal with a group of officers older than him. This science-fiction story sees the war between the two factions grow and threaten to bring down an entire sector of space.

1069 FILM

URUSEI YATSURA: KANKETSU HEN (*Those Obnoxious Aliens, Last Movie: Boy Meets Girl*), Magic Bus, science fiction, 85 min., 2/6. *Urusei Yatsura: Final Chapter*.

When Lamu returns to Uru to find her family, a bad surprise awaits her. Seeing her, her grandfather remembers a pact made on the planet of mushrooms in which he promised to give his granddaughter to Hiji's grandson, a man who saved his life. The handsome Rupa thus goes to Earth to marry Lamu. When the alien princess refuses to follow him, he gives her a ring that makes her lose her powers. Rupa kidnaps Lamu under Ataru's horrified eyes, and he, along with Mendo, Oyuki, Benten, Ran and Rei, tries to rescue her. Carla soon joins them as well. In love with Rupa, she naturally doesn't appreciate the two tying the knot. The group splits up and while Ataru follows Carla, the rest of the gang is captured by Hiji's men who create a doll with Lamu's features in order to fool them.

Urusei Yatsura © Kitty Films. English version © AnimEigo. Licensed to AnimEigo by Compass. All Rights Reserved

The wedding ceremony is interrupted, but Rupa substitutes the fake Lamu for the real one, and the doll declares her love for Rupa in front of an astonished Ataru. A gun shot fired by Carla opens the trap door of the room where the real Lamu is being held prisoner, and she runs to her "little sweetheart." Not knowing about the substitution, Ataru pretends to be in love with Carla and leaves for Earth with her. The two unfortunately bring back mushrooms that grow to incredible sizes and invade the planet. Lamu proposes a pact to the earthlings: the Earth will be saved only if Ataru can catch her and grab her horns, as he did in the first episode. In the meantime, Rupa and Carla finally talk and discover that they are in love with each other. Ataru, in a final and desperate attempt, throws himself against Lamu to hold her against her will. The alien realizes that Ataru has always loved her, and she makes peace with him.

1070 FILM

MAISON IKKOKU LAST MOVIE (*id.*), Kitty, soap opera, 70 min., 2/6.

Before her wedding, Kyoko decides to pay a last homage to the tomb of her deceased husband Soichiro and runs into Godai, who wants to ask for a symbolic consent for the big leap. It's difficult for him to compete with the ghost of the man that Kyoko will always have in her heart, but Godai is very much in love and he doesn't give up. The day of the wedding, the two wear elegant kimonos and after the fateful "yes" they party with their friends who are later joined by tennis master Mitaka and expecting wife Asuna. Kyoko and Godai decide to spend their wedding night at the Ikkoku boarding house, to leave later on their romantic honeymoon. The scene then moves to a few years later, to show the ending of the story. Kozue also gets married, while Asuna, after having given birth to beautiful twins, is already expecting her third child. The two main characters now have a baby girl and Akemi, having received a serious proposal from his employer, decides to settle down. The only one who stays alone is the sweet Ibuki who, having had to give up on Godai, prefers loneliness to other men.

1071 FILM

DORAEMON: NOBITA NO PARALLEL SAIYUKI (*Doraemon: Nobita's Version of Saiyuki*), Shin'ei Doga, comedy, 90 min., 3/12.

Doraemon and his friends create a comedic remake of the famous *Saiyuki*, playing the main characters of the famous fable of the Stone Monkey.

1072 FILM

ESPER MAMI HOSHIZORA NO DANCING DOLL (*Esper Mami: the Ballerina Doll in the Starlit Sky*), Shin'ei Doga, science fiction, 40 min., 3/12.

1073 FILM

ULTRA B BLACK HOLE KARA NO DOKUSAISHA B.B. (*Ultra B: the Dictator From the Black Hole*), Shien'ei Doga, humor, 20 min., 3/13.

1074 FILM

KIDO SENSHI "NU" GUNDAM GYAKUSHU NO CHAR (*Mobile Suit "Nu" Gundam: Char's Counter Attack*), Nippon Sunrise, science fiction, 120 min., 3/12.

In the Universal Century 0093, Char Aznable is head of Neo Jion and is determined to obtain independence for all the people born in the colonies. To reach his goals, he warns the Earth government that the colonies are planning to attack the Earth bombarding it with asteroids. The AEUG (Anti Earth Union Government), rejecting the treaty conditions of Jion, prepares for an inevitable war. Aboard the spaceship Lars Kailum, thirty year-old Amuro Rey is ready to stop Char, piloting a new prototype of Gundam named RX-93 "Nu" Gundam.

1075 FILM

SAINT SEIYA KAMIGAMI NO ASTUKI TATAKAI (*Saint Seiya: The Ardent Divine Encounter*), Toei Doga, fantasy, 46 min., 3/12.

Hyoga, the saint from the constellation of the Swan, rescues a man who is being attacked by mysterious warriors from the polar glaciers. Before he dies, the man warns him: the gods of Asgard are preparing for a confrontation. Hyoga is then attacked as well. Meanwhile, in Tokyo, Saori and the Bronze Saints are preoccupied because they haven't heard from Hyoga, and they go to Asgard to try to find out where he had gone. They are welcomed with high honors by Dolvar, High Priest of Odin, who swears he hasn't seen their friend, but invites them to remain his guests as long as they want. Only the young Freij and his sister Freija show sincere friendship to the Bronze Saints, helping them to find a trace of the presence of Hyoga at the pole, his helmet completely destroyed and hidden amidst the glaciers.

In the meantime, in the palace of the High Priest, an animated discussion is taking place. Freij is strongly against Dolvar's plans for conquest. The evil one wants to capture Saori and subject the world to his will. The discussion gets worse and to prevent any hinderance to his plans, the high priest has the young man put in jail. Saori, sure that Hyoga is in Asgard, goes to the high priest's palace to openly confront him, but Dolvar easily defeats her and, having put her in a trance, he imprisons her in the ship at the feet of the god Odin. This is just the beginning of the battle to save both Saori and the world. During the fight

Midgard, the only masked God Warrior, reveals his true identity — it is, in fact, Hyoga, who is suffering from memory loss. As usual, the final encounter is between Seiya and the head of the enemies, the evil Dolvar. Thanks to the golden armor of the Sagittarius and to the sacrifice of Freij, who freed himself from prison just in time to save Saori, victory belongs once again to the Bronze Saints.

1076 FILM

BIKKURIMAN (*id.*), Toei Doga, humor, 25 min., 3/12.

1077 FILM

HARE TOKIDOKI BUTA (*Serene Partially Pig*), O. Prod., humor, 72 min., 3/12.

1078 FILM

CHIISANA PINGUIN LOLO NO BOKEN (*The Adventures Of Lolo, The Little Penguin*), Life Work, classic, 80 min., 3/12.

1079 FILM

TONARI NO TOTORO (*My Neighbor Totoro*), Tokuma Shoten for Toho, fantastic, 75 min., 4/16. *My Neighbor Totoro*.

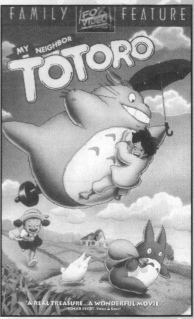

My Neighbor Totoro © Nibariki • Tokuma Shoten. English version released by Fox Video.

Produced by Toru Hara, who lent his expertise to the previous *Nausicaa* and *Laputa*, with a soundtrack by Jo Hisaichi, the movie is set in a warm month of May some thirty years ago. The little Satsuki and Mei are returning home with their father. A mysterious acorn falls on the roof, catching Mei's attention, and the young girl goes outside to discover a strange creature. The girls confide in their nice grandmother, who informs them of the existence of a sweet and shy spirit Susuwatari, visible only to the small children. The characters are involved in a number strange events but it isn't until the first day of school that Mei, thanks to her acute vision, sees the little spirit again. She decides to follow him, and she is soon face to face with Totoro, another spirit identical to the first, but a lot bigger. The girl falls asleep next to her new friend but when she is suddenly awakened by her sister, Totoro has disappeared. Days go by and Satsuki also gets to know the spirits (who have now become three) and who become the inseparable and adventurous companions of the little girls. *Tonari no Totoro* is a movie that is fascinating in its simplicity, reminding adults of their long-lost youth and that stimulates the small ones to discover their own world of fantasy. The movie is a new success for Hayao Miyazaki.

1080 FILM

HOTARU NO HAKA (*Hotaru's Tomb*), Toho, war, 85 min., 4/16. *Grave Of The Fireflies*.

Grave Of The Fireflies ©1988 Akiyuki Nosaka / Shinchosha Co. English version & packaging ©1992, 1998 Central Park Media Corporation. All Rights Reserved

The American B-29s bomb Japan and during a raid, young Seita and his little sister Setsuko are separated from their mother. Their long search ends dramatically and tragically, when the young boy finds his mother burnt to death in a school that served as a refuge, and prefers to hide the truth from his sister. They both seek the help of some relatives who remain indifferent to their needs, and so the siblings decide to move to a cavern near the river. After some time, Seita, unable to find food for his sister, ends up stealing. Taken from a novel by Ayuki Nosaka, the movie, produced by Akira Hara, shows the horrors of war, in part due to the screenplay by Isao Takahata, who is also director. The animation is by Yoshifumi Kondo, the music is by Michio Mamiya and the artistic direction by Fumio Yamamoto.

1081 FILM

TOSHI RAMEN MAN (*Ramen Man, the Fighter*), Toei Doga, Humor, 25 min., 7/9.

1082 FILM

BIKKURIMAN MUEN ZONE NO HIHO (*Bikkuriman: the Secret Treasure of the Abandoned Zone*), Toei Doga, humor, 25 min., 7/9.

1083 FILM

DRAGONBALL MAKAFUSHIGI DAI BOKEN (*Dragonball: the Marvelous Magical Adventure*), Toei Doga, adventure, 46 min., 7/9.

1084 FILM

AKIRA (*id.*), Tokyo Movie Shinsha for Kodansha, science fiction, 124 min., 7/16. *Akira.*

In the year 2030, after the third World War, mysterious preparations are taking place in the area of Neo Tokyo, that will soon be hosting the next Olympic Games. Behind these seemingly innocent preparations, however, is hidden a vast military organization that studies the possibilities of certain children possessing exceptional ESP powers. Amongst these children are Takashi, Masaru, Kyoko and the very powerful Akira, placed in hibernation and "stored" hundreds of meters underground for fear of his uncontrollable powers. The interference of certain young hooligans, headed by the arrogant Kaneda, unleashes a horde of catastrophic events due in part to the destructive fury of Tetsuo, Kaneda's childhood friend who, having discovered his own strange psychic powers, searches for Akira. In the meantime, Kay, who together with her brother Ryu is part of a resistance operation against the super powerful military, tries to discover the mysteries of the secret base and the little mutants. Akira's awakening is inevitable but, incapable of controlling his energy, the little one unleashes a series of events that culminate in a cataclysm of biblical proportions: Akira drags down with him all the mutants whose energy is scattered across the universe. Taken from Katsuhiro Otomo's manga, this is the most expensive and considered the best feature film of the anime library, and offers a unique wealth of special effects, animation and innovation.

Akira ©1989, 1993 Akira Commitee. English version released by Streamline Pictures.

1085 FILM

RYUKO SHIROI HATA NO SHOJO (*Ryuko: the Girl With the White Flag*), Magic Bus, adventure, 80 min., 7/21.

1086 FILM

SAINT SEIYA SHINKU NO SHONEN DENSETSU (*Saint Seiya: the Legend of the Scarlet Saints*), Toei Doga, fantasy, 75 min., 7/23.

The handsome Abel of Phoebos, reincarnation of the god Apollo, sweet-talks Saori into joining him. The Bronze Saints, surprised and distraught by the behavior of their goddess, attempt to stop her with all their might, but the peremptory orders of Saori and the interventions of the Phoebos Saints, faithful to Apollo, render all their efforts in vain. The Saints meet together to try to come up with a plan, but only Seiya still believes in Saori's innocence. Meanwhile, Shiryu goes to Roshi, the master of the five points, and Roshi warns the young Saint that Abel is evil, and has plans to brainwash Saori and rule in her place.

In the meantime, in Greece, the young goddess falls more and more under Abel's charm, but her magical scepter, the symbol of Athena, begins to glow and sends blots of flame towards Abel, marking him as evil. Having been found out, Abel drops his pretense and hits Saori, trying to take what he wants by force. The Cosmos is informed by the Saints, who set out for Apollo's temple. Abel gathers his allies as well, calling in Aphrodite, Camus, Shura, Saga and Death Mask. In the fight, Seiya finds himself protecting Saga, who puts him in the fight only to help him discover his seventh sense, the expression of his full potential. Uniting their powers and wearing the gold armor of the Sagittarius, Aquarius and the Libra, respectively, Seiya, Hyoga and Shiryu finally rescue Saori from the Ade.

1087 FILM
SAKIGAKE!! OTOKO JUKU (*Make Juku get a Move On!!*), Toei Doga, adventure, 75 min., 7/23.

1088 FILM
URUSEI YATSURA NAGISA NO FIANCES (*Those Obnoxious Aliens: Fiancés on the Beach*), Kitty Film, science fiction, 30 min., 8/8. *Urusei Yatsura OVA 5: Nagisa's Fiancé.*

Lamu, Ataru, Mindo and Shinobu visit Ryunosuke's family, who have opened an inn on a little island inhabited by a family of ghosts. Ryunosuke's father has befriended the head of the ghost family, and the two have arranged a marriage between their children. Ryunosuke, a young girl forced by her father to live as a boy, has been promised to the young Nagisa, who, for similar reasons, has been forced to dress and live as a beautiful woman. Like all ghosts, Nagisa must fulfill one mission before ascending to heaven: kiss his future wife.

1089 FILM
URUSEI YATSURA IKARI NO SHARBET (*Those Obnoxious Aliens: Get Upset, Ice Cream Man*), Herald, science fiction, 30 min., 8/8.*Urusei Yatsura OVA 2: Raging Sherbet.*

Lamu, Ran and Benten are sent to Oyuki on Neptune to visit an ice-cream factory run by strange birds with cone-shaped beaks. Ran hopes to earn a fortune by bringing them to Earth, but once on our planet, the birds find it too hot and try to escape.

1090 FILM
HI NO AMEGA FURU (*Fire Rain*), Mushi, adventure, 80 min., 9/15.

1091 FILM
KIMAGURE ORANGE ROAD ANO HI NI KAERITAI (*The Capricious Orange Road: I Want to Turn Back Time*), Studio Pierrot, soap opera, 69 min., 10/8. *Kimagure Orange Road: I Want To Return To That Day.*

Young Hikaru is torn between her ballet practices, where she hopes to learn to become a star, and her love for Kyosuke. However, even though the young man loves Hikaru, he is really attracted to Madoka, their common friend. Kyosuke misses a date with Madoka and compromises any possible future they may have had, when she decides not to see him again. When her teachers don't see her at school anymore, they ask Kyosuke to bring her assignments home. He gathers his courage and phones Madoka, who forgives him. The two get together and Kyosuke's dream comes true, but he still has to deal with breaking up with Hikaru. The young dancer is devastated, but she doesn't give up and vows to get him back.

Urusei Yatsura © Kitty Films. English version © AnimEigo. Licensed to AnimEigo by Compass. All Rights Reserved

Orange Road Movie ©1988 Toho • Studio Pierrot. Subtitled & released by AnimEigo. Licensed by Toho International Co., Ltd. Illustrations (by Takada Akemi) ©1987 Matsumoto Izumi / Shueisha • NTV • Toho. All Rights Reserved.

Hi Atari Ryoko! © M. Adachi / Shogakukan • Toho • Asatsushinsha.

ULYSSE 31

LE MAGICIEN NOIR SISYPHE OU L'ÉTERNEL RECOMMENCEMENT

VIDEOGRAM

Uchu Densetsu Ulysses XXXI © TMS / DIC.

1092 FILM

HI ATARI RYOKO! KASUMI YUME NO NAKA NI KIMI GA ITA (*A Beautiful Ray of Sunshine: Kasumi, You Were in My Dreams*), Group Tack, sport/soap opera, 70 min., 10/8.

1093 FILM

KAITO JIGOMA ONGAKU HEN (*Jigoma, the Robber: Musical Chapter*), Animation Staff Film, 23 min., 11/12.

1094 FILM

CYNICAL MYSTERY HOUR 1 TRIP COASTER (*id.*), Group Tack, adventure, 30 min., 12/24.

1095 SERIES

TOSHI RAMEN MAN (*Ramen Man, the Fighter*), Toei Doga, humor, 1/10 – 9/11/1988.

1096 SERIES

SHOKOSHI CEDEY (*Little Mister Cedey*), Nippon Animation, classic, 43 episodes, 1/10 – 12/25/1988. [*Le Petit Lord*].

Cedric, son of a journalist, lives a carefree youth in America of the 1930s. His father dies suddenly of a heart attack, and Cedric discovers his true family tree, learning that he is the grandson of a rich English count. Impatient to discover his grandfather, he leaves for London with his mother. His grandfather, however, has never accepted the wedding of his son and so he takes the boy away from his mother to bring him up as an English lord. The boy's goodness conquers the old man, who changes his mind about his daughter-in-law and welcomes her to his home. the production is by Junzo Nakajima.

1097 SERIES

SAKIGAKE!! OTOKO JUKU (*Male Juku, Get a Move on!*), Toei Doga, adventure, 34 episodes, 1/10 – 9/11/1988.

The story is centered around a group of rebel students, even if the extreme levels of violence — almost on the same levels as *Hokuto no ken* — render the series almost comical. The Juku are very strict private schools, called "cram schools," that force the students to pass entrance exams or final exams after marathon sessions of studying, leaving less talented students with massive feelings of inferiority or identity crises.

1098 SERIES

UCHU DENSETSU ULYSSES XXXI (*Ulysses XXXI, The Legend Of The Space*), Tokyo Movie Shinsha, science fiction 31 episodes, 2/6 – 4/23/1988. [*Ulysses 31*].

Born of a French/Japanese collaboration, *Ulysses XXXI* is an adaptation of the famous *Odyssey*, set in the future. In the 31st century, Ulysses must find his way back to Earth, a trip made more difficult due to the facts that their route was erased from the computer of the Odyssey spaceship because of the intervention of the gods, while the whole crew is in suspended animation until they return to Earth. Ulysses is helped by his son Telemac, and Temis, an alien friend. The designs are by Shingo Araki and the direction is by Tadao Nagahama. The scenery is by Shinji Ito and Noboru Tatsuike, the music by Studio Osmond.

1099 SERIES

OSOMATSUKUN (*Little Osomatsu*), Studio Pierrot, humor, 86 episodes, 2/25 – 12/23/1988.

1100 SERIES

TSURUPIKA HAGEMARUKUN (*Hagemaru, The Little Bald Man*), Shin'ei Doga, humor, 58 episodes, 3/3 – 8/30/1988.

1101 SERIES

F (*id.*), Kitty Film, sport, 31 episodes, 3/9 – 12/23/1988.

Taken from Noboru Rokuda's manga, the story is set in the car racing world. F tells the story of Gunma Akagi, a Formula 1 champion-in-the-making, thrown out by his father who considers him a degenerate. The young man, relying only on his own abilities and a hard head, gets into a small automobile team and becomes a skillful pilot. The series, produced by Yoko Matsushita, presents a good medley of drama and humor due to the brilliant writing of Hideo Takayashiki. The character designs are by Masaki Kudo, the direction by Koichi Mishino, while Shigeo Shiba assumes the role of art director.

F © Rokuda N. / Kitty / Shogakukan.

1102 SERIES

MOERU ONISAN (*A Brilliant Brother*), Studio Pierrot, adventure, 24 episodes, 3/14 – 9/19/1988.

1103 SERIES

KITERETSU DAIHY AKKA (*The Encyclopedic Kiteretsu*), Studio Gallopp, documentary, 3/27/1988 – today [still running when this book was first published in 1991].

1104 SERIES

DOCTOR CHICHIBUY AMA (*id.*), Ashi, humor, 18 episodes, 4/3 – 7/31/1988.

1105 SERIES

SHIN MANGA MARUHODO MONOGATARI (*The New Conscience Story in Manga*), Dax International, fairy tale, 42 episodes, 4/2/1988 – 1/28/1989.

1106 SERIES

MEISAKU WORLD (*World Masterpiece*), Studio Unio, humor, 4/4/1988 — today [still running when this book was first published in 1991].

1107 SERIES

DONDON DOMERO TO RON (*id.*), Wako, humor, 52 episodes, 4/5/1988 – 3/27/1989.

1108 SERIES

SEKAI MEISAKU DOWA SERIES (*Animated Fairy Tale Series of the World Masterpieces*), Toei Doga, fairy tale, 4/7 – 4/24/1988.

1109 SERIES

CITY HUNTER II (*id.*), Nippon Sunrise, police story/adventure, 62 episodes, 4/2/1988 – 7/14/1989.

The continuing adventures of Ryo Saeba, private investigator, and his lovely but violent assistant Kaori, reach new levels. Oriented towards comedy and slapstick humor, especially with Kaori's willingness to do damage to her boss whenever he ogles female clients, this series doesn't focus on the romance between Ryo and Kaori, partly disappointing the viewers.

Intro
-1962
1963
1964
1965
1966
1967
1968
1969
1970
1971
1972
1973
1974
1975
1976
1977
1978
1979
1980
1981
1982
1983
1984
1985
1986
1987

Index

1110 SERIES

IKINARI DAGON (*Unexpectedly Dagon*), Nippon Animation, humor, 11 episodes, 4/9 – 6/11/1988.

1111 SERIES

TRANSFORMER CHOJIN MASTER FORCE (*Transformer: Supergod Master Force*), Toei Doga, robot, 42 episodes, 4/12/1988 – 3/7/1989.

A new generation of Transformers is being built on Earth to allow the robots to mix with the human beings. Their name is the Pretenders, and their chief, the powerful Metal Hawk, is a robot capable of transforming into a stellar jet.

1112 SERIES

CHO SENSHI BORGMAN (*Borgman, the Supersonic Warriors*), Ashi, science fiction, 35 episodes, 4/13 – 12/21/1988.

Ryo, Chuck and Anice, three people from Earth, decide to have themselves transformed into powerful cyborgs to save the planet from Dust Gead, a powerful and evil tyrant. Thanks to their new found powers, the three youngsters bring peace back to Earth for good.

1113 SERIES

MASHIN HEIYUDEN WATARU (*Wataru, the Legend of the Heroic Magic God*), Nippon Sunrise, robot/humor, 45 episodes, 4/15/1988 – 3/31/1989.

This series, based around the character of the young Wataru Ikusabe, is one of the best from 1988, given accolades for the quality of the animation as well as for the emotions it manages to stir up in the audience. The contagious humor of the secondary characters grabs viewers and keeps them captivated throughout the series. Wataru and his companions face enemies who run the magic robot Ryujinmaru. The little ninja Himiko Shinobite battles with Wotaru with the fantastic abilities of Genjinmaru, the feathered Kurama Wataribe runs the Kujinmaru and the fat Shibaraku Tsurugite completes the team with the Senjinmaru. Buoyed by the success of this series, Nippon Sunrise has produced a sequel in 1990.

1114 SERIES

WHAT'S MICHAEL? (*id.*), Kitty Film, animals, 45 episodes, 4/27/1988 – 3/28/1989.

The Japanese are particularly fond of cats, and many of their popular traditions feature this splendid feline. Michael is a worthy representative of his species: clever, intelligent and opportunistic, he was created by Makoto Kobayashi and, in 1984, he earned much success from his publication in the magazine "Comic Morning." Attentive to the psychology of the animal world, the author manages to draw out the humor in every situation.

1115 SERIES

TOPO GIGIO (*id.*), Nippon Animation, animal, 22 episodes, 4/27 – 9/21/1988.

The famous stuffed animal created by Maria Perego has earned so much success during its tour in Japan that Nippon Animation asked for the rights to produce this series in which the friendly mouse actually ventures outside of the house to find adventure, something which never happened in the original manga.

Cho Senshi Borgman © NTV • Toho.

What's Michael © Makoto Kobayashi / TV Tokyo / Kitty / Kodansha.

1116 SERIES

YOROIDEN SAMURAI TROOPER (*Samurai Trooper: the Legend of the Armor*), Nippon Sunrise, science fiction, 39 episodes, 4/30/1988 – 3/4/1989. *Ronin Warriors* [*Les Samourais De L'Éternel*].

The people of Earth are dismayed because of the return of an ancient kingdom and Arago, its demon ruler. In reality, they have nothing to fear, because Earth is defended by the Samurai Troopers: Ryo Sanada the Fire, ShuLeiFan the Earth, Seiji Date the Light, Shin Mori the Water and Touma Hashiba the Sky. The main characters have each been given a fabulous suit of armor, each of which represents a different virtue: humanity, justice, courtesy, trust and wisdom. Only after a lot of training and concentration, however, are the five able to become one, uniting to form a being with unimaginable powers.

Yoroiden Samurai Trooper © Sunrise • Nagoya TV.

1117 SERIES

HELLO! LADY LIN (*id.*), Toei Doga, soap opera, 34 episodes, 5/12/1988 – 1/5/1989.

1118 SERIES

MAMA O HANASHI KIKASETE (*Mommy, Tell Me a Story*), Staff 21, fairy tale, 5/9 – 9/19/1988.

1119 SERIES

TEKKEN CHINMI (*Chinmi With the Steel Fist*), Ashi, sport, 20 episodes, 7/2 – 12/24/1988.

During a trip, old Lo Shi stops to watch a little boy who is working on a farm. He sees the child cut wood with his hands, throw water pails from the river to the house and do labor that would require at least three men. Impressed by the boy's strength and vitality, the old man, an expert in martial arts, decides to test the boy's potential himself and challenges the child to combat. Satisfied, the old master asks young Chinmi to go with him to the temple on Mount Nanko, to be trained in the field of martial arts. After some initial reluctance, Chinmi accepts. From then on the trials that await him are many, from the entrance exam at the temple to what his teachers put him through, to some disturbing encounters with criminals. Taken from Takeshi Maekawa's manga, *Tekken Chinmi* was less well received than it could have been, mostly because the adaptation ignored the freshness and the humor that had characterized the original manga.

1120 SERIES

BIRITA (*id.*), Shin'ei Doga, humor, 31 episodes, 7/11/1988 – 4/3/1989.

1121 SERIES

SHIN GRIMM MEISAKU GEKIJO (*Grimm's New Masterpieces*), Nippon Animation, fairy tale, 23 episodes, 10/2/1988 – 3/26/1989.

1122 SERIES

YUME MIRU TOPO GIGIO (*Dreaming Topo Giggio*), Nippon Animation, animals, 10/7/1988 – 1/6/1989.

1123 SERIES

HIMITSU NO AKKOCHAN (*Little Akko's Secret*), Toei Doga, magic, 61 episodes, 10/9/1988 – 12/24/1989.

This series delivers a whole set of new designs and adventures for little Akko, the star of a 1969 series. One night a fairy gives Akko a magic mirror, enabling her to become an adult so long as she promises to use her new abilities to help people in need.

1124 SERIES

HAI! AKKO DESU (*Yes! I Am Akko*), Eiken, soap opera, 10/12/1988 – today [still running when this book was first published in 1991].

1125 SERIES

OISHINBO (*The Gourmet Glutton*), Shin'ei Doga, comedy, 10/17/1988 – today [still running in 1991].

Following in the footsteps of the famous series *Mister Ajikko*, here is a new cartoon that concentrates on the Japanese tradition of excellent cooking. This time, however, the story is a touching romance rather than a madcap comedy. The main character is Jiro, a talented chef who works in an elegant Tokyo restaurant. The young man is set in charge of preparing the daily menu, a demanding and difficult task. The restaurant owner believes in his abilities, and Jiro does everything in his power not to disappoint anyone. As usual, happy moments alternate with tough situations, but the main character can always count on the friendly Yuko for support.

1126 SERIES

MEIMON DAISAN YAKYUBU (*The Glorious Third Baseball Team*), Nas, sport, 40 episodes, 10/20/1988 – 1/9/1989.

1127 SERIES

SOEIKE! ANPANMAN (*Go! Anpanman*), Tokyo Movie Shinsha, humor, 24 episodes, 10/3/1988 – 4/3/1989.

1128 SPECIAL

SCIENCE ANIME SPECIAL CHO DEN DO MONOGATARI (*Animated Special on the Story of Science*), Nichiei Shinsha, documentary, 1/16.

1129 SPECIAL

NATSUFUKU NO SHOJOTACHI (*The Girl With the Summer Clothing*), Madhouse, soap opera, 8/7.

1130 OAV

PUTSUN MAKE LOVE VOL. IV KYOFU NO JOKA SANSO NOROI GERENDE (*The Crazy Loves, Vol. IV, the Slant of the Cursed Mountain House of Joka*), Agent 21, erotic, 25 min., 1/14, Toei Video.

A ghost appears in the ski chalet and kidnaps the beautiful Saori. In reality, the ghost is none other than a normal man in disguise, who will do anything to marry the young woman.

1131 OAV

DIRTY PAIR II (*id.*), Nippon Sunrise, science fiction, 50 min., 1/21, Vap. *Dirty Pair Original 2*.

A tragic accident on the fertile planet Hazaru, colonized by believers of the new Tamu religion, causes the death of all the workers of the Jason House company. Our intrepid heroines rush to the planet to lead an investigation but they find themselves involved in their usual 'little incidents' (they end up fighting against the god of the Tamu itself!). The secret of the god's power is sealed in a complex computer system that Yuri and Kei de-

Soeikei! Anpanman © T. Yanase / Playbell / TMS / NTV.

stroy. A new disaster happens on the planet that, deprived of the energy that was binding it together, is victim of a destructive storm. The second episode deals with a group of children who occupy the experimental energy center of the planet Amega to try to put cartoons on every broadcast network. Yuri and Kei are sent to the planet to negotiate with the rebels, but the mission is more difficult than expected. The center's defense system automatically begins its self destruct sequence, and the only way to escape the countdown is to leave the site as fast as possible. Thanks to the Dirty Pair, the children are saved from certain death.

1132 OAV

SHIN CREAM LEMON ETUDE II SESSION CONCERTO (*Cream Lemon New Series: Etude II, Early Spring Concert*), Fairy Dust, erotic, 25 min., 1/21, Fairy Dust.

After having seduced the beautiful Yugo, the guitarist leaves her behind to travel with his group. The young man develops a passionate relationship with a singer, while Yugo, after working through her depression and misery, finally finds her soulmate.

1133 OAV

SCOOPERS (*id.*), ACC, adventure, 58 min., 1/22, Cic Victor.

In the year 2016, in the city of Shambara, a journalist named Yoko and her boyfriend Vito are on the trace of the enigmatic Mister X. One day they receive an invitation from him and they rush to the Tower of the Rainbow, his home, where Yoko is taken hostage. Vito rescues her by destroying the program of the central computer, but only after Mister X escapes.

1134 OAV

KENRO DENSETSU 1 LEINA STOOL (*Leina Stool 1, the Legend of the Wolf's Sword*), Ashi, science fiction, 30 min., 2/5, Toshiba Emi.

Mysterious kidnappings are panicking the female students of a Japanese high school, which leads Leina Stool, a warrior from Cronos, to pass herself off as a student to investigate the matter. The young woman soon befriends a number of the girls, including Sano Yuko, who disappears without a trace during an outing in the city. Leina vows to find the kidnapper at all costs.

1135 OAV

HIGH SCHOOL AGENT (*id.*), Agent 21. adventure, 30 min., 2/12, Toei Video.

Kosuke Kanamori is a high school student who finds himself involved in the NU (National Union) and, for his first mission, is sent to the palace of Madera in Spain to steal the precious Basku egg.

1136 OAV

SALAMANDER (*id.*), Studio Pierrot, science fiction, 50 min., 2/25, Konami Video. [*Salamander*].

The Bacterians, a species of militarized parasite, launch a deadly attack to try to conquer the planet Lattice from the Salamander empire. To save his people, Lord British hires Eddie, Stephanie and Don, three warriors from the rival planet Gladius, who, piloting very sophisticated space transports, manage to destroy the invaders.

Original Dirty Pair © Takachiho & Studio Nue • Sunrise. Released in North America by A.D.V. Films. Packaging Design ©1998 A.D.Vision, Inc.

Original Dirty Pair © Takachiho & Studio Nue • Sunrise. Released in North America by A.D.V. Films. Packaging Design ©1998 A.D.Vision, Inc.

1137 OAV
DIRTY PAIR III (*id.*), Nippon Sunrise, science fiction, 50 min., 2/21, Vap. *Dirty Pair Original 3*.

The first episode turns around Li Suiryu, one of Yuri and Kei's colleagues, who has recently become addicted to gambling. His favorite game is the "meteo," and the Shagrila casino is his second home. It is here that the young women decide to challenge him. During the game, they discover that the casino owner has rigged the entire casino to his advantage. This infuriates Li who, living up to his nickname "Kung Fu Dragon," destroys the place and puts his life back on the right track. In the second episode, the Dirty Pair find themselves investigating a big counterfeit money operation. Yuri and Kei must thus go to the island of Sargicos, a place totally controlled by the Castino family. Yuri comes close to marrying the second son of the clan, while Kei infiltrates the guests and manages to get her hands on the precious printing plates.

1138 OAV
SEISENSHI DUNBINE (*Aura Battler Dunbine*), Nippon Sunrise, science fiction, 80 min., 2/25, Bandai.

A more stylish remake of the original series, Nippon Sunrise launches this movie directly to videocassette. The characterizations and the main events of the story don't vary much at all from the original.

1139 OAV
DRAGON'S HEAVEN (*id.*), AIC, science fiction/fantasy, 45 min., 2/25, Toshiba Emi.

A thousand years have passed since the war between the human beings and invading mechanical creatures when the android Shaian awakes from his ancient sleep. Young Ikuru asks for his help to defeat the evil Elmmedain, head of a Brazilian army. Shaian gives his companion the powerful fire armor that will enable her to defeat the enemy.

1140 OAV
XANADU DRAGON SLAYER DENSETSU (*Xanadu: the Legend of the Dragon Slayer*), Toei Doga, fantasy, 50 min., 3/1, Kadokawa Shoten.

In the year 2035, the courageous Fig sets out in his tank for Xanadu where a war between white and black magic has been fought for centuries. Rieru, the queen of Xanadu, becomes a very good friend of the young man and asks for his help when her enemy Leikswoor kills Rieru's husband to take possession of the precious crystal. Leikswoor's thirst for riches isn't quenched and, to get the second jewel, he kidnaps Rieru. Fig rescues the queen with the magic of the Dragon Slayer sword, given him by the priest Tatson, with which he fights against the perfidious Leikswoor.

1141 OAV
KIZUOIBITO IV MISTY CONNECTION (*The Daredevil IV: Misty Connection*), Madhouse, adventure/erotic, 30 min., 3/5, Bandai.

The GPX sends Misty as a hired killer to murder Keisuke, but after having been defeated in combat, she attempts suicide. Having saved her, Keisuke convinces her to face the organization and fight alongside him.

1142 OAV

HARBOR LIGHT MONOGATARI FASHION LALA YORI (*The Story of the Harbor Light of Fashion Lala*), Studio Pierrot, magic, 50 min., 3/11, Pierrot Project.

A big dance contest is about to take place and almost every aspiring ballerina in the area is taking part. Miho is busy putting the finishing touches on her sister Shuri's costume, but the contest seems to be in danger of cancellation, because Kid, son of the official sponsor, wants to stop it. During the evening before the contest the girls' aunt sadistically tears Shuri's costume, and Miho cries in despair because she doesn't know how to tell her sister. During the night, however, a good fairy appears to Miho and changes her into Lala, an exceptional designer. The movie ends with the discovery that the various events are all part of the main character's dream.

1143 OAV

SOKO KISHI VOTOMS RED SHOULDER DOCUMENT YABO NO RUTSU (*Armor Troopers Votoms: the Red Shoulder Document, the Origins of Ambition*), Nippon Sunrise, science fiction, 56 min., 3/19, Toshiba Eizo Soft.

1144 OAV

CHOJIN DENSETSU UROTSUKIDOJI II (*The Legend of the Superdivinity: the Wandering Boy II*), AIC, horror, 54 min., 3/21, JAVM. *Urotsukidoji: Legend Of The Overfiend. Curse Of The Overfiend.*

A few days after the disaster of the hospital, Nagumo happily comes back to Akemi, not remembering what happened, and goes out with her until the end of the school, watched by Niki, also in love with the girl. From the world of the demons come Kyoki, the spirit of madness and Sakki, the spirit of murder, who offer Niki strength and power in exchange for his soul. To seal the deal, the young man, treated badly by everyone, will have to cut off his own organ. During an evening when Nagumo and Akemi are involved in some heavy petting, Niki kidnaps the girl and, licking her face, he swallows some drops of Nagumo's semen, thus getting part of the Chojin's power. In the meantime, Amano discovers the existence of "Suikakuju the manipulator" who wants to destroy Chojin. A duel between the two devastates the city while Niki, transformed into the intermediate stage of the ultrademon, is fighting against Nagumo. After having destroyed Suikakuju, Amano is thrown in the future where he witnesses, disconcerted, a world devastated by Chojin and a humanity that has given in to lust. Before he can understand how it happened, he is forced to come back to the present.

1145 OAV

DIRTY PAIR IV (*id.*), Nippon Sunrise, science fiction, 50 min., 3/21, Vap. *Dirty Pair Original 4.*

Sandra, Yuri and Kei's ex-friend, becomes the boss of a company that produces steroids, code-named Hussul. To destroy the machine that produces them, the two Lovely Angels face-off with the girl who dies during the fight. Once again, the Dirty Pair have accomplished their mission, but at high cost. In the second episode, Yuri and Kei find Tia, the sole survivor of the disaster of the spaceship Swan, caused by her father's ex-assistant. The insane man had, in fact, used the gas to kill his colleagues and all the passengers in order to take their wealth for himself.

The Ultimate Teacher ©1988 & 1993 Movic/Sony Music Entertainment (Japan) Inc. Package artwork ©1993 Central Park Media. All Rights Reserved.

Balthus: Tia's Radiance ©1988 Media Station Co., Ltd. English version and package ©1997 Kitty. All Rights Reserved.

1146 OAV

SHIN CREAM LEMON MORIYAMA TO SPECIAL II (*Cream lemon New Series: Special to Moriyama II*), Soeishinsha, erotic, 25 min., 3/21, Fairy Dust.

1147 OAV

KYOFUN NO BYONINGEN SAISHU KYOSHI (*The Scary Bionic Man: the Ultimate Teacher*), Animate Film, adventure, 60 min., 3/25, CBS Sony. *The Ultimate Teacher.*

Ganpachi Chaba, a cockroach man who escaped from a center for experimental engineering, begins a teaching career in the Teyo school. His idea of education is to force the students to submit to him through physical brutality, starting with the unscrupulous Hinako Shiratori, the head of a group of hooligans. The young woman has a fetish about her Lucky-Kitty gym shorts, and she can't fight if she is not wearing them. When the teacher reveals her secret to the other students, Hinako drops out of school out of shame.

1148 OAV

MADONNA HONO NO TEACHER (*Madonna, the Fire Teacher*), Studio Unio, humor/soap opera, 50 min., 3/25, Toei Video.

Mako Domon finally finds work as a teacher in a school for maladjusted students. Not able to stand the mischief and trouble created by her students she decides to quit, but the headmaster forces her to become the soccer team's coach. Through sport, Mako will finally make friends with the young rebels.

1149 OAV

ZUKKOKE SANNINGUMI ZUKKOKE GIKU BOKEN (*The Zukkoke Trio: the Adventure of the Zukkokes*), Tama, humor, 57 min., 4/1, Nippon Columbia.

Hachibe, Mochan and Hakase are three young journalists on the elementary school newspaper. One day. when they are trying to discover the secrets of the beautiful teacher Yukiko, they find themselves thrown back to the Edo period. While they try to come back to the present, the children meet the teacher, now dressed as a noble princess.

1150 OAV

PUTSUN MAKE LOVE VOL. V YUKI NO HATSUKOI DAIUNDOKAI (*The Crazy Loves, Vol. V: the Big Match, Yuki's First Love*), Agent 21, erotic, 25 min., 4/8, Toei Video.

A strange young man participates in the school's gymnastics tryouts. Yuki falls madly in love with him, and the problems begin.

1151 OAV

BALTIOS TYA NI IKKI (*Tya, the Most Splendid From Baltios*), Furuta Shoji, erotic, 30 min., 4/10, Uchu Doga. *Balthus: Tia's Radiance.*

1152 OAV

APPLESEED (*id.*), AIC, science fiction, 70 min., 4/21, Bandai.

The beautiful and skillful guerrilla Deunan lives with the cyborg Briareos, isolated from the rest of the world after the great destruction caused by the war. Found by a young explorer, the two are brought to a huge and highly technological city where they become part of the police force. This role, however, reveals itself to be more difficult than expected, as they often receive orders that aren't in line with their morals and values. They stumble on a horrifying discovery: an obscure project of "Worldwide welfare" is striving towards the day when all human beings will be replaced by bioroids. The story of the OAV faithfully follows the first part of Masamune Shirow's original manga.

1153 OAV

DIRTY PAIR V (*id.*), Nippon Sunrise, science fiction, 50 min., 4/21, Vap. *Dirty Pair Original 5*.

While the diplomats and the government army are working on a peace treaty, mysterious armed groups appear and jeopardize the course of the accords. Yuri and Kei are hired to defeat the rebels. In the second episode, we see the Lovely Angels dress up as space truck drivers to investigate a series of accidents that happened to various transportation companies. The case, which also involves the chief of police, is solved when the two discover that the accidents are being created by a big company that sells space cargo.

1154 OAV

HURRICANE LIVE 2032 (*id.*), Artmic, musical, 25 min., 4/24, Toshiba Emi. *Hurricane Live 2032: The Music Of Bubblegum Crisis*.

This musical video is a compilation of the rock group the Knight Sabers' greatest hits, including the most famous from the *Bubblegum Crisis* mini-series. "Tokyo 2032", "Mad Machine" and "Victory" are some of the songs presented by the beautiful Priss, Celia, Linna and Nene.

1155 OAV

KIDO KEISATSU PATLABOR (*Patlabor, the Mobile Patrol*), Studio Dean, science fiction, 30 min., 4/25, Bandai. *Patlabor Original Series, Vol. 1*.

In the year 1990 the Earth's ozone layer slowly begins to thin, giving way to a dramatic environmental imbalance. The polar glaciers begin to melt and the water levels of the oceans and lakes slowly begins to rise. The Babylon Project begins in Tokyo, aimed at preventing the city from sinking into the quickly-rising sea. Labors are created for this purpose, avant-garde construction mechanisms that can extend a pilot's reach and increase his strength. In 1997, to maintain public order in the city, the Tokyo police decides to use the Labor technology to create the robot patrol of the Patlabors. Noa Izumi's story begins here, and the young pilot of the Ingram robot learns to face the worst criminals with unexpected courage and strength. Produced by Mamoru Oshi from a story by Kazunori Ito, the OAV features the character designs of the famous Akemi Takada who, after the success of *Urusei Yatsura* and *Creamy Mami*, proved her flexibility and talent with a new, less caricatured style. The designs are by Yutaka Izubuchi.

1156 OAV

CREAM LEMON ESCALATION SOSHU HEN (*Cream Lemon: the Chapter of the Escalation in Synthesis*), Soeishinsha, erotic, 80 min., 4/25, Fairy Dust.

1157 OAV

KUJAKU O KIDANSAI (*The Peacock King: the Festival for the Return of the Demon*), AIC, horror, 55 min., 4/29, Pony Canyon. *Peacock King: Spirit Warrior — Festival Of The Ogres' Revival*.

Original Dirty Pair © Takachiho & Studio Nue • Sunrise. Released in North America by A.D.V. Films. Packaging Design ©1999 A.D.Vision, Inc.

Hurricane Live 2032 ©1988, 1990 Artmic, Inc & Youmex, Inc. English version ©1992 AnimEigo, Inc.

Patlabor OVA Series ©1988 Headgear / Emotion / TFC. English version and package ©1996 Central Park Media Corporation. All Rights Reserved.

Peacock King ©1988 Makoto Ogino / Shueisha, Inc. / Soeishinsha, Inc. / Pony Canyon, Inc. English version and package ©1997 Central Park Media Corporation. All Rights Reserved.

Dominion Tank Police ©1988 Masamune Shirow / Hakusensha Agent 21 / Toshiba Video Softwares, Inc. English version ©1992 Central Park Media Corporation / Island World Communications Ltd. Package artwork ©1992 Central Park Media Corporation. All Rights Reserved.

The statue of Ashura has been stolen from the temple of Kofuku, and Kujaku has been hired to find it. Ajari, Kujaku's teacher and G.F. Ashura discover that the reason for the robbery is to permit the rise of the demon Seimei Abeno. Kujaku suspects Tatsura of being behind the theft of the statue, and follows him secretly to Hokkaido.

1158 OAV

HIGH SCHOOL AGENT II (*id.*), Agent 21, adventure, 30 min., 5/13, Toei Video.

Kosuke receives the order to steal a gold stone from the submarine UBOOT. Having successfully completed his mission, the young man goes to Oslo where he meets the treacherous Nina, a neo-nazi spy, at the airport. The young woman takes the stone from Kosuke because she claims it had belonged to Hitler and should be the property of the new right-wing national movement. The young man manages to sneak into the group's headquarters, and fight to reclaim the stone.

1159 OAV

SEISENSHI DUNBINE II (*Aura Battler Dunbine II*), Nippon Sunrise, science fiction, 75 min., 5/25, Bandai.

To escape from his enemies, Sho goes to the desert with his companions. Attacked by a whole host of poisonous insects, the group is saved by a horseman of the Roshun family who asks them, in return, to fight the evil Raban. The young people refuse but they are forced to accept when one of the heads of the family takes Lerumu hostage.

1160 OAV

ENSHU NIHON MUKASHI BANASHI (*Erotic Japanese Stories From the Past*), JHV, erotic, 30 min., 5/25, JHV.

1161 OAV

SHIBUYA HONKY TONK (*id.*), Knack, adventure/soap opera, 35 min., 5/25, Tokuma Japan.

Naoya Abe, a fourteen year old from a wealthy family, dreams of becoming a member of organized crime and he gets in the Todogumi clan that controls the Shibuya area in Tokyo. The world that he encounters is a lot tougher than expected. To protect Yoko, his girlfriend, Naoya must kill a member of the rival Tenseikai family. For this reason, he decides to escape to London.

1162 OAV

MAHJONG SHODEN NAKI NO RYU (*The adventurous Legend of Mahjong, the Screaming Dragon*), Gainax/Magic Bus, adventure, 45 min., 5/25, Bandai.

Ryu, better known as Nakino, is a Mahjong champion and, thanks to an enviable ability and uncommon luck, he wins every competition. One day, Ishikawa, a mafia boss, sees him play and offers him the possibility to be part of his clan, an offer that Ryu cannot refuse.

1163 OAV

DOMINION HANZAI GUNDAN (*Dominion, the Criminal Group*), Agent 21, science fiction, 45 min., 5/27, Toshiba, Eizo Soft. *Dominion Tank Police*.

In an unspecified future, the Earth's atmosphere is so polluted that people have to wear gas masks to survive. Crime has grown to frightening proportions and to fight it, Newport

City has formed a special corps, the Tank Police. One of its members is Leona, who, aboard the tank Bonaparte, often confronts the criminal plans of the Buaku band. Capo Buaku and his two sensual companions (cat women created through genetic bio-engineering) create a great deal of trouble for the police organization, while taking only minor losses themselves. Taken from Masamune Shirow's manga.

1164 OAV

GAKUEN BEN RYIYA SERIES ANTIQUES ANTIQUE HEART (*The Series About the Handyman Student: Antique Heart*), Animate Film, horror, 40 min., 6/5, Toshiba Emi.

Three young men are hired to bring down an old school building, but once on the site they meet the spirit of Saki, a beautiful young woman who tells them a tragic story to convince them to abandon their project. However, the young men must obey orders and go ahead with the demolition.

1165 OAV

DOCTOR CHICHIBUY AMAI (*id.*), Fuji/Pony/Canyon/Ashi, humor, 30 min., 6/5, Pony Canyon.

1166 OAV

ROKUSHIN GATTAI GOD MARS JUNANASAI NO DENSETSU (*You Are God in One Body: the Legend of the Seventeen Year Olds*), Tokyo Movie Shinsha, science fiction, 56 min., 6/5, Toho Video.

Marg is rescued by some antigovernment guerrillas who bring him to their village. There, the young man falls in love with the beautiful Lulu. During a feast, however, the soldiers of Zul attack the village and mercilessly massacre the people. The emperor, who had the young man's mother and father killed, couldn't take it when Marg betrayed him to join his brother Mars in opposing the Gishin empire.

1167 OAV

PUTSUN MAKE LOVE VOL. VI SAORI TO YUJI NO NATSU MONOGATARI (*The Crazy Loves Vol. VI; the Summer Story of Saori and Yuji*), Agent 21, erotic, 25 min., 6/11, Toei Video.

Saori and Yuji decide to spend their summer vacation at the beach, but because of a desperate young woman who has decided to commit suicide, and the teacher Akimoto, they are not alone for one instant.

1168 OAV

PROJECT AKO III CINDERELLA RAPSODY (*id.*), Studio Fantasy, science fiction, 50 min., 6/21, Soeishinsha. *Project A-ko : Cinderella Rhapsody*.

This time, A-Ko is involved in the search for a boyfriend and she decides to buy an elegant dress. In order to earn enough money, the young girl finds a job in a fast-food and there, for the first time, she meets K-Kun. The young man who had almost run over C-Ko with his motorcycle, soon becomes the object of A-Ko and B-Ko's eternal rivalry. Their fights are useless, however, because K-Kun is in love with the little, whiny C-Ko.

1169 OAV

AKAI KODAN ZILLION UTAHIME YA KYOKU: BURNING NIGHT (*Zillion, the Red Ray: Nocturn Singer Burning Night*), Tatsunoko, science fiction/musical, 45 min., 6/21, King Record. *Zillion Special: Burning Night*.

Project A-ko 3 ©1988 Soeishinsha/Final-Nishijima/ Pony Canyon. English version & package ©1994 Central Park Media Corporation. All Rights Reserved.

Zillion: Burning Night ©1991 Tatsunoko Production Co., Ltd. Package design ©1991 Streamline Pictures. Released under license by Streamline Pictures

Dominion Tank Police ©1988 Masamune Shirow / Hakusensha
Agent 21 / Toshiba Video Softwares, Inc. English version ©1992
Central Park Media Corporation / Island World Communications Ltd.

Tokyo Vice © Minami Machi Bugyosho / Polydoll.
English version released by AnimeWorks.

Scramble Wars ©1992 Artmic. Licensed by Artmic &
Toshiba EMI, *Ten Little Gall Force* ©1988 Movic/Sony M.E.
Licensed by Toho Intl. English version released by AnimEigo.

The film is a parody of the animated series of the same name. J.J., Champ and Apple are the leaders of a rock group, while their enemies are part of the terrifying Yakuza, the Japanese mafia. Wonderful songs complement an entertaining and action-filled story.

1170 OAV
CREAM LEMON CLIMAX ZENSHO VOL. III (*Cream Lemon, Gathering of Orgasms, Vol. I and II*), Soeishinsha, erotic, 50 min., 6/21, Fairy Dust.

1171 OAV
DOMINION ACT II: HANZAI SENSO (*Dominion Act II: the Criminal War*), Agent 21, science fiction, 40 min., 6/24, Toshiba Eizo Soft. *Dominion Tank Police Act 2.*

1172 OAV
SHIBUYA HONKY TONK VOL. II (*id.*), Knack, adventure/soap opera, 35 min., 6/25, Tokuma Japan.

Hiding in London after murdering his rival, Naoya Abe obtains a job as Aoki's assistant photographer in a publishing firm. When Aoki forces him to steal secret military documents, the young man has to accept and fulfills his mission. When his bosses find out about his criminal past, however, he is ordered to return to his home country.

1173 OAV
KIDO KEISATSU PATLABOR VOL. II: LONG SHOT (*Patlabor, the Mobile Patrol Vol. II, the Risky Hit*), Studio Dean, science fiction, 30 min., 6/25, Bandai. *Patlabor Original Series, Vol. 1.*

Kanukika Kurashi, the New York chief of police, decides to personally escort the mayor on his official visit to Tokyo, in order to ensure his safety. The second Patlabor patrol, knowing that a group of terrorists want to make an attempt on the mayor's life, intensifies its patrols after the discovery of a dangerous bomb under the mayor's car.

1174 OAV
TOKYO VICE (*id.*), Minami Machi Bugyosho, police story, 60 min., 6/25, Polydoll. *Tokyo Vice.*

1175 OAV
KIDO SENSHI SUPER DEFORMED GUNDAM (*Super Deformed Mobile Suit Gundam*), Nippon Sunrise, humor, 30 min., 6/25, Bandai.

After the success earned by the regular movies and series, the Nippon Sunrise brings the exhilerating adventures of *Super Deformed Gundam* to animation. This entertaining and popular film presented the usual characters from *Gundam* in a sitcom-type atmosphere, the characters drawn with huge heads on minuscule bodies in this parody of the original series.

1176 OAV
DOCTOR CHICHIBUYAMA II (*id.*), Fuji/Pony Canyon/Ashi, humor, 30 min., 7/1, Pony Canyon.

1177 OAV
THE TEN LITTLE GALL FORCE (*id.*), Artmic/AIC/Animate Film, humor, 30 min., 7/3, CBS Sony. *Super-Deformed Double Feature: Ten Little Gall Force.*

The craze for Super Deformed has also reached the most feminine space group in Japanese animation. The characters are here reduced to friendly little puppets, involved in adventures that parody the original OAVs.

1178 OAV

VAMPIRE MIYU DAIICHIWA AYAKASHI NO MIYAKO (*Miyu The Vampire: Act I, Metropolis Ghost*), AIC, horror, 30 min., 7/21, Soeishinsha. *Vampire Princess Miyu, Episode 1: Unearthly Kyoto*.

The parents of poor Aiko, a young girl forced by a curse to sleep forever, contact Himiko Se, an expert medium, to free her. To find a cure, the woman begins a long journey that will bring her to an ancient city inhabited solely by vampires.

1179 OAV

CREAM LEMON CLIMAX ZENSHO VOL. III–IV (*Cream Lemon: Gathering of Orgasms, Vol. III and IV*), Soeishinsha, erotic, 50 min., 7/21, Fairy Dust.

1180 OAV

SHONAN BAKUSOZOKU IV HURRICANE RIDERS (*Shonan's Hooligans IV: Hurricane Riders*), Toei Doga, adventure, 50 min., 7/22, Toei Video.

Seiji, Emiko's boyfriend, is a great fan of surfing. He has become a different person, however, since the moment he lost an important summer competition, and desperately seeks a return match. Emiko can't shake him out of his depression and asks Eguchi, the head of Shonan's hooligans, for advice.

1181 OAV

BUBBLEGUM CRISIS IV REVENGE ROAD (*id.*), AIC/Artmic, science fiction/adventure, 30 min., 7/25, Toshiba Emi. *Bubblegum Crisis 4: Revenge Road*.

One night, Priss, one of the Knight Sabers, has a motorcycle accident. In the hospital, she meets a girl who is terrified by the noise motorcycles make while in the streets. The Sabers have to deal with a mysterious executioner aboard a powerful car, who slaughters modern motorcycle riders. The suspicions fall on Gibson, the girl's boyfriend, who would seek revenge on the motorcycle gang who caused his girlfriend's accident.

1182 OAV

KIDO KEISATSU PATLABOR, VOL. III: YON'OKUGOSENMANNEN NO WANA (*Patlabor, the Mobile Patrol Vol. III: A 450 000 000 Year Old Trick*), Studio Dean, science fiction, 30 min., 7/25, Bandai. *Patlabor Original Series, Vol. 1*.

Strange incidents occur in the Bay of Tokyo. People and motor vehicles are being mysteriously dragged into the sea. The second Patlabor patrol, investigating, finds itself in front of an enormous creature that had been thrown in the water by a mad scientist.

1183 OAV

ACE O NERAE! II STAGE I (*Point to the Ace! II Act I*), Tokyo Movie Shinsha, sport, 75 min., 7/25, Bandai.

A chronological sequel to the movie produced by the TMS in 1972. Hiromi leaves for America with Madame Butterfly, Todo and Osaki. There, the two couples will have to rep-

Vampire Princess Miyu ©1988, 1989 Soeishinsha, Inc. / Pony Canyon, Inc. English version ©1992 AnimEigo, Inc. Licensed by Fuji Sankei Communications International, Inc. Released by AnimEigo, Inc.

Bubblegum Crisis ©1988 by Artmic, Inc & Youmex, Inc. Licensed by Youmex, Inc. English version ©1991 by AnimEigo, Inc. All Rights Reserved.

resent Japan in an important tournament. During the American stay, Jin, the young peoples' trainer, to whom Hiromi is linked in a special way, dies of leukemia. Todo is the only one that knows about the death, but he keeps it from Hiromi, certain that her grief would compromise her performance during the competition. Hiromi gets the second place but as soon as she gets home, the bitter surprise awaits her that her loving trainer is dead, leaving her alone to face the uncertain future.

Weeks pass and Hiromi, completely unmotivated, spends her days in her bedroom, refusing to go out. Her attitude preoccupies her friends, especially Todo, who has always been in love with her. Katsura, a Buddhist monk, ex-tennis player and great friend of Jin, unexpectedly shows up and, to honor a promise he made to his friend on his death bed, decides to take care of Hiromi. Slowly, the young woman comes out of her shell and begins to live again and to compete. The four young people must soon make an important decision: whether to become professional athletes or not.

Reika (Madame Butterfly) initially decides not to go the professional route, but she soon changes her mind. Hiromi, insecure as always, relies completely on her new trainer who prepares her, unbeknownst to her, to make a great debut in that world. Todo, instead, convinced that his style of play is mediocre, unexpectedly decides to leave Japan for the United States to work on his technique. Finally, before he leaves, he decides to confess his love to Hiromi. The girl is surprised, but then she realizes that she loves him too.

Once in America, Todo realizes that the road is more difficult than expected but naturally, he doesn't mention that in his letters to Hiromi. The girl senses that something is wrong and she spends all her savings on a trip to New York. After a series of problems and near-misses, she meets Todo by chance and he finally confesses his failures. Hiromi gives him confidence in himself and back in Japan, she becomes motivated to win by herself, so much so that she participates in the professional tournament that awards the prestigious Queen Cup. Needless to say, the young athlete wins the tournament and opens herself up to a great future. This series was split across six OAVs, each one vastly popular.

1184 OAV
ACE O NERAE! II STAGE II (*Point to the Ace! II: ACT II*), Tokyo Movie Shinsha, sport, 50 min., 7/25, Bandai.

1185 OAV
TOYAMAZAKURA UCHUCHO YATSU NO NA WA GOLD (*Cosmic Short Stories of Toyama's Cherries: His Name is Gold*), Toei Doga, adventure/science fiction, 60 min., 7/25, Tokuma Shoten.

In the 21st century, all the great inhabited centers and space colonies are controlled by an enormous computerized system called Edo, through which the five Elder Administrators maintain peace in the Universe. But there is still a dark criminal underground that the general controls can't seem to overcome, so with the authority given him by the police force, Gold, a samurai gifted with the katana laser and harboring cherry blossom tattoos, is left free to act as he pleases. His most important mission begins, however, with the search for his father's murderers, one of the five Elders. The story and the characters are based on the life of Toyoma no Kinsan, a famous hero of ancient Japan.

1186 OAV

WHAT'S MICHAEL? (*id.*), Kitty Film, humor, 45 min., 7/25, Kitty Enterprise.

1187 OAV

WATT POE TO BOKURA NO OHANASHI (*Our Story and the Story of Watt Poe*), Diva, soap opera, 55 min., Konami. [*Watt Poe*].

After the disappearance of Watt Poe, the sea mammal (a cross between a whale, an orca and an arctic mammal), the fishermen from the village can't fish well anymore. The courageous Jamu thus leaves to search for it, wanting to help his family and friends at all costs.

1188 OAV

KAZE NO MATASABURO (*Matasaburo From the Wind*), Project Team, Argos, Adventure, 30 min., 8/20, Konami.

Set in a little mountain school, the story, written by Kenji Miyazawa, tells of the mysterious Saburo Takada, a newcomer to the area. The direction is by Taro Rin.

1189 OAV

GANBARE! KICKERS BOKURA NO DENSETSU (*Let's Go Kids! Our Legend*), Studio Pierrot, sport/musical, 90 min., 8/21, SPO.

1190 OAV

CREAM LEMON CLIMAX ZENSHO VOL. V (*Cream Lemon: Orgasm Gathering, Vol. V*), Soeishinsha, erotic, 50 min., 8/21, Fairy Dust.

1191 OAV

SEISENSHI DUNBINE III (*Aura Battler Dunbine III*), Nippon Sunrise, science fiction, 75 min., 8/25, Bandai.

Lemuru is kidnapped by Laban, and to save her, Sho secretly enters Laban's castle. He is unfortunately discovered but, after being captured, he escapes. Shob, Laban's right hand man, decides to launch an nuclear attack, forcing the two to escape to Earth.

1192 OAV

KIZUOIBITO V KANKETSUHEN FINAL TOUCHDOWN (*The Daredevil V, Final Chapter: the Final Touchdown*), Magic Bus, adventure/erotic, 30 min., 8/25, Bandai.

1193 OAV

NIHON NO OBAKE BANASHI (*Stories of Japanese Ghosts*), O Prod., stories, 30 min., 8/28, Toshiba Emi.

Stories of ghosts remain in the heart and mind of anyone who has sat at the feet of their grandparents and listend to them tell stories, especially in Japan, where ghost stories are fairy tales as well as horror for around campfires. In this series we meet a great number of different ghosts, from the one who wants to avenge his death to the ghost of a girl in love who came back to the world of the living to invisibly stay at her boyfriend's side.

1194 OAV

GEIMOS NO HANAYOME RAN NO KUBIKYOKU (*The Demon's Wife: the Orchid Suite*), Madhouse, horror, 30 min., 8/31, Akita Shoten/Toei Video.

Watt Poe © Konami Industry.

An elegant horror story taken from Etsuko Ikeda's manga. The direction is by Taro Rin, while the designs are by Yuho Ashibe.

1195 OAV
GENSESHIY OSHIN PIYORO IKKA VOL. II–III (*The Piyoro Family, the Guardian of This World Vol. II and III*), Tokyo Movie Shinsha, science fiction, 30 min., 9/1, Akita Shoten.

1196 OAV
LEINA KENRO DENSETSU II (*Leina, the Legend of the Wolf's Sword II*), Ashi, science fiction, 30 min., 9/4, Toshiba Emi.

1197 OAV
NAMAKEMONO GA IMITETA (*Namakemono Has Seen*), Agent 21, Humor, 30 min., 9/23, Toei Video.

The inhabitants of the village of the animals, elephants, bears, goats and cats form a rock group. Taken from Takashi Murakami's manga, this OAV is directed by Akinori Nagaoka, the character designs are by Kinichiro Suzuki, the screenplay is by Yoshio Kurasawa and the artistic direction is by Jiro Kono.

1198 OAV
KIDO KEISATSU PATLABOR, VOL. IV: L NO HIGEKI (*Patlabor, the Mobile Patrol IV: L's Tragedy*), Studio Dean, science fiction, 30 min., 9/25, Bandai. *Patlabor Original Series, Vol. 2.*

The second patrol is temporarily transferred to the Fuji cram school, where strange things soon begin to happen: the bath water becomes red, the ghost of a woman peeps in through a window, while the ghost of a robot comes out of the lake. Curious, Asuma begins to investigate.

1199 OAV
ACE O NERAE! II STAGE THREE (*Point to the Ace! II: ACT III*), Tokyo Movie Shinsha, sport, 25 min., 9/25, Bandai.

1200 OAV
ACE O NERAE! II STAGE FOUR (*Point to the Ace! II: ACT IV*), Tokyo Movie Shinsha, sport, 50 min., 9/25, Bandai.

1201 OAV
SHIBUYA HONKY TONK VOL. III (*id.*), Knack, adventure/soap opera, 35 min., 9/25, Tokuma Japan.

1202 OAV
DONGURI TO YAMANEKO (*The Acorn and the Lynx*), project Team, Argos, animal, 25 min., 9/30, Konami.

On a quiet Saturday night, little Ichiro receives a mysterious invitation to a no-less-mysterious trial that requires his presence.

1203 OAV
CHALK IRO NO PEOPLE (*Chalk Color People*), Watase Seizo, adventure, 54 min., 10/5, Nec Avenue.

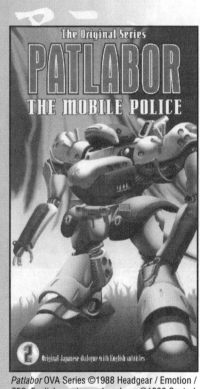

Patlabor OVA Series ©1988 Headgear / Emotion / TFC. English version and package ©1996 Central Park Media Corporation. All Rights Reserved.

1204 OAV

TOP O NERAE! (*Aim For The Top!*), Gainax, science fiction, 55 min., 10/7, Bandai Picture. *Gunbuster, Vol. 1.*

Noriko Takaya is a student at the Okinawa space school and she is the daughter of Captain Takaya, who died under mysterious circumstances. Noriko's greatest desire is to become the pilot of the RX7 robot, to travel in space like her father. The extraordinary abilities of the girl are noticed by the trainer Koichiro Ota who chooses her as a candidate for the Gunbuster secret project.

1205 OAV

SHIN CREAM LEMON AMI SOREKARA... DAI ICHIBU (*Cream Lemon New Series: Ami then... Part I*), Soeishinsha, erotic, 40 min., 10/21, Fairy Dust.

1206 OAV

VAMPIRE MIYU DAI NI WA SO NO UTAGE (*Miyu The Vampire: Act II, Good Boarding School*), AIC, horror, 30 min., 10/21, Soeishinsha/Pony Canyon. *Vampire Princess Miyu, Episode 2: A Banquet Of Marionettes.*

Having moved to another city, Miyu also changes schools, where she meets Key Yasuki, a beautiful boy who likes a girl named Lanka. The young girl becomes interested in him right away, promising him eternal beauty. In the meantime, mysterious disappearances occur in the school.

1207 OAV

ACE O NERAE! II STAGE V (*Point to the Ace! II: ACT V*), Tokyo Movie Shinsha, sport, 50 min., 10/25, Bandai.

1208 OAV

ACE O NERAE! II STAGE VI (*Point to the Ace! II: ACT VI*), Tokyo Movie Shinsha, sport, 50 min., 10/25, Bandai.

1209 OAV

UCHU NO SENSHI (*Space Infantry*), Nippon Sunrise, science fiction, 50 min., 10/25, Bandai.

Carmencita's goal after graduation is to become a spaceship pilot. In love with her, Johnny joins the earthly army to follow her, disregarding his parents' reservations. Once enrolled, the young man finds himself in an environment dominated by strict discipline, and he must soon leave for a distant planet to fight in the war. This first chapter of the series taken from Heinlein's novel *Starship Troopers* faithfully respects the plot and the settings, unlike *Gundam*, which used only the most basic of the book's principles.

1210 OAV

HAJATAISEI DANGAIO II NAMIDA NO SPIRAL KNUCKLE (*The Great-Planet Evil-Destroyer Dangaio II: a Tragic Spiral Knuckle*), AIC, science fiction, 40 min., 10/25, Bandai. *Dangaio 2: Spiral Knuckles In Tears.*

Mia, Roll, Lamba and Pai, after having defeated the Blood DI robot, unite with Tarsan to defeat Galimos once and for all. While doing some repairs on the spaceship, our four characters are attacked by three emissaries from Galimos: Shazarla, Oscar and Domdon.

Gunbuster ©1988,1990 Victor / Gainax / B.M.D. English version and package ©1996 Manga Entertainment, Inc. All Rights Reserved.

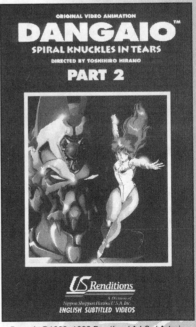

Dangaio ©1988, 1992 Emotion / A.I.C. / Artmic. English version ©1992 U.S. Renditions / E.A.I.C.A.

Demon City Shinjuku ©1993 Hideyuki Kikuchi / Asahi Sonorama / Video Art / Japan Home Video. English subtitled version ©1993 Central Park Media Corporation. English language version ©1994 Manga Entertainment Ltd. Packaging ©1998 Manga Entertainment Ltd. All Rights Reserved.

Gall Force 3: Stardust War ©1988 MOVIC CBS / Sony Group, Inc. English version and package ©1994 Central Park Media Corporation. All Rights Reserved.

During the fight, Lamba recognizes Shazarla as her lady-in-waiting from when she was still princess of her native kingdom. The woman doesn't recognize her, however, as the princess had been erased from her memory. Once aboard the Dangaio, Lamba is forced to hit the adversary robot Aziam The Third with the Spiral Knuckle weapon, causing Shazarla's death.

1211 OAV
MAKAI TOSHI SHINJUKU (*Shinjuku, The City Of The Demons*), Madhouse, horror, 80 min., 25/10, Japan Home Video. *Demon City Shinjuku*.

Under the guidance of Lai the High Priest, Genichiro studies to be initiated to the secret of Nen, but Lebbie Lar, another student, also wants to possess the secret of the great power. Jealous of his study companion, the young man makes a pact with the forces of darkness and defeats Genichiro in a duel in which the land of Shinjuku is also destroyed. The land is then transformed into a possessed land, filled with demons. In exchange for the power given to Labbie Lar, the infernal creatures ask the young man to open a dimensional passage enabling them to come to the world of humans within ten years.

Time passes, and the High Priest is forced to give his esoteric cures to an important government official, the subject of an evil curse set by Lebbie, who can thus act undisturbed through the final phase of his plan. Kyoya, son of Genichiro and heir to his power, leaves for Shinjuku with Sakaya, the daughter of the government official, to stop the infernal rite. After having made their way through a setting of living nightmares, the young man finds the sword that his father had lost some ten years before, and he uses it to launch his final attack on the demonic Lar. The power of Nen and Genichiro's magical wooden sword give Kyoya the edge to defeat the dark menace even as the final sacrifice is about to take place.

1212 OAV
RYUSEIKI SHINSHO A.D. 1990 (*Dragon Century D.C. 1990, Divine Chapter*), AIC, horror, 30 min., 26/10, Kubo Shoten. *Dragon Century*.

A family of dragons and a few human beings are mixed up against their will in the eternal fight between God and the devil. The character designs of this OAV are entrusted to Hiroyuki Kitazume.

1213 OAV
GALL FORCE III: STARDUST WAR (*id.*), Artmic/Animate Film/AIC, science fiction, 60 min., 2/11, CBS Sony. *Gall Force 3: Stardust War*.

Silvy, Lufy, Spia, Ami and Catty reform the group named Gall Force, this time as space spies. On the planet Emblo the five young women must activate a colossal computer to fight against Soruido's army.

1214 OAV
TAIMAN BLUES SHIMIZU NAOTO HEN II (*Lazy Blues: Chapter of Naoto Shimizu II*), Magic Bus, soap opera, 30 min., 10/11, Tokuma Japan.

Naoto is the head of a motorcycle gang, and, as it often happens, the rivalries between groups bring sad consequences. Following an encounter with another gang, the young man ends up in prison.

1215 OAV

KIDO KEISATSU PATLABOR, VOL. V: NIKA NO ICHIBAN NAGAI HI ACT I (*Patlabor, the Mobile Patrol Vol. V: the Longest day of the Second Patrol, Act I*) Studio Dean, science fiction, 30 min., 10/11, Bandai. *Patlabor Original Series, Vol. 2.*

In the winter of 1998 the members of the second corps go back home for a rest period. In the meantime, in Tokyo, the Kekigun group gets ready to attack, strengthened by a nuclear missile from the United States with which it threatens the Japanese government. The patrol must come back to the city where, under Director Goto, they will try to find and stop the entire gang.

1216 OAV

SOKO KISHI VOTOMS KIKO RYOHEI MELLOW LINK (*Armored Troopers Votoms: Mellow Link, the Armed Warrior*), Nippon Sunrise, science fiction, 50 min., 21/11, Vap.

The final chapter of the Votoms is divided into two different OAVs which present the adventures of the courageous warrior and his army. Created by Yosuke Takahashi, the episodes are directed by Takeyuki Kanda and the characterization is by Moriyasu Taniguchi. The design of the mechanical creations is by Kunio Ogawara.

1217 OAV

UCHU NO SENSHI II (*Space Infantry II*), Nippon Sunrise, science fiction, 50 min., 25/11, Bandai.

1218 OAV

SENGOKU KITAN YOTODEN III ENJO NO SHO (*War Stories from the Legend of the Mysterious Sword: Act of the Strong Emotions*), Minami Machi, adventure, 45 min., 25/11, Bugyosho Cic Victor. *Yotoden III.*

Based as usual on spectacular and very well done combat scenes, the plot of this episode sees the duo made up of Kiheiji Dionjo and Kagami (both capable of changing into horrible monsters) confront Ayanosuke, Ryoma and Sakon.

1219 OAV

CRYING FREEMAN (*id.*), Toei Doga for Teoi Video, police story, 50 min., 25/11, Toei Video. *Crying Freeman I: Portrait Of A Killer.*

Taken from the famous manga, also released in Italy, by the Koike/Ikegami duo, this OAV narrates the story of Yo Hinomura, who finds himself caught up against his will in the Chinese mafia. The organization called A Hundred and Eight Dragons takes him in and, with hypnotic conditioning, it makes him into a killer with the code name Crying Freeman. Freeman, because he would like to become one, and Crying, because after having killed someone when he's free from the conditioning, he cries. Seen by the beautiful Emu Hino during an execution, Yo has no other choice than to track her down to kill her. Emu, however, has other plans: knowing that she only has a few hours to live, she asks Freeman to fulfill her last desire and take her virginity. Surprised, Yo, attracted by the young woman, decides to make her wish come true.

In the meantime, both the police and the Japanese mafia are looking for the killer who has two enormous dragons tattooed on his body. Because of that, they are keeping

Intro
-1962
1963
1964
1965
1966
1967
1968
1969
1970
1971
1972
1973
1974
1975
1976
1977
1978
1979
1980
1981
1982
1983
1984
1985
1986
1987
1988
Index

Emu's house under surveillance, as she is the only witness still alive able to describe Freeman. With the police, the members of the Hakushin (the Japanese mafia) break into the villa and, before being destroyed by Yo, they injure Emu. Freeman, now in love with the woman, brings her to the hospital, certain that she will never betray him and tells her that he will be waiting for her at her house on the bay. Healed, Emu succeeds in getting away from the police and meets Yo. Having taken care of the only Hakushin witness who survived the attack at Emu's villa, the two young people, breaking all links with the past, leave for Hong Kong to find the headquarters of the Hundred and Eight Dragons, which Yo is destined to head.

1220 OAV

SHIBUYA HONKY TONK VOL. IV (*id.*), Knack, adventure/soap opera, 35 min., 25/11, Tokuma Japan.

1221 OAV

MEIO KEIKAKU ZEORYMER (*Hades Project Zeorymer*), AIC, science fiction, 30 min., 26/11, Toshiba Emi. *Hades Project Zeorymer: Project 1.*

The Haudragon criminal organization plans to invade the world, using a team of gigantic robots. Zeorymer, the most powerful model, is taken out by his creator Masaki Kihara, who prepares for the counteroffensive. Fifteen years after, Yuratei, the young leader of the Haudragon, decides to go ahead with their plan and kill the rebel Masaki. Robotics are united with biogenetics and the courageous pilot of Zeorymer reveals himself to be the result of a laboratory experiment, as is the copilot as well, transformed into a cyborg and gifted with a great power capable of moving the robot.

1222 OAV

NIHON NO OBAKE BANASHI II (*Stories of Japanese Ghosts II*), O Prod., Humor, 30 min., 26,11, Toshiba Emi.

1223 OAV

SALAMANDER BASIC SAGA MEISO NO PAOLA (*Salamander Basic Saga: Paola in Meditation*), Studio Pierrot, science fiction, 60 min., 30/11, Konami.

On the planet Gladius, Stephanie, Don and Eddy are fighting against the Bacterian aliens. During their search for the leader of Gladius, they find a spaceship in which they find a beautiful young woman named Paola, fast asleep. Awakened, the young woman reveals a prophecy of the Bacterian invasion and claims to know where their planet is situated. The planet is the 7th of the C3 zone, and the three characters leave to search for it to defeat the enemy on its own territory. Taken from the famous video game bearing the same name, this OAV is enriched by the captivating characterization of Haruhiko Mikimoto and by the meticulous mechanical design by Tatsuharu Moriki. It is directed by Hisayuki Toriumi, from a concept by Kazusane Hirashima.

1224 OAV

ICHI POUND NO FUKUIN (*A One Pound Gospel*), Studio Gallopp, comedy, 50 min., 2/12, Shogakukan. *One-Pound Gospel.*

Kosaku, a 19 year old boxer and Angela, a nun who really cares about the young man, meet on the stairs of a church, where Angela helps an exhausted Kosaku. The boxer trains hard and keeps his form by throwing punches in the air in prevision of an important fight. Twice, he even hits an innocent passerby who, strangely enough, doesn't react, leaving both times with his face covered. Kosaku loves boxing as much as eating, and his meals make him rapidly gain weight and put him at risk of having to change weight categories. Sister Angela personally sees to it that the young man follows a diet, and Kosaku, not to disappoint her, decides to intensify his training. The day of his medical visit, the boxer has never felt better and, having gone back to his original weight, is ready for the fight. His opponent shows up with an embarrassing black eye and he reveals himself to be the innocent passerby who takes the occasion to avenge himself. Kosaku seems to be losing but, when he receives a hard blow to the stomach, losing his mouthguard, things change. Slipping on the mouthguard, in fact, the opponent becomes an easy target for Kosaku who knocks him out easily.

1225 OAV
GAI YOMA KAKUSEI (*Gai, The Demon's Disillusion*), Toei Doga, horror, 6/12, Uchu Doga. *Guy: Double Target.*

1226 OAV
KIDO KEISATSU PATLABOR, VOL. VI: NIKA NO ICHIBAN NAGAI HI ACT II (*Patlabor, the Mobile Patrol Vol. VI: the Longest Day of the Second Patrol, Act II*), Studio Dean, science fiction, 30 min., 10/12, Bandai. *Patlabor Original Series, Vol. 3.*

The story initiated in the previous episode continues, in which the second patrol must face Kakigun.

1227 OAV
SHINSHU RINIHEN KAN NO ICHI OGON NO RYU (*Fantastic War in the Kingdom, Part I: the Golden Dragon*), Magic Bus, fantasy, 30 min., 10/12, Japan Communication.

1228 OAV
KAZE O NUKE! (*Faster than the Wind*), Madhouse, adventure, 60 min., 16/12, Victor Music.

1229 OAV
UCHU NO SENSHI III (*Space Infantry III*), Nippon Sunrise, science fiction, 50 min., 17/12, Bandai.

1230 OAV
SOKO KISHI VOTOMS KIKO RYOHEI MELLOW LINK II (*Armored Troopers Votoms: Mellow Link, The Warrior With The Weapon II*), Nippon Sunrise, science fiction, 50 min., 21/12, Vap.

The main character is once again Mellow Link, who battles a new enemy in an unchanged screenplay. Because of Link's desertion, the army which he commanded is destroyed, and the main character thus decides to leave to avenge his companions.

1231 OAV
VAMPIRE MIYU DAISANWA MOROKI YOROI (*Miyu The Vampire, ACT III, Fragile Armor*), AIC, horror, 30 min., 21/12, Soeishinsha. *Vampire Princess Miyu, episode 3: Fragile Armor.*

The Ultimate In Science Friction!

Guy Double Target ©1990, 1992 Media Station. English version ©1994 A.D.Vision.

Vampire Princess Miyu ©1988, 1989 Soeishinsha, Inc. / Pony Canyon, Inc. English version ©1992 AnimEigo, Inc. Licensed by Fuji Sankei Communications International, Inc. Released by AnimEigo, Inc.

Violence Jack
Original story & trademark ©1973/1996 Go Nagai /
Dynamic Productions Inc. Animated version © 1988
Dynamic Planning • Soeishinsha • Japan Home Video.
The trademark "Violence Jack" is used under
permission of Dynamic Planning Inc and by courtesy of
the Dynamic Group of Companies (Europe). English
version ©1996 Dynamic Planning, Inc. All rights
Reserved. Uncut version released by Critical Mass.

Bubblegum Crisis ©1988 by Artmic, Inc & Youmex,
Inc. Licensed by Youmex, Inc. English version
©1991 by AnimEigo, Inc. All Rights Reserved.

1232 OAV
UCHU KAZOKU CARLBINSON (*Carlbinson, the Cosmic Family*), Doga Kobo, Tokuma Shoten.

1233 OAV
YOSEI O (*The King of the Fairies*), Madhouse, adventure, 60 min., 21/12, CBS Sony.

1234 OAV
VIOLENCE JACK JIGOKU GAI (*Violence Jack: the Infernal Chapter*), Studio 88, horror, 60 min., 21/12, Japan Home Video. *Violence Jack, Part 1: Evil Town.*

The Shinjuku underground shopping center in Tokyo has been buried under the ruins provoked by an earthquake. The survivors trapped in the ruins are forced to practice cannibalism, turning the underground shopping center in some sort of hell run by three different factions. One day, Violence Jack succeeds in entering the underworld complex, and Aira, the leader of the C zone, pleads with him to help her group against the incursions of B zone. Following the colossal character, Aira and her followers manage to see the sun's light once more and return to a quieter life.

1235 OAV
GINGA HEIYU DENSETSU VOL. I (*The Legend of the Heroes of the Galaxy, Vol. I*), Artland, science fiction, 30 min., 21/12, Kitty Enterprise.

1236 OAV
RYUSEIKI MASHO R.C. 297 RURISHA (*Dragon Century, Demon Chapter, R.C. 297 Rurisha*), AIC, horror, 30 min., 25/12, Kubo Shoten. *Dragon Century.*

1237 OAV
BUBBLEGUM CRISIS V: MOONLIGHT RAMBLER (*id.*), AIC/Artmic, science fiction/adventure, 30 min., 25/12, Toshiba Emi. *Bubblegum Crisis 5: Moonlight Rambler.*

Because of a flight incident, a space shuttle crashes. The Knight Sabers investigate on the Genom organization to determine their responsibility, and to dismantle it once and for all.

1238 OAV
GINGA HEIYU DENSETSU VOL. II (*The Legend of the Heroes of the Galaxy, Vol. II*), Artland, science fiction, 30 min., 28/12, Kitty Enterprise.

FOURTH PART

Index

INDEX OF THE ORIGINAL TITLES

Intro
-1962
1963
1964
1965
1966
1967
1968
1969
1970
1971
1972
1973
1974
1975
1976
1977
1978
1979
1980
1981
1982
1983
1984
1985
1986
1987
1988
Index

Intro
-1962
1963
1964
1965
1966
1967
1968
1969
1970
1971
1972
1973
1974
1975
1976
1977
1978
1979
1980
1981
1982
1983
1984
1985
1986
1987
1988
Index

Intro
-1962
1963
1964
1965
1966
1967
1968
1969
1970
1971
1972
1973
1974
1975
1976
1977
1978
1979
1980
1981
1982
1983
1984
1985
1986
1987
1988

Index

Intro
-1962
1963
1964
1965
1966
1967
1968
1969
1970
1971
1972
1973
1974
1975
1976
1977
1978
1979
1980
1981
1982
1983
1984
1985
1986
1987
1988
Index

Intro
-1962
1963
1964
1965
1966
1967
1968
1969
1970
1971
1972
1973
1974
1975
1976
1977
1978
1979
1980
1981
1982
1983
1984
1985
1986
1987
1988
Index

Intro
-1962
1963
1964
1965
1966
1967
1968
1969
1970
1971
1972
1973
1974
1975
1976
1977
1978
1979
1980
1981
1982
1983
1984
1985
1986
1987
1988
Index

INDEX OF THE LITERAL ENGLISH TITLES

Intro
-1962
1963
1964
1965
1966
1967
1968
1969
1970
1971
1972
1973
1974
1975
1976
1977
1978
1979
1980
1981
1982
1983
1984
1985
1986
1987
1988
Index

Intro
-1962
1963
1964
1965
1966
1967
1968
1969
1970
1971
1972
1973
1974
1975
1976
1977
1978
1979
1980
1981
1982
1983
1984
1985
1986
1987
1988
Index

Intro
-1962
1963
1964
1965
1966
1967
1968
1969
1970
1971
1972
1973
1974
1975
1976
1977
1978
1979
1980
1981
1982
1983
1984
1985
1986
1987
1988
Index

Intro
-1962
1963
1964
1965
1966
1967
1968
1969
1970
1971
1972
1973
1974
1975
1976
1977
1978
1979
1980
1981
1982
1983
1984
1985
1986
1987
1988
Index

Intro
-1962
1963
1964
1965
1966
1967
1968
1969
1970
1971
1972
1973
1974
1975
1976
1977
1978
1979
1980
1981
1982
1983
1984
1985
1986
1987
1988
Index

Intro
-1962
1963
1964
1965
1966
1967
1968
1969
1970
1971
1972
1973
1974
1975
1976
1977
1978
1979
1980
1981
1982
1983
1984
1985
1986
1987
1988
Index

Intro
-1962
1963
1964
1965
1966
1967
1968
1969
1970
1971
1972
1973
1974
1975
1976
1977
1978
1979
1980
1981
1982
1983
1984
1985
1986
1987
1988

Index

Intro
-1962
1963
1964
1965
1966
1967
1968
1969
1970
1971
1972
1973
1974
1975
1976
1977
1978
1979
1980
1981
1982
1983
1984
1985
1986
1987
1988
Index

Intro
-1962
1963
1964
1965
1966
1967
1968
1969
1970
1971
1972
1973
1974
1975
1976
1977
1978
1979
1980
1981
1982
1983
1984
1985
1986
1987
1988
Index

Intro
-1962
1963
1964
1965
1966
1967
1968
1969
1970
1971
1972
1973
1974
1975
1976
1977
1978
1979
1980
1981
1982
1983
1984
1985
1986
1987
1988
Index

Intro
.-1962
1963
1964
1965
1966
1967
1968
1969
1970
1971
1972
1973
1974
1975
1976
1977
1978
1979
1980
1981
1982
1983
1984
1985
1986
1987
1988

Index

INDEX OF THE ITALIAN TITLES

Intro
-1962
1963
1964
1965
1966
1967
1968
1969
1970
1971
1972
1973
1974
1975
1976
1977
1978
1979
1980
1981
1982
1983
1984
1985
1986
1987
1988
Index

Intro
-1962
1963
1964
1965
1966
1967
1968
1969
1970
1971
1972
1973
1974
1975
1976
1977
1978
1979
1980
1981
1982
1983
1984
1985
1986
1987
1988
Index

Intro
-1962
1963
1964
1965
1966
1967
1968
1969
1970
1971
1972
1973
1974
1975
1976
1977
1978
1979
1980
1981
1982
1983
1984
1985
1986
1987
1988
Index

INDEX OF THE FRENCH TITLES

KEY

FR = Shown in France

QC = Shown in Quebec (French-Canada)

Intro
-1962
1963
1964
1965
1966
1967
1968
1969
1970
1971
1972
1973
1974
1975
1976
1977
1978
1979
1980
1981
1982
1983
1984
1985
1986
1987
1988

Index

INDEX OF THE TITLES SHOWN OR AVAILABLE IN NORTH AMERICA

Intro
-1962
1963
1964
1965
1966
1967
1968
1969
1970
1971
1972
1973
1974
1975
1976
1977
1978
1979
1980
1981
1982
1983
1984
1985
1986
1987
1988
Index

Intro
-1962
1963
1964
1965
1966
1967
1968
1969
1970
1971
1972
1973
1974
1975
1976
1977
1978
1979
1980
1981
1982
1983
1984
1985
1986
1987
1988
Index

Intro
-1962
1963
1964
1965
1966
1967
1968
1969
1970
1971
1972
1973
1974
1975
1976
1977
1978
1979
1980
1981
1982
1983
1984
1985
1986
1987
1988
Index

Intro
-1962
1963
1964
1965
1966
1967
1968
1969
1970
1971
1972
1973
1974
1975
1976
1977
1978
1979
1980
1981
1982
1983
1984
1985
1986
1987
1988
Index

KEY

TV = Shown on television
VHS = Released on video cassette
DVD = Released on DVD

A18 = Anime 18 (CPM)
ADV = A.D.Vision (ADV Films)
AE = AnimEigo
AP = Antartic Press
AW = AnimeWorks (Media Blasters)
B = Bandai Entertainment, Inc
BFV = Best Film & Video
BV = Buena Vista (Disney)
CE = Celebrity Home Entertainment
CPM = Central Park Media
CVG = The Congress Video Group
FHE = Family Home Entertainment
FN = FUNimation
FV = Fox Home Video
HG = Harmony Gold U.S.A.
HTV = Hi-Tops Video
KM = Kidmark
KV = Kitty Video (Media Blasters)
ME = Manga Entertainment
MGV = Malibu Graphics Video
OR = Orion Video
P = Pioneer
PBE = Palm Beach Entertainment
PV = Parade Video
RS = The Right Stuf International
SP = Streamline Pictures (Streamline Entreprises)
SS = Software Sculptors (CPM)
THV = Tyndale Home Video
UAV = United American Video
USM = U.S. Manga Corps (CPM)
USR = U.S. Renditions (Nippan)
VE = Voyager Entertainment
VR = Video Rarities
VV = Viz Video (Viz Communications)

Numbers in parenthesis are either the catalog number or the year(s) of the release.

Intro
-1962
1963
1964
1965
1966
1967
1968
1969
1970
1971
1972
1973
1974
1975
1976
1977
1978
1979
1980
1981
1982
1983
1984
1985
1986
1987
1988
Index

LIST OF THE MAIN NORTH AMERICAN ANIME RELEASERS

A.D. Films (ADV)

Labels: A.D.Vision, ADV FanSubs, SoftCel Pictures.

Southwest Plaza Building
5750 Bintliff #217
Houston, TX 77036-2123

Ph: (713) 977-9181
Fx: (713) 977-5573
E-mail: sales@advfilms.com
Web: www.advfilms.com

AnimEigo (AE)

P.O. Box 989
Wilmington, NC 28402-0989

Ph: (800) 24A-NIME (242-6463)
    (910) 251-1850
Fx: (910) 763-2376
E-mail: questions@animeigo.com / orders@animeigo.com
Web: www.animeigo.com

Bandai Entertainment (B)

Labels: AnimeVillage.com, Bandai Entertainment

P.O. Box 6054
Cypress, CA 90630-6454

Ph: (877) 77A-NIME (772-6463)
Fx: (714) 816-6708
E-mail: support@bandai-ent.com
Web: www.bandai-ent.com / www.AnimeVillage.com

Central Park Media (CPM)

Labels: Anime 18 (A18), Central Park Media (CPM), Software Sculptors (SS), U.S. Manga Corps (USM)

250 West 57th Street, Suite 317
New York, NY 10107

Ph: (800) 626-4277
Fx: (212) 977-8709
E-Mail: info@teamcpm.com
Web: www.centralparkmedia.com
     www.software-sculptors.com
     www.animeone.com
     AOL: Japanimation Station, Keyword: Japanimation

Media Blasters (MB)

Labels: AnimeWorks (AW), Kitty Media (KV)

265 West 40th Street, Suite 700
New York, NY 10018

Ph: (212) 532-1688
Fx: (212) 532-3388
E-mail: info@media-blasters.com
Web: www.media-blasters.com
     www.kittymedia.com

Manga Entertainment (ME)

Label: Manga Video.

727 N. Hudson Street, Suite 100
Chicago, IL 60610

Ph: (312) 751-0020
Fx: (312) 751-2483
E-mail: manga@manga.com
Web: www.manga.com

Distributed in Canada by Sony Music Entertainment ((416) 391-3311).

Pioneer Entertainment (P)

Pioneer Animation
PO Box 22782
Long Beach, CA 90801-5782

Ph: (213) PIONEER (746-6337)
Fx: (310) 952-2791
E-mail: help@pioneeranimation.com
Web: www.pioneeranimation.com / www.pioneer-ent.com

Also distribute: Bandai Entertainment (B), Video Video (VV)

The Right Stuf International (RS)

Labels: The Right Stuf (RS), Critical Mass (CM).

P.O. Box 71309
Des Moines, IA 50325

Ph: (800) 338-6827
Fx: (515) 252-0555
E-mail: info@rightstuf.com
Web: www.rightstuf.com

Also sell all products from all other anime releasers.

Urban Vision Entertainment (UV)

5120 W. Goldleaf Circle, Suite 280
Los Angeles, CA 90056

Fx: (323) 292-9854
E-mail: info@urban-vision.com
Web: www.urban-vision.com

Viz Video (VV)

Viz Communications, Inc.
P.O. BOX 77010
San Francisco, CA 94107

Ph: (800) 394-3042
Fx: (415) 546-7086
E-mail: info@viz.com / shopbymail@viz.com
Web: www.viz.com

For a list of other anime distributors or retailers, you can check *Protoculture Addicts'* web page: www.protoculture.qc.ca/PA/FAQ.htm or www.protoculture.qc.ca/PA/webIndex.htm.

AN ESSENTIAL BIBLIOGRAPHY

AN ESSENTIAL ANIME & MANGA BIBLIOGRAPHY

GROENSTEEN, Thierry. *L'Univers des Mangas. Une Introduction à la Bande Dessinée Japonaise.* Casterman, 1996. 143 pg. ISBN 2-203-32606-9.

LEDOUX, Trish & RANNEY, Doug. *The Complete Anime Guide. Japanese Animation Film Directory & Resource Guide.* Tiger Mountain Press, 1997. 214 pg. ISBN 0-9649542-5-7. $19.95 US.

LEVI, Antonia. *Samurai From Outer Space. Understanding Japanese Animation.* Chicago, Open Court, 1996. 169 pg. ISBN 0-8126-9332-9.

McCARTHY, Helen & CLEMENTS, Jonathan. *The Erotic Anime Movie Guide.* London, Titan Books, 1998. 191 pg. ISBN 1-85286-946-1. £12.99.

McCARTHY, Helen. *Anime! A Beginner's Guide to Japanese Animation.* London, Titan Books, 1993. 64 pg. ISBN 1-85286-492-3. £6.99.

McCARTHY, Helen. *The Anime! Movie Guide. Movie-by-Movie Guide to Japanese Animation.* Woodstock, The Overlook Press, 1997. 285 pg. ISBN 0-87951-781-6. $17.95 US.

POITRAS, Gilles. *The Anime Companion. What's Japanese in Japanese Animation?* Berkeley, Stone Bridge Press, 1999. 163 pg. ISBN 1-880656-32-9. $16.95 US.

SCHODT, Frederik L. *Dreamland Japan; Writings On Modern Manga.* Berkeley, Stone Bridge Press, 1996. 360 pg. ISBN 1-880656-23-X. $16.95 US.

SCHODT, Frederik L. *Manga! Manga! The World of Japanese Comics.* New York/Tokyo, Kodensha, 1983. 260 pg. ISBN 0-87011-752-1. $16.95 US/3,000¥

——— *Kaboum! Explosive Animation from America and Japan.* Sydney (Australia), Museum of Contemporary Art, 1994, 159 pg. ISBN 1-875-632-32-8. $19.95 AUD.

MAGAZINES

Many anime magazines have been published in the past years (*Animag, Anime Fantastique, Anime FX, Anime UK, Animenominous, Anime-Zine, Manga Max, Mixx-Zine, Tokyo Pop, V-Max,* etc.), but only those three remain in publication and can be considered as essential references:

Animeland. Le premier magazine de l'Animation et du Manga. Anime Manga Presse, c. 98 pg. (full color), monthly. ISSN #1148-0807. 35 FF. Published in French.

Animerica. Anime & Manga Monthly. Viz Communications, c. 96 pg. (56 pg color), monthly. ISSN #1067-0831. $4.95 US.

Protoculture Addicts; The Anime & Manga Magazine. Protoculture Enr., c. 64 pg. (12 pg color), bi-monthly. ISSN #0835-9563. $4.95 US/Can. The oldest anime magazine in publication (in November 2000 it has celebrated its 13th anniversary).

REFERENCES

We used those Japanese references to confirm information and for illustrations.

Anime Video Collectors Guide. Tokyo, Genkosha Publ., 1986. 178 p. ¥880.

AX Magazine. Sony.

Newtype Magazine. Kadokawa Shoten.

Osamu Tezuka Cartoons 40 Years. Tokyo, Akita Shoten, 1984. 178 p. ISBN 4-253-00776-7.

Osamu Tezuka Theatre: The Animation Filmography of Osamu Tezuka. Tokyo, Tezuka Production, 1991. 96 p.

Super Robot Encyclopedia (Dengeki Selection). Tokyo, Media Works/Shufu No Tomo Publ., 1997. 128 p. ¥1650. ISBN 4-07-305544-5.

Tatsunoko Pro Anime Super Data File. Tokyo, Tatsumi Publ., 1998. 160 p. ¥2000. ISBN 4-88641-277-7.

This Anime Is Great! (Takarajima Extra #293). Tokyo, Takarajima, 1997. 240 p. ¥1000. ISBN 4-7966-9293-2.

INTERNET RESOURCES

A Fan's View (Convention Reports): www.fansview.com

Anime News Network: www.animenewsnetwork.com

Anime Web Guide: www.tcp.com/~doi/alan/webguide/awgHome.html

Anime Web Turnpike: www.anipike.com

Gilles Poitras' Service to Fans Page: www.sirius.com/~cowpunk/

Those are the essential resources. From there, you can find more. You can also check *Protoculture Addicts*' web page: www.protoculture.qc.ca/PA/FAQ.htm or www.protoculture.qc.ca/PA/webIndex.htm for more anime & manga related links.

Intro
-1962
1963
1964
1965
1966
1967
1968
1969
1970
1971
1972
1973
1974
1975
1976
1977
1978
1979
1980
1981
1982
1983
1984
1985
1986
1987
1988
Index

ACKNOWLEDGEMENTS

ACKNOWLEDGEMENTS OF THE ORIGINAL ITALIAN EDITION

The publisher wishes to thank for their kind assistance throughout the editing of the text and for giving the permission to reproduce the images: Miss Asatsura (Kitty Film), Aono Shiro and Yoshida Satoji (Tokyo Movie Shinsha), Masaharu Omodaka (Tezuka Prod.), Chieko Matsumoto and Hideaki Matsuda (Mushi Prod.), Shigeru Miyazaki (Tatsunoko Prod.), Hiroshi Kato (Ashi Prod.), Akiyoshi Takei (Kodansha Video), Hiroyuki Kurano and Michio Yokoo (Tokuma Shoten), Buichi Terazawa and Junko Ito (All Girl Co.). As well as Fujio Production, Shingo Araki, Kensuke and Tetsuya Chiba, Michi Himeno, Ryoko Ikeda, Hayao Miyazaki, Go Nagai, Monkey Punch, Mitsuteru Yokoyama.

A special thanks to: Reiji Matsumoto, Kenji Nagai (Dynamic Production), Satoko Sasaki, Kazuhiko Uramoto, Yoshi Hatano and to all the staff in Toei Doga's studio and offices.

An additional thanks to: Emiko Ando (Toei Doga), Mika Suzuki Moretto, Naoko Daga, and to Frederico Colpi who has lend us his precious assistance from Japan.

Grateful thanks, finally, to the editors of this book: Andrea Accardi, Nives Aiuola, Giancarlo Carlotti and Enrico Fornaroli, let alone to the authors for their continuous collaboration.

Furthermore, we apologize to copyright holders whom we were not able to contact in order to ask permission to publish their images.

ACKNOWLEDGEMENTS OF THE ENGLISH EDITION

First, the publisher wishes to thank his staff: Miyako Matsuda, for her loving assistance, and Martin Ouellette, for his great and constant support.

We also want to thank Adeline D'Opera (for the translation), Hilary Doda (for the proofreading of the text), Francine Pelletier (for additional translation), as well as the authors of the book, Andrea Baricordi, Massimiliano De Giovanni, Andrea Pietroni, Barbara Rossi, and Sabrina Tunesi, for their great work. An additional thanks to Serena Varani (Kappa Edizioni).

We want to express our gratitude and special thanks to all the people of the North American anime industry who have constantly supported our work on this project and on our magazine *Protoculture Addicts*, particularly: Janice Williams, Matt Greenfield and Ken Wiatrik (ADV), Robert Woodhead and Luray Carroll (AnimEigo), Nobu Yamamoto and Jerry Chu (Bandai Entertainment), John O'Donnell, Masumi Homma O'Donnell, and Mee-Lise Robinson (Central Park Media), Maki Terashima (I-G USA), John Sirabella and Lance Schwulst (Media Blasters), Mike Egan, Matt and Danielle Opyt (Manga Entertainment), Hiroe Tsukamoto and Chad Kime (Pioneer), Shawne Kleckner (The Right Stuf), Therese Garnett (Sony Music Canada), Kara Redmon (Urban Vision), Seiji Horibuchi and Ann Ivan (Viz Communications).

We also want to thank our friends, collaborators and all other people who helped this project one way or another, particularly: Ghislain Barbe, Aaron Dawe, Asaka Dawe, Keith Dawe, Jean-François "Jeff" Fortier (Dream Pod 9), Yvan West Laurence, Carlo Lévy, Cédric Littardi, Michael Liu, Carl Macek, Pierre Ouellette (Dream Pod 9), Fred Patten, Frederik L. Schodt, James S. Taylor, Dominique Veret, Vincent Wilson, Yui Yuasa and Nene Tamaki, and the people of CD Japan, HobbyLink Japan, Nikaku Animart, Planet Anime.

Finally, we want to thank all the Japanese animation creators and producers for giving us such a great entertainment, and all the anime fans for giving life to this industry.

NOTES

Princess Knight   1967

Star Blazers 1975

little lulu and her friends 1976

Space battleship Yamato   1977

Dangard Ace   1977

Farewell to spacebattle Yamato: in the name of love 197

Conan, the boy from the future 1978

Galaxy express 999   1978

Yamatoll the space cruiser 1978

lun-lun, the girl from the flowers 1979

Anne with the red hair 1979

Doraemon 1979

the rose of Versailles 1979

Towards the Earth 1980

Phoenix 2772 1980

Tom Sawyer 1980

Cyborg 009 1980

Foomon 1980

Goodbye, Galaxy express 999: Andromeda, end of the line 1981

Swiss family Robinson   1981

Vengeance of the space pirate 1982

Memol with the pointy hat 1984

Night on the Galactic railroad 1985

Minky Momo, the princess of Magic. circle of my dream 1985
The chocolate panic picture show 1985
Doteraman 1986

NOTES

NOTES

NOTES

NOTES

NOTES

Payette & Simms inc.

Achevé d'imprimer en décembre 2000 sur les presses de
Payette & Simms inc. à Saint-Lambert (Québec)